Children's Literature

Children's Literature

Discovery for a Lifetime

FOURTH EDITION

BARBARA D. STOODT-HILL

JOHN TYLER COMMUNITY COLLEGE

LINDA B. AMSPAUGH-CORSON

UNIVERSITY OF CINCINNATI

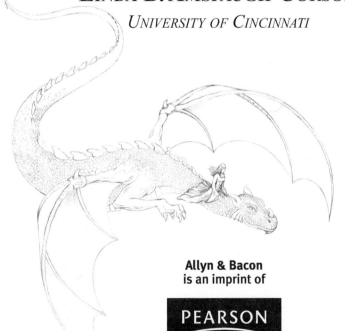

**Allyn & Bacon
is an imprint of**

PEARSON

Boston   New York   San Francisco
Mexico City   Montreal   Toronto   London   Madrid   Munich   Paris
Hong Kong   Singapore   Tokyo   Cape Town   Sydney

Vice President and Editor in Chief: Paul A. Smith
Senior Editor: Linda Ashe Bishop
Senior Project Manager: Mary M. Irvin
Editorial Assistant: Demetrius Hall
Design Coordinator and Cover Design: Diane C. Lorenzo
Cover Image: Greg LaFever
Operations Specialist: Laura Messerly
Director of Marketing: Quinn Perkson
Marketing Manager: Krista Clark
Marketing Coordinator: Brian Mounts

Photo Credits: Anthony Magnacca/Merrill, 138 and 235; Kenneth P. Davis/PH College, 168; all other photos by Barbara Stoodt-Hill.

For related titles and support materials, visit our online catalog at www.pearsonhighed.com

Library of Congress Cataloging-in-Publication Data

Stoodt, Barbara D.
  Children's literature : discovery for a lifetime / Barbara D. Stoodt-Hill & Linda Amspaugh-Corson.
    p. cm.
  Includes bibliographical references and index.
  ISBN 978-0-13-158939-1
  1. Children's literature—Study and teaching (Elementary)   2. Children—Books and reading.
I. Amspaugh, Linda B.   II. Title.
LB1575.S86 2009
372.64—dc22

2008002658

**Allyn & Bacon
is an imprint of**

Printed in the United States of America
10 9 8 7 6 5 4 3   [EB]   12 11 10

To Sarah Price, Kyle Neu, Matthew Price,
and Andrew Price, with much love,
Grandma Barbara

For my favorite children's librarians:
Susan, Tari, Victoria.
Thank you, Linda

Preface

The values of literature are well established. Publishers, libraries, and bookstores offer a rich array of children's books. Television commercials urge parents to read to their children. Athletes, movie stars, and politicians urge children to read, and various programs provide books to children for their reading pleasure. Children's books are available on the Internet, and students can learn about authors on Internet sites.

Yet in spite of the availability of literature and the widespread recognition of its importance, there is a dilemma. Every U.S. state has some form of objectives or standards that students need to achieve. This often leads teachers to force-feed facts to students so they will pass mandated tests. While we recognize teachers' needs to ensure students pass their tests, we believe read-aloud time and time for literature experiences can better promote children's growth and development than short-term responses to tests. Research supports the idea that optimizing children's literary experiences enhances their learning and knowledge retention.

This book is the product of our many experiences as teachers, professors, parents, and grandparents. Our goal is to help teachers, librarians, and parents infuse literature into children's lives and to promote a lifelong interest in books. Our theme is "literature for a lifetime" because we hope to prepare teachers to positively impact children's reading by:

- Selecting books that will enhance children's learning and development.
- Implementing literature that will support the classroom curriculum and meet established standards.
- Identifying books children will respond to.
- Sharing literature that will stimulate children's and young adolescents' responses.
- Infusing literature into elementary and middle school classrooms and homes.
- Choosing relevant and authentic literature for English language learners.
- Identifying books that portray children with special needs.

- Enhancing literature experiences with the computer and the Internet.
- Choosing literature that develops children's cultural consciousness.

The Organization of the Text

We present the ideas and information in this text in the following order. Chapters 1 through 3 create a foundation for understanding literature and appreciating children's literature, as well as ways of incorporating literature in classrooms and libraries. These chapters also provide guidance for selecting children's books. Chapter 3 is a new chapter focusing on contemporary issues in selecting children's books.

Chapters 4 through 11 explore the formats and genres of children's literature in picture books, poetry, traditional literature, fantasy, realistic fiction, historical fiction, nonfiction, and biography. Authors and illustrators are emphasized through profiles that appear throughout the book. In these profiles, we hope to acquaint students with authors and illustrators and their works, as well as offer models for classroom study.

Chapter 12 introduces literature for children who experience daily challenges of physical, sensory, or emotional disabilities. Chapter 13 focuses on sharing multicultural literature inclusive of children from various cultures. These two chapters serve a dual purpose. First, they afford children opportunities to identify with those who have had similar experiences. Second, they give readers opportunities to appreciate their own culture and the cultures of others.

Chapters 14, 15, and 16 present ways of nurturing children's engagement with, and response to, literature. Chapter 14 engages children with literature through oral and silent reading experiences; Chapter 15 explains how to encourage children's response to literature. Finally, Chapter 16 presents sample guides and units that teachers have used in developing classroom experiences with literature.

Each chapter opens with a list of key terms, guiding questions, and classroom snapshots that give examples of teachers and children involved with literature. These snapshots serve as classroom models for others. Throughout the book, additional authentic classroom experiences are meant to develop deeper cognitive and affective understanding and aesthetic awareness.

Each chapter concludes with *Thought Questions and Applications* and *Research and Application Experiences* that align IRA/NCTE standards (objectives) to the experiences. Also included at the end of each chapter are bibliographies of cited books that include genre identification and suggested grade levels. Where appropriate, asterisks (*) indicate books that will appeal to reluctant readers.

New to This Edition

Users of the third edition of *Children's Literature: Discovery for a Lifetime* will find that this fourth edition reflects major revisions in every chapter and important pedagogical changes.

- Every chapter is extensively updated with recent children's literature.
- The vignettes have been updated to "classroom snapshots," which are classroom and text centered.

- Chapter 3 is entirely focused on issues in children's literature.
- Two asterisks (**) identify classic literature.
- Fantasy is emphasized throughout the text because it is very important for today's students.
- Middle-school literature is included throughout the text.
- Graphic novels and manga are discussed in several chapters.
- Series books are recognized throughout the book because they interest students of all ages.

Children's literature enhances lifelong learning, intellectual growth, and self understanding. Therefore, teachers, librarians, and parents who read to children of all ages are offering them a priceless gift.

Acknowledgments

We wish to express our sincere appreciation for the support and encouragement of our editor, Linda Bishop. We would also like to thank the following reviewers: Nancy Berbrich, State University of New York–Potsdam; Linda H. Cox, Baylor University; Georgianna Duarte, University of Texas–Brownsville; Shirley B. Ernst, retired from Eastern Connecticut State University; and Dee Storey, Saginaw Valley State University.

Brief Contents

Contents

Children's Literature

1

Introduction to Children's Literature

KEY TERMS

children's literature   literary transaction
graphic novels   literature
literary criticism   manga

GUIDING QUESTIONS

Did you have a favorite book in childhood? Did you enjoy Dr. Seuss's delightful books or did you prefer time-honored tales like "Goldilocks and the Three Bears"? What books do today's children enjoy? How do you choose books to read? Do you consult reviews or ask friends about the books they read? Think about the following questions as you read this chapter.

1. How is children's literature different from adult literature?

2. What value does literature have in children's lives?

3. What are the major considerations when selecting media to use in the classroom?

Introduction to Children's Literature

"The power of story is not to be denied. In prehistoric caves, during Irish famines, in Nazi concentration camps, stories were as important as food. . . . Children's literature is the inheritance of this tradition" (Hearne, 1999, pp. 4–5). In this chapter, we explore the nature of children's literature and its values in children's lives to help create a foundation for those concerned with fostering children's literary experiences.

Stories are a natural part of life. "Offering stories to children is the way our print-dominated society carries on a habit even older than writing and as common as bread—telling stories and listening to them" (Meek, 1977, p. 36). Constructing stories in the mind is a fundamental way of making meaning. Through stories and language, humans record, explain, understand, and control their experience. Stories are behind the nightly news, the comics, and the 11 o'clock sports report. When you ask a friend about her experiences in a hurricane, she creates a narrative to tell what happened, helping both of you understand her experience. Through telling, retelling, believing, and disbelieving stories about one another's past, future, and identity, we come to know one another.

What Is Children's Literature?

The term *literature* refers to a body of written works; it is an art form in which language is used in creative, artistic ways. *Children's literature* is written specifically with children's interests and experiences in mind; this literature fosters children's passion for reading. Children's literature explores, orders, evaluates, and illuminates the human experience—its heights and depths, as well as its pains and pleasures. Most importantly, children's literature entertains children, while giving them access to the accumulated experience and wisdom of the ages. Memorable authors of children's literature adeptly engage readers with information, language, unique plots, and many-faceted characters.

1

Authors consider their audiences' experiences and their life events as they create order and form in their writing. The major difference between children's literature and adult literature is the more limited life experience of the younger audience.

What Are the Values of Children's Literature?

Literature affects all of our lives deeply, motivating thinking, enhancing language and cognitive development, and encouraging children to read and to continue reading, thus accelerating learning (Pressley, 2001). Books take readers beyond everyday experiences, broadening their world knowledge, developing their imaginations and senses of humor, and enabling them to grow in humanity and understanding (Galda, Ash, & Cullinan, 2001). Aesthetics, understanding, imagination, knowledge, cognition, and language are values attributed to literature (Gallas, 2000). However, foremost among literature's values is enjoyment. Readers have to find pleasure in books if they are to experience the values literature offers (Sloan, 2002). Individuals who enjoy literature read often and find pleasure in the books they read. Well-crafted stories and poems enchant readers. The fascinating information and knowledge imparted in fine literature for children attracts readers to all types of works, including humorous stories, informational books, fiction, nonfiction, and poetry.

Humor

Humor is an important value of literature, one that contributes to children's development and interest in reading. Gilles Bachelet's *My Cat, the Silliest Cat in the World* demonstrates humor for children because the "cat" behaves like an ordinary cat, but he is like no cat anyone has ever seen. Although the storyteller accepts the fact that the animal is a cat, readers conclude that someone should tell this character that he is very confused! The "cat" is actually an elephant acting like a cat. Children laugh throughout this story. Humor is an important theme in poetry, too. Adam Rex uses a variety of media and literary techniques to create hilarious poetry in *Frankenstein Makes a Sandwich*. The characters in this poetry book include the creature from Black Lagoon (who refuses to listen to his mother), and Count Dracula—who with spinach stuck in his teeth is not too scary but just scary enough that no one has the nerve to tell him about the food in his teeth. The "Zombie, Zombie" poem creates unforgettable images. If you like to laugh, this is the book for you, whether you are child or adult.

Informational Books

Informational books pique readers' interest in new topics and whet their appetite for knowledge. In their book, *Sky Boys: How They Built the Empire State Building*, Deborah Hopkinson and illustrator James Ransome capture the drama of men working high above New York City. This book views the construction through the eyes of a boy who lived in the time period of this construction. Poetic text and rich detail help readers understand this human accomplishment.

Fiction, Nonfiction, and Poetry

Fiction, nonfiction, and poetry are artistic interpretations of experiences, events, and people. They are forms of literature, each of which expresses meaning in different ways. Picture books and book illustrations add the dimension of visual art, which interacts with language to tell a story, create a poem, or impart information. Aesthetics pertain to the beauty that readers perceive in a literary work. Literature is verbal art that helps readers appreciate the beauty of language, thereby adding new dimensions to their lives.

Literature and Language Arts

The language arts include speaking, listening, reading, and writing. Children's literature is essential to teaching and learning the language arts. Much of the content for teaching the arts of speaking, listening, reading, and writing is derived from children's books. Reading to children builds their sense of story and enhances their understanding of the ways authors structure and organize text. Moreover, literature builds knowledge. Jon Agee's book, *Terrific,* is an example of an exceptional book for developing the language arts. *Terrific* is the story of a pessimist who wins a trip to Bermuda and then responds to his good fortune by saying that he will probably get a sunburn. He continues to predict calamity after calamity. Ultimately, his parrot is the only one who can help him.

Literature provides writers with ideas and inspiration, as well as a means to create models for organizing ideas in text; therefore, immersing children in literature prepares them for writing. For example, *The True Story of the 3 Little Pigs* and *The Stinky Cheese Man and Other Fairly Stupid Tales,* both by Jon Scieszka, are guaranteed to tickle everyone's sense of humor and motivate children to read and write.

Literature as a Language Model

Language and thinking are so closely interrelated that the ability to think depends upon one's mastery of language. Literature enlarges children's sensitivity to and understanding of language, thereby enabling them to choose the words and create the syntax that best express their thoughts. Fiction, nonfiction, and poetry help readers remember what they have read, promote their sense of the ways in which discourse may be structured, and discover patterns for structuring their own writing. Children need many opportunities to interact with others using language that is essential to acquiring higher-order thinking. Social activities such as conversations, hearing and telling stories, and discussing books enhance language development. Experiences with literature create a language foundation for listening, reading, and writing. Writers create richer language models in books than in everyday conversation because they tend to use elaborate sentences and sumptuous words, whereas speakers employ the same few words again and again.

Leo Lionni used exquisite language in many of his books (Lionni, 1963). For example, his book *Swimmy* includes a lobster that walks like a "water-moving machine" and an "eel with a tail that is too long to remember." This writing expands children's language repertoire, enabling them to develop greater facility in thinking, imagining, reading, and writing. Jack Prelutsky creates poetry that offers linguistic delight to readers and listeners. His book *Behold the Bold Umbrellaphant and Other Poems* includes Ballpoint Penguins who "do little else but write and write," and an Umbrellant that stays dry in the rain. These unusual creatures offer glee and zing to both readers and listeners. In *Arithmetickle*, J. Patrick Lewis uses word play. The subtitle of this book is *An Even Number of Odd Riddle-Rhymes*, which illustrates Lewis's word play. (Poetry is discussed in more detail in Chapter 5.)

Research reveals that the stories children write reflect the characteristics of their reading materials.

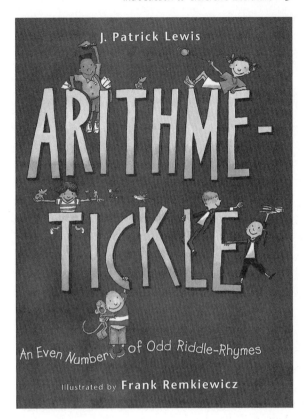

These poems will make you laugh at math.

Children whose reading reflects a wide range of writing structures, complex sentence patterns, and rich vocabulary exhibit these characteristics in their own writing, whereas those who read simple, repetitious stories write in a simple, repetitive style. Reading and discussing a wide variety of stories seems to help students discover the ways authors create meaning in written language, as these children are more sensitive to plot, character, setting, and writing style than their less-well-read peers (Calkins, 1986; Graves, 1983). The elements of stories are discussed in Chapter 2.

Literature and Understanding the World

"Children are growing up in a very complicated and difficult world, and they will have tough decisions to make throughout their lives. Literature plays an important role in teaching them what the world is like" (Lowry, 2002). Books stimulate readers' emotional responses. Characters like Edward Tulane, a toy rabbit in Kate DiCamillo's *The Miraculous Journey of Edward Tulane,* invite readers to care about them.

Edward Tulane, a toy rabbit, is transformed through his journey—as are readers. Edward discovers answers to the important questions: "What difference does one person make?" and "What is the value of love?" As they read, children begin to realize that people around the world share their hopes, dreams, and fears. Through stories, they learn that many life experiences, such as happiness, sadness, fears, warm family relationships, death, and loneliness, are universal experiences. Kate DiCamillo observes that stories that begin with "long ago and far away" and "once upon a time" give both readers and storytellers the distance needed to bring life into focus and to tell the truth. She also says that a story about love "is about learning how to open your heart over and over again." (DiCamillo, 2007, p. 38). (Fantasy is discussed in more detail in Chapter 6.)

Reading about story *characters'* feelings and actions develops children's abilities to understand and appreciate how others feel. Children who come to understand and appreciate various cultures are more likely to understand the shared aspects of human life and to appreciate the cultures that comprise the United States, as well as the world at large. In *Love to Langston,* a biography in poetry, Tony Medina uses poetic language to give readers insight into the life of Langston Hughes and the importance of his writing in all of our lives.

Literature and Imagination

Imagination is a creative, constructive power that is intimately related to higher-order thinking skills. Every aspect of daily life involves imagination. People imagine as they talk and interact with others, make choices and decisions, analyze news reports, or assess advertising and entertainment. Critical and creative thinkers strive to develop or invent novel, aesthetic, and constructive ideas. Literature illustrates the unlimited range of the human imagination and extends readers' personal visions of possibilities (Frye, 1964; Gallas, 2000). Literature stirs and stretches the imagination, providing new information, ideas, and perspectives so that readers can imagine possibilities. Audrey Wood illustrates the possibilities of imagination in *Little Penguin's Tale.* In this way, it expands the readers' ability to express imagination in words and images.

Many children's books inspire readers' creative thought and imaginations. For example, Jeanette Winterson, the author of *Tanglewreck,* created a gothic

Audrey and Don Wood have written and illustrated many books. Readers return again and again to Little Penguin's Tale, only to discover that some of us can just hear a story—and others have to experience it.

tale that is set in an England where time is an article of trade, creating unusual mixtures of the past and present. Silver, the protagonist of the story, lives in *Tanglewreck* because it reminds her of her lost parents and sisters. She is unaware of the villains who live underground and of the Timekeeper, who is hidden in the house. Winterson has created a story that balances humor and adventure.

Literature and Cognition

Literature is a way of thinking that serves as a source of knowledge and a sounding board for children's reasoning. It plays a role in developing a sharp and critical mind (Langer, 1995). All literature, stories, and poems, as well as nonfiction, stimulate thinking by giving readers substance for reflection. Literature can provoke readers to analyze, synthesize, connect, and respond thoughtfully, which facilitates cognitive development. Literature is a forum that offers readers diverse perspectives on familiar topics by giving them a safe medium for trying different roles, imagining new settings, and puzzling out unique problem solutions. Many books model thinking processes such as problem solving, inferring, evaluative thinking, relational thinking, and imagining. Readers of Jon Scieszka's *Math Curse* will be stimulated to discover the many times they confront mathematical reasoning in their lives.

Literature and the Curriculum

Literature supports learning across the curriculum because it widens the reader's world beyond the immediate time and place. Reading is an instrument for accessing ideas and information. Moreover, it gives students opportunities to interact with one another and to understand the ways that others think and respond. For example, students who read are able to generate hypotheses and cultivate multiple perspectives, ways of thinking that are used in all subject areas. Children who read recognize the connectedness of separate subjects and the patterns of knowledge and carry knowledge from one subject to another. An integrated curriculum is one in which teachers plan for students to learn language at the same time they are learning something else, which may be science, social studies, math, or art, or even a project such as planning an assembly program. Literature enhances the curriculum with thematic and topical units and literature-based instruction. A good example of a book that supports learning is Claudia Logan's book *The 5,000 Year Old Puzzle: Solving a Mystery of Ancient Egypt,* which takes readers beyond mere facts and descriptions. Readers learn how real archaeologists conduct an actual dig; students also get a picture of how archeologists think and communicate and learn about life in ancient Egypt as well. (Nonfiction is discussed in more detail in Chapter 10.)

Literature Experiences in Classrooms

The values of literature emerge in children's lives when they have coherent, planned experiences with carefully selected literature. The following principles have emerged from research and experience:

1. Cultivating a love of reading first is the most compelling reason for literature and libraries in schools. Love of reading leads to increased reading, which is followed by students' highly developed literacy skills. However, using literature as a drill for facts or skills can eliminate the enjoyment (Rand 2002; Rosenblatt, 1995).

2. Literature programs should have a coherent structure. "Literature can be used as a way of understanding the world, or appreciated as a work of art that has value in and of itself" (Serafini, 2003).

3. Literature programs give students opportunities to appreciate the author's language, meaning cues, and literary conventions. Three principles are frequently used to organize literature programs: genre studies (categories of literature), elements of literature studies (plot, character, setting, style, theme), and authors' and illustrators' studies (recognized writers in the field of children's literature, and artists who illustrate children's books). (Literary genre, elements, and authors are discussed more fully in Chapter 2.)

4. Children's response to literature is an important part of the literary experience. We believe in the transactional perspective: that authors and readers create meaning together (Krashen, 2004; Rand, 2002; Serafini, 2003). Response refers to readers' feelings about a work of literature. Readers use the author's meaning cues, extracting and constructing meaning as they interact with text and relate to life as they know it. "Each time we talk about a book we discover our sense of it, our ideas about it, our understanding of what it is and means, even the details we remember have changed and shifted and come to us in different arrangements, different patterns" (Chambers, 1983, p. 167). Readers' responses are cultivated by giving them occasions to read, discuss and discover, consider, represent, and reread to make their own meanings. Figure 1.1 illustrates the reader-response transaction. (Chapter 15 explores responses to literature in more detail.)

Fine literature is important to the preceding goals; however, the focus of this text is learner-centered

---

FIGURE 1.1 Literary response continuum.

BOOK READER

| Uninterested, does not finish book | Somewhat interested | Enjoys book, finds it satisfying | Excited, wants to share feeling about book | Finds book totally absorbing |

literary experiences with quality children's books. The literature suggested in this text establishes touchstones or benchmarks that are quality standards designed to help you select inspiring literature that stimulates children's appreciation and responses.

Trends in Children's Literature

As the values of children's literature are recognized in children's lives, publishers are producing many excellent children's books. Adults often discover that children's books have changed dramatically since their childhood. Modern life and culture impinge on publishing and on children's reading interests. Publishers are expanding the quality and number of books available on subjects that were "all but invisible in literature for youth" (Horning et al., 2006). Today's authors address death, birth, anger, mental illness, alcoholism, and brutality in explicit terms. Students read gothic novels that seem dark to adults. Futuristic worlds, science fiction, and imaginary characters and settings are found in popular literature.

Adolescent Literature

Adults who have not read recently published children's or adolescent literature may find the realism shocking; nevertheless, contemporary realism contributes to children's self-understanding. In Esckilsen's *The Outside Groove,* the protagonist, Casey LaPlante, is an accomplished student with high aspirations, but her parents are more focused on the performance of her older brother, Wade, who participates in stockcar races. So Casey decides to take up driving in the races herself. With the backing of her uncle Harvey and her all-girl pit crew, Casey becomes so successful that she is a threat to her brother's success. Casey's parents then forbid her to race and steal the spotlight from him. The plot has excitement, mystery, and romance.

Adolescents have a larger number of books addressing their interests than ever before, and they are responding by purchasing more books. Adolescent readers are defined in various ways, ranging from age 11 to 16, or from grade four to college (Bucher & Manning, 2005). Middle-school and intermediate students may be defined in various ways, with the most common being grades five or six through grade eight.

Adolescent readers are a diverse group because some adolescents are more like elementary students, while others may be ready for high school or adult reading (Sutton, 2007). Of course, the intermediate grades tend to have parameters similar to middle school.

Chapter Books

Chapter books are more plentiful for children beginning in second and third grade. Many of the chapter books for this level are part of a series. Interesting books for this age group are very important because they are moving into more independent reading. *Scaredy Squirrel Makes a Friend* by Melanie Watt is the second in a series about Scaredy Squirrel. *Martin Bridge: Sound the Alarm!* by Jessica Kerrin is the second in a series about a boy who loves the superhero Zip Rideout. Sara Pennypacker's *The Talented Clementine* is the story of 8-year-old Clementine and her search for a talent because her class is having a talent show to raise money for a class trip.

Series Books

Series books attract many children to reading, developing both motivation and fluency along with other values. Series books add to "the reservoir of experiences and ideas created from the sum total of all their reading"; the richer this reservoir of experience and ideas, the more effective children's transactions with literature will become over time (Purves & Monson, 1984).

Series books do have value for young readers. The experience of making patterns, putting stories together, extrapolating, and confirming may be providing a crucial step toward reading more sophisticated books and toward a broader literary understanding. When I was in fourth grade, I eagerly read all of the books in the Nancy Drew series. Recently, "Good Morning, America" presented a program featuring outstanding women who had read all of the Nancy Drew books. Each one commented on their pleasure in reading this series and in the values of these books. They agreed that they learned independence and the belief they could do things without help. Of course, they realized these values in retrospect.

Series books are very popular with today's readers, and many new series are available in a wide range of genre and topics. Outstanding authors have written popular series, such as J. K. Rowling's *Harry Potter* series (all ages) and Brian Jacques's *Redwall* series (intermediate). Students eagerly await new books in their favorite series. Kathryn Lasky's series entitled *Guardians of Ga'Hoole* (middle school) is about a kingdom where barn owls dwell. The clerks at my local bookstore assure me that the books in this series are extremely popular and sell out as quickly as they come in. When librarians compiled bibliographies of what their students read, they learned that students became momentarily addicted to series books and comic books and then they moved on (Mackey, 1990, p. 488). These materials seem to be as much a part of one's literary maturation as are the children's classics.

Graphic Novels and Manga

Graphic novels and *manga* are very popular with students; both have huge audiences. Graphic novels are modern comic books that are printed on higher quality paper. Manga are Japanese comic books that are read from back to front. Both types of books have huge audiences, as students tell one another about them. Barnes & Noble and Borders bookstores devote large sections to these books. Many graphic novels are being adapted to film, and superheros are popular subjects. One teacher asked her sixth-grade class how many had read manga, and discovered that 75 percent had read and enjoyed manga (Bucher & Manning, 2005). Another interesting trend is writing graphic novels; when visiting the large sections of graphic novels in major bookstores, I observed a large number of books about how to write graphic novels, and I talked with students who were writing them.

Fantasy

Fantasy and science fiction have expanded significantly in recent years due to the Harry Potter phenomenon. Parents and children have discovered fantasy and science fiction, and they want more. The Harry Potter series by J. K. Rowling, in particular, could be termed a phenomenon, as readers of all ages—from young children to college students to senior citizens—eagerly wait for the publication of each new book in the series; the Harry Potter books have an international popularity as well and have been translated into many other languages.

Nonfiction

A larger number of excellent nonfiction books on a wide variety of topics is available. The authors of these nonfiction works have created inviting, well-written books. Children find the real world and real events fascinating, and reading enables them to participate in experiences that go far beyond learning mere facts. Trade books give readers a sense of people, times, and places that textbooks do not. For example, in *Team Moon: How 400,000 People Landed Apollo 11 on the Moon*, Thimmesh gives an exciting behind-the-scenes account of the first manned moon landing. This account turns chilling when the author introduces seven challenges that threatened to abort the landing and turn it into a tragedy. The text is enhanced with color photographs of the mission.

In Eve Bunting's *Pop's Bridge*, young readers learn about a high iron man who works on the Golden Gate Bridge; the story is told through the eyes of his son, Robert. When a scaffold falls, Robert and his friend Charlie see the accident through binoculars. San Francisco is also the subject of an interesting historical novel in Laurence Yep's *The Earth Dragon Awakes: The San Francisco Earth Quake of 1906*. This story is told from the point of view of Henry and his friend Chin, a Chinese immigrant. These and other nonfiction books enhance children's understanding of a variety of subjects.

Multicultural Literature

Readers today have a larger array of relevant multicultural literature to choose from. For example, *Angelina's Island* by Jeanette Winter is the story of a new immigrant from Jamaica who finds it difficult to adjust to New York City. *La Linea* by Ann Jaramillo is a coming-of-age story about Miguel who crosses the line from Mexico to the United States and subsequently realizes that life is a series of lines to be crossed. (Multicultural literature is presented more fully in Chapter 13.)

 # Selecting Children's Literature

A *literary transaction* involves the meaning constructed when an individual reads a specific book, views a film or Internet site, or listens to a tape recording (Rosenblatt, 1978). Because children should have many opportunities to make literary transactions that appeal to their own interests, purposes, and motivation, we believe in exposing children to a wide variety of genre, themes, characters, settings, and subject matter to help them develop interests and a sense of literary quality.

The major considerations in selecting and helping children select books are summarized in Figure 1.2.

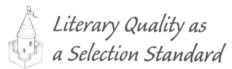

Literary Quality as a Selection Standard

Literary quality, which is the focus of *literary criticism*, falls into three categories: work(text)-centered criticism, which focuses on the quality of the book or media; child-centered criticism (focused on children's response to the work, text, or media); and issues-centered criticism, which focuses on appropriate presentation of social, cultural, and political diversity (issues that are discussed in more detail in Chapter 3). A book may present social issues accurately while failing to achieve in storytelling, while a book of excellent literary quality may not appeal to children. All three categories are factors to consider when choosing literature for children.

Splendid Stories

Librarians and teachers are concerned with literary quality because they strive to put excellent books in children's hands—books of honesty, integrity, and vision. There is no room for cutesy books, dull books, or books that talk down to children (Hearne with Stevenson, 1999). What qualities do truly great books for children have? Why do so many children return to these books year after year? First of all, they tell splendid stories that resonate with children's experiences and their imaginations. Books like Margaret Mahy's *The Boy Who Was Followed Home* tell stories that delight children. In this story, Robert is thrilled

when a hippopotamus follows him home, but the 43 hippos who gather on his family's lawn complicate the situation. A witch is called in to convince the animals to leave, leading to an unexpected climax.

Memorable Characters

Second, appealing literature has memorable and well-drawn characters, who live on in our adult minds—consider Peter Pan and Captain Hook. Another unforgettable character is Tsynq Yr, an alien who crashes to earth and is forced to inject his mind into a skunk's body in Pamela Service's *Stinker from Space*. Look for this book in the library, and you will find only well-worn copies . . . unless they are all checked out.

Vivid Illustrations

Third, many great books unite memorable text with vivid illustrations. Books such as Beatrix Potter's *The Tale of Peter Rabbit* and Maurice Sendak's *Where the Wild Things Are* illustrate this union of text and illustration. The true classics of literature are books that remain popular because children want to read them.

Award Books

Books that receive special awards are recognized as being of high literary quality, and therefore are a good beginning place for getting acquainted with worthwhile literature. The Newbery Award and the Caldecott Awards are the best-known of the book awards. These awards are given by the American Library Association. The details of these awards are in the following boxes. Additional award information is in the Appendix.

Another award, the Robert F. Sibert Informational Book Award, established in 2001, is given annually to the author of the most distinguished informational book published during the preceding year. The American Library Association administers the award. See the Appendix for a winners' list.

Other awards include the following (see the Appendix for a more complete list):

- The Hans Christian Andersen International Medal is awarded to living authors and artists by the International Board on Books for Young People.
- The International Reading Association presents the Children's Book Award to authors with unusual promise.

FIGURE 1.3 Criteria for the Newbery Award.

1. In identifying distinguished writing in a book for children, committee members must:

   a. consider:
      - interpretation of the theme or concept
      - presentation of information, including accuracy, clarity, and organization
      - development of plot
      - delineation of characters
      - delineation of setting
      - appropriateness of style

   NOTE: Because the literary qualities to be considered will vary depending on content, the committee need not expect to find excellence in each of the named elements. The book should, however, have distinguished qualities in all the elements pertinent to it.

   b. consider excellence of presentation for a child audience

2. Each book is to be considered as a contribution to literature. The committee is to make its decision primarily on the text. Other aspects of a book are to be considered only if they distract from the text. Such other aspects might include illustrations or overall design of the book.

   NOTE: The committee should keep in mind that the award is for literary quality and quality of presentation for children. The award is not for didactic intent or for popularity.

From: Peterson, L. K. & Solt, M. L. (1982). Newbery and Caldecott Model and Honor Books, p. 399. New Providence, NJ: Bowker.

FIGURE 1.4 Criteria for the Caldecott Medal.

1. In identifying a distinguished picture book for children, committee members must:

   a. consider the excellence of:
      - execution in the artistic technique employed
      - pictorial interpretation of story, theme, or concept
      - appropriateness of style of illustration to the story, theme, or concept
      - delineation of plot, theme, characters, setting, mood, or information through the pictures

   b. consider the excellence of presentation in recognition of a child audience

2. The only limitation to graphic form is that the form must be one that may be used in a picture book (film photography is not considered, but still photography is).

3. Each book is to be considered as a picture book. The committee is to make its decision primarily on the illustrations, but other components of a book are to be considered, especially when they make a book less effective as a children's picture book. Other components might include elements such as the written text or the overall design of the book.

   NOTE: The committee should keep in mind that the award is for distinguished illustrations in a picture book and for excellence of pictorial presentation for children. The award is not for didactic intent or for popularity.

From: Peterson, L. K., & Solt, M. L. (1982). Newbery and Caldecott Medal and Honor Books, p. 400. New Providence, NJ: Bowker.

- The Laura Ingalls Wilder Award is given to authors or illustrators who have made lasting contributions to children's literature.
- The Boston Globe/Horn Book Award is presented to authors of fiction and nonfiction and to illustrators.
- The Coretta Scott King Award is given to the best books for children about the black experience.
- The Pura Belpré Award is given to the best books for children about the Latino experience.
- The Consortium of Latin American Studies Programs (CLASP) gives the Americas Award in recognition of books that authentically and engagingly portray Latin America, the Caribbean, or Latinos in the United States.
- The Orbis Pictus Award recognizes outstanding nonfiction books. The National Council of Teachers of English sponsors this award.

Criticism of Awards

Children's book awards are valuable examples of literary quality for teachers and students. However, some award books have been criticized on several counts. First, such awards may be given to books appealing to only a small segment of the population, selected not on the basis of popularity with children but only on the basis of literary quality. And since concepts of literary quality can differ dramatically from individual to individual, giving awards on this basis can create the problem of elitism.

Second, many children's favorites are outstanding works that did not receive the prestigious Newbery Award, books such as the Little House books by Laura Ingalls Wilder and *Charlotte's Web*** by E. B. White. (Although *Charlotte's Web* did not receive the Newbery Award, it was recognized as an Honor book by the Newbery Award Committee.)

Readers' Motivation, Experiences, and Interests as Selection Guides

Students find friends' book recommendations most valuable. Every teacher has seen a book move through a class because friends recommended it to friends, who then recommended it to other friends until all or most of the students read it. Teachers' and librarians' booktalks also attract students to books. (Booktalks are discussed in more detail in Chapter 14.) Many teachers advocate children's free choice of literature as an important element for promoting reading in classrooms. Some suggest that children themselves should be the ultimate critics of their literature, that children's preferences for certain kinds of books not only should be honored, but also should form a basis for evaluating books.

Personal Appeal

Betsy Hearne (1999) stresses the importance of personal appeal and involvement in selecting children's books. She suggests that adults choose books that meet their standards but these books must appeal to children. She maintains that children's responses to books are as important as experts' recommendations. The power of personal attraction to a book cannot be underestimated. During their school years, children will read many types of literature, and the appeal of some books will not be apparent to adults.

Motivation

Students must have the desire or motivation to read a book for engagement to occur. They need an interest in the book's subject. Recent studies of children's reading motivations and interests shed some light on this subject. Edmunds and Bauserman studied 37 teachers and 831 students in grades pre-K through grade five, using the conversational interview portion of the Motivation to Read Profile (Gambrell et al., 1996). They identified six categories that motivated children to read (see Figure 1.5).

The Motivation to Read Profile

The Motivation to Read Profile was an instrument used in a study of adolescents' motivation to read (Pitcher et al., 2007). The study involved 384 adolescents and spanned a wide variety of geographic settings. The

---

> **FIGURE 1.5** Summary of students' motivation for reading.
>
> *Children chose narrative literature for these reasons:*
> - The books related to their personal interests.
> - The characteristics of the books appealed to them.
> - The students were given choices.
>
> *Expository books were chosen for these reasons:*
> - They gained knowledge from the books.
> - The books related to their personal interests.
> - The students were given choices.

findings of this study show what teachers and librarians need to do:

A. Acknowledge the multiple literacies that students engage in outside of the classroom and find ways to incorporate them in the classroom. Preferred literacies may differ from individual to individual. Taylor et al. (2005) found that some students who were not motivated to read school materials were motivated to read other materials. For example, Taylor's own son was a very successful reader in the elementary grades, but later was an unsuccessful reader who viewed himself as a poor reader who disliked reading. However, he was able to use written text to teach himself complex computer languages. Taylor suggests there is a gender gap in reading because boys seem to exhibit differences in preferred literacies more frequently than girls.

B. Model their own reading enjoyment.

C. Embrace engaging activities such as book clubs and reading circles into regular instruction in secondary schools.

D. Include reading materials of varied formats, levels, and topics in the classroom.

E. Incorporate elements of choice in readings and projects.

Identifying Personal Preferences and Interests

Literature preferences and interests are highly individual phenomena that change from reader to reader and book to book (Galda et al., 2001). Understanding readers, the texts they choose to read, and the contexts in which they read is very complex. Therefore, observations, discussions, and booktalks are the best ways to identify books that will energize children's reading. Observations regarding the engaging books that students choose to read and making notes about their choices are the most valid ways to identify their interests. Teachers can identify individual children's reading interests through techniques like the following:

1. Observe children as they engage in classroom activities, noting and recording interests exhibited during class assignments, oral discussions, group projects, and so forth. Children in second grade and beyond should keep their own records of books read and their response to the books.

2. Conduct informal discussions with the children themselves, their parents, peers, and others, which will reveal some interests.

3. Engage children in booktalks about a specific group of books, observe the students' responses to these books, and make notes about the books that the students responded to.

4. Conduct interest inventories, which take a variety of forms, asking children directly about their reading interests. Children can list their favorite book titles, respond to questions through a multiple-choice format, or complete sentence starters (see Figure 1.6).

5. Encourage children to choose books independently and observe their choices.

Recommended Reviews and Reading Lists

Teachers, librarians, and parents will find the following reviews and lists helpful when selecting books. In addition, a variety of review journals and recommended reading lists are available in print and on the Internet.

> *Adventuring with Books: A Booklist for PreK through 6,* 13th edition, published by the National Council of Teachers of English.
>
> Bowker, R. R. *Subject Guide to Books in Print.* New York: Bowker.
>
> *The Bulletin of the Center for Children's Books,* published for the University of Illinois Graduate School of Library and Information Science by the Johns Hopkins University Press. The Internet site is www.press.jhu.edu/journals.
>
> The Child Study Children's Book Committee of Bank Street College compiles an annual list of

---

FIGURE 1.6 Interest inventory.

1. I like to read _____ books.
2. I visit the library every _____.
3. I like to read when _____
4. I like to read more than I like to _____.
5. I watch television every _____.
6. My favorite television shows are _____.
7. I use a computer every _____.
8. I play computer games every _____.
9. I think books about sports are _____.
10. I think mysteries are _____.
11. I like "chick lit" _____.
12. My favorite author is _____.
13. I read funny stories about _____.
14. I like make-believe stories _____.
15. When I have spare time, I _____.
16. I like to read in _____.
17. Good books make me feel _____.
18. The best books are about _____.
19. The most boring books are about _____.
20. My favorite movie is _____.
21. My favorite video is _____.
22. I read _____ because my friend told me about it.
23. I own these books: _____.

Scoring : Score one point for each positive answer. Positive answers are ones that indicate the student enjoys reading and has identifiable reading, listening, and viewing interests.

16–23—Child has a positive attitude toward reading and has developed interests.

10–15—Child has average interest in reading.

1–9—Child needs guidance and support to develop an interest in reading.

---

30 books categorized as primary (grades K–2), intermediate (grades 3–5), and advanced (grades 6–8).

Children's Catalog is published annually by Wilson Publishing.

The Horn Book reviews books and includes articles about children's literature and authors. The Internet site is magazine@hbook.com

The Horn Book Guide to Children's and Young Adult Books is published by The Horn Book twice a year.

Language Arts is published by The National Council of Teachers of English and includes book reviews in each issue.

The Reading Teacher and the *Journal of Adolescent & Adult Literacy* are published by the International Reading Association and include book reviews in each issue.

Winkel, L. (Ed.). (Biannually). *The elementary school library collection: A guide to books and other media*. Philadelphia: Brodart Foundation.

Zarnowski, M., Kerper, R., & Jensen, J. (Eds.). (2002). *The best in children's nonfiction, The reading, writing and teaching Orbis Pictus award books*. Urbana, IL: National Council of Teachers of English.

Selecting Literature for English Language Learners

"Students learning English as a new language are the fastest growing group in U.S. schools today" (Vardell, Hadaway, & Young, 2006). Literature plays a critical role in immersing children in a new language. Both school and classroom libraries are integral to the literacy process because access to books encourages more reading. Students in classsroms with libraries read 50 percent more books than students in classrooms without them (Neuman, 1999). According to Vardell et al, the following guidelines are appropriate for English language learners:

Content accessibility. This refers to the familiarity of the topic, story, or concept. When the English language learner is familiar with the content in his or her language, the English content will be easier to understand.

Language accessibility. The language of the book should be simple and direct. Simple phrases or sentence patterns, a limited amount of text on each page, and predictable, repetitive text give English language learners a good beginning level.

Visual accessibility. Abundant illustrations give readers cues to help them figure out the meaning of the text.

Genre accessibility. English language learners need exposure to various styles of writing and text organization. Both the school and classroom libraries should have a variety of genres and topics.

Children's Literature and Media

Children's literature today includes media such as movies based on children's books and books that are based on popular movies. Movies based on books, such as *Pirates of the Caribbean, The Chronicles of Narnia,* and *Harry Potter,* are popular with youngsters. The Internet provides sites where students can learn about authors and read book reviews. Students can communicate with others who are reading the same books. They can create films about their favorite stories and poems. Students can view literature and media with multiple perspectives. Throughout this text, we will introduce film and Internet literature, as well as related Internet sources. Lists of useful Internet sites can be found on the companion web site.

Audio books, electronic books, television, movies, Internet sites, and videos provide legitimate forms of literature that are here to stay. High-quality media actively involve children with the literature they are experiencing—an advantage that children may carry into other literary experiences. *Reading Rainbow*, a television show aired on local PBS stations, has received many awards that attest to its high quality.

The availability of media-based literature is growing rapidly: Listening Library now offers more than 200 unabridged children's recordings (*Horn Book,* 2007). Although these media do not replace books, they do offer a different dimension, and narrators and actors can make stories come alive for children. Many children will go on to read books they have been exposed to through various media; others will not because the media offer an alternative route to literature they could not access otherwise.

Videos such as *The Very Hungry Caterpillar* (Disney) offer animation and music to enhance this well-loved story. The various genres of children's literature are represented in videos. For example, The James Marshall Library (Children's Circle/Scholastic) includes popular fairy tales that primary-grade children will enjoy. Videos include feature-length films such as *Beethoven Lives Upstairs. The Children's Literature Web Guide* on the Internet can direct you to multimedia materials that have been evaluated by parents' groups and the American Library Association.

CD–ROM drives are standard on computers today, creating easy access to excellent media. Living Books features various children's authors, such as Mercer Mayer (Random House/Broderbund).

Busy, Busy Town by Richard Scarry has received the Parents Award for Quality (Paramount International). Microsoft published some of the *Magic School Bus* titles, which children find fascinating, on CD–ROM. The interactive, involving nature of computerized books adds to their popularity and their value for children.

Media-based literature should not be designed to offer alternative editions of existing books; rather, it should offer additional dimensions. Some writers create original literature for CD–ROM rather than converting existing literature to a media format. *Freddi Fish and the Case of the Missing Kelp Seeds* (Humongous Entertainment) is another entertaining and original computer story.

Horn Book (2007) reviewed various audiobooks and listed these excellent examples: *The Last Dragon* by Silvana De Mari, *The Miraculous Journey of Edward Tulalne*, by Kate DiCamillo, and *Lon Po Po* by Ed Young. *Horn Book* reviews media periodically; the reviews are often available in public libraries as well as college and university libraries. *School Library Media Activities Monthly* is also an invaluable resource for identifying media, Internet sites, and curriculum and standards connections.

Evaluating Media-Based Literature

The media deluge all of us with information and news. Teachers, librarians, parents, and students have to assess the value and accuracy of media. The first question that students ask about media is "which information is believable?" Students who are interested in issues can develop critical reading and critical viewing skills (Hobbs, 2001). Questions like these will help them evaluate media:

- What makes you believe what you've read or heard?
- Why did that story get in the news?
- Is that really true?
- Isn't that just your point of view?
- Why wasn't the information included in our textbook? (Hobbs, 2001)

The American Library Association

Another source of media evaluation is The American Library Association, which reviews and evaluates media for children. Consulting their reviews and standards can be very helpful to librarians and teachers. The standards for literature identified earlier in this chapter are also applicable to media presentations of literature.

1. The literature must tell a good story or be a wonderful poem or give accurate, interesting information (check the guidelines established in the genre chapters).
2. The literature must actively involve viewers or listeners.
3. The literature should convey the essence of the literature so that plot, theme, characterization, and setting are authentic, although the style may differ according to the medium.
4. The literature should meet all of the standards set for written literature; for instance, informational literature should meet nonfiction standards, and the difference between theory and fact should be apparent.
5. The literature should have all illustrations in scale and accurately identified.
6. The literature should not be simplified so that it loses literary quality; literature prepared for film, computer, video, and so forth may require changes, but these can be achieved without loss of quality.
7. The literature should not trivialize the story, for instance, by making the presentation too "cute."

Literature and the Standards Movement

There is widespread concern in the United States about curriculum knowledge and student performance. As a result, many states and professional organizations have developed standards and high-stakes tests that define what students should know in a specific content subject. The tests are used to appraise students' progress toward achieving those standards or goals. For example, language arts standards define what students should know about language and be able to do with language (NCTE & IRA, 1996). Standards for the English language arts jointly developed by the International Reading Association (IRA) and the National Council of Teachers of English (NCTE) are shown in the following box. Throughout this book, we relate literature and standards to building this foundation for learning.

FIGURE 1.7 IRA/NCTE Standards for the English language arts.

The vision guiding these standards is that all students must have the opportunities and resources to develop the language skills they need to pursue life's goals and to participate fully as informed, productive members of society. These standards assume that literacy growth begins before children enter school as they experience and experiment with literacy activities—reading and writing, and associating spoken words with their graphic representations. Recognizing this fact, these standards encourage the development of curriculum and instruction that make productive use of the emerging literacy abilities that children bring to school. Furthermore, the standards provide ample room for the innovation and creativity essential to teaching and learning. They are not prescriptions for particular curriculum or instruction.

Although we present these standards as a list, we want to emphasize that they are not distinct and separable; they are, in fact, interrelated and should be considered as a whole.

1. Students read a wide range of print and nonprint texts to build and understanding to texts, of themselves, and of the cultures of the United States and the world; to acquire new information; to respond to the needs and demands of society and the workplace; and for personal fulfillment. Among these texts are fiction and nonfiction, classic and contemporary works.

2. Students read a wide range of literature from many periods in many genres to build an understanding of the many dimensions (e.g., philosophical, ethical, aesthetic) of human experience.

3. Students apply a wide range of strategies to comprehend, interpret, evaluate, and appreciate texts. They draw on their prior experiences, their interactions with other readers and writers, their knowledge of word meaning and of other texts, their word identification strategies, and their understanding of textual features (e.g., sound-letter correspondence, sentence structure, context, graphics).

4. Students adjust their use of spoken, written, and visual language (e.g., conventions, style, vocabulary) to communicate effectively with a variety of audiences and for different purposes.

5. Students employ a wide range of strategies as they write and use different writing process elements appropriately to communicate with different audiences for a variety of purposes.

6. Students apply knowledge of language structure, language conventions (e.g., spelling and punctuation), media techniques, figurative language, and genre to create, critique, and discuss print and nonprint texts.

7. Students conduct research on issues and interests by generating ideas and questions, and by posing problems. They gather, evaluate, and synthesize data from a variety of sources (e.g., print and nonprint texts, artifacts, people) to communicate their discoveries in ways that suit their purpose and audience.

8. Students use a variety of technological and informational resources (e.g., libraries, databases, computer networks, video) to gather and synthesize information and to create and communicate knowledge.

9. Students develop an understanding of and respect for diversity in language use, patterns, and dialects across cultures, ethnic groups, geographic regions, and social roles.

10. Students whose first language is not English make use of their first language to develop competency in the English language arts and to develop understanding of content across the curriculum.

11. Students participate as knowledgeable, reflective, creative, and critical members of a variety of literacy communities.

12. Students use spoken, written, and visual language to accomplish their own purposes (e.g., for learning, enjoyment, persuasion, and the exchange of information).

The curriculum standards movement has become a force in education because, in many states, students must achieve specified scores in order to pass to the next grade level, not to mention graduate from high school. The "high-stakes" tests can create tension for both teachers and students. Teachers recognize that an education involves more than memorizing facts specified in the various standards. In fact, students need to create cognitive connections among facts in order to understand and remember them. Literature can develop deeper understandings and memories.

Creating Effective Literary Experiences...

Hearing literature read aloud is usually children's first introduction to literary experience. Through read-aloud experiences, children can be introduced to genre, elements of literature, and authors/illustrators (these issues are discussed in more detail in Chapter 2 and Chapter 14). These experiences and subsequent literature reading experiences can be structured through teacher and librarian (media specialist) planning. Children can participate in reading circles, webquests, reading discussions, and Internet programs

CLASSROOM SNAPSHOT

CONNECTING IDEAS AND LANGUAGE

Janet Rosario chose *My Teacher Likes to Say* by Denise Brennan-Nelson to show her students the connections among ideas and language in books. After reading the book aloud, Janet asked the children to identify phrases, clichés, proverbs, etc., that the teacher in the story liked to say. She wrote the children's responses on the overhead transparency. Following is the list they compiled:

Full of beans

Ants in your pants

Two heads are better than one

Button your lip

I'm hungry as a bear

The pen is mightier than the sword

The early bird gets the worm

After identifying the sayings, the students discussed the meaning of each one and reviewed the way the sayings were illustrated in the book. Then Janet gave them a homework assignment to remember sayings they had heard and write them down. She also suggested that they ask their parents and grandparents about their favorite sayings. Her plans included having each student make a picture book of their collected sayings. The author of *My Teacher Likes to Say* explained in fine print the history of the sayings; Janet used this fact to plan an activity that she hoped would lead her students into researching the sayings they discovered.

---

relating to printed books, taped books, and videos. Clusters of related books, booklists, and media are suggested in this text and on the companion web site.

Exploring Literature

The ways that literature is presented influence children's literary response. How books are read and what is read, the frequency of read-alouds, and active discussions build children's reading interests and response to literature (Galda et al., 2001). Reading books aloud and discussing them helps students construct meaning. Increasing the connections that students can make with literature content (including media-based materials) through discussion and response activities also increases comprehension and appreciation.

Media-based literature is easy to present: It can be done as simply as turning on a switch. It should always, however, be a part of a planned literary experience. The parents, teachers, or librarians presenting the literature should share the experience with the children. First, creating a context for the experience by introducing the piece and helping the children see connections to themselves will help ensure their active involvement and response; afterward, adults can discuss the experience with the children and share their responses. Discussion

and opportunities to respond are just as important for media as for books. The suggestions in Chapter 15 will be helpful in planning responses to literature.

Summary

This chapter introduced children's literature as literature that children understand and enjoy. Moreover, the text established the importance of literature in elementary classrooms, as a means of exploring and seeking meaning in human experience. Children's literature includes all types of books that entertain and inform children, including picture books, traditional literature, realistic fiction, historical fiction, biography, fantasy, poetry, and nonfiction, among other media such as narratives, videos, verbal stories, and the fine arts. The content of children's literature is limited only by the experience and understanding of the reader. Successful teachers involve their students with literature daily by reading aloud and providing time for students to read on their own.

Literature knowledge enables teachers and other adults to select appropriate literature and to guide literature experiences. Selecting literature and media that appeals to children and motivates them to read is essential to help students learn to appreciate and understand literature. Children should have opportunities to get acquainted with fiction, nonfiction, and poetry. English language learners should have literature that they can understand.

Thought Questions and Applications

1. Write your own definition of children's literature.

2. How does literature develop children's imagination?

3. Which values of literature are most important, in your opinion?

4. How is a good children's book like a good adult book? How is it different from an adult book?

5. What do you think you need to learn in order to select children's literature?

6. Could the same criteria be used to evaluate both adult and children's literature? Why or why not?

7. Do you think computers and software will replace literature?

8. What touchstone or benchmark books have you discovered?

9. Access one of the Internet sites related to children's literature.

Research and Application Experiences

1. Interview three of your friends to determine their favorite childhood books, and then interview three children. Compare their responses.

2. Read three new children's books (published within the last five years). How are they like the ones you read as a child? How are they different? Make file cards for each of these books to start your children's literature file.

3. Interview three teachers. Ask them how often they read aloud and what books they choose to read aloud.

4. Read several books by the same author to help you become acquainted with a children's author. What did you learn about the author from his or her writing? Look up the author on the Internet and add that information to what you have already learned. Add these books to your children's literature file.

5. If you are participating in an internship experience accompanying this course, observe the following in your classroom:

   a. How often does the teacher read aloud?

   b. What does the teacher read aloud?

   c. How often do the children independently read trade books?

6. Read one of the children's books mentioned in this chapter and compare your response to the book with the author's comments about it.

7. If you are participating in an internship experience related to this course, ask the students to identify their favorite authors.

Classroom Activities

ACTIVITY 1.1   UNDERSTANDING AND APPRECIATING WRITING PATTERNS

Jon Agee's book, *Terrific*, develops readers' word understanding and appreciation as well as language structure. In this story the central character has a negative response for each positive event, creating a pattern. Each of the following books also has a pattern: *Fortunately* by Remy Charlip; *The Important Book* by M.W. Brown; and *Meanwhile* by Jules Feiffer. Students at all levels will learn words that increase comprehension; they can use the writing patterns to structure their own writing and their own stories. Older students can learn about pessimism and optimism from Jon Agee's book, and this study can be extended to a study of Agee's other books.

Children's Literature References

Note: Books designated with an asterisk (*) are recommended for reluctant readers.

Agee, J. (2005). *Terrific*. New York: Hyperion. K–2;3–4;7+. MF

A negative man continually finds the negative when something good happens.

Bachelet G. (2006). *My cat, the silliest cat in the world*. New York: Abrams. K–2. PB*

This picture book is about an elephant who thinks it is a cat.

Balliett, B. (2004). *Chasing vermeer*. New York: Scholastic. 3–4;5–6. CRF

Petra and Calder have to find a Vermeer painting that disappeared.

Brennan-Nelson, D. (2004). *My teacher likes to say.* Chelsea, MI: Sleeping Bear. K–2;3–4. CRF*

Teachers use some sayings over and over, such as "two heads are better than one."

Brown, M.W. (1999). *The important book*. New York: Harper. K–2. PB

Discusses the most important thing about common objects.

Bunting, E. (2006). *Pop's bridge.* New York: Harcourt. K–2;3–4. INF

The story of building the Golden Gate Bridge.

Charlip, R. (1993). *Fortunately*. New York: Aladdin. K–2;3–4. PB

This story is written in the fortunately unfortunately pattern.

Crow, J. M. (2006). *Counting coup*. Washington D.C.: National Geographic. 3–4;5–6. INF

The author writes about his experiences as a warrior.

Davies, N. (2006) *Extreme animals*. New York: Candlewick. K–2;3–4. INF

The author includes fascinating information about animals that will appeal to children.

DiCamillo, K. *The miraculous journey of Edward Tulane.* New York: Candlewick. 3–4;5–6. MF

This is the story of a vain, cold-hearted china rabbit who searches for love.

Dowell, F.O. (2005). *Chicken boy.* New York: Atheneum. 5–6;7+. CRF

Tobin faces a variety of problems, including a nearly certifiable grandmother and a pack of juvenile delinquent siblings.

Eschilsen, E. (2006). *The outside groove.* Boston: Houghton Mifflin. 5–6;7+. CRF

Casey becomes a female race car driver.

Feiffer, J. (1997). *Meanwhile.* K–2;3–4. PB

This nonsense story illustrates absorption in a book.

Hardinge, F. (2006). *Fly by night.* New York: Macmillian. 5–6;7+. MF

A traveling wordsmith finds himself in a place where culture is suspect and the politics are complex.

Harper, C. (2007). *Just grace.* Boston: Houghton. K–2;3–4. CRF*

Just Grace is one of three girls named Grace in third grade.

Hopkinson, D. (2006). *Sky boys: How they built the Empire State Building* (J. Ransome, Illus.). New York: Schwartz & Wade. K–2;3–4. INF*

Jacques, B. (2007). *Eulalia (Redwall).* New York: Philomel. 3–4;5–6. MF

The Badger King of Salamandastron envisions his own death so he searches for a successor.

Jaramillo, A. (2006). *La linea.* Roaring Brook, CT: Roaring Brook Press. 5–6;7+. CRF

Miguel and his sister leave Mexico for California and barely survive the journey.

Kerrin, J. & Kelly, J. (2007). *Martin Bridge: Sound the alarm.* New York: Kids Can Press. K–2;3–4. CRF

Shows how the Empire State Building was built.

Lasky, K. (2007). *The guardians of Ga'hoole.* New York: Scholastic. 5–6;7+. MF

Coryn and friends preside over a New Golden age.

Lewis, J. P. (2002). *Arithmetickle* (F. Remkiewicz, Illus.). New York: Harcourt. K–2;3–4. P

This book is an even number of odd riddle-rhymes.

Lionni, L. (1963). *Swimmy*. New York: Pantheon. K–2. MF

After a fierce tuna eats his family, Swimmy sets out to see the world.

Logan, C. (2002). *The 5,000 year old puzzle: Solving a mystery of ancient Egypt.* New York: Farrar. 3–4;5–6. INF

The story of an archaeological expedition that took place in 1924.

Mahy, M. (1993). *The boy who was followed home.* New York: Puffin. K–2. MF

A boy is followed home by a hippopotamus. This makes him happy until more and more hippos gather in the yard.

Medina, T. (2002). *Love to Langston* (C. Christie, Illus.). New York: Lee & Low. 4–9. P

Superb poetic biography of Langston Hughes.

Newman, J. (2006). *Hippo! no, rhino!* New York: Little Brown. K–2. MF

A rhino is upset when a zookeeper puts up the Hippo sign in front of his home.

Pennypacker, S. & Frazee, M. (2007). *The talented clementine.* New York: Hyperion. 3–4.

Jennifer, a third grader, is searching for a talent to perform in the school talent show.

Potter, B. (2006). *Beatrix Potter Complete Tales.* London:Warne.

A complete unabridged collection of Potter's stories.

Prelutsky, J. (2006) *Behold bold umbrellephant.* New York: Greenwillow. K–2;3–4. P

Each poem is about an animal and an inanimate object.

Rex, A. (2006). *Frankenstein makes a sandwich.* New York: Harcourt. K–2;3–4. P

A humorous collection of poetry.

Rowling, J. & GrandPré (2007). *Harry Potter and the deathly hallows.* 3–4;5–6;7+. MF

This is a hero's mission.

Scieszka, J. (1989). *The true story of the 3 little pigs by A. Wolf* (L. Smith, Illus.). New York: Viking. K–2;3–4. MF*

Mr. A. Wolf gives his version of what happened to the three little pigs.

Scieszka, J. (1992). *The stinky cheese man and other fairly stupid tales* (L. Smith, Illus.). New York: Viking. K–2;3–4;5–6. MF*

This is a collection of fractured fairy tales that delight all ages.

Scieszka, J. (1995). *Math curse* (L. Smith, Illus.). New York: Viking. K–2;3–4;5–6. INF*

This book tells of the problems of living in a world where math is so important.

Sendak, M. (1963). *Where the wild things are.* New York: Harper & Row. K–2. MF*

Max is wild, so his mother sends him to bed without dinner; he discovers he is loved.

Service, P. (1989). *Stinker from space.* New York: Fawcett. 3–4;5–6. MF

Karen dreams about adventures in space and encounters an alien in the body of a skunk.

Thimmesh, C. (2006). *Team moon: How 400,000 people landed Apollo 11 on the moon.* Boston: Houghton Mifflin. 3–4;5–6;7+. INF

A behind the scenes look at the first Apollo moon landing.

Watt, M. (2007). *Scaredy Squirrel makes a friend.* New York: Kids Can Press. K–2. F

Scaredy is lonely, but he is afraid of making friends.

White, E. B. (1952). *Charlotte's web* (G. Williams, Illus.). New York: Harper & Row. 3–4. MF

Charlotte the spider saves Wilbur the pig's life with a unique solution to his problem.

Wilder, L. W. & Williams, G. (2006). *A Little House collection: The first five novels.* New York: Harper Collins. 3–4;5–6. HF

The early years of Laura Ingalls Wilder.

Winter, J. (2007). *Angelina's island.* New York: Farrar. K–2;3–4. CRF

Angelina is homesick for Jamaica, but Mama helps her find a new island in the sun.

Winterson, J. (2007). *Tanglewreck.* New York: Bloomsbury. 3–4;5–6. MF*

Eleven year-old Silver and her aunt live in a strange house filled with clocks.

Wood, A. (1993). *Little Penguin's tale.* New York: Harcourt. K–2. PB

Little Penguin dances with his imagination.

Yep, L. (2006). *The earth dragon awakes: The San Francisco earthquake of 1906.* New York: Harper Collins. 3–4;5–6;7+. CRF

The San Francisco Earthquake is told through the experiences of two fictional families.

Professional References

Baumann, J., Hooten, H., & White, P. (1999, September). Teaching comprehension through literature: A teacher-research project to develop fifth graders' reading strategies and motivation. *The Reading Teacher, 53,* 38–51.

Beach, R. (1993). *Reader-response theories.* Urbana, IL: National Council of Teachers of English.

Bruner, J. (1986). *Actual minds, possible worlds.* Cambridge, MA: Harvard University Press.

Bucher, K. & Manning, M. (2005). *Young adult literature: Exploration, evaluation, and appreciation.* Upper Saddle River, NJ: Merrill/Prentice Hall.

Calkins, L. (1986). *The art of teaching writing.* Portsmouth, NH: Heinemann.

Chambers, A. (1983). *Introducing books to children.* Boston: Horn Book.

DiCamillo, K. (2007). The Miraculous Journey of Edward Tulane. *Horn Book* LXXX. No 4 Pg. 417.

Frye, N. (1964). *The educated imagination.* Bloomington: Indiana University Press.

Galda, L., Ash, G. E., & Cullinan, B. (2001, April). Research on children's literature. *Reading Online, 4 (9)*, 1–42.

Gallas, K. (2000, Winter). Why do we listen to stories? *New Advocate, 13*, 35–40.

Gallo, D. (1977). Teaching writing: Advice from the professionals. *Connecticut English Journal, 8,* 45–50.

Gambrell, L., Palmer, B., Codling, R., & Mazzoni, S. A. (1996). Assessing motivation to read. *The Reading Teacher,* 49, 518–533.

Graves, D. (1983). *Writing teachers and children at work.* Portsmouth, NH: Heinemann.

Hearne, B. (1999). *Choosing books for children.* Urbana, IL: University of Illinois Press.

Hobbs, R. (April, 2001). Classroom strategies for exploring realism and authenticity in media messages. *Reading Online, 4* (9).

Horn Book (2007). "Listening Library." Hornbook Online. www:Hornbook.

Horning, K., Lingren, M., Rudiger, H., & Schliesman, M. (2006). *CCBC choices 2006.* Madison: University of Wisconsin.

International Reading Association and the National Association for the Education of Young Children. (1998). *Learning to read and write: Developmentally appropriate practices for young children.* Newark, DE: International Reading Association.

Langer, J. A. (1995). *Envisioning literature: Literary understanding and literature instruction.* New York: Teachers College Press.

Lowry, L. (2002, Spring). Censorship and challenge: One author's perspective. *Journal of Children's Literature, 28,* (1), 11–13.

Mackey, M. (1990). "Filling in the gaps: The Baby Sitters Club, the series book and the learning reader." *Language Arts,* 67, 484–489.

Meek, M. (1977). Introduction. In M. Meek, A. Warlow, & G. Barton (Eds.), *The cool web: The pattern of children's reading.* London: Bodley Head.

National Council of Teachers of English and International Reading Association. (1996). *Standards for the English language arts.* Urbana, IL: National Council of Teachers of English.

Neuman, S. (1999). Books make a difference: A study of access to literacy. *Reading Research Quarterly,* 34(3) 266–311.

Paterson, K. (1981). *The gates of excellence: On reading and writing books for children.* New York: Dutton.

Pitcher, S., Lettie, K., Albright, C., Walker, N., Seunarinesingh, K., Mogge, S., Headley, K., Ridgeway, V., Peck, S., Hunt, R., Dunston, P. (2007). Assessing adolescents' motivation to read. *Journal of Adolescent and Adult Literacy.* 50(5), 378–396.

Pressley, M. (2001, September). Comprehension instruction: What makes sense now, what might make sense soon. *Reading Online, 5* (2), 3–35.

Purves, A., & Monson, D. (1984). *Experiencing children's literature.* Glenview, IL: Scott Foresman.

Rand Corporation. (2002). *Reading for understanding: Toward an R and D program in reading comprehension.* Washington, D.C.: Rand Corporation.

Rosenblatt, L. M. (1978). *The reader, the text, the poem: The transactional theory of the literary work.* Edwardsville: Southern Illinois University.

Rosenblatt, L. M. (1995). *Literature as exploration* (5th ed.). New York: Modern Language Association.

Sensenbaugh, R. (1997). Phonemic awareness: An important early step in learning to read. *ERIC Clearinghouse on Reading, English, and Communication Digest, 119,* 1–4.

Serafini, F. (2003, February). Informing our practice: Modernist, transactional, and critical perspectives on children's literature and reading instruction. *Reading Online, 6* (6), 1–7.

Short, K. (1993). Making connections across literature and life. In K. Holland, R. Hungerford, & S. Ernst (Eds.), *Journeying: Children responding to literature* (284–301). Portsmouth, NH: Heinemann.

Sloan, G. (2002). Reader response in perspective. *Journal of Children's Literature, 28* (1), 22–30.

Sutton, R. (2007). Problems, paperbacks, and the printz: Forty years of YA books. *Horn Book, 83* (3), 232–243.

Taylor, B., Peterson, D., Pearson, P., Rodriguez, M. (2005). Looking inside classrooms: Reflecting on the "How" as well as the "What" in effective Reading Instruction. *Reading Education Policy: A Collection of* Articles from the International Reading Association. Newark, DE.

Vardell, S., Hadaway, N., Young, T. (May, 2006). Matching books and readers: Selecting literature for English learners. *The Reading Teacher, 58,* (8), 734–741.

Vygotsky, L. (1978). *Mind in society.* Cambridge, MA: Harvard University Press.

Weaver, C. (1994). *Reading process and practice.* Portsmouth, NH: Heinemann.

Weaver, C. (1998). *Reconsidering a balanced approach to reading instruction.* Urbana, IL: National Council of Teachers of English.

Wells, G. (1998, September). Some questions about direct instruction: Why? To whom? How? And when? *Language Arts, 76,* 27–35.

Wilks, S. (1995). *Critical and creative thinking.* Portsmouth, NH: Heinemann.

2 Understanding Literature

KEY TERMS

chapter books

climax

conflict

contemporary realistic
  fiction

denouement

dramatic plot

episodic plot

fantasy

genre

historical fiction

literary conventions

nonfiction

picture books

plot

poetry

setting

traditional literature

GUIDING QUESTIONS

What type of literature is your favorite (poetry, fantasy, science fiction, nonfiction, etc.)? Why do you like the type of literature that you identified?

1. How would you describe a plot?

2. How is book selection related to understanding literature?

3. How do the genre, plots, and characters in adult books differ from those in children's books?

4. How do the elements of literature influence readers' understanding of the books they read?

Introduction to Understanding Literature

Genre is a French word that means "kind or type." A genre approach to exploring literature emphasizes the pattern or structure of literary works, which gives readers a structure for thinking about and understanding literature. Each genre has universal *literary conventions* that are elements of form, style, or content (Morner & Rausch, 1991). Books belonging to a specific genre share characteristics in plot, characters, settings, tone, mood, and theme. Genre patterns create rules for literary elements that are the same for children's literature and adult literature. As you read, refer to the touchstone books introduced throughout the chapter.

Literary Genre

Children's literature is usually classified into these *literary genres*: graphic novels, contemporary realistic fiction, modern fantasy, historical fiction, traditional literature, poetry, and nonfiction books. Table 2.1 summarizes the distinguishing characteristics of each genre. Picture books include all genre; the stories in these books are told with words and pictures. Chapter books also belong to all genre. Through experiences with literature, children learn to recognize that nonfiction differs from fantasy. For example, authors of fantasy use elements of make-believe: perhaps a

TABLE 2.1

Distinguishing characteristics of various genres.

Genre	Distinguishing Characteristics
Graphic Novel	Novel told in comic book style
Contemporary Realistic Fiction	Could happen in the contemporary world
Modern Fantasy	Could not happen in the real world; science fiction is fantasy set in the future
Historical Fiction	Set in the past
Traditional Literature	Based on the oral tradition, the stories are spread through word of mouth rather than print
Poetry	Intense, imaginative writing in rhythmic language structured in shorter lines and verses

place where magical things happen, a futuristic time setting, or another fantastic element the author chooses to invent. Authors make unbelievable events acceptable to readers.

Margaret Peterson Haddix made unbelievable events acceptable in her absorbing science fiction work, *Double Identity*. In this story, the 12-year-old central character, Bethany, lives in an average environment with overprotective parents. So Bethany is puzzled when her parents suddenly travel to Aunt Myrlie's home and leave her with her aunt. She was becomes convinced that they are running from some terrible problem; the only clue she has is hearing her father tell Aunt Myrlie, "She doesn't know anything about Elizabeth." The mystery intensifies when she receives a package from her father containing four different birth certificates from four different states and a large sum of money. Then a strange man appears, who asks endless questions. By the end of the book, readers have many theories about the mystery and its effect on Bethany. Readers also will have theories about Bethany's response to the secret. *Double Identity* is certain to hold readers' attention. Beware! Once students and teachers begin reading this book, they won't be able to stop.

Graphic Novels

Graphic novels have grown popular over the last 10 years. They are related to both wordless picture books and comic books. Graphic novel stories may be told through pictures or through both pictures and words. Jon Scieszka created the graphic novel, *Nightmare on Joe's Street* based on the *Time Warp Trio*, a popular television series. Joe and Sam, the central characters, learn about horror stories when they are caught up in a nightmare of their own. Graphic novels are discussed in more detail in Chapter 4.

Chapter books are books that are written in chapters. Chapter books are popular with children who are not yet ready for novels. Many younger children are excited when they read their first "chapter book" because it is a symbol of growing up. *Gooney Bird Greene* by Lois Lowry is a chapter book about an unusual student who likes to be the center of attention. She entertains her second-grade classmates and the teacher with true stories about herself. *Gooney Bird Greene* is a chapter book that would be considered realistic fiction.

Contemporary Realistic Fiction

The characters in *contemporary realistic fiction* could be real, the settings could exist, and the plots could happen, although they are products of an author's imagination rather than actual history or fact (Morner & Rausch, 1991). In *Click Here* by Denise Vega, Erin, who is in middle school, keeps a computer diary on her private page, which she plans never to post on the Internet. Erin's experiences are written in middle-school language with middle-school drama. She is a computer nerd who accidentally posts her blog to the Internet.

Fantasy

Fantasy is characterized by one or more imaginary elements, such as a make-believe world, characters with magic powers, magical events related to time, or imaginary events. Imaginative language and visuals mesh. *The Palace of Laughter: The Wednesday Tales No. 1* is an intriguing fantasy. In this story, Jon Berkeley has fashioned a complicated plot with odd characters and surprising twists that support his dramatic climax. The central character is Miles Wednesday, who has escaped an orphanage and lives contently in a barrel until a tiger comes by and notices that Miles smells "like a circus." Miles decides to find out whether the tiger is real and whether he belongs to a circus that has just come to town. He embarks on a variety of dangerous adventures as he seeks to learn about his heritage, saving many individuals he meets along the way.

Historical Fiction

Authors of *historical fiction* tell a story associated with historical events, characters, incidents, or time periods. However, historical setting alone is not enough to make a book worthwhile; it has to tell a good story as well. For example, Paulsen's *The Legend of Bass Reeves: Being the True and Fictional Account of the Most Valiant Marshal in the West* has a central character who escapes slavery and hides in Indian territory until the Civil War is over. After the war, a federal judge recruits Bass to clean up the lawlessness in the region. Using knowledge he developed while living many years with the Creek Indians, Bass becomes an authentic western hero. He is the kind of hero that legends are written about.

Picture Books

Picture books are perhaps the most recognizable book format in children's literature. In these books the story is told through pictures and words; neither could exist without the other, although wordless picture books tell their stories entirely in pictures. Jane O'Connor combined children's attraction to miniature worlds and snow globes to create *The Snow Globe Family*. In this story, the snow globe people live parallel lives with the big family. The snow globe people wait for the big people to shake the globe, so they can play in the snow. This book is excellent.

Traditional Literature

Traditional literature is based on oral tradition. For instance, stories such as "Cinderella" were passed from one generation to the next by word of mouth and were not written until the scholars collected these tales (Morner & Rausch, 1991). Among the oral conventions traditional stories share are formulaic beginnings and endings: "Once upon a time" and "They lived happily ever after." The settings are created in a sentence or two, and the characters are stereotypes. The rags-to-riches story of *Dick Whittington and his Cat* as told by Margaret Hodges is a version of a tale that storytellers have told and retold in various media. In Hodges's version, Tom is a destitute orphan who travels to London to seek a fortune. After arriving in London, Tom purchases a cat to chase the rats and mice that disturb his sleep. Tom's cat is so successful that a rich merchant purchases the cat for a huge sum of money, which makes Tom very wealthy. He goes on to marry the merchant's daughter and to do many good works. The author includes a brief history of Tom's story in the book.

Poetry

Poetry is described as intense and imaginative literature. Poets strive to capture the essence of an experience in imaginative language that creates a greater concentration of meaning than is found in prose. Poetry differs visually from other types of literature in that it generally has short lines that may or may not rhyme and is written in verse form. In *Mites to Mastodons: A Book of Animal Poems,* Maxine Kumin uses rhyming, consonance, and assonance to create lyrical poetry that makes enjoyable read-alouds; Pamela Zagarenski uses mixed-media to create delicate and humorous illustrations. (Poetry is discussed more fully in Chapter 5.)

Nonfiction

Nonfiction is organized and structured around main ideas and supporting details that present information and explain it in several styles, such as description, cause and effect, sequential order, comparison, and enumeration. Authors of nonfiction books identify key ideas and themes to grab readers' attention and motivate them to read more about the topic. *Sea Horse: The Shyest Fish in the* Sea is bound to attract children who find sea horses fascinating. In this book, readers learn that this fish does not behave like a fish. The illustrator uses textured vinyl and wood prints and highlights the illustrations with watercolor wash. (Nonfiction is discussed in more detail in Chapter 10.)

COMPARING WRITING STYLES

Third-grade teacher Gale Smithers read *Mites to Mastodons: A Book of Animal Poems* by Maxine Kumin to her language arts students. Many of the children asked her to read their favorite poems again. Then Matthew said, "This poetry reminds me of *Beast Feast*, which is my all time favorite poetry book." Haley joined in with "This book reminds me of *Beast Feast*, but the way the poems are written is different." Gale listened and then commented, "Tomorrow we will compare these books; be sure to bring your own copies if you have them and check with Mrs. Doyle in the library for copies."

The following day, Gale used overhead transparencies of poems from each collection. The children compared the writing style in each of the books, identifying the various rhyme schemes in Kumin's book and the witty style of Douglas Florian in *Beast Feast*. The students chose their favorite styles and wrote their own poems in that style.

Later the students compared the informational books *Weird Friends* by Jose Aruego and Ariane Dewey and the *Bug Scientists* by Donna Jackson and wrote poems about the animals and bugs that interested them.

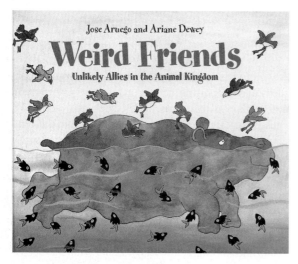

These weird friends help one another.

Through reading and listening to a broad range of genres, children develop *schemata* (cognitive networks of knowledge and experience) that facilitate their understanding of literature (Applebee, 1978). This knowledge enables them to focus on the ways authors create stories, poems, and information. Children develop schemata and implicit understandings of genre through hearing and reading books with plot, character, setting, theme, and style. They use these schemata to construct meaning and predict outcomes.

The classroom snapshot illustrates some of the ways the genre are important in classroom instruction.

Literary Elements

Joseph Conrad (1922) stated that the novelist's aim is "to make you hear, to make you feel—it is, before all, to make you see." Authors employ narrative style to help readers see their stories. In much the same way that readers use their own lives as a basis for understanding literature, writers create plot, character, setting, and theme out of their own experiences. Authors create coherent sequences highlighting dramatic events to tell an exciting story. Even when telling true or nonfiction stories, writers organize events that would otherwise be too chaotic to form a coherent story. In the process, they take liberties with reality, just as memories do when we reflect on experiences. We remember the high points in life—the dramatic events.

Plot

A *plot* is a chain of interacting events, as in our own lives. Each of us is involved in many plots as our lives unfold. These various plots, based on our own experiences, are the raw material for stories. Each story leads to another because life happens that way. Children need books where the story is at the center of the writer's attention and where the plot matters (Wadham, 1999). The plot holds the story together, making it a critical element in fiction. Wyndham and Madison (1988) describe plot as "a plan of action devised to achieve a definite and much desired end—through cause and effect" (p. 81). Their definition is similar to Giblin's (1990), who calls plot the blueprint of the story, or the path it will follow from beginning to end.

In developing plot, the author weaves a logical series of events, explaining why events occur. "A well-crafted plot, like some remarkable clockwork, can fascinate us by its sheer ingenuity" (Alexander, 1981, p. 5). Credible plots unfold gradually, building a logical cause-and-effect sequence for story incidents. Story events inserted without adequate preparation make a contrived and uninteresting plot. Interesting plots usually have unique characteristics to grab children's attention. In *Dad, Jackie, and Me*, Myron Uhlberg tells the story of a young Chinese immigrant who identifies with the trials of Jackie Robinson. Although the young Chinese boy and his father have a tender, respectful relationship, problems arise when the deaf father cheers for Jackie Robinson and embarrasses the young boy. However, his Dad's devotion wins the boy over.

Story characters act out the causes and effects of story incidents. *Cause* establishes the main character's line of action to solve a problem, get out of a situation, or reach a certain goal; *effect* is what happens to the character as a result of the action taken. Storytellers can make all sorts of imaginary events credible by laying the groundwork for them (Alexander, 1981). *Foreshadowing* is the groundwork that prepares for

A father and son enjoy baseball together.

future story events through planted clues in situations, events, characters, and conflicts. In *Gooney Bird Greene* by Lois Lowry, foreshadowing occurs immediately when Gooney Bird arrives in the second grade from Paris (Texas), sporting an unusual hair style, unusual clothing, and an unusual lunch. Then she announces, "I want a desk right smack in the middle of the room because I like to be right smack in the middle of everything." This dramatic entrance signals that Gooney Bird is a character to watch.

Conflict

Story conflicts increase tension to arouse readers' suspense. Interesting plots are based on difficulties to overcome, problems to solve, and goals to achieve. Believable conflicts and problems provide the story with shape, movement, tension, and drama. *Conflict* is "the struggle that grows out of the interplay of two opposing forces in a plot" (Holman & Harmon, 1986, p. 107). One of these opposing forces is usually the main character in the story, who struggles to get what he or she wants and is vigorously opposed, either by someone who wants the same thing or by circumstances that stand in the way of the goal (Wyndham & Madison, 1988).

A conflict implies struggle, but it also suggests that motivation exists behind the conflict or a goal that can be achieved through the conflict. The central problem or conflict must remain out of the main character's reach until near the end of the story. Nevertheless, readers are aware that a fateful decision is at hand that will precipitate a crisis in the principal character's affairs, although the outcome of this struggle is never certain.

In Andrea Spalding's *Secret of the Dance*, the conflict is between the Canadian government and the aboriginal people who were not allowed to participate in potlatches. Potlatches are important cultural ceremonies that celebrate milestones such as marriage and death; therefore, the aboriginal people were compelled to go underground to celebrate their ceremonies. In the book, one night a boy sneaks out and accidentally sees his father participating in an illegal ceremony. The boy has to make a decision about what he has seen.

The conflicts that writers commonly use are summarized in the following list:

1. a struggle against nature;
2. a struggle against another person, usually the antagonist;

3. a struggle against society; and

4. a struggle for mastery by two elements within the person (Holman & Harmon, 1986).

Climax

The protagonist's most intense struggle occurs at the *climax*, which is the highest point of interest in the story, the point at which readers learn how the conflict is resolved. A strong conflict keeps readers turning pages to discover whether the protagonist makes the right decision. In Elise Broach's *Shakespeare's Secret*, the conflict is between Hero and her new classmates. Hero hates her name because it was chosen by a Shakespearian scholar, and, in her new school, one of her classmates has a dog named Hero. Then Hero befriends Danny, who is the most popular guy in school. When Hero meets an elderly neighbor she discovers the woman has mysterious stories to tell about a million-dollar diamond. This story is a quick read, and many secrets are revealed.

Denouement

Denouement is the falling action that occurs during the unwinding of the story after the climax. This part of the story ties up the various threads of the plot into a satisfying, logical ending, although not necessarily a "happily ever after" ending. Jack and his tiger, Lily, live in a lovely apartment and do everything together in Diane Goode's *Tiger Trouble*. Their life is perfect until a grumpy new landlord demands that Lily move out of the building. However, Lily catches burglars, becomes a hero, and saves the day.

Types of Plot

Dramatic and episodic plots are the most common types of plot structure, but several others also appear in children's books, such as parallel plot and cumulative plot. Parallel and cumulative plots are often associated with traditional literature and picture books.

Dramatic Plot. *Dramatic plots* establish setting, characters, and conflicts with fast-moving action that grabs children's attention and creates enough tension to hold their interest until the exciting climax. (Figure 2.1 illustrates a dramatic plot line.) Philip Reeve creates a dramatic plot in *Larklight: A Rousing Tale of Dauntless Pluck in the Farthest Reaches of Space*. Motherless siblings Art and Myrtle Mumby live in an alternative

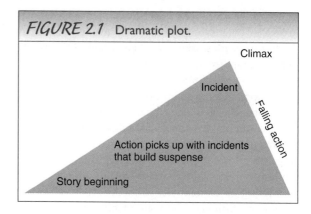

FIGURE 2.1 Dramatic plot.

universe with their ichyomorphologist father who studies exotic specimens. He and the children are invited to the Royal Xenological Society in London where he meets Mr. Webster, who turns out to be a giant spider. After the spider kills their father, the children find safety in an escape barrel. But the drama increases when flesh-eating larvae encase them in pods. A pirate, Jack Havock, and his loyal crew of aliens are their only hope.

Episodic Plot. *Episodic plots* are quite similar to dramatic plots. The major difference is that in a book with an episodic plot each chapter is a "mini-plot," or a story within the main story. Each *episode* or incident is connected and relates to the same main character or characters. The conflict runs through the total book, and the book is unified by the common theme of the main story. (Figure 2.2 illustrates an episodic plot.) *Just Grace* by Charise Harper is an episodic book. Each chapter or episode is based on situations that Grace fails to succeed in. For example, she does not get to be the magician's helper at her own birthday party. There are four "Graces" in her class; the teacher

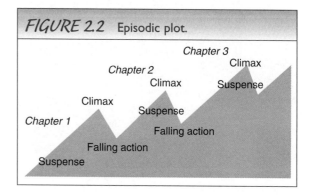

FIGURE 2.2 Episodic plot.

gives each one a slightly different name, but she misunderstood Grace's request to be called "Grace"; therefore, she is called "Just Grace." Her empathy is like a "teeny tiny superpower" that makes Grace do things that she doesn't want to do, like smile at a loathsome boy. Grace's empathy leads her to help other people.

Gary Schmidt's *The Wednesday Wars* has episodes based on each month of Holling Hoodhood's seventh-grade school year. Each episode is another step in Holling's progress toward finding out who he is.

Parallel plot. *Parallel plots* include two plots that unfold side by side. These plots usually are intertwined into a single story as the book winds down, so that the intertwining may occur near the story's climax. Carl Hiaasen used parallel plots to tell the story of *Hoot*. One plot line is told from the point of view of a middle-school boy named Roy, and the other plot line develops from the point of view of a policeman named Dana. The

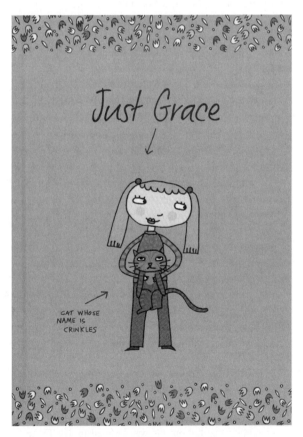

Grace wanted her own identity.

connection between the plots gradually emerges as the story evolves. A movie of *Hoot* is available; children will enjoy comparing the movie to the book.

Cumulative plot. *Cumulative plots* unfold through a pattern of repetition in which characters or events are added to each other, with each new character or event paralleling a previous character or event, building toward a climax that solves the problem. Cumulative plot stories, which usually appear in traditional literature or picture books such as *The Three Little Pigs,* often contain repeated refrains.

Circular plot. *Circular plots* unfold with the story starting in one place, then departing from that point before the climax, and returning to the beginning point. This plot is illustrated in *My Last Best Friend* by Julie Bowe. After her best friend moves away and doesn't write to her, Ida May vows to never have another best friend. Then Stacey Merriweather moves to town. Stacey is friendly, sparkly, and popular. She smiles at Ida May, who has to force herself not to smile back. In the end, Ida May and Stacey become best friends.

Characters

Characters propel the plot of a story; they make things happen in the story. In a way, they are like actors who direct and bring the plot to life in movies and on stage. Skillful authors create believable, memorable characters (Holman & Harmon, 1986). Readers care about believable characters with whom they can identify and feel truly involved. A variety of strategies make characters live and breathe in readers' minds. One is telling the details of a character's thoughts, feelings, motivations, and attitudes. Another is depicting characters in ways that are consistent with their social background, educational level, and age. Portraying the human qualities, emotions, desires, hopes, dreams, and motivations that distinguish characters as individuals creates memorable characters.

Developing Characters

Jeanne Birdsall has a talent for creating unforgettable characters. In *The Penderwicks: A Summer Tale of Four Sisters, Two Rabbits, and a Very Interesting Boy,* she creates Rosalind, who is a kind mother figure; Skye, who is intelligent and has a temper; Jane, a dreamy romantic; Batty, who wears detachable butterfly wings;

and Hound, the family dog. When they arrive at their summer cottage, they meet the landlady's son, Jeffrey. Some of the tension in this story arises from the children's personalities. All of the characters, including the dog, are captivating. The story is humorous, although it has some poignant scenes related to the landlady and her boyfriend. Jeffrey and the sisters have plans to eliminate the conflict. Remember: If there were no conflict, there would be no story (Wyndham & Madison, 1988).

In this book, the sisters are *protagonists* and the landlady's boyfriend is the antagonist. The villain, or antagonist, has traits that provide a complete contrast to those of the protagonist. An antagonist lends excitement and suspense to a story but is developed with less detail than a protagonist.

Supporting Characters

In literature, some characters are developed with less depth than the protagonist. These are the supporting characters, who often lack the depth and complexity of the protagonist. These characters may be built around a single dominant trait or a quality representing a personality type (Morner & Rausch, 1991). Supporting characters are needed as part of the interactive background; their primary function is to advance the protagonist's development. Fully portraying these characters would make the story too complex for children. Supporting characters often include the protagonist's best friend, a teacher, or parents. In the *Penderwicks* story, Batty is a supporting character.

Stereotypes are flat characters who lack individualizing characteristics and instead represent traits generally attributed to a social group as a whole (Morner & Rausch, 1991). They exhibit a few traits representative of conventional mothers, fathers, friends, or teachers and are developed quickly with brief bits of information so that drawing their characters does not interrupt the story flow. In traditional literature, all characters are stereotypes representing traits such as good, evil, innocence, and wisdom.

Dynamic and Static Characters

Dynamic characters. *Dynamic* or *developed characters* change significantly during the course of a story as incidents cause their personalities to emerge and expand. In the *Penderwicks*, readers see each of the sisters develop through the story events.

Static characters. *Static* or *delineated story characters* are the opposite of developed characters. They seem impervious to experience and remain essentially the same throughout the story. These are the "Peter Pan" characters who never grow up. The principal character in Astrid Lindgren's *Pippi Longstocking* is static. Pippi, a 9-year-old Swedish girl, is well-rounded and fully described. She lives alone with a monkey and a horse and has many novel adventures. Pippi never changes; she remains irrepressible as ever.

Character Interaction

Authors may use any number of character interactions to help readers get acquainted with characters. In Gary Schmidt's *The Wednesday Wars,* Holling Hoodhood interacts with his teacher, Mrs. Baker, with classmates, and with his parents. He begins the school year believing that his teacher hates him because he is the only student in class on Wednesday afternoons, as all of the other students are having religious instruction at that time. When he asks his sister for help, he points out that it is like "asking Nova Scotia to go into battle with you."

Getting to Know the Story Characters

Readers come to know characters the way we come to know an acquaintance—from the way the person talks and acts, the way the characters interact with others, and their reactions to and thoughts about the character. Character traits are revealed through a number of narration techniques. First-person narration, in which the main character is usually the narrator, allows readers to infer traits from what the main character says and how others react. Similarly, a limited narrator may tell the story from the main character's point of view. An omniscient narrator, however, may tell all about the main character and also tell about others from their points of view.

The book *Surviving the Applewhites* by Stephen Tolan includes a wide array of characters who interact with Jake Semple. Jake's thoughts in the following extract reveal how he views himself:

> Jake was beginning to feel he was disappearing altogether. Nobody except E. D. and Destiny noticed when he swore. Nothing he's done before to show people who he was and what he stood for worked here. He couldn't even chill out the way he used to. No TV to watch. His Walkman was useless without earphones.

If he dared to smoke where he could be seen, somebody was sure to snatch away his cigarette. (p. 85)

Authors often use conversations to help readers know characters; manner of speaking and subject matter are revealing, especially when combined with the characters' actions. A character's traits may be revealed through conversation with another character.

In the following extract, Jake is talking with E. D. Applewhite.

"Better not light that thing," she said.

The boy reached into his pocket and pulled out a yellow plastic lighter. "You can't have a smoke-free environment outdoors," he said.

"We can have it anywhere we want—this is our property, all sixteen acres of it."

Jake looked her square in the eye and lit the cigarette. He took a long drag and blew the smoke directly into her face so that she had to close her eyes and hold her breath to keep from choking on it. (pp. 5–6)

Character traits, descriptions, and actions are usually developed through illustrations and language in picture books. In these books, the words and the pictures are integrated to reveal details about the characters, such as in *The Penderwicks* by Jeanne Birdsall, who uses her photography background to depict the characters, action, and setting.

Setting

Setting is the story's time and place. Vivid settings give a story reality; they give readers a sense of being there. The importance of setting varies from story to story. In some it creates the stage for the characters' actions; in others it is indefinite, a universal setting that is secondary to the story. The story itself dictates the importance of setting.

Once the general location and time are identified, authors decide on the specific details of the setting. Some setting are very specific, such as "a certain district in London, England, in the summer of 1993"; other settings are more universal, requiring fewer details and a more indefinite time and place. Time and location dictate many of the story's other details: the type of home and furniture, the scenery, and the flora and fauna of the surrounding countryside. The social environment, foods, newspapers, magazines, and games are also aspects of the setting.

Zilpha Snyder is well known for writing about big houses that are settings for adventures, as she does in *The Treasures of Weatherby*. The details about the house give reality to the story and the mystery, as well as to the mysterious character who appears and contributes to the growth of Harleigh, the main character.

Illustrations develop setting in some books, whereas other books portray the setting through words. Some stories are closely tied to the setting, whereas others are not. Mini Grey uses details very successfully in *Traction Man*. The action figure, Traction Man, has an adventurous life. He escapes the "poisonous dishcloth" and adopts a "scrubbing brush" as a pet. He undertakes a rescue mission with a triumphant outcome. Grey shows the ingenuity of a young boy who imagines adventures for a Christmas present.

Mood

The mood or tone of a story is created through the setting. The author uses words and the artist uses illustrations to create the feelings readers should experience. The three sisters in Ursula Dubosarsky's *The Red Shoe* live in a world of uncertainty. The Cold War setting depicts how world events impinge on the lives and moods of these three young women. An unstable father and an absent mother add to the intense feelings of growing up in a nervous time.

The words and phrases used in this story create a feeling for the life and times; they express the author's interpretation of the significance of the place and time. The author writes about the end of summer along the ocean and describes the sounds of the waves as being "Like people shouting, wanting her attention." The author's language reflects the tone and theme of this coming-of-age-story.

Theme

The *theme* is defined as the point, the message, or the central idea that underlies a book. Fine writers subtly weave their themes into stories. Children, like adults, prefer authors who trust their readers to infer theme from story events, characters, and setting rather than preaching or explicitly stating the theme. In poetry, fiction, and drama, it is the abstract concept that is made concrete through the characters, plots, mood, and images created. The theme of a story has both a subject and a predicate; it tells what the book means. Another way of explaining theme is that it expresses "lessons about life" (Barton, 2001). Holling Hoodhood in *The Wednesday Wars* begins to find out who he is through his experiences in seventh grade. He reads Shakespeare, acts in a Shakespearen play, becomes a runner, and helps his sister when his parents refuse to help. His teacher helps him, but he then prepares his teacher for success when the school board visits.

Multiple Themes

Literature usually has multiple themes. Moreover, different readers discover different messages in the same story because readers' unique schemata influence the themes they identify in a specific book (Barton, 2001). Carl Hiaasen's *Hoot* contains several themes. First, Roy Eberhardt, the protagonist, is the new kid in school—again. Second, he stumbles into an effort to save endangered burrowing owls from bungling adults. Third, he discovers that school bullies do serve a greater purpose in the world. Fourth, he makes friends as he works to save the burrowing owls. Carl Hiaasen, the author, points out that he wrote the book as a parody of the state of Florida because he reveals the good and bad of that state. Children may also discover other themes in this novel.

The most common themes in children's books are associated with fundamental human needs, including:

1. the need to love and be loved;
2. the need to belong;
3. the need to achieve;
4. the need for security—material, emotional, spiritual; and
5. the need to know (Wyndham & Madison, 1988).

These universal themes are expressed through the ideas, characters, plots, and settings developed in fiction, nonfiction, and poetry.

Children's Response to Theme

Building meaning is a complex developmental process. A 3-year-old understands a story differently than an 8-year-old; younger children can, however, identify theme. Although older children are better able to talk about the themes in stories, children in kindergarten are "able to identify thematically matched books 80% of the time for realistic fiction and 35%

for folktales, thus indicating that thematic identification is a fairly early developmental strategy" (Lehr, 1991, p. 67).

Themes are subject to readers' interpretation; therefore, they are open to individual responses. Nevertheless, the dominant idea or theme should be apparent to readers. Individuals respond differently to the same story because response is based on individual experience; readers use their schemata to interpret and understand the material. Individuals remember what is important to them and see what they expect to see or are capable of seeing. The varying responses of students are explored in greater depth in Chapter 15.

Many stories offer readers opportunities to respond at different levels of understanding. Readers can take as much or as little from literature as their developmental levels and experiential backgrounds permit. For example, Carl Hiaasen's book *Hoot* has several thematic layers. At the highest level, readers may recognize the story as satire revealing "the good, the bad, and the screwy state of Florida" (dust jacket). Readers at another level will identify the struggles of a boy who has been the "new kid" many, many times. Another theme in the book involves the way children have to guide bungling adults in some situations.

Theme and Topic

Theme is concerned with the central idea, or meaning, of a literary work. Topic, however, may be thought of as the general subject of discussion or discourse. For example, a topic or subject could be "saving endangered animals," as in the book *Hoot*. No proper theme is simply a subject (topic) or an activity.

Style

Authors express their *style* through the language they use to shape their stories: the words they choose, the sentences they craft, the dialogue they create, and the amount and nature of the descriptive passages. Authors arrange words in ways that express their individuality. "Style is a combination of the two elements: the idea to be expressed and the individuality of the author" (Holman & Harmon, 1986, p. 487). No two styles are exactly alike. Ultimately, the author's use of language determines the lasting quality of a book.

Language Devices

Author style is most apparent in the language devices used to achieve special effects or meanings; authors stimulate their readers through the use of figurative language, imagery, allusion, hyperbole, understatement, and symbolism. Readers then use these devices to infer and connote individual interpretations based upon their experiential background. *Connotation* refers to an association or emotional response a reader attaches to a particular word that goes beyond the dictionary definition, or *denotation*; the connotation is the meaning drawn from personal experience. For example, many people associate warm, loving feelings with the word *mother*, feelings that go far beyond the literal denotation of a "female parent."

Figurative language. Figurative language is connotative, sensory language that incorporates one or more of the various figures of speech such as simile, metaphor, repetition, and personification (Holman & Harmon, 1986). Figurative language is used to develop character, show mood, and create setting.

Imagery. Sensory language widens the mind's eye and helps the reader build images that go beyond the ordinary to new and exciting experiences. These experiences can be the sensory kind, in which one sees or hears new things, or they can be an intellectual experience in which one thinks new things. In Janet Wong's book *The Dumpster Diver*, the pages are full of movement and unusual imagery. The children assisting the dumpster diver have to hose off the beetles and roaches and spiders that emerge en mass from the dumpster. They discover "millions of legs living two hundred feet away." After they find a pair of roller skates and a ripped parasol, disaster strikes when the dumpster trash collapses and Steve (the dumpster diver) is badly hurt. The children invent a new plan for sorting trash because Steve needs a wheelchair.

Allusion. *Allusion* is a figure of speech that makes indirect reference to a historical or literary figure, event, or object (Holman & Harmon, 1986).

Hyperbole. *Hyperbole* is exaggeration used to make a point. In *The Wednesday War*, Holling Hoodhood uses allusion and hyperbole when he says that the "Presbyterian pastor is old enough to have known Moses."

Understatement. *Understatement* is almost the opposite of hyperbole. It plays down a situation or person and is often used for comic effect as when Molly McGinty in *Molly McGinty Has a Really Good Day* by Gary Paulsen engages in converation with Tommy Adams, the scariest boy in the school who says, "I didn't beat him up; I just stuffed him in a locker."

Symbolism. *Symbols* express deeper meanings in children's literature (Barton, 2001). They can be persons, objects, situations, actions, or words that operate on two levels of meaning. A symbol has both a literal meaning—a concrete meaning—and an inferential meaning, one that is implied. Linda Sue Park uses her Korean name as a symbol of the Japanese harassment in *When My Name Was Keoko*.

Point of View

Point of view is the perspective or stance from which the author tells a story. It is the eye and mind through which the action is perceived (Morner & Rausch, 1991). The point of view determines the vocabulary, sentences, and attitudes expressed. Essentially, authors can use two general narrative points of view, first person and third person. A first-person narrator actually appears within the story and tells the tale using the pronoun "I." The first-person point of view has some advantages; one is its conversational nature, which makes readers feel they know the narrator. First-person narrators tell the reader what they are thinking and feeling, giving readers an intimate experience. Plot, setting, and character are more likely to be unified when the main character says, "This is what happened to me, this is where it happened, this is how I felt" (Sebesta & Iverson, 1975, p. 78).

Linda Sue Park chose first-person narration for the central characters in *When My Name Was Keoko*. This stylistic choice is appropriate because she is narrating her own experiences and those of her brother in a parallel plot. Each person tells of his or her experiences during the Japanese occupation of Korea during World War II, at which time all Koreans had to choose a Japanese name.

A third-person narrator, unlike a first-person narrator, stands outside the story and tells the tale using pronouns such as *he, she,* and *they*. Third-person narration has two commonly used variations: omniscient perspective and limited omniscient perspective.

Children's literature most frequently uses omniscient perspective to tell stories.

With omniscient perspective, the narrator sees all, knows all, and reveals all to the reader. This narrator has access to and reveals the thoughts and motives of all the characters; knows the present, past, and future; and also comments on or interprets the actions of all of the characters. A major advantage of this style lies in the freedom a narrator has in unfolding the story. For instance, authors can speak directly to readers, telling whatever they choose to tell or speaking over the heads of the characters in an aside to help readers understand the significance of an event or a character (Sebesta & Iverson, 1975). Narrators with limited perspective focus on the thoughts of a single character and present the other characters externally (Morner & Rausch, 1991). In this approach, the author typically follows one character throughout the story. The reader knows only what this one character knows and sees only those incidents in which that character is involved. In Gary Schmidt's *The Wednesday Wars,* the protagonist, Holling Hoodhood, is the character through whom readers learn about the characters, actions, and feelings in the story.

Literary Experiences That Enhance Understanding

Literary experiences can motivate children to read, as well as enhance their understanding. Getting to know authors, as well as their experiences, writing techniques, and interests, are among the most powerful literary experiences. Authors make their stories come alive with details, stylistic devices, genre, and the elements of literature. What writers create comes from hearsay, incidents, people, places, and truths they have experienced. Betsy Byars (1993) says, "I always put something of myself into my books, something that happened to me. Once . . . a wanderer came by the house and showed me how to brush my teeth with a cherry twig. That went in *The House of Wings.*"

Many writers describe themselves as storytellers. Paula Fox (1991) says:

> I am a storyteller and I have been one for more than 30 years. When I finish one story, I watch the drift

in my head, and very soon am thinking about another story. All one's experience shapes one's stories. However, readers expect authors to take them "there" to help them recreate the writer's reality; what matters is what they make of it—what they do with it.

Simply reporting incidents and characters as they took place is not enough to draw in readers; the author must create illusions with the facts. Illusion—what writers make of their experiences—must convince readers that it is reality by resonating with their emotions and moving them to new feelings and insights (Alexander, 1981).

Discussion as Literary Experience

When a group of 5 or 6 students discuss a book they have all read, they stimulate one another to think about the story from different perspectives. For example, *The Wednesday Wars* has different meanings for seventh graders and eighth graders. Holling (the protagonist), a seventh grader, considers eighth graders to be penitentiary bound due their behavior and attitudes. Discussion is a valuable tool for enhancing the understanding and response of each person in the group. Moreover, each time a different group of children discusses a story, they bring up ideas that no one has mentioned.

Literary Experiences

The best literature-based activities are those that grow naturally out of the literature and relate to the plot, theme, setting, characters, or style of the book. Activities that grow out of the literature encourage students to think critically and enable readers to demonstrate or share their response to the book. Later chapters discuss experiencing literature in much greater detail.

When working on developing an understanding of genre, select titles that are clear examples of the genre being studied. Picture books are useful for developing genre activities because they are appealing and are clear and direct examples for teaching genre. They are also useful for developing an understanding of plot, theme, style, characterization, setting, and style. The suggested activities are suitable for individuals, pairs, small groups, or whole classes. Figure 2.3 is a map of literary activities.

DISCUSSING AND COMPARING PICTURE BOOKS

Gina Sims's second-grade class was studying the picture books of Janet Stevens. They had read and discussed *Tops and Bottoms, Epossumondas,* and *Cock-a-Doodle-Doo.* The animal characters and funny plots delighted the children. They enjoyed the animal characters and the funny plots; in fact, they wanted the teacher to reread these books every day. Then Gina received a new Janet Stevens book, *The Great Fuzzy Frenzy.* She told the children they had a big surprise coming, but they had to wait until story time.

At story time the children were anxious to learn about the surprise; when Gina held up the new book they applauded. Then she asked the children whether they knew anything about prairie dogs. Several of them had seen prairie dogs in zoos, and they explained how prairie dogs liked to pop their heads out their holes. Gina explained that prairie dog holes were very important in the story she was going to read.

She read the story aloud and the children laughed. In this story, a dog drops a green tennis ball down a prairie dog hole; of course, the ball makes a commotion among the prairie dogs. The bully Big Bark comes to take a look, but before he can, Pip Squeak touches and shouts, "It's fuzzy." The prairie dogs strip the green fuzz off the ball and adorn themselves with it, but Big Bark objects and war breaks out. When the prairie dogs collapse with exhaustion, Big Bark steals all of the green fuzz and announces that he is "King of the Fuzz." His

The fuzz on a tennis ball becomes very important in the frenzy.

moment of glory is shattered when an eagle decides he would make a good lunch. However, he does survive.

Then Gina asked her students to identify the beginning, middle, and end of the story. Then they compared this story with *Tops and Bottoms.* The following day, the children asked to hear the story again, and the discussion of their favorite parts and the illustrations continued.

Summary

Genres are literature classifications with each member of a classification exhibiting common characteristics. Genre classifications give teachers, librarians, and students the language to discuss and analyze books. The genres of children's literature include: traditional literature, modern fantasy, contemporary realistic fiction, historical fiction, biography, poetry, and informational literature. All these categories of genres have the same characteristics as adult literature. Picture books represent all genre.

Through many experiences with stories, readers gradually discover the elements that comprise literature: story, plot, characters, setting, theme, and style. As their experience with literature grows, they develop schemata, cognitive structures that enable them to make sense of what they read and to anticipate what the author will say, thus enriching their understanding. Children's understanding of literature exceeds their ability to verbalize story knowledge, but concerned adults can help them expand their appreciation and understanding. As one of those concerned adults, your understanding of the elements and organizational patterns of fiction discussed in this chapter will assist you

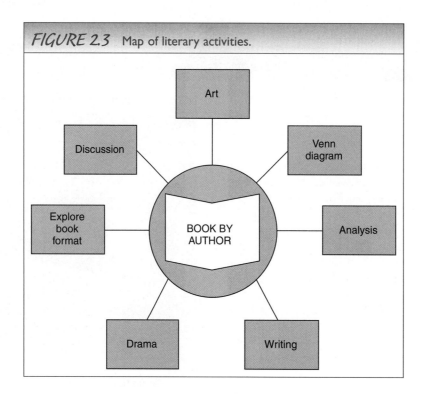

FIGURE 2.3 Map of literary activities.

in choosing books and planning literary experiences. The figure on p. 37, *Elements of Fiction,* reviews the elements of fiction and suggests some questions to ask yourself when reviewing a piece of literature.

Thought Questions and Applications

1. What value do the elements of literature have for students?

2. What is author style? Identify the components of style.

3. Compare a picture book character with a character in a novel. How do they differ in development and the amount of detail included?

4. What themes have you discovered in the children's books you have read thus far?

5. Why do you think teachers choose to read fiction aloud more often than nonfiction?

Research and Application Experiences

1. Choose a fiction book to read and identify each of the elements of literature in that book. Map the story grammar of the book.

2. Choose a nonfiction book and identify the patterns of organization in it.

3. Compare two characters in two different realistic fiction books.

4. Compare a poem, a story, and a nonfiction book that are on the same topic.

5. Survey an elementary school class. Ask the students to identify the structures in various types of literature. Which type of literature do the students seem to know the most about? Why do you think this is true?

6. Identify any weaknesses revealed, keeping in mind that fewer traits are exhibited in a shorter story.

Classroom Activities

ACTIVITY 2.1   LITERARY ELEMENTS

IRA/NCTE Standards: 3, 6, 11. Develop comprehension, genre, elements of literature, and vocabulary in this specific book, science and conservation.

This activity deals with analyzing the literary elements of a piece of realistic fiction. Although all of the elements are mentioned here, in an actual classroom you would probably choose to discuss only one of the elements, such as plot, characterization, or setting. This realistic fiction could be compared with a fantasy to clarify the genre characteristics.

Book: *Hoot* by Carl Hiaasen

1. Introduce the book, asking questions to help students predict the elements.

    A. What might the title indicate about the story?

    B. What can the dust jacket help you predict about it?

    C. Where do you think the story takes place? Who is the main character? How old is the main character?

2. Have students silently read the story.

3. Discuss the story with the students, encouraging them to think about the plot. Discuss the parallel plot in this book.

    A. Describe Roy at the beginning of the story. How does he change in the story? What events cause him to change?

    B. Describe Officer Delenko at the beginning of the story. How has he changed at the end of the story?

    C. Why does Roy say, "Dana was just a big stupid bully; the world was full of them"?

    D. What is the theme of this story? What makes you think this is the theme?

    E. What is the climax in this story? Did the story end the way you thought it would?

    F. What are the comical events in this story?

    G. Now that you have read the story, what do you think the significance of the title is?

    H. Describe Carl Hiaasen's writing style in this book.

4. Use extension activities to allow students to respond to the story.

    A. Make a timeline for this story that shows its key events.

    B. Write a note to a visitor thanking him or her for the visit.

    C. Write a review for this book that will cause another person to want to read it.

    D. Read *Surviving the Applewhites* and compare the characters in that book with those in *Hoot*, or read *Mary Ann Alice* by Brian Doyle and compare the plots in these stories.

ACTIVITY 2.2   STORY GRAMMAR

IRA/NCTE Standards: 3, 11, 12. Comprehension, genre, elements of literature, and vocabulary.

A *story grammar* is a set of rules that describes the possible structures of well-formed stories (Rumelhart, 1975; Stein & Glenn, 1979). Most researchers agree that story grammars include character, setting, a problem or conflict, and a series of one or more episodes. Story grammars give readers a way of describing and discussing what they read, which helps refine their comprehension and gives them a means of organizing their recollections. The story grammar in this activity is based on Kate DiCamillo's *The Tale of Despereaux.* After studying this story have students create a story grammar to learn about plot.

Story grammar.	
Book:	*The Tale of Despereaux* by Kate DiCamillo.
Setting:	Castle/Dungeon.
Characters:	Despereaux mouse family, princess, jailer/Gregory.
Efforts to solve problems:	1. Family rejects. 2. Princess likes him. 3. Sent to dungeon. 4. Saved by princess.
Resolution:	Lives in princess castle.

ACTIVITY 2.3   COMPARE CHARACTERS OR SETTING IN A VENN DIAGRAM

IRA/NCTE Standards: 2, 3. Compare/contrast to comprehend.

In this example, students compare two characters: the title character from *Epossumondas* and Big Dog from *The Great Fuzz Frenzy* (see figure). The following characters are also good for comparison:

> *The White Giraffe* (St. John) and *Double Identity* (Haddix)
>
> *My Last Best Friend* (Bowe) and *Just Grace* (Harper)
>
> *The Wednesday Wars* (Schmidt) and *Chicken Boy* (Dowell)

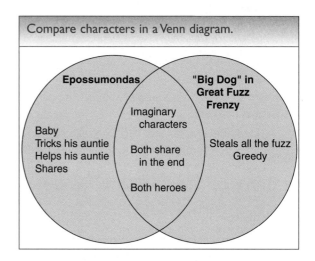

Compare characters in a Venn diagram.

Epossumondas — Baby / Tricks his auntie / Helps his auntie / Shares

Imaginary characters / Both share in the end / Both heroes

"Big Dog" in Great Fuzz Frenzy — Steals all the fuzz / Greedy

ACTIVITY 2.4   STORY INTRODUCTION

IRA/NCTE Standards: 2, 3, 4, 5, 6, 12. Summarize, synthesize, and persuade.

This story introduction is based on *The White Giraffe* by Lauren St. John. This mystery begins in London and moves to Africa where Martine goes to live with her grandmother on an African game preserve. Even before she meets her grandmother, Martine realizes that she is part of a mystery. Then she hears stories about a mythical white giraffe that no one has been able to find.

Martine learns the truth about herself and the white giraffe.

Suggested individual literary experiences.

Teachers can suggest these activities for students to perform individually or in groups of two or three.

1. Prepare discussion questions for the book. (Students may need to be given models of open-ended questions until they become adept at creating such questions.)
2. Prepare a Venn diagram that compares and contrasts this book with another.
3. Prepare a diorama of an important scene or setting from the book.
4. Act out a scene from the book.
5. Prepare a poster or commercial for the book.
6. Keep a reading journal summarizing each day's reading and responding to the reading experience.
7. Prepare a story grammar or story map. (See the model in this chapter.)
8. Draw a plot line for the story. (See the models in this chapter.)

ACTIVITY 2.5   LEARNING ABOUT PLOT

IRA/NCTE Standards: 2, 3, 6, 12. Compare/contrast, comprehend, and discussion.

Listen to a taped version of *The Teacher's Funeral* and compare it with the book. Discuss the two versions.

Draw a plot line for the taped book. (See the models in this chapter and in the figure below.)

Elements of fiction.

PLOT

1. Does the plot grab the reader's attention and move quickly?
2. Are the story events sequenced logically, so that cause and effect are clear?
3. Is the reader prepared for story events?
4. What is the conflict in this story (e.g., character with another character, character and society, character and a group, within the character)?
5. Is there a climax?
6. Is the denouement satisfying?

CHARACTER

1. Does the main character seem like a real person?
2. Is the main character well-rounded with character strengths and weaknesses revealed? (In a shorter story fewer traits are exhibited.)
3. How are character traits revealed (e.g., conversation, thoughts, author tells reader, actions)? Does the author rely too much on a single strategy?
4. Does the character grow and change?
5. Is the character a delineated character?
6. Are the character's conversations and behavior consistent with age and background?

SETTING

1. Where does this story take place?
2. When does this story take place?
3. How are time and place related to the plot, characters, and theme?
4. Is this a universal setting?

THEME

1. What is the theme?
2. Is the theme developed naturally through the actions and reactions of story characters?
3. Does the author avoid stating the theme in words (except in traditional literature)?
4. Is the abstract theme made concrete by the story?

STYLE

1. What stylistic devices characterize the author's writing (e.g., connotation, imagery, figurative language, hyperbole, understatement, allusion, symbol)?
2. What is the mood of the writing (e.g., gloomy, happy, evil, mysterious)?
3. What point of view is used?
4. Is the point of view appropriate to the story?

Children's Literature References

Note: Books designated with an asterisk (*) are recommended for reluctant readers.

Aruego, J., & Dewey, A. (2002). *Weird friends: Unlikely allies in the animal kingdom.* New York: Gulliver Books\Harcourt. K–2;3–4. INF*

Animals help one another in this book.

Birdsall, J. (2005). *The Penderwicks.* New York: Knopf. 3–4;5–6. CRF

The Penderwicks spend summer in a cottage and have a great time.

Bowe, J. (2007). *My last best friend.* New York: Harcourt. 3–4. CRF

After her best friend moves, the protagonist decides to never have a best friend.

Broach, E. (2006). *Shakespeare's secret.* New York: Walker. 5–6;7+. CRF

Hero's name was chosen by her father, who loved Shakespeare.

Butterworth, C., & Lawrence, J. (2006). *Seahorse the shyest fish in the sea.* New York: Candlewick. K–2;3–4. INF*

This informational book follows the life and development of the seahorse.

Dowell, F. O. (2007) *The chicken boy.* New York: Aladdin. 3–4;5–6. CRF

Tobin's mother died and his family fell apart. He finds a supportive friend.

Florian, D. (1998). *Beast feast.* New York: Voyager. K–2;3–4. P*

A collection of poetry about animals.

Goode, D. (2001). *Tiger trouble.* New York: Scholastic. K–2. P

The landlord wants the tiger to move until the tiger catches a burglar.

Grey, M. (2005). *Traction man is here!* Atlanta: Peachtree. K–2. MF

Traction man is an action figure who has an adventurous life.

Haddix, M. (2007). *Double identity.* New York: Aladdin. 5–6;7+. CRF

Bethany has led a sheltered life until she encounters a mystery.

Harper, C. (2007). *Just grace.* Boston: Houghton Mifflin. 3–4. CRF

Confusion results when three Graces are in the same classroom.

Hiaasen, C. (2002). *Hoot.* New York: Knopf. 5–6;7+. CRF*

The story of a boy who works to save owls.

Hodges, M. (2006). *Dick Whittington and his cat.* New York: Holiday House. K–2;3–4. Traditional Literature.

A new version of the traditional story.

Jackson, D. (2002). *The bug scientists.* New York: Houghton Mifflin. K–2;3–4. INF

These scientists like to study bugs of all sorts.

Kumin, M. (2006). *Mites to mastodons: A book of animal poems.* Boston: Houghton Mifflin. K–2;3–4. P

A collection of poems about animals of all sizes.

Lindgren, A. (1950). *Pippi Longstocking* (L. Lamborn, Tran.; S. Glanzman, Illus.). New York: Viking. K–2. MF

Pippi is an unusual character who never grows up or changes.

Lowry, L. (2002). *Gooney bird greene* (M. Thomas, Illus.). Boston: Houghton Mifflin. K–2. CRF*

Gooney Bird likes to be the center of attention.

Park, L. S. (2002). *When my name was Keoko.* New York: Clarion. 5–6;7+. HF

The story of a Korean girl and her life under the Japanese occupation.

Paulsen, G. (2006). *The legend of Bass Reeves.* New York: Wendy Lamb Books. 3–4;5–6. B

Bass Reeves escapes slavery and becomes a law man.

Peck, R. (2005). *The teacher's funeral.* New York: Dial. 5–6;7+. HF*

The teacher's death and funeral generates interesting and humorous problems.

Reeve, P. (2006). *Larklight: A rousing tale of dauntless pluck in the farthest reaches of space* (D. Wyatt, Illus.). New York: Bloomsbury. 5–6;7+. MF

In this science fiction book children search for their father, who was killed by spider.

Salley, C. & Stevens, J. (2002). *Epossumondas.* New York: Harcourt. K–2;3–4. PB

Epossumondas is a baby possum.

Schmidt, G. (2007). *The Wednesday wars*. New York: Houghton. 5–6;7+. MF

This is the story of Holling Hoodhood's seventh-grade school year.

Scieszka, J. (2006). *Nightmare on Joe's street (time warp trio vol. 1)*. New York: Harper Trophy. 3–4; 5–6. MF

A graphic novel and horror story.

Sendak, M. (1963). *Where the wild things are*. New York: Harper & Row. K–2;3–4. MF

Max is sent to bed without his supper, and his imagination takes over.

Snyder, Z. (2006). *The treasures of Weatherby*. New York: Atheneum. 5–6;7+. CRF

Raleigh experiences a mystery in the Weatherby house.

Spalding, A. (2006). *Secret of the dance*. Custer, WA: Orca Publishing. 5–6;7+. HF

This book portrays the conflict between aboriginal people and the Canadian government.

Stevens, J. & Crummel, S. (2005). *The great fuzz frenzy*. New York: Harcourt. K–2. PB

A tennis ball becomes a treasure.

Stevens, J. & Crummel, S. S. (Reprint 2005). *Cock-a-doodle-doo*. New York: Voyager. K–2. PB

This story is about a proud rooster.

Stevens, J. (1995). *Tops & bottoms*. New York: Harcourt. K–2. PB

The trickster agrees to take half of the crop.

St. John, L. (2007). *The white giraffe*. New York: Dial. 3–4;5–6. CRF

A mysterious white giraffe appears in Africa; hunters try to catch it, but a young girl stops them.

Uhlberg, M. (2005). *Dad, Jackie, and me* (C. Boatman, Illus.). New York: Peachtree. K–2;3–4. PB

A deaf father and his son share a love of baseball.

Vega, D. (2005). *Click here*. New York: Little Brown. 3–4;5–6;7+. CRF

Erin is a computer nerd who has an accident with her blog.

Wong, J. (2007). *The dumpster diver*. Candlewick. K–2. CRF

The dumpster diver hunts for treasures and then finds ways to use them.

Professional References

Adams, S. M., & Collins, A. (1986). A schema-theoretic view of reading. In H. Singer & R. Ruddell (Eds.), *Theoretical models and processes of reading* (pp. 404–425). Newark, DE: International Reading Association.

Alexander, L. (1981). The grammar of story. In B. Hearne & M. Kaye (Eds.), *Celebrating children's books* (pp. 3–13). New York: Lothrop, Lee & Shepard.

Applebee, A. (1978). *The child's concept of story*. Chicago: University of Chicago Press.

Barton, J. (2001). *Teaching with children's literature*. Norwood, MA: Christopher-Gordon.

Byars, B. (1993). Writing for children. *Speech*. Durham, NC: Southeastern Children's Writers Association.

Conrad, J. (Ed.) and Simmons, A. (Ed.). (1922). Preface to a career. In *The nigger of the Narcissus*. New York: Doubleday.

Fox, P. (1991, September). Writing: The village by the sea. *Book Links, 1*, 48–50.

Giblin, J. (1990). *Writing books for young people*. Boston: The Writer.

Hardy, B. (1977). Narrative as a primary act of mine. In M. Meek, A. Warlow, & G. Barton (Eds.), *The cool web: The pattern of children's reading* (pp. 12–23). London: Bodley Head.

Holman, C. H., & Harmon, W. (1986). *A handbook to literature* (4th ed.). New York: Macmillan.

Koskinen, P., Blum, I., Bisson, S., Phillips, S., Creamer, T., & Baker, T. (1999, February). Shared reading, books, and audiotapes: Supporting diverse students in school and at home. *The Reading Teacher, 52* (5), 430–444.

Kucan, L., & Beck, L. (1996, June). Four fourth graders thinking aloud: An investigation of genre effects. *Journal of Literacy Research, 32* (2), 269–287.

Lehr, S. (1991). *The child's developing sense of theme*. New York: Teachers College Press.

Morner, K., & Rausch, R. (1991). *NTC's dictionary of literary terms*. Lincolnwood, IL: National Textbook.

Rumelhart, D.E. (1975). Notes on a schema for stories. In D. G. Bobow & A. M. Collins (Ed.), *Representation and Understanding* (pp. 573–603.) New York: Academic Press.

Sebesta, S., & Iverson, W. J. (1975). *Literature for Thursday's child.* Chicago: Science Research Associates.

Stein, N.L. & Glenn, C. G. (1979). An analysis of story comprehension in elementary school children. In R.O. Tierney (1990, March). Redefining reading comprehension. *Educational Leadership, 47*, 37–42.

Van Vliet, L. (1992). *Approaches to literature through genre.* Phoenix, AZ: Oryx.

Wadham, T. (1999). Plot does matter. *The Horn Book, LXXV*, 445–450.

Wyndham, L., & Madison, A. (1988). *Writing for children and teenagers.* Cincinnati, OH: Writer's Digest Books.

3
Issues Relating to Literature for Children and Young Adolescents

KEY TERMS

bibliotherapy   stereotype

dialect   word choice

didacticism   writing style

GUIDING QUESTIONS

1. Why are certain books banned or challenged by some adults?

2. Where will you find lists of books that have been challenged or banned in schools and libraries?

3. Why is it important for teachers to examine the language that is used in children's books?

4. What impact does testing have on how much and what kinds of books children read?

Introduction to Issues That Impact Using Children's Literature in Classrooms

This chapter will examine several issues that impact literature for children and young adolescents. Books are often challenged or banned by adults who think the books are inappropriate for younger readers. There are several areas that seem to be especially problematic: language, sexuality and violence. There are other issues related to children's books that are not necessarily being challenged: didacticism and stereotypes. Two last areas of concern are related to school issues: bibliotherapy and No Child Left Behind legislation. Both of these last areas relate to the quality of the literature available as well as to how the books are used with children.

Challenged or Banned Books

Adults who choose books for children and young adolescents make their selections based on a number of different criteria (see Chapter 2). There are several other considerations. For example, all authors express their values in the books they write, whether it be in the language used, the role of men and women, the activities of the characters, or the stereotypes that are used. Some adults are uncomfortable with the values expressed in certain books. Therefore, teachers need to be familiar with the content in the books that they use in their classrooms so that they are prepared in the event that some community members may object to a chosen book. An open marketplace of ideas encourages children to think critically and to develop their own values, not necessarily those of the adults around them. This is often why books are challenged or banned.

However, parents certainly have the responsibility to be familiar with the books their children are reading and to state their objections about them if there is content that they feel is unacceptable. Parents may even request that their child not read a particular book and that the teacher give him or her an alternative book to read. However, do parents have the right to prevent all the children in the class or school from reading that book by having the book removed from the library? This has been an issue that is faced in many classrooms. Most school districts have a policy regarding what to do if a parent challenges the use of a particular book. Teachers need to familiarize themselves with the policy as well as with the books that they hope to use in their classrooms.

Books in every genre have been challenged. The Harry Potter Series (fantasy) by J. K. Rowling were the most frequently challenged books of the twenty-first century. The American Library Association (ALA) reported that there were more than 3,000 attempts to remove this series of books from schools and libraries between 2000 and 2005 (ALA, 2006). In 2005, two of the most challenged books were informational books that were often not being used in the classroom but were only in the school library: *It's Perfectly Normal* and *It's So Amazing*, both by Robie Harris. Also on the 2005 list of most challenged books were two books of contemporary realistic fiction: a Newbery Honor book, *Crazy Lady* by Jane Leslie Conly, and *Whale Talk* by Chris Crutcher. In other years, books in every genre have also been challenged or banned.

Why are many books for children and adolescents challenged or banned? According to the American Library Association (ALA), there are many reasons. One of the most common reasons is sexual content. Other challenges are because of offensive language, homosexuality, a perceived anti-family perspective, violence, and the very common "unsuited to age group." Even the "Alice" series by Phyllis Naylor Reynolds was on ALA's 2006 list of most challenged books, being cited for sexual content and offensive language.

An interesting case regarding a challenged book is in the courts. The Miami-Dade school district took a book off the shelves because the information it contained was full of factual omissions (deLuzuriaga, 2007). The school board removed the book because it didn't accurately depict life in Cuba. The outcome of this case has the potential to affect how the First Amendment is applied as librarians and teachers select books.

Teachers and others who want to know why specific titles have been challenged are encouraged to go to the American Library Association web site (www.ala.org/). At this same web site, they can find out what to do if a book they have chosen has been challenged. There are many links to other resources about this topic provided by the ALA.

The National Council of Teachers of English web site also has many suggestions for dealing with challenged or banned books. The form in Figure 3.1 can be used when questions arise.

Language

There are several language issues that impact literature for children and young adults. The first is *word choice.* Authors who choose simple words because they want to make reading "easy" for children may actually be disrespecting them. E. B. White, author of *Charlotte's Web*, wrote in 1969 in *The Paris Review,* "Some writers for children deliberately avoid using words they think a child doesn't know. This emasculates the prose and, I suspect, bores the reader. Children are game for anything. I throw them hard words, and they backhand them over the net. They love words that give them a hard time, provided they are in a context that absorbs their attention" (Neumeyer, 1994, p. 242).

For example, in the 2007 Newbery Award winner, *The Higher Power of Lucky,* Susan Patron uses the word *scrotum* on four different pages. Immediately after winning the award, opinion pieces and editorials criticizing the use of that word were published. Some people appeared to believe that this single word made the book unsuitable for children to read. Probably many young readers would be like Lucky, the protagonist, who didn't even know what the word meant. Lucky is finally able to ask her guardian for the definition, at which point, the word choice becomes a non-issue.

In most of Chris Crutcher's books, the use of swearing is an integral part of his writing style. This has also been severely criticized, and his books are regularly challenged and often taken off the shelves. However, Crutcher (2007) is also a child and family therapist and bases many of his characters on the lives and issues his clients are experiencing. He has suggested that if he didn't include the language that real people use that his stories would not reflect their struggles. The vocabulary he uses is a form of respect for the difficult situations in which many young people find themselves.

FIGURE 3.1 A form used when a book is challenged.

Citizen's Request for Reconsideration of a Work

Author _____

Paperback _____ Hardcover _____

Title _____

Publisher (if known) _____

Request initiated by _____

Telephone _____

Address _____

City _____

Zip Code _____

Complainant represents

_____ Himself/Herself

_____ (Name organization) _____

_____ (Identify other group) _____

1. Have you been able to discuss this work with the teacher or librarian who ordered it or who used it?

    _____ Yes _____ No

2. What do you understand to be the general purpose for using this work?

    a. Provide support for a unit in the curriculum?

       _____ Yes _____ No

    b. Provide a learning experience for the reader in one kind of literature?

       _____ Yes _____ No

    c. Other _____

    d. Did the general purpose for the use of the work, as described by the teacher or librarian, seem a suitable one to you?

       _____ Yes _____ No

    If not, please explain.

    _____

    _____

3. What do you think is the general purpose of the author in this book?

    _____

    _____

4. In what ways do you think a work of this nature is not suitable for the use the teacher or librarian wishes to carry out?

    _____

    _____

5. Have you been able to learn what is the students' response to this work?

    _____ Yes _____ No

6. What response did the students make?

    _____

    _____

7. Have you been able to learn from your school library what book reviewers or other students of literature have written about this work?

    _____ Yes _____ No

8. Would you like the teacher or librarian to give you a written summary of what book reviewers and other students have written about this book or film?

    _____ Yes _____ No

9. Do you have negative reviews of the book?

    _____ Yes _____ No

10. Where were they published?

    _____

11. Would you be willing to provide summaries of the reviews you have collected?

    _____ Yes _____ No

12. What would you like your library/school to do about this work?

    _____ Do not assign/lend it to my child.

    _____ Return it to the staff selection committee/department for reevaluation.

    _____ Other-Please explain

    _____

    _____

13. In its place, what work would you recommend that would convey as valuable a picture and perspective of the subject treated?

    _____

    _____

Signature _____

Date _____

Source: NCTE

There are many other books in which the characters may use cuss words or in which sex and drug use are described. Those who want to challenge books may be looking for examples of books that include these kinds of words or incidents. However, in well-written literature, use of certain words or events is integral to the characters and the setting in which the plot takes place. For example in *Saint Iggy*, Iggy Corso was born drug-addicted; his mom is off "visiting" and is not expected to return to the home; his dad is stoned and has passed out from excessive use of alcohol. Iggy has gotten into big trouble at school, but he makes the kind of decisions that may help him grow up to be somebody. The use of what might be considered inappropriate language in another setting is right for this setting. The use of swear words, drugs, and sex are not the focus of the story but simply the vehicles that are used in this coming-of-age novel by K. L. Going.

A second issue, *writing style,* or how the author puts together the words and sentences, impacts the readability of books. For example, in many of the easier (or transitional) chapter books the authors seem to have "written down" the text, trying to make them easy to read. These books are often not appealing to children or to those who pick fine literature for them. An example of a well-written book for this audience is *That Crazy Eddie and the Science Project of Doom* by Judy Cox. Cox writes in a simple style but the language is interesting and realistically describes the events and actions.

A third area of language to be considered is the use of a *dialect.* Every person speaks a form of a dialect, which may be defined as a difference from what is considered the "standard." Dialects vary in three ways: sentence structure (my brother, he), vocabulary (tennis shoes/sneakers), or pronunciation (pen pronounced as "pen" or "pin"). Authors use dialect to convey information about the characters implicitly. Sometimes the use of a dialect conveys a negative stereotype, as when an author may have a character from a cultural group speak differently from other characters in a story. Sometimes the dialect is used to simply provide extra information about the protagonist, the time, or the setting. For example, in *A Strong Right Arm: The Story of Mamie "Peanut" Johnson* by Michelle Y. Green, dialect is used to convey the times and the people involved. "I don't want no trouble, sir," I said, "and Mr. Sarge here says I ain't breaking no laws" (p. 31).

Two other good examples of books in which dialect represents the culture and setting of the story are *The Girl Who Spun Gold* by Virginia Hamilton and *Gator Gumbo: A Spicy Hot Tale* by Candace Fleming. The dialect used in both helps to convey the stories in a credible manner. The dialect is integral to the presentation.

The problem of dialect use arises when it is used to convey negative connotations about a particular group of people, when the author is saying that the character(s) does not have the intelligence to speak as an educated person does and therefore is of less value.

CLASSROOM SNAPSHOT

A FOCUS ON LANGUAGE

The children in Ms. Mattingly's class were in literature circles, discussing their books. The conversation of the group that was reading *The Great Gilly Hopkins* by Katherine Paterson seemed to be especially feisty. Ms. Mattingly stopped to listen to their conversation.

Lily said, "Look, Ms. Mattingly. Gilly is using a word that my mom says we shouldn't use."

Jason got into the conversation: "I told Lily that Gilly used that word because of who she was—she didn't have the same kind of families that we have."

Gena responded, "I don't think we should read this book any more. If my Aunt Janie sees this word, I'm going to be in trouble."

Ms. Mattingly was prepared for this kind of discussion, having used this book for literature circles several times previously. The whole class got in on the discussion about *word choice*, when certain words are appropriate to use and when they are not. The children then discussed why some books are challenged or banned and explored their feelings about their use. The discussion went well beyond the words used in this book, and the children had an opportunity to have a valuable exploration of ideas.

Another problem may be if the dialect interferes with comprehension of the content. Because the spelling of the words, the sentence structure, or the words chosen may be unfamiliar to the reader, the reader may not fully understand what is being read. If one is reading the book aloud, dialect usage may also be an issue, especially if the reader does not speak the dialect.

Writing style and dialect use are important language considerations when choosing high-quality books for children and young adults; nonetheless, they are rarely the basis for a book being challenged. Word choice, however is often the basis for a challenge.

Sexuality

Books have been challenged because of both heterosexual and homosexual content. Although both areas have been challenged, it has only been relatively recently that more books that explore being gay and coming out have been published for young adolescents. Brent Hartinger, who addressed the gay and lesbian issue in *The Geography Club,* writes, "One of the big concerns that editors relayed to us, when they were turning us down, was that the book did not have library potential. They didn't think libraries would be able to purchase the book because the subject matter is 'controversial.' Around 2000 it somehow became acceptable for libraries to shelve this kind of book . . . I am now on the list of acceptable books for libraries" (Emert, 2004, p. 13).

Kathleen T. Horning (2005) suggests that our society has made significant progress over the past 40 years regarding the recognition of gays and lesbians in the mainstream culture: "Many kids now go to schools where they have openly gay teachers and can join a Gay Straight Alliance group. There is also a growing body of gay literature for teens and even younger children in which they can see themselves in a positive light" (p. 52).

Alex Sanchez (2004) believes that gay and lesbian writers have a responsibility to readers. "Through my writing I hope to give readers an insight into the lives of gay and lesbian teenagers, their families, their friends, and communities—the daily name-calling and bullying they experience, their courage, struggles, hopes and dreams for a better life for both themselves and for those (of) you (who) come after them" (p. 1).

Although all of the above books and writers focus on books for teenagers, there are also books available

A frequently challenged book.

for younger children. These books focus more on families in which there are two parents of the same gender. Judith Snow has addressed this issue in *How It Feels to Have a Gay or Lesbian Parent: A Book by Kids for Kids of All Ages*. Some of these books are reviewed in Chapter 8, Contemporary Realistic Fiction.

Although more books are now available that include both heterosexual and homosexual events, nine of the ten most challenged books in 2006 were challenged because of sexual content and/or homosexuality (ALA, 2006). Those choosing books for children and young adolescents need to be aware that there will probably be those in the community who may object to these books being available to readers. However, for the sake of those children living in homes with same-gender parents and for students who may be harassed by their peers in middle or high school because of their gay or lesbian identities, books about gay/lesbian families and individuals need to be available. Although there may be political stumbling blocks when choosing literature on this topic, "When teachers and teacher educators, librarians, and parents have access to quality literature with gay and lesbian characters, and when educators remember that public schools should include all students, attitudes may change so there is greater tolerance for gay and lesbian students and parents" (Hermann-Wilmarth, 2007, p. 348).

Violence

Violence is an ever-increasing issue in the world today. Osofsky (1999) reports that violence in the United States might be considered a "public health epidemic." There is a higher homicide rate among young men in the United States than in almost any other country, the exceptions being in a few developing countries and in actual war zones. Violent behavior occurs in families as well as on the streets. This violence is depicted in some books, especially in realistic fiction, and is often a concern as one selects and uses literature for children and young adults. Although violence appears in all genres, it appears most realistically in contemporary and historical realistic fiction. Even though there is also much violence in traditional literature, that violence often does not seem as "real" to readers because of the settings.

Franzak and Noll (2006) state that, "The ubiquitous presence of violence is so much a part of our consciousness that for many of us it has a numbing effect. We are at a loss as to how to make meaning of the violent context of our social reality" (p. 662). It is for this reason that teachers need to have focused discussions about violence as it is portrayed in literature. Doing so can help students understand how violence impacts their lives. These discussions can help students see how violence functions. "If we can understand how we interpret violence, we are perhaps better equipped to resist violence in our midst" (p. 671).

A book for students in middle grades is *Harry Sue* by Sue Stauffacher. In the story, Harry Sue's dad throws her out of a window when she is four. After her parents are sent to prison, she is placed in the custody of her paternal grandmother. Granny runs a daycare center in which the children are in danger of being harmed. When one of the children almost dies, Harry Sue must take action and, in so doing, finds hope for her life and that of her best friend, a quadriplegic.

A much more complex book, *Just Listen* by Sarah Dressen, is the story of a teenager, Annabel, with a variety of significant problems. Annabel finally reveals that she was a victim of sexual assault, and this

has been at the root of many of her problems. Fortunately, this is a book that ends on a positive note, and the resolution is hopeful.

Many adults do not understand the use of graphic reality and violence as portrayed in some genres, and thus it is an area that is ripe for challenges. Because of this, some teachers are reluctant to introduce these books and to have the discussions with their students. Harris et al. (2001) found that preservice teachers tended to be conservative and did not introduce books into their classrooms that might be complex or controversial. However, teachers need to realize that many times they may be the only adults a student will trust, so it seems that teachers should be familiar with books that portray these important, but potentially challengeable, topics. Certainly, no books are "right" or "wrong" in and of themselves; the issue is whether a specific book is right or wrong for a specific reader. This implies that the adult should be familiar with both the book and the reader before making recommendations.

Other Issues

The last three issues discussed in this section are not ones about which there are usually challenges. Didacticism and stereotyping do, however, impact the quality of the writing, so they do need to be taken into consideration.

Didacticism

Didacticism, or presenting obvious, heavy-handed moral messages or instructions, alienates many readers. Some authors find literature for children and young adults an irresistible platform for sharing *their* beliefs and values. They believe that young people lack proper values and should be taught through didactic literature. The issue here is not a concern for the specific values espoused, but the way in which they are presented. One of the differences between well-written fiction and poorly written fiction is the way beliefs and values are expressed. In well-written fiction, the beliefs and values are implicit. They emerge from the characters' actions, conversations, and decisions. In poorly written fiction, the theme or message gets in the way of the story itself.

Stereotyping

A *stereotype* is created when a group of people is described as having specific characteristics without recognizing that individuals in that group may not have those characteristics. For example, often in books for children, grandmothers are portrayed as having gray hair and baking cookies for their grandchildren. These two characteristics are indeed true for many grandmothers but not all. The danger of stereotyping is that there is always some truth in the traits ascribed to the group but the assumption cannot be made that every individual within the group has those traits. Lots of grandmothers do bake cookies but probably an equal number will be just as happy to buy them at the store—or some grandmothers may not think cookies are important at all!!

All groups of individuals have stereotypes, or a variety of specific characteristics, associated with them. Regardless of the race, gender, culture, age, occupation, lifestyle, or place of residence, those who are outside the group will see similarities among the individuals and then make generalizations that all who are in the group will have the same characteristics. Truth is, however, that members of any group must be regarded as unique individuals with their own values, beliefs, and opinions, not merely as representatives of the group.

Authors use stereotypes in their writing because they make the assumption that readers will understand the implicit characteristics associated with the individual/setting so less description will be needed. For example, in traditional literature, stepmothers are generally not nice people. Authors do not need to go into any extensive descriptions about "badness" but based on the stereotypes plus the stepmothers' actions, readers learn to anticipate evil deeds if a stepmother is involved.

Stereotypes in literature can perpetuate biases toward individuals who are members of a particular group. If children only read books in which females are passive or dependant and males are the ones who take charge of a situation or who make the important decisions, then girls may take away the message that they need to learn to be passive themselves. "If young children are repeatedly exposed to biased representations through words and pictures, there is a danger that such distortions will become a part of their thinking, especially if reinforced by societal biases" (Anti-Defamation League, 2003, p. 1).

Picture books, used both with younger and middle-school aged children, can be the basis for critical discussion of complex issues. Books by Patricia Polacco are especially good for this purpose. In *Rotten Richie and the Ultimate Dare,* siblings Trish and Richie each choose an activity that is thought of as gender-specific—Trish likes ballet and Richie likes hockey. Because of their dare, Trish plays hockey on her brother's team and scores the winning goal; Richie dances in her ballet recital, taking a lead part. In *Thank You, Mr. Falker*, Trish has a reading disability and is made fun of by the other students. Her teacher takes the time to help her learn to read. Both of these books present the opportunity to discuss stereotypes often held by children and young adolescents.

School-Related Issues

The last two issues in this chapter relate to how books are used by adults as they interact with children. Many children, of course, will read books that they find on library shelves just because they are interested in the topics. Other children will read only what is required by their teachers or their reading program. In either case, the books available to them are chosen by adults. How those books are used may impact whether or not the children become lifelong readers or "I only read what I have to read" readers. The issues in this section relate to classroom practices: bibliotherapy and the No Child Left Behind legislation.

Bibliotherapy

Bibliotherapy literally means "helping with books." According to Bernstein (1989), bibliotherapy involves the "self examination and insights gained from reading" (p. 159). Historically, doctors, therapists and other health-care professionals have used bibliotherapy as a strategy to help their patients solve a problem.

There are four stages in bibliotherapy. In the first, *identification*, the reader becomes personally involved in the book, generally identifying with the character who has a similar problem. The second stage is *catharsis*, the emotional release that occurs when readers identify with the character. The reader may know for the first time that other people have similar problems. The third stage is *insight*. This is a form of self-discovery, which may allow the reader to gain knowledge about his or her situation. The fourth stage is *application*. As a result of going through the first three stages, the reader may demonstrate attitudinal or behavioral changes.

Although bibliotherapy was originally used by therapists, many teachers have applied these four principles when they have had students who have had problems. For example, sibling rivalry is often an issue for young children. A teacher may read a selection of books, including an information book, *Bratty Brothers and Selfish Sisters: All about Sibling Rivalry* by R. W. Alley, and a picture book, *Buttons and Bo* by Satoshi Itaya, to the class. Talking about the situations in the informational book and about bear siblings in the picture book may allow the children to discover that most siblings have disagreements. As they share their experiences, children can gain insights that they can apply to their lives.

Children's responses to books are central to the concept of bibliotherapy. Teachers, however, must use careful judgment during the discussions. Some children, during a group discussion, may share more than they should about their feelings. This may make them very vulnerable to unkind remarks by some of their classmates. It is often a better practice to have children share their personal feelings about the ideas in writing or drawing. Bibliotheraphy is not something that teachers should do without careful preparation and professional study.

Maeve Visser Knoth (2006) suggests that, rather than using a book to help a reader address a current problem, reading about problems before a specific problem occurs in the reader's life is the better approach. "Rather than address what is happening in the present, I am inclined to prepare children for emotional experiences *before* they occur" (p. 273). She gives the example of having read a book about the death of a grandparent long before her own grandmother died. She took what she remembered from that book and applied it to her own life. As a librarian, she tries to introduce children to emotionally complex books on a regular basis so that the children have a better chance of being prepared for events that happen to them and their family or peers.

There is no question, however, that books that are carefully used can help children cope with current problems (Stanley, 2002; Myracle, 1995). However, teachers and parents must not assume that simply reading about a character who has a similar problem will "cure" the grief resulting from a death or even something relatively simple like sibling rivalry. It is simply one strategy that is available that can be used to help readers who are experiencing difficulties in their lives.

No Child Left Behind Legislation and its Relationship to Literature

Many educators have expressed frustration with the current emphasis on preparation for testing and getting high test scores. Teaching for the test, which is done in many classrooms, often means that there is less time for reading and enjoying fine literature. "Books no longer hold a prominent place in many classrooms; instead, they are being increasingly replaced by programmed reading instruction, highly codified textbooks, and leveled readers, all focused upon isolated skills" (Chatton, 2007, p. 490). Teachers have important decisions to make as they work with students. How will they best prepare their students for doing well on the tests as well as helping them develop attitudes so that they will be lifelong readers?

It is the belief of many professionals that when children like to read, they will read regularly and will learn more information than is necessary to pass the tests. Of course, students need to learn test-taking strategies, but as they read well-written literature, they are able to explore ideas beyond those on which they are being tested. "In good books, no child has to be left behind. Because young people are the protagonists in their stories, and because stories are written to give a sense of hope and inspiration for the possibilities life holds, children's literature challenges the prevailing idea that it is success on reading tests that will determine success in life" (Chatton, p. 490).

Books have been written for children about testing. These can help children know that others are experiencing anxiety about the tests they must take. Nancy Poydar tells the story of how older students (who have experienced testing before) try to make the younger children even more anxious in *The Biggest Test in the Universe*. After the test, these children pass on the exaggerated stories about the tests. In *Testing Miss Malarky* by Judy Finchler, it is the teachers, parents, and administrators who are most anxious about "THE TEST."

Summary

The books and issues described in this section are ones about which teachers almost always have strong opinions. Teachers often "self-censor" because they may be afraid that some books may cause a controversy either with the parents or the school district. Although it is important that teachers check to see if their district has a policy about which books may or may not be used in classrooms, there may be times when books that would be very appropriate for individuals to read are not available to readers. This is an issue that needs to be discussed by all of those concerned with educating all students.

Thought Questions and Applications

1. Do you think that teachers should read books that have swear words in them orally to their classes? Why? Why not?

2. What will you do to be assured that your students will do well on standardized tests and at the same time learn to love to read?

3. Will you use a book that has been challenged in your classroom? Why? Why not?

Research and Application Experiences

1. Go to your local public library and ask to see their criteria for book selection. Do you think that these criteria will assure that the library has a balanced collection of books?

2. Compare and contrast the violence that children may read about in books with the violence that they view on TV, either in the news or in other shows. What conclusions do you draw?

3. Choose a favorite children's book and examine the writing style the author uses. Now find a book you didn't like very well and examine the writing style in it. Was the writing part of the reason you liked one and didn't like the other?

Classroom Activities

ACTIVITY 3.1   READING, GRAPHING, AND WRITING

IRA/NCTE Standards: 1, 5, 6, 7, 9, 12.

This activity is a way to integrate literature with making graphs in mathematics. Have students look at the following differences and count the numbers of instances each is found in the books, by genre, they are reading. Graph the results.

> Boys as main characters
>
> Girls as main characters
>
> Characters with a physical challenge (mobility, vision, hearing, etc.)
>
> Characters from a variety of races and cultures.

Other categories, as appropriate to the lesson, can be used. For example, the number of women and men who are scientists as found in informational books can be graphed.

At the conclusion of the graphing, write a descriptive essay on what was found, comparing results by the different genre read.

Activity 3.2 Author Study: Patricia Polacco

IRA/NCTE Standards: 1, 2, 7, 9, 11, 12.

Patricia Polacco has written almost 50 books, many of which are about characters and situations that dispel some commonly held stereotypes. Collect as many of these books as possible (have the students collect some, too) and use them for discussions, research, and connections with other areas; include discussions on her artwork as well. Other information and activities can be found at patriciapolacco.com.

Activity 3.3 Challenged Books

IRA/NCTE Standards: 1, 2, 3, 4, 5, 7, 9, 12.

When working with older students and getting permission from the school administration, go to the American Library Association web site (www.ala.org/) and print out lists of books that have been challenged. Choose several that are appropriate for this age group. After reading these books, use them as a basis for discussion and ascertain why they may have been challenged. Follow-up activities could involve letter writing, opinion pieces, and other activities to share what was learned.

Children's Literature References

Alley, R. W. (2007). *Bratty brothers and selfish sisters: All about sibling rivalry*. St. Meinrad, IN: One Caring Place. K–2. INF

Sibling rivalry is the focus of this book.

Conley, J. L. (1993). *Crazy lady*! New York: HarperCollins. 5–6;7+. CRF; NewH

Vernon learns to change his view of people and events.

Cox, J. (2005). *That crazy Eddie and the science project of doom* (B. Sims, Illus.). NY: Holiday House. K–2;3–4. CRF

Eddie is creative, and this often gets him in trouble.

Crutcher, C. (2001). *Whale talk*. New York: Greenwillow. 7+. CRF

TJ puts together a swim team made up of misfits.

Dressen, S. (2006). *Just listen*. New York: Viking. 7+. CRF

Annabel was a victim of sexual assault.

Finchler, J. (Reprint 2003). *Testing Miss Malarky*. NY: Walker Books. K–2. CRF; PB

Miss Malarky is worried about the test, too.

Fleming, C. (2004). *Gator gumbo: A spicy hot tale* (S. A. Lambert, Illus.). NY: Farrar, Straus and Giroux. K–2;3–4. MF; PB

An original folk tale.

Going, K .L. (2007). *Saint Iggy*. New York: Harcourt. 7+. CRF

Iggy's family does not help him learn to make good decisions. He finds other support.

Green, M. Y. (2002). *A strong right arm: The story of Mamie "Peanut" Johnson*. New York: Scholastic. 3–4;5–6. HF; B

An African American baseball player wants fair treatment.

Hamilton, V. (2000). *The girl who spun gold* (L. Dillon and D. Dillon, Illus.). New York: Blue Sky Press. K–2;3–4. MF; PB

Retelling of a traditional tale.

Harris, R. (Updated edition, 2004). *It's perfectly normal: Changing bodies, growing up, sex and sexual health* (M. Emberly, Illus.). Cambridge, MA: Candlewick. 5–6;7+. INF

A book about facts and issues relating to puberty.

Harris, R. (Reprint, 2004). *It's so amazing: A book about eggs, sperm, birth, babies, and families* (M. Emberly, Illus.). Cambridge, MA: Candlewick. 5–6;7+. INF

Answers about reproduction and birth.

Hartinger, B. *Geography club.* New York: Harper. 7+. MRI

Itaya, S. (2004). *Buttons and Bo.* New York: North South Books. K–2. PB; MF

A fantasy book about sibling rivalry.

Naylor, P. R. Alice Series. New York: Atheneum. 3–4;5–6;7+. CRF

A series about a girl who lives with her dad and older brother.

Patron, S. (2006). *The higher power of Lucky.* New York: Atheneum. 5–6;7+. CRF; New

Lucky lives with her father's ex-wife after her mom dies.

Paterson, K. (1978). *The great Gilly Hopkins.* New York: Crowell. 5–6;7+. CRF

Gilly is a foster child who has been in several different homes.

Polacco, P. (2001). *Thank you, Mr. Falker.* New York: Philomel. 3–4;5–6. CRF

Trish has difficulty learning to read.

Polacco, P. (2006). *Rotten Richie and the ultimate dare.* New York: Philomel. K–2;3–4. CRF; PB

Siblings dare each other to try new activities.

Poydar, N. (2005). *The biggest test in the universe.* New York: Holiday House. K–2. CRF; PB

The first-graders are afraid of the big test.

Rowling, J. K. The Harry Potter Books (M. GrandPré, Illus.). New York: Scholastic. 3–4;5–6;7+. MF

A series of fantasy books about magicians-in-training.

Snow, T. (2004). *How it feels to have a gay or lesbian parent: A book by kids for kids of all ages.* New York: Harrington Park Press. 4–6;7+.

Children talk about the confusion and prejudice they encounter. Discrimination is an issue for them.

Stauffacher, S. (Reprint, 2007). *Harry Sue.* New York: Yearling. 3–4;5–6. CRF

Harry Sue has lived in abusive situations since she was young.

White, E. B. (1952). *Charlotte's web.* New York: HarperCollins. 3–4;5–6;7+. MF

A spider saves a pig's life.

Professional References

ALA: American Library Association web site: www.ALA.org. Accessed July 1, 2007.

Anti-Defamation League, (2003). Assessing Children's Literature. http://www.adl.org/education/assessing.asp. Accessed, July 1, 2007.

Bernstein, J. E. (1989). *Bibliotherapy:* How books can help young children cope. In Bernstein, *Books to help children cope with separation and loss* (2nd ed.) (pp. 166–178). New York: Bowker.

Chatton, B. (2007). No Child Left Behind: Literature that captures what standardized texts can't measure. *Language Arts, 84,* 490–497.

Crutcher, C. (2007). Presentation at the 2007 Wilmington College Children's Literature Conference, Wilmington, Ohio.

DeLuzuiaga, T. (2007). *Miami Herald,* July 7, 2007. (MiamiHerald.com).

Emert, T. (2004). Interview with Brent Hartinger. *Signal Journal 27,* 12–14.

Franzak, J., & Noll, E. (2006). Monstrous acts: Problematizing violence in young adult literature. *Journal of Adolescent & Adult Literacy, 49,* 662–672.

Harris, V. J. et al. (2001). Controversial issues in children's literature. *The New Advocate, 15,* vii-viii.

Hermann-Wilmarth, J. M. (2007). Full inclusion: Understanding the role of gay and lesbian texts and films in teacher education classroom. *Language Arts, 84,* 347–356.

Horning, K. T. (2005). On spies and purple socks and such. *Horn Book, 81,* 49–52.

Knoth, M. V. (2006). What ails bibliotherapy? *Horn Book, 82,* 273–276.

Myracle, L. (1995). Molding the minds of the young: The history of bibliotherapy as applied to children and adolescents. *The ALAN Review, 22.*

National Council of Teachers of English web site: NCTE.org

Neumeyer, P. F. (1994). *The annotated Charlotte's Web.* New York: HarperCollins.

Osofsky, J. D. (1999). The impact of violence on children. *The Future of Children, 9,* (3).

Sanchez, A. (2004). Crossing two bridges: Coming out: The power of images in YA Lit. (Remarks adapted from panel discussion at the 2003 NCTE Convention.) *The ALAN Review, 32,* (1).

Stanley, J. (2002). *Reading to heal: How to use bibliotherapy to improve your life.* London: Vega.

4
Picture Books: Visual and Verbal Art

KEY TERMS

benchmark

graphic novels

illustrated book

picture book

visual literacy

wordless picture book

GUIDING QUESTIONS

1. Why are picture books such an important form of literature?

2. How are graphic novels similar to picture books?

3. Why are picture books valuable for all ages?

4. Who is your favorite picture book illustrator?

Introduction to Picture Books

Children's first experiences with literature are usually with picture books. However, more and more picture books are appearing in middle-school classes because they present complex ideas and concepts in an easy-to-access format. *Picture books* bring images and ideas together in a unique and exciting art form that adults and children can explore at many levels. "A picture book has a collective unity of story-line, theme, or concept, developed through the series of pictures of which the book is comprised" (Matulka, 2002). Fine picture books give children a window on the world. Moreover, the visual literacy and graphic imagery in picture books enable authors and artists to tell stories, share poems, and convey information.

One of the fine current picture books is *The Runaway Dinner* by Allan Ahlberg, an absurdly funny story that integrates pictures and languages. At the outset of this story, Banjo (a boy) sits down to eat, but the sausage named Melvin darts off the plate. Melvin is followed by the table and three peas named Percival, Paul, and Peter. They all run down the street followed by Banjo, his mother and father, and the cat. The illustrations drawn by Bruce Ingman are naïve, childlike drawings in acrylic. Banjo almost grabs Melvin when the sausage gets tired, but Banjo's mother tells him not to eat the sausage because it has been on the ground. Ahlberg's technique of naming the foods and the names he chooses contribute to the humor of the situation. By the way, a hungry Banjo does eat a plum pie named Joyce when he returns home. This story is an excellent comparison to the classic story of "The Gingerbread Boy."

The Nature of Picture Books

Picture books are an introduction to *visual literacy,* which "is the ability to interpret, use, appreciate, and create images and video using 21st century media in ways that advance thinking, decision making, communication, and learning" (NCREL, 2003). Throughout their school years, students will read about and create graphics from the World Wide Web, videos, film, three dimensional rotations of film, and many other sources. Exploring picture books gives children opportunities to understand color, scale, object placement, and so forth, which will provide a good beginning toward developing visual literacy.

This chapter includes examples of excellent picture books available to enrich your understanding of picture books and their value in children's lives. *Benchmarks,* or standards of quality, are represented in the exemplary books discussed in this chapter. We suggest that you read some of these books to develop your own taste and standards of quality. Your ability to identify picture books that students will appreciate and that will extend their learning experiences will increase with experience. This chapter introduces picture books and graphic novels in a genre organization because all literary genre appear in the picture book format.

Artistic Expression

Picture books are a form of artistic expression that is ideally suited to reinterpreting and representing the world to an audience (Lewis, 2001). The pictures and the text in picture books function as different forms of communication; each is incomplete without the other (Nikolajeva & Scott, 2001). Caldecott Medalist Ed Young (1990) believes "there are things that words do that pictures never can, and likewise, there are images that words can never describe." Picture books are "as close to drama or a thirty-two page movie, as it is to either literature or art" (Wood & Wood, 1986, p. 556). Pictures stimulate dramatic, active responses in children that compare with their responses to theater or film.

Researchers have found that illustrations contribute to readers' understanding, as well as to intellectual and emotional development (Kiefer, 1995). Although the text itself is generally brief, the interaction of text and illustrations makes picture books complex literature. Because picture books usually contain 2,000 words or fewer, with 60 words per page and only 32 pages per book, the author can only give the bare bones of a story. These textual constraints mean that writers must be downright stingy with their words, while creating characters, setting, plot, and theme, along with enough suspense to make readers turn the pages. Each double-page spread must lead readers to turn the page.

A Blending of Text and Art

This blending of text and art is illustrated in *Leaf Man* by Lois Ehlert. A Leaf Man who is composed of brilliantly colored autumn leaves appears on the book

The Leaf Man flies away for adventures.

cover. Ehlert used only 207 words to tell the story, which takes only 10 minutes to read. The art inside the book amplifies the rhythmic language, while creating visual and auditory images. The story line of *Leaf Man* begins, "But yesterday the wind blew Leaf Man away." Then ducks and geese composed of leaves appear in the art, but the author points out that "A Leaf Man's got to go where the wind blows." Ehlert encourages readers to speculate about the places the wind will take Leaf Man, and the brilliant colored pictures call readers' attention to the bright green fields, golden prairie meadows, and lakes and rivers below. Children's attention is drawn to the leaf characters that occupy the various scenes. The author challenges readers to listen to and look at everyday objects in different ways and suggests that readers may find "a Leaf Man waiting to go home" with them.

Illustrations and Illustrators

Lois Ehlert enjoys illustrating her books with common things found in the environment. She is fascinated by nature and is a keen observer of the natural world (Ehlert, 2005). Certainly this book resonates with young students who will listen for the rustle of leaves and look for the shapes composed of leaves.

This book reminds me of a first-grade student who observed that the leaves on my windowshield looked like sharks. *Leaf Man* was illustrated with leaves the author collected for many years and from many places. Her love of nature is apparent in other books, *Nuts to You* and *Mole Hill.* Ehlert observes that her books are difficult to categorize because they are both fiction and nonfiction. She writes about actual events and information, but her perspective is that of a storyteller.

Artistic Styles

Illustrators are artists who create the visual components of color, shape, line, texture, and dimension to create visuals that tell and interpret stories. Illustrators consider the nature of the story or subject as they make careful selections of technique, and style. The key to "telling stories with pictures" is creating a flow of graphic images that is readable, coherent, and obviously related to the text (Shulevitz, 1985). Artists strive to evoke the essence of a work rather than to simply "make pictures."

For his wordless picture book, *Flotsam,* David Wiesner chose bold colors and rich detail to develop readers' understanding of "flotsam," which he defined as anything that floats. The illustrations show a boy looking through a magnifying glass at the objects he finds on the seashore. When a camera washes up, he has the film developed, and his imagination goes into action. The rich detail and the watercolors involve readers with the fantasy of the book.

In Jim Murphy's Irish ghost story, *Fergus and the Night-Demon,* illustrator John Mandeers brings the tale to life with a spooky setting and characters with very expressive faces. The artist skillfully illustrates the movement of characters, wind, and water as Fergus faces and escapes the dreadful demon with red eyes.

Christlow (1999) demonstrated the different ways that illustrators can interpret the same story by following two illustrators as they created dramatically different illustrations for *Jack and the Bean Stalk.* Most libraries will have additional versions of this story, and students enjoy comparing different versions and examining the reasons for the various interpretations.

Artists combine visual elements and artistic media to create styles expressing their thoughts, feelings, and interpretations. Authors choose words and sentences to create text, while artists choose style, *medium,* technique, and color to interpret a particular piece of literature. Both words and art are parts of reading picture books. Artistic styles are summarized with examples in Table 4.1, and popular media are summarized in Table 4.2.

Types of Picture Books

Traditional Style Picture Books

Traditional picture books like *How I Became a Pirate* tell a story through the interaction of pictures and words. This hilarious book was written by

TABLE 4.1
Artistic styles commonly used in picture books.

Style	Example
Cartoon	
The artist uses a cartoon style based on line drawings.	*Meanwhile*—by Jules Feiffer
Graphic style (as in graphic novels)	*To Dance* by Siena Siegel and Mark Siegel
Folk or primitive art	
The artist uses bold lines and colors.	*A Gift for Abuelita* by Nancy Luenn
Impressionism	
The artist suggests or gives an impression.	*Between Earth & Sky* by Joseph Bruchac
Realistic	
The artist depicts subjects as they actually appear.	*Home Run* by Robert Burieigh

TABLE 4.2

Popular media for illustrations in children's picture books.

Medium	Example
Pastels, mixed-media collage	*This Jazz Man* by Karen Ehrhardt, illustrated by R.J. Roth
Watercolors	*How to Make Friends with a Giant* by Gennifer Choldenko
Line and watercolor paintings	*Once Upon a Banana* by Jennifer Armstrong, illustrated by David Small
Pen and ink drawings	*Wee Gillis* by Munro Leaf
Collage	*Alexander and the Wind-Up Mouse* by Leo Lionni
Color photos	*Cave Sleuths* by Laurie Lindop
Oil on wood	*The Pilgrims of Plimoth* by Marcia Sewall

Melinda Long and illustrated by David Shannon. When the pirate comes ashore, he asks Jeremy where he is and is surprised to learn that he has landed on the wrong beach. Then the pirate decides to take Jeremy Jacob on the pirate ship to be a "digger" of treasure. Jeremy is excited because he expects to learn what pirates do, but Jeremy discovers what pirates don't do and decides that he does not want to be a pirate. This picture book illustrates the integration of text and pictures to tell a story. This is a perfect book for dramatization and/or readers' theater.

Wordless Picture Books

Illustrators of *wordless picture books* use their artistic talents to create character, setting, plot, theme, and style without using any words at all. Each frame or page leads readers to the next. In *Sidewalk Circus* by Paul Fleischman, the story begins with a girl watching a worker put up posters announcing the arrival of the circus. Fleischman gives readers a grandstand seat for the neighborhood circus. The young girl in the book watches a construction worker walking on a beam like a tight rope walker and a young man carrying a side of beef on his back like Goliath the Strongman in the circus. This is how she discovers a neighborhood circus.

Wordless picture books give students opportunities to practice predicting, questioning, and retelling skills, which are essential to reading comprehension (Trinkle, 2006). The following wordless picture books are helpful for developing readers' comprehension:

Banyai, I. *Zoom.* Puffin Books, 1998.

Lehman, B. *The Red Book.* Houghton Mifflin, 2004.

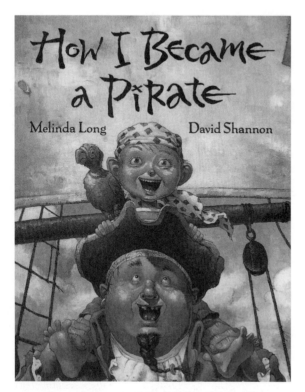

Pirates' lives are not all fun and games.

Liu, Jae Soo. *The Yellow Umbrella.* Kane/Miller, 2002.

Wiesner, D. *Tuesday.* Clarion, 1997.

Graphic Novels

Graphic novels are like comic books; however, graphic novels are longer (Carter, 2007). *Nightmare on Joe's Street* by Jon Scieszka is a popular graphic novel based on the television series of the same name. The author introduces each character prior to introducing the plot. At the outset of the story, Joe, the hero, and his friend, Sam, have warped into a time and space where they have to find THE BOOK, which Joe uses to warp into different times and places; he has to find THE BOOK in this new time and place, so he and Sam can get back to where they came from. They are caught up in a horror story and meet Frankenstein's monster. This story is told in comic book style with strips of pictures and balloons containing text and sound effects.

Illustrated Books

Illustrated books have fewer illustrations than picture books; these illustrations simply depict characters, story events, or setting. In illustrated books the text can stand alone to tell the story, while the illustrations help readers visualize characters and so forth. Lois Lowry's *Gooney Bird Greene* is an illustrated book. The vast majority of illustrated books are for children in second grade and above. Illustrated books have pictures, but fewer than a picture book or a graphic novel. For example, *Outbreak: Plagues that Changed History* by Bryn Barnard is an illustrated book with stunning pictures that elaborate the dense text. In this nonfiction book, Barnard explores the invisible world of microbes and how they have shaped human destiny. He raises questions such as: "Did yellow fever help the slave trade?" and "Did cholera pave the way for modern Manhattan?" (He answers "yes in each case.") This fascinating book is clearly intended for students in grades five through nine or older. In fact, this adult couldn't put the book down!

Picture Books for Older Students

Picture books can play important roles in the development of older students. Teachers will find that picture books appeal to all ages because "the best children's writers say things to a five-year-old that a fifty-year-old can also respect" (B. Hearne, 1999, p. 9). Both a 5-year-old and a 50-year-old appreciate picture books, albeit in different ways. For instance, the sheer power of the life-like illustrations in *Sky Boys: How They Built The Empire State Building* establishes the theme of how workers built the Empire State Building, which was the tallest building in the world at that time. Hopkinson and Ransome obtained photographs taken 75 years ago for the end papers of this book. This book is an excellent companion to Eve Bunting's *Pop's Bridge,* which tells the story of building the Golden Gate Bridge. Bunting writes about this edifice in ways that appeal to child readers, and C. F. Payne illustrates the opening of the bridge in his contemplative style. *Pop's Bridge, Sky Boys,* and *Brooklyn Bridge* by Lynn Curlee are excellent subjects in a unit for older students. These titles are excellent for comparison and contrast.

The Magic School Bus and the Science Fair Expedition is an excellent picture book for older students. The scientific information is carefully researched and accurate. Miss Frizzle and her flying school bus are well known to school students. Their creators, Joanna Cole and Bruce Degen, are dedicated to making learning fun, and they are certainly successful. The quality of their work is widely recognized, and many awards attest to their success.

An entirely different picture book style appears in Jules Feiffer's *Meanwhile*—which is illustrated with cartoons. Raymond, the main character, learns to use the word *meanwhile* to escape difficult situations. This imaginative book will appeal to all ages. Many readers will choose to use *Meanwhile* to escape their own difficult situations or they might search for their own magic word.

A bear is an important character in Jon Agee's book *Milo's Hat Trick.* Milo is a magician who has failed miserably in his chosen profession. However, he has one last chance . . . he must get a rabbit to jump out of his hat. He finds a bear instead, but the bear cooperates. Now he has a bear in his hat; all he has to do is whistle and the bear jumps out to the crowd's astonishment. Milo encounters several problems, but his solutions are revealed through the illustrations. The humor of Jon Agee's picture books is appealing to middle-school students.

Picture books have many layers of meaning, some of which resonate most readily with older students. Furthermore, picture books are an excellent choice for introducing concepts, literary elements, genre, and writing. Besides, they are just plain fun. The following classroom snapshot illustrates a middle-school class using a picture book.

USING DISCUSSION TECHNIQUES

Lisa James read the book *So You Want to be President* by Judith St. George and David Small because it received the Caldecott Medal. As Lisa read, it occurred to her that the book might interest her sixth-grade students who were studying political cartoons and Presidents. To introduce the book, she showed the book cover to the class and asked the students to identify the four Presidents on the cover (the cover is Mt. Rushmore). After the class identified George Washington, Thomas Jefferson, Theodore Roosevelt, and Abraham Lincoln, she asked the students how they identified the Presidents. In class discussion, the students distinguished the exaggerated characteristics that made the Presidents identifiable, such as Roosevelt's glasses and mustache, Lincoln's nose and chin, and so forth. Lisa then showed the double-page spreads in the book and asked the students to identify as many of the Presidents as possible. The students recognized a number of them.

Lisa asked, "Would you want to be President?"

Some of the students answered, "Yes, because you could do whatever you want, live in the White House, travel in Air Force 1, and have lots of vacations. You get a lot of money." However, others responded, "No, everyone criticizes you all the time. It's too hard to be President. There are wars, shootings, and all the other countries that don't cooperate."

Then Lisa read the book. Following the reading, the students discussed these points:

A. positive and negative aspects of being President;

B. unusual characteristics of the Presidents;

C. the pros and cons of being President; and

D. creating cartoons of the Presidents.

Following the reading and discussion, the students chose Presidents to be subjects of their cartoons. They decided to branch out and create cartoons for local notable people, including the principal. Some students chose to do research to identify the quirks of people that could be made into cartoons, and they made class books of their cartoons.

 Genre in the Picture Book Format

Realistic fiction, modern fantasy, traditional literature, biography, historical fiction, poetry, and informational books are all genres of children's literature found in picture books. Picture books must be alive to grab readers' attention and hold it (B. Hearne, 1999). The picture books we include in this chapter will hold students' interest. In the following segment, we address each genre.

Realistic Fiction

As you read earlier in this text, realistic fiction has characters like people we know. Settings are contemporary, and the characters encounter problems that occur in actual life situations. Lynne Rae Perkins tells such a story in *Pictures from Our Vacation*. She incorporates snapshots, notebook entries, art, maps, and details that a primary-grade child would notice. The narrator realizes that some of the fun cannot be expressed in photos, but she realizes that those memories will remain in her mind.

Nadia Wheatley's picture book, *Luke's Way of Looking,* gives realistic fiction an imaginative angle. The protagonist, Luke, looks at things differently than all the boys in his class. When the teacher looks at Luke's paintings, the teacher goes ballistic! Then Luke discovers a museum and discovers a place where his way of looking at things is valued. As a result of this experience, his world changes.

Good Boy Fergus is realistic because the story is a one-sided conversation between David Shannon (the author/illustrator) and the Shannon family's West Highland terrier, Fergus. On his morning walk Fergus manages to do everything wrong, as shown in the illustrations. Readers who have dogs, especially, will laugh at Fergus's antics and understand that this is a very realistic story because they will have had similar experiences with their own pets!

Picture Book/Fantasy

Picture book fantasy has elements of make-believe, but readers enjoy good fantasy so much that they want to believe it is true. Fantasy is especially popular in picture books because readers can interpret the text in imaginative ways. The book *Pirate Bob* is the story of a happy pirate ship, the Blackbird. Author Kathryn Lasky explains in words that Pirate Bob has a huge scar, while illustrator David Clark uses watercolor to illustrate the scar, which runs from the pirate's nose to his ear. Yellow Jack, Bob's best friend, is "the color of a very pale lemon" because he has scurvy. Pirate Bob, Yellow Jack, and their parrot are memorable characters, and the book is an excellent addition to a collection of pirate stories.

Henry P. Baloney is a different kind of student in Jon Scieszka and Lane Smith's *Baloney.* Henry P. is from another planet, but he has problems just like earthlings. He has to come up with a very good excuse for being late, or he will have permanent lifelong detention. Imagination serves Henry P. well, because he creates amazing stories about his adventures and misadventures. Strange words appear in the text because Henry uses words from many languages. Thankfully, the authors provide a "decoder" page to help readers. Does Henry's magic work? His teacher, Miss Bugscuffle, is not taken in by the tale, but she explains that the day's assignment is to compose a tall tale and suggests that Henry get busy writing his story. The artist has created Henry with green skin color, large eyes, and pointed ears, showing that he is clearly from another galaxy, as is Miss Bugscuffle.

Some picture book fantasies feature children in unusual situations, often including unusual characters. Tina, the girl in Richard Waring's *Alberto the Dancing Alligator,* receives an egg for a gift, which hatches into an alligator. Tina enjoys spending time with her pet, especially dancing the tango. Unfortunately, the alligator falls into the toilet and descends into the world underneath the city. The alligator has fun for a while, but when he tries to return home, he climbs into other peoples' bathrooms. The rumor spreads that 1,000 alligators are on the loose and all bathrooms are at risk, resulting in expert

alligator hunters going after the alligator. How does Tina save her friend? Read this fantastic book and find out. Children will enjoy thinking of ways to save Alberto from the alligator hunters.

Picture Book/Poetry

Handsprings by Douglas Florian joins simple spring poems with joyful water color paintings. On the cover, a child somersaults out of a daisy, inviting children into this picture book.

Calef Brown's *Dutch Sneakers and Flea Keepers* is a collection of 14 "stories" about unusual items. For example, readers meet a runaway waffle and donut beetles marching across a sugar beach. They discover a mysterious fish, tattlesnakes, and 7 bad teeth!

Picture Book/Traditional Literature

Traditional literature consists of the written form of stories based on the oral tradition; picture books are a popular format for traditional literature. In fact, selecting picture books to include in this group was a challenge because there are so many! Mary Quattlebaum retells a witty story in her book, *Sparks Fly High: The Legend of Dancing Point*. The dancer in this tale is Colonel Lightfoot, who has a "waggy, braggy tongue." The devil challenges the braggart Lightfoot to dance for a patch of land, and it appears that Lightfoot will lose, until he realizes that the devil has a weakness like his own, pride.

Picture Book/Historical Fiction

Historical fiction addresses actual events and ways of living, and picture books are an advantageous format for this genre because the artist can create settings that are authentic to the time. Irene Kelly's *A Small Dog's Big Life Around the World* is an excellent example of historical fiction. Kelly relies on facts as much as possible. An actual event is the plot for this story, and a dog named Owney is the central character. Owney lives at the post office in Albany, New York. He makes newspaper headlines as he travels from coast to coast, and then he travels around the world. After his death, he is preserved and can be seen in the National Postal Museum.

Picture Book/Biography

The life and art of Romare Bearden is presented in Claire Hartfield's book *Me and Uncle Romie: A Story Inspired by the Life and Art of Romare Bearden*. The biography is told through fictionalized diary entries written by James, who is visiting Harlem from North Carolina. James discovers the wonders of his uncle's art and explores the wonders of Harlem. The rich illustrations are Romare Bearden's collages. This is a wonderful picture book for introducing different points of view, art, and diary or journal writing.

According to author Barbara Kerley, there was a time when almost no one in the world knew what a dinosaur looked like. That was before a Victorian artist named Waterhouse Hawkins, whose story is revealed in *The Dinosaurs of Waterhouse Hawkins*. Hawkins spent over 30 years building the first awe-inspiring, life-sized dinosaur models. His passion and courage

Tails are important to animals.

created an extraordinary legacy for us. The book's illustrator, Brian Selznick, creates a visual masterpiece with paintings to tell the story of this complex, fascinating individual. Dinosaur lovers of all ages will love this book.

Nonfiction/Picture Books

Informational picture books are popular with writers and readers because illustrations clarify and illustrate nonfiction. *What Do You Do with a Tail Like This?* by Steve Jenkins and Robin Page explores fascinating feats animals can perform with their ears, eyes, mouths, noses, feet, and tails. The interactive style of the text encourages children to think and imagine. The illustrations enhance the text and ignite children's interest in animal behavior.

 ## Visual Literacy

Reading pictures is very much like reading text; the objectives are the same. *Visual literacy* is the ability to interpret and evaluate illustrations as well as the visual elements of media and artistic style the artist uses (Camp & Tompkins, 1990). Visual texts are not as simple as they appear; they are complex, multilayered texts that communicate meaning (Moline, 1995).

Illustrations convey meaning to readers and viewers because they are the artist's rendering of plot, theme, setting, mood, and character. Readers need to integrate visual images and language. Visual literacy is increasing in importance due to computers, digital images on cell phones, games, advertising, and so forth.

Seeing the big picture is the first level of developing visual literacy (Muth and Kitalong, 2004). At this level, readers ask themselves, what is the whole image? What attracts my attention? What story does this picture tell? Teachers may choose to have children tell their stories, thus interpreting the picture in language. The interpretations of different students will differ because they use their individual schemata to understand the picture and to relate language with the picture.

Applying Visual Literacy

Little Smudge by Lionel Le Neouanic is a newly discovered fantastic book. In this book, Little Smudge is lonely. His mood is immediately apparent because he is a little, black smudge, all alone in the corner of an otherwise blank page. Color and position on the page communicate loneliness, although there are no words on the page. On the next page, the text says, "Little smudge is bored, all alone in the corner." Then his mommy suggests that he find some friends. He hears some shouting among squares, triangles, and circles, but they call him a dirty smudge and tell him to go away. His daddy tells him a secret. He learns to transform himself into a monster, a man, and other shapes that are pictured against the white background of the book pages. When the other shapes see what he can do they are interested, so he teaches them how to transform. Then they become good friends. With very simple shapes on stark white pages, Le Neouanic tells a wonderful, creative story that has many applications to developing visual literacy.

Visual Literacy and Wordless Picture Books

Wordless picture books are another vehicle for exploring visual literacy. For example, the first page in *Flotsam* shows a sea creature whose eyes express surprise; why is the sea creature surprised? The eye in the background probably shocked him. The following double-page spread creates a context for the story because readers see a boy with a magnifying glass on a beach with the ocean in the background and a sandcastle nearby. His parents are sitting nearby with the usual equipment for a beach vacation. The following double-page spread shows him studying a crab; he is tumbled over by the waves and then an underwater camera washes up and the action picks up. Younger children can tell a story based on the pictures, which could be recorded. Children who are little older could write the story and compare their various written versions.

Thinking Skills and Visual Literacy

We know that children respond to visual texts to construct both cognitive and affective meaning (Kiefer, 1995). Children usually see more in pictures than adults. As a former first-grade teacher, I remember the elaborate stories that children who could not read created from the pictures. Children who have many opportunities to describe, compare, interpret, and value illustrations in picture books learn to interact with visual information (Stewig, 1992). For instance, the *I Spy* books by Walter Wick and Jean Marzollo are excellent beginning books for kindergarten and primary-level children, who enjoy examining these puzzles and later creating their own. Many editions and versions of the *I Spy* books are available. Books like Joan Steiner's *Look-Alikes, Jr.* develop similar skills.

Chris Van Allsburg's books are essential for developing thinking and visual literacy. *Probuditi!* is his newest book, and, like his other books, the reader is drawn into the story. The sepia color and the varied textures and patterns encourage varied viewpoints. In the book, Calvin likes to tease his younger sister, Trudy. After he attends a magic show, he hypnotizes Trudy, but he is unable to break the spell. You have to read the last page of the book to truly appreciate the story! Each of his books has the quality of drawing the reader into the pictures and the story. Students can identify the ways they are drawn into the pictures. Another of Van Allsburg's books, *Z was Zapped,* is not an alphabet book but an alphabet drama. Van Allsburg draws readers into his illustrations, so study all of his books.

Comparing Picture Books

Comparing two or more versions of the same story, such as *Cinderella, Stone Soup,* or *Goldilocks,* builds children's visual literacy. *The Marvelous Mouse Man* by Mary Ann Hoberman is a new and different version of the *Pied Piper of Hamelin,* providing a delightful comparison to the original.

Teachers should provide children with opportunities to focus on illustrations, describe them, and compare them. As children explore the work of various artists, they will develop preferences for illustrators and styles of art.

Selecting and Evaluating Picture Books

What makes a picture book an outstanding example of the format and genre? This question is at once simple and complex, just as are fine picture books. Most importantly, a good picture book is one that children enjoy. They ask to hear the story again and again. Whenever possible, they pore over the pictures. Creating superb picture books is not easy, due to the short and simple text that must be interesting while also retaining freshness and quality through many readings. Picture books have well-drawn characters, suspenseful plots, authentic settings, and accurate information, all factors that contribute to literary excellence in the various genre of literature. The art is integrated with the narrative and is appropriate to the mood and subject matter. Arnold Lobel (1981) established the most important standard: "A good picture book should be true. That is to say, it should rise out of the lives and passions of its creators" (p. 74).

Internet Evaluation Sites

The Internet can be invaluable in helping media specialists (librarians) and teachers in locating and evaluating books. The National Center for Children's Illustrated Literature, located in Abilene, Texas, sponsors exhibits and educational programs and maintains a web site. The site, currently located at www.nccil.org/children, has illustrations, biographies, and teaching activities. The Children's Literature Web Guide is a rich source of information; most publishers of children's picture books, such as Houghton Mifflin, Random House, Rising Moon, and Simon & Schuster, maintain web sites that include book information, author information, and teaching ideas. Web locations and addresses often change, so we suggest that you include key words into your search engine that will pull up a list of web sites for you to explore.

Qualities of Excellent Picture Books

In choosing picture books to read, consider the visual components of color, line, shape, space, texture, and perspective, as well as the standards suggested for that particular genre, because picture books encompass all genres. The best indicators for picture books that children will enjoy, however, are these qualities:

1. The book is appropriate for the age and stage of development of the potential readers or listeners. Fine picture books are works of art appropriate for a broad range of students.

2. Children can identify with the main character. Consider whether the main character is developed as a multidimensional character or a one-dimensional stereotype. (Stereotypes are appropriate characters in traditional literature, of course.)

3. Children can understand the plot, which has an identifiable climax and an identifiable ending. Stories have beginnings, middles, and endings.

4. The theme grows out of characters, and the plot is appropriate for children.

5. The story is told in interesting, expressive language with simple narrative, and the author avoids long descriptions—the story is a "page turner."

6. Nonfiction is accurate and presented in an interesting, authentic style.

7. The illustrations enrich the text, are integrated with the text, and are appropriate to the mood and subject matter.

Summary

Children are usually introduced to literature through picture books because the majority of picture books are read-alouds. Wordless picture books and graphic novels are also included in the picture book format. Picture books are complex art forms that include all genre of literature. In picture books, the text and illustrations interact to tell a story or, in nonfiction works, to convey information. Neither pictures nor text tell the story alone. The brevity of text in picture books forces authors to choose their words carefully, and the artists' work becomes very important to telling a good story. Many illustrators are artists who experiment with a variety of styles, media, and colors to achieve the interpretation they feel is appropriate for the text.

Picture books are essentially ageless literature; books like Robert McCloskey's *Make Way for Ducklings* and Maurice Sendak's *Where the Wild Things Are* are classics and should be read again and again. Picture books tell good stories, humorous stories, and sad stories; they include words and illustrations relating to science, history, poetry, and a wide variety of informational topics.

Thought Questions and Applications

1. What is a picture book? Why is it a format rather than a genre?

2. Identify your favorite picture book illustrations. Why are these illustrations favorites? Who created these illustrations?

3. What are the advantages of using picture books with older students?

4. How can you use picture books to extend children's aesthetic experience?

Research and Application Experiences

1. Read three picture books to a group of children. Ask them to choose their favorites and explain why they are their favorites.

2. Choose a picture book and identify its beginning, middle, and ending.

3. Read *Talking with Artists* (vol. 3), compiled and edited by Pat Cummings (1998), or *Side by Side* by Leonard Marcus (2001). Which team of artist and writer do you especially enjoy? How could you use these books in your classroom?

4. Visit a children's bookstore and study the picture books. Which genre was represented with the most books? Can you identify any trends in the subject matter?

5. Create a picture book of your favorite traditional story.

6. Write a book and have a friend illustrate it. What problems in interpretation did you encounter?

7. Create a list of picture books that parents could read to their children.

Classroom Activities

Picture books are written to be read aloud while the listeners look at the pictures, creating an integral part of the literary picture book experience. (Chapter 14 gives information regarding oral presentations of literature.) Children often cluster in a group to listen so that they can better see the illustrations, frequently asking the teacher to read the book again; they do benefit from hearing the story multiple times. Placing the book nearby where children can pick it up and pore over the pictures at their own pace builds their interest in literature and reading. This section presents strategies and activities to engage students with picture books, encourage response, and develop visual literacy. Many of the suggestions focus on the illustrations and careful observations of them. Although these activities are based on picture books, they are also applicable to other forms of literature.

ACTIVITY 4.1   READING A PICTURE BOOK TO CHILDREN

IRA/NCTE Standards: 3, 4, 6. Listening comprehension, oral language, and visual literacy.

1. Introduce the book. An introduction can motivate listeners and anticipate the ideas in the book. Show students the cover and title, and tell them the names of the author and illustrator.

2. Read the story aloud to give students the opportunity for appreciative listening. Make sure that all the children have the chance to view the pictures as you read.

3. Discussion following appreciative listening enhances understanding. Ask the students what things they noticed in the book. Encourage children to compare themselves and their experiences to the picture book and its illustrations. Does the main character look like them? Act like them? Would they do the same things the character did? Would they like to have the character as a friend?

4. Use extension activities to allow students to respond to the story and enrich their understanding. Exploring the ways the author and artist express meaning in text and illustrations is useful. Comparing and contrasting experiences are very helpful to learning.

ACTIVITY 4.2 COMPARING FOLK TALE VARIATIONS

IRA/NCTE Standards: 1, 3, 6, 11. Understanding of print and nonprint texts. Use a variety of strategies to understand, interpret, and evaluate figurative language and participate in a literacy community.

1. Older students can do the previous Activity 4.1 as a writing activity.

2. Students can create their own versions of "Red Riding Hood" (or another favorite).

3. Students can compare the written text of various versions of "Red Riding Hood."

4. Additional aesthetic experiences can involve making puppets, drawing or painting pictures, painting friezes, designing bulletin boards, creating posters, and doing craft projects.

5. Retelling stories through creative drama and story-telling gives children opportunities to respond to the language of picture books. Encourage students to relate prior knowledge to picture clues to construct understanding.

6. Writing stories, poems, or informative pieces based on picture books gives children additional literary experiences. They could even develop their own illustrations to accompany their written responses.

7. Choosing music that fits the mood of a book extends the aesthetic experience.

ACTIVITY 4.3 DEVELOPING A UNIT OF STUDY ON THE TOPIC OF UNUSUAL CHARACTERS

IRA/NCTE Standards: 3, 6, 11.

Select several appropriate books for a teaching unit on strange characters, which could extend over a week or more. A partial list of good picture books about strange characters appears at the end of this activity. Although this unit focuses on characters, the topic could be virtually anything—trees, giants, boys, girls, teachers, mothers, or fathers.

1. Introduce the book you have selected and encourage the students to make predictions from the title and the cover of the book or from the opening sentences.

2. Read the story aloud to give students the opportunity for appreciative listening. Ask them to think about how this character is similar to strange characters they have seen on television, in movies, in books, or characters they have imagined.

3. Discuss the story with the children and encourage them to think about the story. Ask appropriate questions to start discussion, such as:

   a. Do the pictures look like real characters or make-believe characters?

   b. How is this character special (unique)?

   c. What things did the character do in the story?

   d. How is this character special?

e. Do you think this character has unusual abilities that make him or her special?

f. Could an ordinary character do the special things this character can?

g. If you could talk to the author or illustrator, what questions would you like to ask?

4. Use extension activities to allow students to respond to the story.

a. After reading several books to the children, and allowing them to enjoy the illustrations, have them think of ways to compare and contrast the characters. They may suggest things such as size, color, personality, special powers, whether they are real or make-believe, and so forth.

b. Have students draw pictures of their favorite one and tell or write why this is their favorite.

c. Have students tell or write about a special character they would like to have as a friend and explain why.

d. Ask older students to compare the characters by creating grids such as the one in the figure.

The following are suggested picture books for a unit on strange characters:

- *Beware, Take Care: Fun and Spooky Poems* by Lilian Moore
- *Frankenstein Makes a Sandwich* by Adam Rex
- *The Closet Ghosts* by Uma Krishnaswami
- *Miss Mingo and the First Day of School* by Jamie Harper
- *The Shivers in the Fridge* by Fran Manushkin
- *My Buddy Slug* by Jarrett J. Krosoczka

Grid for comparing characters.				
Title	Character's Looks	Character's Personality	Character's Actions	Character's Likable Characteristics

ACTIVITY 4.4   EXPLORING A SINGLE BOOK IN DEPTH

IRA/NCTE Standards: 3, 4, 11.

Book: *Seen Art* by Jon Scieszka and Lane Smith.

The narrator is looking for art. When the narrator accidentally goes into the Museum of Modern Art to look for art, the docent escorts him through galleries in the museum. The docent asks him questions that focus his attention on the masterpieces. Each of the works of art that he visits are identified at the end of the book.

a. Why did the narrator go to the Museum of Modern Art?

b. When looking at Van Gogh's "Starry Night," the guide asks the narrator in the book if he could feel the restlessness, the color, the emotion. How would you describe your feelings about this painting?

c. Read each page of the book, and the words the author used to talk about the painting.

d. Think of other words to express your feelings about the paintings and objects.

e. Why do you think a helicopter is in the museum?

f. What things are found in the museum that are not paintings?

g. What other items could be placed in this museum? Remember this is a museum of modern art.

h. Choose one painting or object in the museum, find out everything you can about it, and tell why it was chosen for the museum.

i. Did the narrator ever find art? Explain your answer.

ACTIVITY 4.5   ARTIST/ILLUSTRATOR PROFILES

Studying illustrators yields many benefits to young readers. Readers who know something about the person who illustrated a picture book have a better understanding of it. Finding connections between books and their creators challenges children to think in new ways, which widens their life experiences. Artists often project their own experiences into their work. The accompanying profile of Chris Van Allsburg demonstrates this.

A Biographical Profile: Chris Van Allsburg

Chris Van Allsburg was born near Grand Rapids, Michigan, and grew up in and near Grand Rapids. In Grand Rapids, he lived on a street that looked like the one on the cover of *Polar Express,* a street bordered with huge elm trees.

In high school, he was interested in math and science, and his high level of achievement led the University of Michigan to offer him early admission. His admission interview revealed that he had not chosen a major, but he liked to draw, so the admissions officer suggested an art program. However, the head of the department was unconvinced because Van Allsburg had had no art classes in high school. Eventually he talked his way into the program. He became interested in sculpture because he could use the skills and craftsmanship learned in building model boats and cars.

After finishing his degree, he went to graduate school at the Rhode Island School of Design. Upon graduation, he set up a sculpture studio and married an art student who taught elementary school. He exhibited his sculptures in a New York city art center. Meanwhile, he began drawing at night. Athough he did not think his drawings were valuable, they were exhibited at the Whitney Museum of Art. His wife and a friend, David McCauley, believed that he should do a picture book. McCauley introduced him to his editor at Houghton Mifflin, who believed that Van Allsburg could do the illustrations and text of a book. He created *The Garden of Abdul Gasagi,* which was awarded the Caldecott Honor Medal. His book, *Jumanji,* received the Boston Globe Book Award, and the National Book Award. *Jumanji* also was made into a popular feature film. The *Polar Express* received the Boston Globe Book Award and was made into a feature film. The *Mysteries of Harris Burdick* received the Boston Globe Book Award. Van Allsburg has received the Regina Medal for his lifetime achievement in children's literature.

Chris Van Allsburg has two children and lives in Rhode Island.

The material for this author/illustrator study was taken from Chris Van Allsburg's official site on the Internet.

ACTIVITY 4.6   EXPERIMENTING WITH MEDIA

IRA/NCTE Standards: 10, 11, 12.

Students can experiment with the media that artists use and make their own picture books. You may choose to involve the art teacher in this experience and explore media such as paint, collage, chalk, photographs, pencil, lithograph, watercolor, fabric, or quilt paintings. Students could create a picture book or photographic essay using photographs they have taken. They can create a composition based on the photographs, write the text, make a cover, and bind the book.

ACTIVITY 4.7   USING ILLUSTRATIONS TO LEARN MORE ABOUT STORIES

IRA/NCTE Standards: 5, 6.

Students can examine the illustrations in a book to glean information that is not presented in the story. Answering questions like the following will guide their studies (Stewig, 1992). These questions and their answers are based on an illustration from *Chicken Little* by Steven Kellogg.

1. What can we tell from the characters' clothing? (The animals are wearing clothing, which suggests that the story is make-believe. They are not wearing cold-weather clothing, so it is probably not winter.)

2. Where do you think Chicken Little is going? Why? (She is carrying a lunch box and pencil, which suggests that she is going to school.)

3. How did the fox happen to see Chicken Little? (He is using binoculars.)

4. Why does the fox have a book in the car? (It is a poultry recipe book. He is planning to cook Chicken Little.)

5. What can we infer about the time of year? (It is probably fall, because school is in session, but it is not cold yet, because the leaves are green and acorns are on the tree.)

6. How does the fox plan to kill Chicken Little? How do you know? (With a hatchet, because the picture of his imagination shows one.)

7. What do we learn about the fox? (He likes to eat chickens.)

Children's Literature References

Note: Books designated with an asterisk (*) are recommended for reluctant readers.

Agee, J. (2001). *Milo's hat trick.* New York: Hyperion. 3–4;5–6. PB

   Milo learns to be a magician, but a bear comes out of his hat.

Ahlberg, K. (2006). *The Runaway Dinner.* Cambridge, MA: Candlewick. K–2;3–4. PB

   This story gives new meaning to fast food.

Aston, D., & Long, S. *An egg is quiet.* New York: Chronicle. K–2. INF

   This book is a naturalist's diary of an egg.

Babbitt, N. (1998). *Ouch!* New York: HarperCollins. 3–4. PB

   In this little known Grimm tale, Marco begins life as an ordinary boy.

Barnard, B. (2005). *Outbreak: Plagues that changed the world.* New York: Crown 3–4;5–6. PB

   A well-written study of specific plagues.

Brown, C. (2000). *Dutch sneakers and flea keepers.* New York: Houghton Mifflin. K–3. P

   This collection of poetry features 14 poetic stories.

Bruchac, J. (1996). *Between earth and sky* (T. Locker, Illus.). K–2;3–4. PB

   A collection of native American legends.

Bunting, E. (2006). *Pop's bridge.* New York: Harcourt. K–2;3–4. PB

   Pop helped build the Golden Gate Bridge.

Burleigh, R. (1998). *Home run* (M. Wimmer, Illus.). San Diego: Silver Whistle. 3–4;5–6. PB

   Narrates the career of Babe Ruth.

Cole, J., & Degen, B. *The magic school bus and the science fair expedition.* New York: Scholastic Press. 3–4;5–6. PB

   Another Miss Frizzle adventure.

Curlee, L. (2001). *Brooklyn bridge.* New York: Harcourt. K–2;3–4. PB

   A picture book about the construction of the Brooklyn Bridge.

Ehlert, L. (2005). *Leaf man.* New York: Harcourt. K–2. PB

   Ehlert shares her love of Nature.

Feiffer, J. (1997). *Meanwhile—.* New York: Harper Collins. K–2;3–4;5–6. PB

   Raymond discovers that meanwhile . . . can take him to another place.

Fleischman, P. (2004). *Sidewalk circus.* Cambridge, MA: Candlewick. K–2;3–4. PB

A circus is coming to town, but a young girl discovers a circus in everyday events.

Florian, D. (2006). *Handsprings.* New York: HarperCollins. K–2;3–4. P

A collection of poetry and illustrations honoring spring.

Hartfield, C. (2002). *Me and Uncle Romie.* New York: Dial. 3–4;5–6. B

This is the story of Romare Bearden, the artist, told from a child's point of view.

Hoberman, M. (2002). *The marvelous mouse man* (F. Freeman, Illus.). New York: Harcourt. K–2;3–4. PB

A marvelous version of the "The Pied Piper of Hamlin."

Hopkinson, D. & Ransome, J. (2006). *Sky boys.* New York: Schwartz & Wade. 3–4;5–6. PB

A nonfiction picture book about building the Empire State Building.

Jenkins, J. (2003). *What do you do with a tail like this?* Boston: Houghton Mifflin. K–2;3–4.PB

The author shows the importance of tails.

Kellogg, S. (2006, Reissue). *Alexander and the wind-up mouse.* New York: Dial. K–2.

Alexander is confused with a live mouse.

Kelly, I. (2005). *A small dog's big life around the world.* New York: Holiday House. K–2,3–4. HF

This true story features a traveling dog.

Kerley, B. (2001). *The dinosaurs of Waterhouse Hawkins* (B. Selznick, Illus.). New York: Scholastic. 3–4;5–6. PB

Waterhouse Hawkins spent more than 30 years studying and constructing model dinosaurs.

Lasky, K. (2006). *Pirate Bob.* New York: Charlesbridge. K–2. PB

The outlaw pirate hopes to steal enough money and goods to retire.

Leaf, M. (2006, Reissue). *Wee Gillis.* New York: NYR Children's Collection. 3–4;5–6. PB; CalH

Wee Gillis lives in Scotland, and the setting is beautifully illustrated.

Le Neouanic, L. (2006). *Little Smudge.* New York: Boxer Books. K–2;3–4;5–6. PB

Little Smudge learns to transform and makes friends.

Lindrop, L. (2004). *Cave sleuths: Solving science underground.* New York: 21Century. 3–4. INF

Long, M. (2003). *How I became a pirate.* New York: Harcourt. K–2. PB

A boy becomes a pirate, but discovers they don't live like he does.

Lowry, L. (2002). *Gooney Bird Greene* (M. Thomas, Illus.). Boston: Houghton Mifflin K–2. CRF

Gooney Bird Greene is a unique character.

Luenn, N. (1998). *A gift for Abuelita* (R. Chapman, Illus.). Flagstaff, AZ: Rising Moon. K–2.

A gift for grandmother.

Murphy, J. (2006). *Fergus and the night demon.* New York: Harper. K–2;3–4. PB

Younger children will enjoy the humor in this book.

Perkins, L. (2007). *Pictures from our vacation.* New York: Greenwillow. K–2;3–4;5–6. PB

A family looks at pictures to reflect on their vacation.

Quattlebaum, M. (2006). *Sparks fly high: The legend of dancing point.* New York: Farrar. K–2;3–4. TF

Colonel Lightfoot dances with the devil to determine who is the better.

Raczek, L. T. (1999). *Rainy's powwow* (G. Bennett, Illus.). Flagstaff, AZ: Rising Moon. K–2;3–4. PB

Rainy is planning to dance at the Thunderbird Powwow.

Scieszka, J. (2006). *Time warp trio: Nightmare on Joe's street.* New York: Harper.

This graphic novel is a new entry in a popular series.

Scieszka, J., & Smith, L. (2001). *Baloney. (Henry P.).* New York: Viking. K–2;3–4. PB

Henry P. Baloney is an alien with a problem. He is late for school.

Shannon, D. (2006). *Good boy Fergus.* New York: Blue Sky. K–2. PB

Fergus is a playful dog who makes readers laugh

Stevens, J., & Crummel, S. T. (2001) *And the dish ran away with the spoon* (J. Stevens, Illus.). New York: Harcourt. K–2. PB

A new version of the old rhyme.

St. George, J. (2000). *So you want to be president* (D. Small, Illus.). New York: Philomel. 3–4;5–6. PB

The author and illustrator profile Presidents' quirks.

Van Allsburg, C. (2006). *PROBUDITI!* New York: Houghton Mifflin. K–2;3–4. MF

Calvin hypnotizes his sister but cannot break the spell.

Waring, R. (2002). *Alberto the dancing alligator* (H. Swain, Illus.). Cambridge, MA: Candlewick. K–2. PB

Tina and Alberto the alligator love to dance, until Alberto is accidently flushed.

Wheatley, N., & Ottley, M. (2001). *Luke's way of looking.* LaJolla, CA: Kane/Miller K–2;3–4. PB

The school does not like Luke's art, but the museum helps him appreciate his thinking.

Wick, W. (1998). *Walter Wick's optical tricks.* New York: Cartwheel/Scholastic. K–2. PB

A wonderful collection of optical illusions.

Wiesner, D. (2006). *Flotsam.* New York: Clarion. K–2;3–4. PB; Cal

A wordless picture book of a boy's experiences at the seashore.

Professional References

Ardizzone, E. (1980). Creation of a picture book. In S. Egoff, G. Stubbs, & L. Ashley (Eds.), *Only connect: Readings on children's literature* (pp. 289–298). New York: Oxford University Press.

Camp, D. J., & Tompkins, G. E. (1990). Show–tell in middle school? *Middle School Journal, 21,* 18–20.

Carter, J. (Ed.) (2007). *Graphic novels.* Urbana, IL: National Council of Teachers of English.

Christlow, E. (1999). *What do illustrators do?* New York: Clarion.

Cianciolo, P. (1990). *Picture books for children* (3rd ed.). Chicago: American Library Association.

Cummings, P. (1998). *Talking with artists* (Vol. 3). New York: Bradbury.

Dillon, L., & Dillon, D. (1992b). Leo's story. In P. Cummings (Ed.), *Talking with artists* (pp. 22–23). New York: Bradbury.

Hearn, M. P. (1999). *David Wiesner: Master of incongruity.* Abilene, TX: National Center for Children's Illustrated Literature.

Hearne, B. (1999). *Choosing books for children: A commonsense approach.* Urbana, IL: University of Illinois Press.

Kiefer, B. (1995). *The potential of picturebooks.* Upper Saddle River, NJ: Merrill/Prentice Hall.

Lacey, L. E. (1986). *Art and design in children's picture books.* Chicago: American Library Association.

Lewis, D. (2001). *Reading contemporary picturebooks: Picturing text.* New York: Routledge/Falmer.

Lobel, A. (1981). A good picture book should. . . In B. Hearne & M. Kaye (Eds.), *Celebrating children's books* (pp. 73–80). New York: Lothrop, Lee & Shepard.

Marcus, L. S. (2001). *Side by side.* New York: Walker.

Matulka, D. (2002). Picturing books: A site about picture books. http://picturingbooks.org.

Moline, S. (1995). *I see what you mean.* York, ME: Stenhouse.

Muth, M., & Kitalong, K. (2004). *Getting the picture.* New York: Bedford/St. Martins.

NCREL. (2003). *Text Comprehensions.* Naperville, IL: NCREL.

Nikolajeva, M., & Scott, C. (2001). *How picturebooks work.* New York: Garland.

Schwarcz, C. (1991). *The picture book comes of age: Looking at childhood through the art of illustration.* Chicago: American Library Association.

Shulevitz, U. (1985). *Writing with pictures: How to write and illustrate children's books.* New York: Watson Guptill.

Smith, L. H. (1991). *The unreluctant years.* New York: Viking.

Stewig, J. (1992). Reading pictures, reading text. *New Advocate, 5,* 11–22.

Trinkle, C. (2006). Teaching prediction and questioning strategies by using wordless picture books. *School Library Media Activities Monthly, 23,*11–12.

Wood, D., & Wood, A. (1986). The artist at work: Where ideas come from. *Hornbook, 60,* 556–565.

Young, E. (1990). Caldecott acceptance speech. *Hornbook, 66,* 452–456.

Zelinsky [Online]. Available: http://www.nccil.org/exhibit/zelinsky.html [2000, March 23].

5 Poetry for Every Child

KEY TERMS

alliteration	metaphor
assonance	nonsense poetry
concrete poetry	onomatopoeia
epics	personification
figurative language	rhyme
free verse	rhythm
haiku	simile
imagery	

GUIDING QUESTIONS

Do you enjoy poetry? What factors have led you to either like or dislike poetry? Do you think your early experiences affected the way you feel about poetry now? What was the last poem you read? Keep these questions in mind as you read.

1. What is poetry?

2. Why is poetry valuable in children's lives?

3. Who are some of the popular contemporary poets who write specifically for children?

4. How can teachers engage children with poetry?

Introduction to Poetry

The teachers and librarians of today are living in what may be the "golden age" of poetry. A wide range of poetry on topics that appeal to children are available in books, tapes, CDs, and on the Internet. Every imaginable subject exists in poetry for children, teachers, and librarians to enjoy.

"Poetry . . . is something very close to dance and song" (Frye, 1964). *Imagery* enables poets to create dense meaning with few words. Poets' words "reflect subtle shadows, images, and symbols that lead children to see beyond the literal and surface-level meanings" (Cullinan, Scala, & Schroder, 1995, p. 3). Poetry's *rhythm*, sound patterns, *figurative language*, compactness, and emotional intensity set it apart from prose. "You can't say anything much more briefly than a poem or folktale says it, nor catch a fact or feeling much more expressively" (Hearne, 1991, p. 107). One word in a poem says much more than a single word in prose. Poets use words economically, choosing each word for its meaning and its sound and polishing each one like a gem to create associations in readers' minds.

This characteristic is illustrated in Walter Dean Myers's *Here in Harlem: Poems in Many Voices*. Myers tells the dreams and sorrows of Harlem's residents. In each of his 54 poems, readers hear the voice of the person featured in the poem. Elementary and middle-school students delight in the language, cadence, and rhythm of Myers's poems.

Marilyn Nelson creates a somber tone in *A Wreath for Emmett Till*. The illustrator, Philippe Lardy, explains in the artist's note that the poem is structured like a painting. Lardy translates the symbols, layers, colors, geometry, and sense of space in the poetry into the accompanying illustrations. For example, he uses the color red and a tree cut in half to symbolize the sheer horror of Emmett Till's murder. In one scene, crows surround a picture of Emmett Till

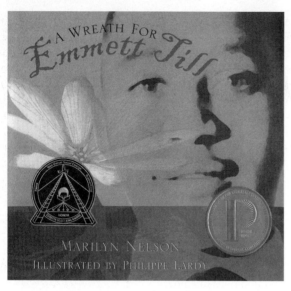

A memorial to a hero.

because crows represent death in some cultures. A superb web site related to this actual event is available at www.pbs.org/wgbh/till.

Poetic language expresses and interprets experience through its intense, imaginative, and rhythmic form. The rhythms of movement and song are illustrated in Lee Bennett Hopkins's *Song and Dance*. The poems in this book draw children into the dancing rhythm of language. Poets use language in ways that not only re-create the rhythms of oral language, but extend them to include novel and unusual applications.

Poetry Is Concentrated Meaning

The rich imagery of poetry permits a far greater concentration of meaning than what is found in prose (Morner & Rausch, 1991). A poem can start us thinking and talking about feelings and subjects. It can also express feelings that we cannot put into words ourselves. Poetry's economy of expression is comparable to the terseness of a conversation between long-time friends—it relies on the ring of familiarity in voice inflections and images to create meaning.

Emotional Intensity

Poetry, rooted in the world of emotions as well as in the mind, is emotionally intense. Poets capture universal feelings by writing about experiences that have affected them in such a way that they believe the experiences will affect readers as well. The experiences may be everyday happenings that have been commemorated with an emotional intensity that meets the needs and interests of listeners and readers. For instance, Margarita Engle articulates the bitterness of Manzano's life as a slave in *The Poet Slave of Cuba: A Biography of Juan Francisco Manzano*. Engle writes from three perspectives, alternating among Manzano, his parents, and his owner, a madwoman. Engle uses Manzano's autobiographical notes to create a complex picture of growing up in slavery.

Expressing Feelings and Moods

Poetic language may be unpretentious and the number of words limited, but the emotional intensity of poetry makes it a natural form for expressing feelings. Jack Prelutsky, the first children's Poet Laureate, is an unpretentious poet. In *Good Sports: Poems about Running, Jumping, Throwing, and More*, he uses ordinary words in short lines to capture the feelings and thoughts of children playing various sports. He has a new collection, *Aunt Giraffe's Green Garden*, which is a collection of whimsical, poetic pictures of people, animals, and events. Paul Janeczko also uses short lines to write about baseball players and fans in *That Sweet Diamond: Baseball Poems*. His poem "The Pitcher" is from this collection.

A general discussion of poetry can be organized in various ways; we have chosen to organize our discussion of poetry around poetic form, content, theme, and audience appeal.

Elements of Poetry

Poets use words in melodious combinations to create singing, lyrical qualities. Sound patterns and figurative language connote sensory images appealing to sight, sound, touch, and smell. These images build on children's experiences and relate to their lives. Douglas Florian uses poetic language to celebrate the exuberance of spring in *Handsprings,* which completes his set of seasonal poetry books. In this lyrical volume, the poet captures the sensory responses children experience when smelling flowers and picking them to make garlands. In the illustrations, readers see whimsical pictures of a boy with a flower for a nose, a boy with leaves over his eyes, and a girl with flowers in her hair. Adding to the joy of spring is a boy with a large baseball bat.

Jack Prelutsky's *It's Snowing! It's Snowing!: Winter Poems* is based on familiar winter experiences; the poems' vivid descriptions of the first snowfall, snowball fights, ice skating, and catching cold make for an interesting contrast with the poems celebrating spring in *Handsprings*. Both books will stimulate sensory responses in children.

Poetic Language

The words in a poem are carefully chosen to imply a range of ideas, images, and feelings. Each word implies and suggests more than it literally says. Poets create rich *metaphors* that summon hundreds of associations to stimulate readers' thoughts and emotions. Readers' individual connotative understandings are based on their emotional responses to words or concepts. For instance, readers who live in the Blue Ridge Mountains will likely have different responses to poetry about mountains than those who have never seen mountains, but both groups of readers will respond to the rich, sensory language of poetry (see Table 5.1).

Joyce Sidman's *Song of the Water Boatman and Other Pond Poems* gives readers the feeling of the spring thaw at a pond. The poet's words and the illustrator's hand-colored wood cuts give readers a sense of the drama of the world of the pond. The poet portrays a unique view of life underwater at the edge of the pond. The scientific accuracy makes this book a good choice to pair with a nonfiction book.

TABLE 5.1
Examples of sensory language.

Sense	Imagery
Vision	Fire-engine red, gigantic, elongated
Touch	Soft, hard, rough
Sound	Crunch, rumble, squeak
Smell	Rotting leaves, wet dog, bread baking
Movement	Hop, skip, trudge
Taste	Sweet, salty, bitter

Diane Ackerman engaged in word play when she composed *Animal Sense*. She created fresh images when she wrote "Consider the owl: a pair of binoculars with wings." She wrote about the cow, "every meal is grass with a side order of grass / plus huge drollops of grass smothered in grass, followed by grass chops and for dessert more grass." This language delights readers as they look at the owl and the cow in new ways.

Sound Patterns

Children learn the sound patterns of language before they learn words; in fact, sound patterns appear to be instrumental in children's acquisition of language. The sounds of poetry attract young children, who realize early on that words have sounds as well as meanings. "They love to rhyme words, to read alliterative tongue twisters, to laugh at funny-sounding names" (Fleischman, 1986, p. 553). Sound patterns are a delight to the ear of everyone, young and old. Rhyme, alliteration, onomatopoeia, and assonance are several devices commonly used by poets to achieve these sound patterns; often, these devices are combined to give sound effects to a poem.

The delightful sound patterns of nursery rhymes, combined with their brevity and simplicity, invite children to roll them over their tongues. "Hickory Dickory Dock" is a good example. Repeat it aloud to yourself or read it to a young child. Think about your own or the child's response to its patterns of sound. How many devices can you identify in this verse?

> *Hickory, dickory, dock,*
> *The mouse ran up the clock.*
> *The clock struck one,*
> *and down he run.*
> *Hickory, dickory, dock.*

Rhyme

Rhyme is one of the most recognizable elements in poetry, even though poetry does not have to rhyme. Rhyme is based on the similarity of sound between two words such as *sold* and *mold* or *chrome* and *foam*. "When the sounds of their accented syllables and all succeeding sounds are identical, words rhyme" (Morner & Rausch, 1991). A good rhyme, a repetition of sounds, pleases readers. It gives order to thoughts and pleasure to the ears (Livingston, 1991). Rhyme gives poetry an appealing musical quality.

The most common form of rhyme in poetry is end rhyme, so named because it comes at the end of the line of poetry (Morner & Rausch, 1991). End rhyme is illustrated in Rhoda Bacmeister's poem "Galoshes." Internal rhyme occurs within a line of poetry; an example of internal rhyme can be found in Karla Kuskin's poem "Hughbert and the Glue" in May Hill Arbuthnot's poetry anthology, *Time for Poetry*. Rhyming patterns in poetry are grouped in stanzas. A common end rhyming pattern is to rhyme the last word in every other line.

> *My garden is a soft green.*
> *Blue water flows over my waterfall.*
> *My flowers have a red sheen.*

The stanzas thus formed have special names depending on the number of lines in the rhyming pattern:

two lines: couplet

three lines: tercet

four lines: quatrain

five lines: quintet

six lines: sextet

seven lines: septet

eight lines: octave

Alliteration

Alliteration is achieved through repetition of consonant sounds at the beginning of words or within words. It is one of the most ancient devices used in English poetry to give unity, emphasis, and musical effect. Jack Prelutsky uses alliteration when he repeats the P sound in his poem, "Peanut Peg and Peanut Pete." This poem is found in *The Frog Wore Red Suspenders*.

Onomatopoeia

Onomatopoeia gives poetry a sensuous feeling. Onomatopoeia refers to words that sound like what they mean. For example, the word *bang* sounds very much like the loud noise to which it refers. In *Stories to Begin On*, Rhonda Bacmeister uses the words *splishes, sploshes, slooshes*, and *sloshes* in the poem "Galoshes" to create the sounds of walking in slush.

Assonance

Assonance is the close repetition of middle vowel sounds between different consonant sounds such as the long /a/ sound in *fade* and *pale*. Assonance creates near rhymes, rather than true rhymes; the use of assonance is commonly found in improvised folk ballads (Morner & Rausch, 1991). Assonance gives unity and rhythmic effect to a line of poetry. Maxine Kumin writes with traditional couplets or ABAB rhyme schemes to which she adds texture with assonance and consonance. Consonance is repetition of consonants as a rhyming device as in stick, march, stack, larch.

Rhythm

Rhythm is the patterned flow of sound in poetry created through combinations of words that convey a beat. Rhythm can set the sense of a story to a beat, but it can also emphasize what a writer is saying or even convey sense on its own. David McCord's "Song of the Train" in *Far and Few* demonstrates this. In traditional English poetry, rhythm is based on *meter*, the combination of accent and numbers of syllables (Morner & Rausch, 1991). Meter and rhythm are created when patterns of accented and unaccented syllables and of long and short vowels work together.

Wordplay

Wordplay is an inviting characteristic of children's poetry. The sound patterns in poetry create the playful language that children find pleasurable. They roll interesting words over their tongues and repeat them, savoring their flavor. Calef Brown is a skilled "wordplayer" who has again demonstrated his skill in *Flamingos on the Roof*. He makes familiar things into something different; for instance, a crystal ball becomes a crystal bowling ball that predicts your bowling fortune. He has illustrated this book with acrylic paintings that show people and places in unusual colors with quirky details.

Figurative Language

Writers use figures of speech, also called *figurative language*, to express feelings and create mental pictures (images). Figures of speech offer writers many possibilities for expressing thoughts and feelings. One of the major challenges in creating poetry is to choose figures of speech that offer fresh images and that uniquely express the poet. In fact, a poet's facility in using figures of speech is what makes the major difference between pleasant verse and fine poetry

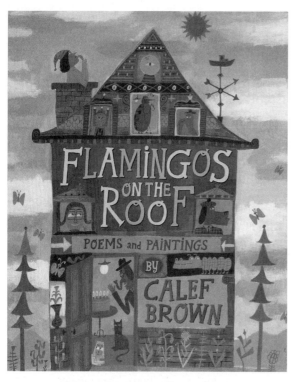

The interesting title introduces imaginative poems.

(Livingston, 1991). The best-known figures of speech are simile, metaphor, and personification.

Simile

A *simile* is a figure of speech using the words *like* or *as* to compare one thing to another. Most of you will recognize that "white as snow" is a simile, but it is so time-worn that it has become a cliché. Poets must be acute observers, seeing and hearing in new ways to offer fresh figures of speech. Look for the similes used by Valerie Worth in "Frog," a poem from her book *Animal Poems*.

Metaphor

Metaphor, like simile, is a figure of speech comparing two items, but instead of saying something is *like* something else, metaphor says that something *is* something else. Langston Hughes uses metaphor to arouse the reader's feelings and imagination in his poem "Dreams," calling life a "broken-winged bird" and a "barren field! Frozen with snow." These metaphors create images that clarify our thoughts about dreams.

The reader recognizes, of course, that life is not actually a bird or field (Livingston, 1991); however, these comparisons communicate vivid, unique images. A poet writing about baseball in spring might choose the attributes of a baseball player, using the words *swings, pitches, throws, catches, slides, bunts*, and *tags*. Can you write a poem with these words?

Personification

Personification attributes human characteristics to something that does not actually have these qualities. Poets have a talent for endowing inanimate objects with life, as Myra Cohn Livingston does in the poems in her book, *A Circle of Seasons*: "Spring brings out her baseball bat, swings it through the air."

 ## Types of Poetry

Free verse has become the most popular form for contemporary children's poetry, whereas older poetry follows traditional forms. Authorities divide poetry into three categories—narrative, dramatic, and lyric, although these elements are often combined in a single poem (Bagert, 1992). Poets choose and combine poetic forms to create the one that best tells their ideas and feelings. This means that attempts to categorize poems by type are usually impossible. In the section that follows, we examine poetic form and introduce examples to clarify understanding.

Narrative Poems and Epics

Narrative poems tell stories. The story elements—plot, character, setting, and theme—make narrative poems especially appealing because everyone enjoys a good story. Narrative poems that tell about the adventures of young characters or characters who are childlike make compelling reading for children. In *The Friendly Four*, Eloise Greenfield tells the story of four friends who build a pretend cardboard town called Goodsummer. The children play together while inventing their town. This enjoyable poem could also be used for children's theater.

Book-length narrative poems are called *epics*. Byrd Baylor and her illustrator, Peter Parnall, share their love of the desert with readers in their illustrated epic, *The Other Way to Listen*.

Dramatic Poetry

Dramatic poetry often appears in the form of a monologue, in which a single character tells about a dramatic situation (Morner & Rausch, 1991). Many examples of dramatic form are found in traditional ballads. Author Gary Soto has a gift for capturing everyday moments in the lives of middle-school students with direct, vivid emotions. In his book, *A Fire in My Hands: Revised and Expanded Edition,* middle-school students will recognize themselves and their daily experiences during this critical period in their lives. (The cover of this book reveals that the fire in Soto's hand, alluded to in the title, is an orange.)

Lyric Poetry

Lyric poems are short, personal poems expressing the poet's emotions and feelings. They speak of personal experience and comment on how the writer sees the world. Originally such poems were written to be sung to the music of a lyre, so it is not surprising that lyric poetry has a feeling of melody and song (Livingston, 1991). Lyric poetry is the most common form for children's poetry. It can be identified through the use of the personal pronouns *I*, *me*, *my*, *we*, *our*, and *us* or related words (Livingston, 1991).

Emotion, subjectivity, melodiousness, imagination, and description are distinguishing characteristics of dramatic poems (Morner & Rausch, 1991). Lyric poems can be found in Nikki Grimes's book, *A Pocketful of Poems.* The voice in the book belongs to Tiana, who uses words she likes to say and tells us, "I slip under its silver light / and pull it to my chin, like a quilt."

Haiku

Authentic *haiku*, a poetic form that originated in Japan, describes nature and the seasons. Haiku are patterned poems based on syllables, words, and lines. The first line contains five syllables, the second contains seven, and the third contains five for a total of 17 syllables in three lines. Paul Janeczko and J. Patrick Lewis collaborated on *Wing Nuts: Screwy Haiku,* a humorous collection of poems that are a contrast to the usual Japanese haiku.

Free Verse

Free verse differs from traditional forms of poetry in that it is "free" of a regular beat or meter (Morner & Rausch, 1991). Free verse usually does not rhyme, does not follow a predetermined pattern, and has a fragmentary syntax. Free verse incorporates many of the same poetic devices that writers of structured poetry employ, but writers of free verse are more concerned with natural speech rhythms, imagery, and meaning than with rhyme and meter. Valerie Worth's *Animal Poems* paint word pictures in exquisite poetry. Jellyfish "rising under water / like transparent / Ghost-bells / of lost lands . . ."

Concrete Poetry

The form of *concrete poetry* is inseparable from the content. Concrete poetry merges visual, verbal, and auditory elements, arranging the words and letters to suggest something about the subject of the poem. For example, a poem about a rock might be written in the shape of a rock, or a poem about a cloud may be written in the shape of a cloud. In addition, several carefully selected words may be suspended on a mobile so that, as the air moves the mobile, the words move and a poem evolves, with each person seeing a different poem.

A marvelous collection of shape poems is found in J. Patrick Lewis's *Doodle Dandies: Poems That Take Shape.* Douglas Florian also includes a room-shaped concrete poem, "The Gecko," in his book *Lizards, Frogs, and Polliwogs.*

Nonsense Poetry

Nonsense poetry ordinarily is composed in lyric or narrative form, but does not conform to the expected order of things. It defies reason. Nonsense poetry is playful; the meaning is subordinate to sound (Morner & Rausch, 1991). "Nonsense is a literary genre whose purpose is to rebel against, not only reason, but the physical laws of nature. It rejects established tenets and institutions, pokes fun at rational behavior, and touts destruction. It champions aberrations" (Livingston, 1981, p. 123).

Writers of nonsense poetry create unusual worlds in which objects and characters are recognizable but do absurd things and become involved in absurd situations. They know, for example, that cows cannot jump over the moon, but they like the fun of such implausible antics as those in the following lines.

> *Hey diddle diddle*
> *The cat played the fiddle,*
> *The cow jumped over the moon.*

Edward Lear, the master of nonsense, wrote poems that appealed to all ages. Although his *Complete Nonsense Book* was published in 1948, it remains popular today. J. Patrick Lewis shows that he is an outstanding student of Lear in his book *Boshblobberbosh: Runcible Poems for Edward Lear*. And funky nonsense is also the theme of Calef Brown's appealing book, *Polkabats and Octopus Slacks: Fourteen Stories*.

Nonsense writers use a variety of strategies in their craft. They invent words, as Laura Richards does in "Eletelephony." Alliteration is the technique Lear uses in "Pelican Chorus." Personification also lends itself well to nonsense verse, as animals, objects, and even pieces of furniture take on human characteristics. Exaggeration is a useful device to writers of nonsense, as Shel Silverstein shows in "Sarah Cynthia Sylvia Stout Would Not Take the Garbage Out," one of many nonsense poems in his book, *Where the Sidewalk Ends*.

Content of Poetry

The subject matter of poetry is unlimited, as poets find no activity too humble and no object of daily living too minor for their poems. For instance, Douglas Florian featured birthday cake in "Cake Mistake" from *Bing Bang Boing*.

Poetry embodies life and reveals its complexity; it is a part of the fabric of life. Poets look at ordinary things and events more closely than the rest of us and see the things we overlook. Constance Levy fosters new ways of seeing the everyday world in the poems featured in *A Crack in the Clouds and Other Poems*. She uses simple language and varied cadences to tell about cricket songs, icicles, weeds, and comets. Pat Mora's book, *Love to Mama*, features Latino poets, who celebrate mothers, grandmothers, and great-grandmothers—women who are always there for their families.

Garbage to Fairy Tales

A plethora of poems on subjects ranging from garbage to fairy tales and from topics that are side-splittingly funny to serious are readily available. Teachers can find that poems fitting every mood, interest, and topic are available in any form. Content is more important than form when selecting poetry for children.

Although the range of content in poetry is far too broad to catalog here, we will highlight humor as one of the most popular subjects in children's poetry. Jack Prelutsky is a poet well known for his zany poems. He uses splendid words such as *disputatious* and *alacrity*, and his poems have unexpected twists that delight his readers. Perhaps most important, all children (including boys, who are sometimes hard to interest in poetry) love his poems. His book, *Something Big Has Been Here*, has many ridiculous images to delight readers. In "The Turkey Shot Out of the Oven," the turkey shoots out of the oven because it is stuffed with unpopped popcorn. Then there is the character in "Denson Dumm" who plants light bulbs in his hair so that he will be forever bright. Like all of Prelutsky's books, however, this one offers a diverse range of topics, including serious poems such as "Don't Yell at Me."

Comets, Stars, the Moon, and Mars by Douglas Florian is another outstanding book of poetry. He writes stellar poetry about the earth, the moon, galaxies, and other space-related topics. He speaks to both children and adults. A good book to use with Florian's is *Science Verse* by Scieszka and Smith. Although the topics are different, the perspective is similar.

The Natural World in Poetry

Again, space constrains us from cataloging the variety of ways to treat subjects in poetry, but we will briefly

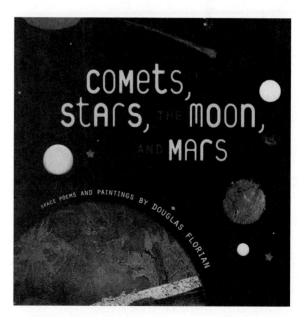

The poet explores the heavens in this book.

discuss the poems of three different poets who have all written on a popular topic, "The Natural World." Each poet chose different stylistic devices and perspective to portray the natural world: The poems could be categorized as realistic fiction or even informational compositions because they communicate the essence of each topic. Each poet focuses on a different aspect of the natural world.

The first poet, Avis Harley, writes undersea-themed poems in his book *Sea Stars: Saltwater Poems.* In one poem, a crab claims that his imagined image comes from a toe-pinching scrimmage. A conservationist orders, "Do not pollute." The book is illustrated with stunning photographs.

The second poet, Jorge Arugeta, in *Talking with Mother Earth: Poems / Hablando con Madre Tierra: Poemas,* writes in the voice of an Indian boy named Tetl who tells about his connection to the natural world. The simple poetry provides colorful visual imagery. The poetry is written in both English and Spanish.

And in a different vein, the third poet, Joyce Sidman, in *Butterfly Eyes and Other Secrets of the Meadow,* uses melodious language to write "poetry riddles" that present related elements in spreads that answer the riddles and offer details. The elegant scratchboard illustrations reflect precise observation.

A different take on the natural world is presented with the following artifacts from a middle-grade insect unit that began with Douglas Florian's *Insectlopedia.*

Middle grade students integrate Insectlopedia with science.

The poem "Locusts" was written by a student after reading *Insectlopedia.*

Locusts
Eating is mostly what this insect does
Swerving around looking for food
Locusts
Swarming and exploring
Food every where and then gone
Born in North America
The nymph is still young
Looking for amusement
Soon it grows and sheds its dry skin
Growing to soon swarm like bees
But stinging the land instead of
innocent humans
They are energized and they swarm and
buzz everywhere rubbing and bumping
into each other mating season
Soon enough a great grassland is bare
A forest is soon a barren land
Covered with dead trees
Eating leaves at all costs
Consuming some of our lives in yield
Wishing for more to eat
More
More
More
Always more
Like a bull they charge to their red,
green leafs

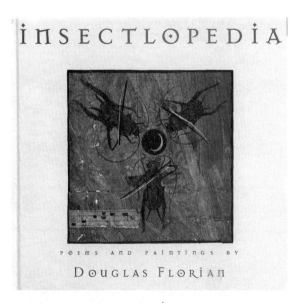

Insects can be poetic.

Great green leafs full of water and flavor
Eating more and still not full
Consuming all the vegetation they can see
And for farmers there goes money
Groceries
Every thing for them
These beasts
Short horned grasshoppers
Swerving
Chewing
Eating
Flying
Locusts covering the sky like a solar
eclipse just as if we had no
Sun
The plants die
And so do we
Still they're pondering how to get more
food
Destroying countries
Swarming by the thousands
Eating and nothing more
Luckily, other insects aren't like that
Eating till nothing exists any more
They survive for a short while
Finally dying out when winter comes
Giving the land a much needed break.
by
Kyle Neu

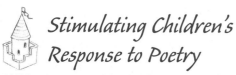

Stimulating Children's Response to Poetry

Children's poetry has experienced a renaissance in recent years. Contemporary children's poets such as Jack Prelutsky, Paul Fleischman, Paul Janeczko, Eloise Greenfield, and Douglas Florian are very popular. "More than ever before, poetry for children has climbed to its proper station" (Hopkins, 1998, p. 4). Teachers, librarians, and parents have the opportunity to choose from a wide variety of poems and poetry books to nurture children's interests.

Poetry speaks to the emotions and the intellect. It is pleasurable and comfortable, amusing and relaxing. Poetry can be an important part of children's literary life, clarifying and illuminating experience and enriching

daily life. For example, Jack Prelutsky's "What a Day It Was at School" speaks to readers of "over-loaded back-pack," and fractions, but it also includes the good parts of the day like field trips. The rhythms of poetic language appeal to children; they stick in memory and children repeat the rhythms by marching, tapping, skipping, and so forth. They also enjoy repeating interesting rhymes again and again, savoring the feel of the rhymes on their tongues. Poetry lifts spirits and stimulates imaginations, stirring readers to communicate in interesting ways (Peck, 1979).

Poetry appreciation begins with the premise that poems merit a prominent place in children's lives. "Poetry must flow freely in our children's lives; it should come to them as naturally as breathing, for nothing—nothing—can ring and rage through hearts and minds as does poetry" (Hopkins, 1998).

Adults who wish to engage children's interest in poetry will be pleased to learn that extensive technical knowledge is unnecessary. Although sometimes helpful, expertise regarding poetic form is not as important as having many experiences with interesting poetry. Response to poetry is largely a matter of experience. Presenting a variety of poems gives children opportunities to identify their favorites; with experience, adults can acquire a discriminating sense for the poetry, and they may even discover an unrealized passion for it.

Poets and Their Poetry

Learning about the people who create poetry will motivate children to read more. When choosing a poet to study, the teacher may do read-alouds that focus on a single poet's works. Children can immerse themselves in the work of a single poet, focusing on one they like very much. Children who lack experience with poetry, however, may have to experience more poetry to find a favorite.

We chose Jack Prelutsky for a poet's profile because he is a favorite of children all over the United States with his keen sensitivity to children's fears, pleasures, and funny bones (Behr, 1995). This poet's profile was prepared with materials from the *Highlights' Teacher Net*, www.teachingk–8.com and *Children's Books and Their Creators* (Silvey, 1995).

USING POETRY IN THE CLASSROOM

Chip Russell, a fourth-grade teacher, decided to immerse his students in poetry for a month. He obtained posters of poems to post in his room and left the bulletin boards empty for the children to complete as a part of the study. His goal was to have children experience a variety of poetry, so they could identify favorites.

On Monday morning, he greeted the students with a stack of poetry books, including Calef Brown's *Flamingos on the Roof*, Jack Prelutsky's *Good Sports*, J. Patrick Lewis's *Once Upon a Tomb: Gravely Humorous Verses*, and Adam Rex's *Frankenstein Makes a Sandwich.*

When Chip announced, "We are doing to 'do' poetry for a while," he was met with groans from several boys. He then said, "I am going to read a poem from each of these books and you are to focus on one of those poems. I'll place the books on this table, so you can refer to them later, if you need to. Relax and take a listening attitude."

After reading the poems, Chip initiated a discussion. He asked, "What did the poem you chose make you think about?"

Chris said, "I liked Frankenstein, and it made me laugh and I thought about some of the monsters on television."

Emily liked "Martian Men" because there was a lot of alliteration in it. That made the words interesting, they sounded like martians.

Chip said, "Have you ever seen pictures of martians?" She responded, "No."

Chip said, "Now I would like you to join your reading circles and continue discussing the poems."

Later in the day, he gave the children a list of Internet sites. Their assignment was to go on the Internet to one of the sites, listen to a poem, and think of two things they liked about the poem or two things they would like to change in the poem.

A Biographical Profile: Jack Prelutsky

Jack Prelutsky says that he was probably a challenge to parents and teachers because schools and parents are not always prepared for individuals with great creativity. His multifaceted talents are demonstrated by his various occupations, including musician, photographer, truck driver, entertainer, and sculptor.

When a publisher expressed an interest in Prelutsky's poems, even though he was really trying to sell his photographs, he was shocked. He did not like poetry due to his experiences in school. In fact, he thought poets were very strange people. Moreover, he grew up in a tough Bronx neighborhood where poets were generally considered boring, sissies, or dead.

Prelutsky's goal is to write fresh, contemporary poems with humor as a basic ingredient. He believes that life does not have to be so serious, so his poems are almost always humorous, and he throws in a good bit of nonsense. Prelutsky is recognized for his irreverent style, technical versatility, and awareness of what children like.

Prelutsky loves what he is doing, writing poems and traveling around the United States meeting and talking with children. He likes writing, travel, and people, and he likes to see how children are growing through his books. Among his more than 30 volumes are:

Rolling Harvey Down the Hill

The New Kid on the Block

The Baby Uggs Are Hatching

The Dragons Are Singing Tonight

Something Big Has Been Here

Selecting and Evaluating Poetry

The following books contain both exemplary poetry and suggestions for classroom activities:

Let's Do a Poem! by Nancy Larrick

Pass the Poetry, Please! by Lee Bennett Hopkins

Tiger Lilies, Toadstools and Thunderbolts: Engaging K–8 by Iris Tiedt

Students with Poetry by Iris Tiedt

The Place My Words Are Looking For by Paul Janeczko

Near the Window Tree by Karla Kuskin

Poem-Making: Ways to Begin Writing Poetry by Myra Cohn Livingston

One of the very best ways to cultivate confidence with poetry is by reading many poems and deciding which poems and poets you like the best. Once you have discovered a poem or a poet who speaks to you, look for more poems by the same poet. Through this process your own taste will evolve, and you will find it easier to share poetry that you really enjoy. Develop your own wide collection of poems, both for your own use and to engage children's interests.

Offer a variety of poems in read-aloud sessions. A particular poem or book, however, may not be for everyone. It is for those individuals who relate to the feelings and ideas expressed. In the introduction to *A Tune Beyond Us*, Myra Cohn Livingston (1968) cautions readers: "Every poem in this collection will not speak for you. But perhaps one, or two, will. And that will be enough" (p. iv).

The brevity of poems motivates some children. Despite their brevity, however, poems should be read at a leisurely pace to allow readers to savor the words and ideas (Hearne, 1991). Brevity and a leisurely pace are two features of Mary Ann Hoberman's book, *You Read to Me, I'll Read to You: Very Short Stories to Read Together*. This unique book "in two voices" uses rhyme, rhythm, and repetition in poetry. The end flap of this book says, "Here's a book with something new—You read to me! I'll read to you."

Children relish poetry in classrooms and other settings where it is cultivated as a natural happening, a part of daily life. Reading a poem to celebrate holidays, rainy days, snowy days, pets, funny incidents, and sad events gives children opportunities to read and listen.

Locating Poetry

Poetry appears in several types of books: anthologies, specialized collections, and book-length poems. Poetry anthologies are collections of poetry that include many types of poems on many subjects. One of the most comprehensive is *The Random House Book of Poetry for Children* (Prelutsky, 1983), edited by Jack Prelutsky and illustrated by Arnold Lobel, which includes poems arranged in broad categories. Specialized collections are books of poems that focus on a specific theme or topic. All of the poems in Jane Yolen's *Dinosaur Dances* relate to dinosaurs—more specifically, dancing dinosaurs. A lengthy single poem may be published as an entire book, usually a picture book, as is Byrd Baylor's *The Other Way to Listen*.

Evaluating anthologies can be especially difficult because the poems represent such a broad range of subject matter and style, but reviewing the table of contents and examining the literary quality of a few poems in different sections can identify the range of topics. An anthology can provide appropriate poetry at a moment's notice for everyday reading needs—holidays, weather, and daily incidents. Of course, one or two good anthologies cannot fulfill all the poetry needs of children. Poetry should be a part of planned experiences as well as incidental experiences. Table 5.2 presents several examples of anthologies, specialized collections, and book-length poems.

Children's Preferences

Children's appreciation of poetry is enhanced when adults thoughtfully choose literature reflecting children's experiences and interests. Of course, asking children what they like has obvious value. Research suggests that visual appeal is a factor in children's choices. They like poetry that is generously spaced and tastefully illustrated (Sebesta, 1983). Fisher and Natarella (1982) report that primary-grade children's poetry preferences include narrative poems and limericks, poems about strange and fantastic events, traditional poems, and poems that use alliteration, onomatopoeia, and rhyming.

TABLE 5.2

Examples of poetry.

Author	Title	Grade Level
Anthologies		
Beatrice Schenk de Regniers	*Sing a Song of Popcorn*	K–8
Tomie dePaola	*Tomie dePaola's Book of Poems*	1–6
Jack Prelutsky	*The Random House Book of Poetry for Children*	1–8
Ann McGovern	*Arrow Book of Poetry*	3–7
Nancy Larrick	*Piping Down the Valleys Wild*	3–7
Specialized Collections		
Zena Sutherland	*The Orchard Book of Nursery Rhymes*	Preschool–1
Valerie Worth	*Animal Poems*	K–2
Mary Ann Hoberman	*Yellow Butter, Purple Jelly, Red Jam, Black Bread*	K–3
Nancy Larrick	*Mice Are Nice*	K–3
Edward Lear	*Of Pelicans and Pussycats: Poems and Limericks*	K–4
Jack Prelutsky	*Something Big Has Been Here*	K–4
Aileen Fisher	*When It Comes to Bugs*	K–6
Karama Fufula	*My Daddy Is a Cool Dude*	1–5
Robert Froman	*Seeing Things: A Book of Poems*	1–6
Nancy Larrick	*On City Streets*	1–6
David McCord	*One at a Time*	1–6
Jack Prelutsky	*Rolling Harvey Down the Hill*	1–6
Paul Fleischman	*Joyful Noise: Poems for Two Voices*	2–6
Arnold Adoff	*Sports Pages*	4–7
Cynthia Rylant	*Waiting to Waltz: A Childhood*	4–8
Single-Book Poems		
Nadine Bernard Westcott	*Peanut Butter and Jelly: A Play Rhyme*	K–2
Myra Cohn Livingston	*Up in the Air*	K–4
Robert Frost	*Stopping by Woods on a Snowy Evening*	1–6
Arnold Adoff	*All the Colors of the Race*	3–8
Byrd Baylor	*The Desert Is Theirs*	3–8
Byrd Baylor	*The Other Way to Listen*	3–8
George Ella Lyon	*Together*	K–6

Intermediate-grade students like poems related to their experiences and interests, humorous poems, and those with rhythm and rhyme (Bridge, 1966). They respond better to contemporary poems than to traditional ones and also prefer poems that address familiar and enjoyable experiences, funny poems, and those telling a story (Terry, 1974). Narrative poems and limericks are the most popular form with fourth, fifth, and sixth graders, whereas haiku and free verse are among the least popular (Terry, 1974).

Later studies of children's poetry preferences are consistent with the earlier studies (Ingham, 1980;

Simmons, 1980). The weight of research indicates that children prefer humorous poetry and poetry addressing familiar experiences. Children prefer poems by Shel Silverstein and Dennis Lee to traditional poetry (Ingham, 1980), because the poetry of Silverstein and Lee communicates, inspires, informs, and tells of things that are, were, may be, and will never be (Peck, 1979). When selecting poetry, ask these questions:

1. Can children understand it?

2. Does the poem stir emotions such as humor, sadness, empathy, and joy?

3. Does the poem create sensory images such as taste, touch, smell, or sight?

4. Does the poem play with the sounds of language? Does the sound echo the senses (Cullinan et al., 1995; Lenz, 1992)?

5. Does the rhythm enhance the meaning? Does the poem bring the subject to life? (Literary critics agree that fine poets bring an experience or emotion to life, making it live for others.)

6. Will this poem motivate children to read other poetry?

7. Does the poem evoke a response in the listener/reader?

Using such guidelines, however, is no substitute for old-fashioned observation: Children's eyes light up over a splendid poem that speaks directly to them; they grimace over ones they do not like. The clearest signal that you have read a winner is, of course, a request to read it again.

 Enriching Poetic Experiences

Children's responses to poetry are closely linked to the ways in which they customarily explore the world: observing and manipulating. As they explore the nature and parameters of language, poetry can give children access to specific characteristics or elements not found in their everyday experience (Parsons, 1992).

Surround Children with Poetry

Display poems, posters, and books related to classroom activities and studies. Place poem posters (that you or the children make and laminate) around the classroom. Recite or read poems whenever opportunities arise. Celebrate poets and poetry books that the children especially enjoy. Play tapes of poets reading their own work. Make up poems on the spur of the moment that fit classroom events and studies.

Poetry experiences begin with listening and chanting. Poetry comes to life when read or said out loud. Children enjoy repeating and intensifying the magic of poetry; they like to hear it again and again and object to changes in delivery or attempts to leave out verses (Parsons, 1992). Children love to chime in with the reader, clap with the rhythm, mime facial expressions, act out events, or just repeat the words. Such oral experiences intensify their appreciation of poetry.

The poet's use of unfamiliar words and combinations of words, definite rhythms, vocal stress on words and syllables, and even the poem's ideas, however, can complicate reading poetry aloud. Practice reading poetry so you can read fluently, at a comfortable rate. A tape recorder can be helpful in practicing oral reading.

Read Poetry Daily

Children need to hear poetry daily, particularly appealing poems that help them develop an ear for the rhythm and sound of poetry. Daily poetry readings should be both incidental and planned. Incidental poetry reading occurs in conjunction with an event such as a birthday or a new baby in the family. Holidays and events, such as the first day of spring and the first day of winter, are good reasons to read a poem. Rain, sunshine, snow, and the first robin of the spring are all events to be marked with poetry. Planned poetry reading occurs when the teacher chooses poetry that fits the curriculum or develops thematic units with poetry; the diversity of subject matter and form in poetry makes such planning easy. A few unit suggestions are included at the end of this chapter.

Rhythm

Sound Effects

Students can express the rhythms of poetry through sound effects. Teachers may organize a team to create background sound effects as a poem is read aloud (Larrick, 1991); for instance, for "The Merry-Go-Round Song," a sound effects team could re-create the up-and-down rhythm of a carousel by repeating the sounds OOM-pa-pa, OOM-pa-pa in the rhythm of the song. Encourage the children to vary the sound effects and work at identifying the most effective sounds for poems they enjoy. Groaning, snapping fingers, stomping feet, and rubbing hands together may be appropriate sound effects for some poems. For other poems, students might make crying sounds, or laugh, moo, or cluck. They may even invent sounds.

Repetition

Young children enjoy repeating sounds, words, and phrases they hear. Joining in on the repeated lines in nursery rhymes, ballads, camp songs, spirituals, and traditional play rhymes is a fine way to involve them with poetry. Invite them to join in on the repeated parts during reading or singing such songs and rhymes as "The Muffin Man," "John Brown's Baby Had a Cold Upon His Chest," "The Wheels on the Bus Go Round and Round," or "He's Got the Whole World in His Hands."

Echo

Echoing lines and words is another way of inviting children into poetry. Repeated words or phrases can be treated like an echo or a series of echoes (Larrick, 1991), as seen in the traditional folk song "Miss Mary Mack." The echo can be developed in a number of ways: One individual can read or recite the poem with another echoing the repeated words; or groups can do the parts instead of individuals. Another variation is to

emphasize the beat on the repeated words by clapping with the chant on those words.

Choral Reading

Activities such as repetition and echoing prepare children for choral reading of poetry. Many poems lend themselves to choral reading. "The Poor Old Lady Who Swallowed a Fly," shown in Figure 5.1, can be a choral reading involving two or three groups of students. Assign the various stanzas to different groups and have the repeated words chanted in unison by the entire group. You can literally find hundreds of poems for this and similar activities; the examples here are provided to give you an idea of what to look for. If you try a poem and it does not work out, try others until you find some that you and the students enjoy. Material for choral reading should be meaningful, have strong rhythm, have an easily discernible structure, and perhaps rhyme. Some good ones are:

- "The Pickety Fence" by David McCord, in *Far and Few, Rhymes of the Never Was and Always Is*.
- "The Umbrella Brigade" by Laura Richards, in *Time for Poetry* by Karla Kuskin.
- "Godfrey, Gordon, Gustavus Gore" by William B. Rand, in *Time for Poetry* by Karla Kuskin.
- "Yak" by William Jay Smith, in *Oh, That's Ridiculous* by Jane Yolen.

CLASSROOM SNAPSHOT

POETRY FOR RHYTHM AND WORDPLAY

Poetry fun in the primary grades is obviously different than in middle school or intermediate grades. Poetry has to move for these children because they are on the move. Rhythm, words, and humor are major attractions. Courtney Rogers, a second-grade teacher, chose "The Polliwogs" from Douglas Florian's *Lizards, Frogs, and Polliwogs*. As the children listened, they picked up on the rhythm and the wordplay. On the second reading they joined in chanting appealing words such as *polliwoggle and polliwiggle*; *wriggle*; *quiver and shiver*; and *jiggle, jog, and frog*. A number of the children moved with the words, thereby resembling a group of polliwogs.

Courtney then printed the poem on a large chart, so the children could read it themselves. She noticed the children copied the movement words on their own papers. Many of the children chose to draw pictures of polliwogs to accompany the words they wrote. As she expected, the students asked for more poems from this collection. This vignette demonstrates that children have a natural affinity for poetic language and language play. They relish inventing words and rolling them over their tongues. They respond to the rhythms of jump rope rhymes, advertising jingles, and rap music (McClure, 2002). Unusual combinations of words intrigue children, who respond to the musical, rhythmic qualities of the words.

> **FIGURE 5.1** The Poor Old Lady
> Who Swallowed a Fly.
>
> There was an old lady
> who swallowed a fly.
> I don't know why she swallowed a fly.
> Perhaps she'll die.
> There was an old lady who swallowed a spider;
> that wriggled and jiggled and tickled inside her.
> She swallowed the spider to catch the fly.
> I don't know why she swallowed a fly.
> Perhaps she'll die.
> There was an old lady who swallowed a bird.
> How absurd, to swallow a bird!
> She swallowed the bird to catch the spider.
> She swallowed the spider to catch the fly.
> I don't know why she swallowed the fly.
> Perhaps she'll die.
> There was an old lady who swallowed a cat.
> Think of that, she swallowed a cat!
> She swallowed the cat to catch the bird.
> She swallowed the bird to catch the spider.
> She swallowed the spider to catch the fly.
> I don't know why she swallowed the fly.
> Perhaps she'll die.
> There was an old lady who swallowed a dog.
> She went the whole hog and swallowed a dog.
> She swallowed the dog to catch the cat.
> She swallowed the cat to catch the bird.
> She swallowed the bird to catch the spider.
> She swallowed the spider to catch the fly.
> I don't know why she swallowed the fly.
> Perhaps she'll die.
> There was an old lady who swallowed a cow.
> I don't know how she swallowed a cow!
> She swallowed the cow to catch the dog.
> She swallowed the dog to catch the cat.
> She swallowed the cat to catch the bird.
> She swallowed the bird to catch the spider.
> She swallowed the spider to catch the fly.
> I don't know why she swallowed the fly.
> Perhaps she'll die.
> There was an old lady who swallowed a horse.
> She died of course.
> *Unknown*

Movement

The rhythm of poetry gives it a feeling of movement, making it difficult for children to be still when listening to it. "Poetry is not irregular lines in a book, but something very close to dance and song, something to walk down the street keeping in time to" (Frye, 1964). "Or jog down the trail keeping time to. Or do the dishes by. Or jump rope on the playground with" (Hearne, 1991). Being involved with poetry makes it more appealing. "Doing" creates opportunities for children to respond to, to participate in, and to be involved with the poetry. "Doing" can involve chanting, singing, dancing, tapping, and swinging to the rhythms of poetry (Larrick, 1991). Children appreciate the rhythmic aspect of poetry and rhymes. Tapping, clapping, and swinging arms with poetry sensitizes participants to the rhythms and involves them with poetry. They need opportunities to hop, skip, jump, and march to poetry. They enjoy trying out various assignments such as: "Walk with confidence. Tiptoe stealthily. Walk flatfoot like a clown. Walk like a sad old man. Imagine you are picking up a heavy sack of apples and carry it on your shoulder . . . Swim like a fish. Fly like a bird" (Larrick, 1991).

Movement is a natural introduction to poetry. Some traditional singing games such as "If You're Happy and You Know It, Clap Your Hands" and "The Wheels on the Bus Go Round and Round" are excellent vehicles for making students more aware of rhythm. Movement is an important element in Lillian Morrison's *Rhythm Road: Poems to Move To*. This fresh, inventive collection of nearly 100 poems is an excellent introduction to the genre and to motion for all ages. Morrison has arranged the poems in sections that include dancing, riding, watching water, and hearing music; other sections include the topics of living things, active entertainments, sports, work, television, technology, and the mind. When using this book in the classroom, read the poems aloud and encourage listeners to move with the sounds.

Lillian Morrison has accommodated the need for movement in much of the poetry she has written. *The Break Dance Kids* is just one of her books that stimulates poetic movement. *A Rocket in my Pocket*, compiled by Carl Withers, is a collection of rhythmic chants, songs, and verses that are part of U.S. folklore. The works in this volume also encourage movement.

Riddle-Poems

Riddle-poems delight young children; their brevity encourages readers. In riddle-poems, the reader uses hints hidden in the verses and in illustrations. Such poems introduce a sense of fun and wordplay. In *Riddle-Lightful: Oodles of Little Riddle-Poems*, J. Patrick Lewis indirectly describes common objects such as a fire truck, a raisin, and a kite. Both children and adults enjoy solving the riddles in Brian Swann's *The House with No Door: African Riddle-Poems* and *Touching the Distance: Native American Riddle-Poems.*

Themes and Topics

One way of organizing poetry experiences and activities is through themes and topics. Topics are subjects that serve to focus and integrate classroom experiences, such as transportation, bridges, baseball, and so forth. Even houses can be topics for poetry as Mary Ann Hoberman demonstrates in her picture book, *A House Is a House for Me.* She explores the concept of houses with interesting ideas such as a glove (a house for a hand).

Themes of love, courage, patriotism, friendship, and so forth appear in poetry. Poetry is often used to introduce themes and topics, and such units may include all types of literature or poetry. Chapter 16 discusses units in greater detail.

Listening is the theme in Byrd Baylor's book, *The Other Way to Listen.* After reading this poem, children may want to listen in different places at different times, observing what happens and writing their own poems or stories about the experience.

Animals, Birds, and Insects

Animals, birds, and insects are frequent subjects for poets and favorite subjects of children, and no shortage of books exists from which to build a topical unit. William Jay Smith's *Birds and Beasts* is both a poetry collection and an art book. Smith's poems and the graphic images created by Jacques Hnizdovsky's woodcuts combine to create a funny, lighthearted tone. Myra Cohn Livingston's *If the Owl Calls Again: A Collection of Owl Poems* views owls from many perspectives. Many readers will be surprised at the number of great poets from various cultures who have written about owls.

Insects are the topic of Paul Fleischman's Newbery Award book, *Joyful Noise: Poems for Two Voices.* These poems are wonderful fun in the classroom because two or more individuals must read them, and they can be the basis for creating choral readings. In these poems, sounds create the images, movements, and appearance of many insects. Douglas Florian also writes about bugs that creep, crawl, and fly in *Insectlopedia.*

Holidays

Poetry is a natural part of holiday celebrations, and holidays are a good time for integrating poetry in classrooms. Almost every holiday or season has more than enough poetry written about it to serve as the basis for a unit of study at the appropriate time of year. Look on the Internet and book reviews for holiday poetry.

Discussion

Many people are unsure about discussing or asking questions about poetry. Poetry is art and many of us agree that it should not be overanalyzed, but does that mean that it cannot be discussed or examined at all? Discussions of poetry should avoid overanalysis as well as overgeneralization.

The best guide for poetry discussion comes from Perrine (1969):

1. Consider the speaker and the occasion. Discuss who wrote the poem, whether the speaker or character is the same person as the poet, and the point of view the poet uses.

2. Consider the central purpose of the poem. Discuss why the poet wrote it and what type of poem it is: a circus poem, a wildlife poem that celebrates nature, and so on.

3. Consider the means by which that purpose is achieved: rhythm, rhyme, imagery, or repeated words, phrases, or lines, and so on.

As children become fluent readers, they can prepare poems to read aloud either as individuals or as groups, implementing some of the suggestions in the activity section that follows. One way of generating student participation in poetry is to write a poem on a chart, then cut it apart and give each student the part they are to read. The parts can be numbered to assist the students.

Playing music as a background when reading poetry dramatizes it. Puppets, pantomime, and creative drama are appropriate activities for many poems because they tell stories. Nursery rhymes such as "Jack and Jill" or "Humpty Dumpty" are appropriate to these activities, as are many other poems. "The Poor Old Lady Who Swallowed a Fly" works well for puppets or drama. Children may experiment and explore with the sounds of poetry through their voices, create their own poetry, examine various themes, and relate poetry to the arts.

Summary

Poetry is compressed language and thought that implies more than it says. Poetry is literature in verse form. The good news about children's poetry is its plentiful supply. Current poetry addresses contemporary themes and experiences that children can appreciate. Children see poetic language as natural unless they have had negative experiences that turn off their interest in this form. Unfortunately, many adults view poetry with a mixture of awe and insecurity because they believe they must have academic knowledge in order to do justice to it in the home or the classroom. However, teachers, librarians, and parents can read poetry with and to children as an organic part of their daily experiences and celebrations. Oral read-aloud experiences are the best way to introduce poetry to children.

Adults should acquire a wide variety of poetry for students. Adults need to be acquainted with all forms and types of poetry so they can discover children's preferences. A wide-ranging collection of poetry enhances children's opportunities to find their favorites. Children enjoy the rhyme, humor, rhythm, and movement of poetry. Emphasizing meaning, response, and enjoyment is important when incorporating poetry into children's lives.

Thought Questions and Applications

1. How is poetry different from prose?
2. What are the major characteristics of poetry?
3. Why does poetry appeal to children?
4. How can you as a teacher build children's response to poetry?
5. Do you think poetry is natural for children? Why or why not?
6. How should poetry be presented in classrooms? Why?
7. Identify three strategies for presenting poetry that you plan to use as a classroom teacher. Why do you like these strategies?

Research and Application Experiences

1. Start a poetry file or collection for use in your classroom. This collection should relate to everyday events, holidays, and the curriculum.
2. Start a thematic collection of poetry. The themes you identify will depend upon the ages of the children with whom you will be working.
3. Compare the treatment of a single subject in poetry, prose, and informational writing.
4. Survey the teachers in an elementary school. Ask them how often they use poetry in their classrooms and what the children's favorite poems are. What conclusions can you reach based on your research?
5. Survey students at one grade level and ask them to identify their favorite poems. Create a graph that shows the titles, poets, and types of poems they enjoy most.
6. Practice reading three poems aloud. Tape yourself, so that you can realize your progress in the oral interpretation of poetry.
7. Examine three or more anthologies of poetry. Which one would you find most useful in the classroom? Why?

Classroom Activities

ACTIVITY 5.1   HUMOR

IRA/NCTE Standards: 2,3,4,5,6,12. Language comprehension, figurative language, communication, range of literature and language use.

Read orally or silently selected books and discuss them using the guide question.

Suggested Book List

- *Faint Frogs Feeling Feverish* by Lillian Obligado
- *If I Were in Charge of the World* by Judith Viorst
- *Frankenstein Makes a Sandwich* by Adam Rex
- *Rolling Harvey Down the Hill* by Jack Prelutsky
- *The Complete Nonsense Book* by Edward Lear
- *Where the Sidewalk Ends* by Shel Silverstein
- *You Read to Me, I'll Read to You* by John Ciardi

Guiding Questions

1. What makes you laugh? Think about television shows, books, poems, and real-life events. Some people laugh at exaggeration, wordplay, jokes on other people, or unexpected events.

2. Can you think of other things that make people laugh? Make a list with your classmates.

3. Listen to the poems that your teacher reads. Which ones did you think were the funniest? Which ones were not funny?

4. How did the poet make you laugh? What techniques, elements, forms, and so forth did he or she use?

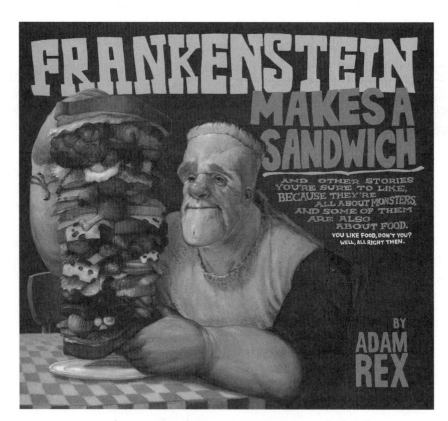

Frankenstein makes a very interesting sandwich.

5. Why did the poet write this poem?

6. What poems made your classmates laugh? Why did they laugh?

7. Vote for the funniest poem or poems of those your teacher reads. Find out why these were the funniest.

8. Make a bulletin board display to tell the school about funny poems and the ways authors make them funny.

9. Find more funny poems and make a class book. Read funny poems to your family and friends to find out what poems make them laugh.

ACTIVITY 5.2   INTERACTIVE INTERNET POETRY READING & WRITING SITES

IRA/NCTE Standards: 2, 3, 4. Language comprehension, figurative language, read a wide range of literature, and adjust language to communicate.

Visit the following Internet sites and identify ways that they can be used in classrooms.

www.KidzPage.org

http://gardenofsong.com/didzpage

www.shadowpoetry.com/magnet.html

www.rif.org/readingplanet/gamestation/poetry/splatter

www.poetryexpress.org

http://pbskids.org/arthur/games/poetry

ACTIVITY 5.3   POETRY FAIR

IRA/NCTE Standards: 1, 2, 4, 5, 11. Students read a range of texts and genre for a variety of purposes including personal fulfillment; students communicate with a variety of audiences for different purposes.

At a poetry fair, students read aloud poetry they have written or poetry by their favorite poets. Some poems are solo performances; some are readers' theater, explained in Chapter 14. Some poems are chanted by the students. They perform for an invited audience, and they may also perform for other classes. Following is an invitation to a poetry fair; the invitation includes a poem written by the teacher and a program for the fair.

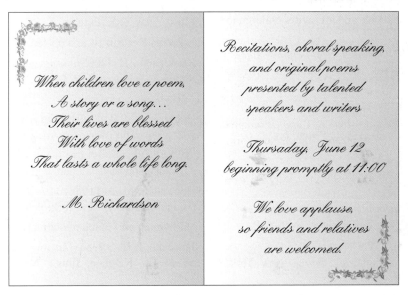

When children love a poem,
A story or a song...
Their lives are blessed
With love of words
That lasts a whole life long.

M. Richardson

Recitations, choral speaking,
and original poems
presented by talented
speakers and writers

Thursday, June 12
beginning promptly at 11:00

We love applause,
so friends and relatives
are welcomed.

ACTIVITY 5.4   POETRY-RELATED MEDIA

The Internet site www.poetry.com will provide a variety of poetry-related links, including one to the Poetry Society of America.

For Teachers:
Refer to *Book Links, School Library Media Activities Monthly,* and *Tiger Lilies, Toadstools, and Thunderbolts: Engaging K–8 Students with Poetry,* by Iris McClellan Tiedt, for additional ideas.

Children's Literature References

Note: Books designated with an asterisk (*) are recommended for reluctant readers.

Ackerman, D. (2003). *Animal sense* (P. Sis, Illus.). New York: Knopf. K–2;3–4. P

   Animal poetry.

Arbuthnot, M. (Ed.). (1951). *Time for poetry.* Chicago: Scott, Foresman. K–2;3–4;7+. P

   An anthology of poetry.

Bacmeister, R. W. (1940). *Stories to begin on* (T. Maley, Illus.). New York: Dutton. K–2. P

   Poetry for younger children.

Baylor, B. (1978). *The other way to listen* (P. Parnall, Illus.). New York: Scribner's. 5–6;7+. P

   Introspective poetry.

Brown, C. (2006). *Flamingos on the roof.* Boston: Houghton Mifflin. K–2;3–4. P

   Brown's exuberant poetry and art invites children to read.

Brown, C. (2004). *Polkabats and octopus slacks: Fourteen stories.* New York: Houghton Mifflin. K–2;3–4. P

   A delightful collection of poetry.

Engle, M. (2006). *The poet slave of Cuba: A biography of Juan Francisco* (S. Manzano, Illus.). New York: Holt. 5–6;7+. P

   The poet is sad in his youth, but he overcomes his sadness.

Fleischman, P. (1988). *Joyful noise: Poems for two voices* (E. Beddows, Illus.). New York: Harper. 3–4;5–6. P

   Insect poems for two voices.

Florian, D. (1994). *Bing bong boing.* New York: Harcourt. 3–4;5–6. P

   A collection of humorous short verse.

Florian, D. (1998). *Insectlopedia.* New York: Harcourt Brace. K–2;3–4. P

   Poems about insects.

Florian, D. (2001). *Lizards, frogs, and polliwogs.* New York: Harcourt. K–2;3–4. P

   A collection of amphibian poems.

Florian, D. (2006). *Handsprings.* New York: Greenwillow. K–2;3–4. P

   Poetry about movement in sports.

Gollub, M. (1998). *Cool melons—turn to frogs!: The life and poems of Issa* (K. Stone and K. Smith, Illus.). New York: Lee & Low. 3–4;5–6. P

   Haiku.

Greenfield, E. (2006). *The friendly four.* New York: HarperCollins. K–2. P

   A group of four friends are the topic of this poem.

Grimes, N. (1999). *A pocketful of poems* (J. Steptoe, Illus.). New York: Putnam. K–2;3–4. P

   Poems that can fit in a pocket.

Hopkins, L. B. (2005). *Song and dance.* New York: Simon & Schuster. K–2;3–4. P

   Rhythmic poetry.

Hoberman, M. A. (2001). *You read to me, I'll read to you: Very short stories to read together.* New York: Little Brown. K–2. P

   One person reads a poem and the second responds.

Hoberman, M. A. (1982). *A house is a house for me* (B. Fraser, Illus.). New York: Penguin. PreK–2. P

   Rhyming verses tell about many kinds of houses.

Janeczko, P. B. (1998). *That sweet diamond: Baseball poems* (K. Katchen, Illus.). New York: Atheneum. 3–4;5–6. P

   Baseball poetry.

Janeczko, P. B., & Lewis, P. (2006). *Wing nuts: Screwy haiku.* New York: Little Brown. K–3. P

Unusual haiku.

Janeczko, P. (2005). *A kick in the head* (C. Raschka, Illus.). Cambridge, MA: Candlewick Press. K–2;3–4. P

Poetry for fun.

Lear, E. (1948). *The complete nonsense book.* New York: Dodd, Mead. 3–4;5–6;7+. P

Classic nonsense.

Levy, C. (1998). *A crack in the clouds and other poems* (R. Corfield, Illus.). New York: McElderry. 3–4;5–6. P

Sun shines through the clouds.

Lewis, J. P. (1998a). *Boshblobberbosh: Runcible poems for Edward Lear* (G. Kelley, Illus.). New York: Creative Editions. 5–6. P

Nonsense.

Lewis, J. P. (1998b). *Doodle dandies: Poems that take shape* (L. Desimini, Illus.). New York: Atheneum. K–2;3–4. P

A collection of concrete poems.

Lewis, J. P. (1998c). *Riddle-lightful: Oodles of little riddle poems.* New York: Knopf. 3–5. P

Riddles.

Livingston, M. C. (1990). *If the owl calls again: A collection of owl poems* (L. Frasconi, Illus.). New York: McElderry. 3–4;5–6. P

All kinds of owl poems.

Livingston, M. C. (1982). *A circle of seasons* (L. E. Fisher, Illus.). New York: Holiday House. K–2;3–4. P

A collection of seasonal poetry.

McCord, D. (1952). *Far and few, rhymes of the never was and always is* (H. B. Kane, Illus.). New York: Little Brown. K–2;3–4. P

A collection of rhythmic poems.

Mora, P. (2001). *Love to mama* (B. Barragan, Illus.). New York: Lee & Low. 3–4;5–6. P

The poet writes about his mother.

Morrison, L. (1985). *The break dance kids.* New York: Lothrop. 3–4;5–6. P*

Poetry in a break-dance rhythm.

Morrison, L. (Selector). (1988). *Rhythm road: Poems to move to.* New York: Lothrop. K–2. P*

Rhythmic poetry for moving in the classroom.

Myers, W. D. (2005). *Here in Harlem: Poems in many voices.* New York: Harper. 5–6;7+. P

Readers hear the individual voices of the people in this poem.

Nelson, M. (2005). *A wreath for Emmett Till.* Boston: Houghton Mifflin. 5–6;7+. P

This poetic memorial for Emmett is well illustrated.

Prelutsky, J. (Comp.). (1983). *The Random House book of poetry for children* (A. Lobel, Illus.). New York: Random House. K–2;3–4;5–6. P

An anthology.

Prelutsky, J. (2006). *It's snowing! It's snowing!: Winter poems.* New York: Harper Trophy. K–2;3–4. P

A winter poem.

Prelutsky, J. (2006). *What a day it was at school.* New York: Greenwillow. K–2;3–4. P

A bad and good day from a student's point of view.

Prelutsky, J. (2007). *Good sports* (C. Raschka. Illus.). New York: Knopf. K–2;3–4. P

Sports poetry.

Prelutsky, J. (1990). *Something big has been here* (J. Stevenson, Illus.). New York: Greenwillow. K–2; 3–4. P

This collection includes unusual characters.

Richards, L. (1983). *Eletelphony* (A. Lobel, Illus.). In J. Prelutsky (Ed.) *The Random House book of poetry for children.* New York: Random House. K–2;3–4. P

A funny nonsense poem.

Shaik, F. (1997). *The jazz of our street* (E. B. Lewis, Illus.). New York: Dial. 3–4;5–6;7+. P

The music of the street.

Sidman, J. (2005). *Song of the boatman and other pond poems* (B. Prange, Illus.). New York: Houghton Mifflin. 3–4;5–6. P

Poetry about water and boats.

Silverstein, S. (1974). *Where the sidewalk ends: The poems & drawings of Shel Silverstein.* New York: Harper. 3–4;5–6;7+. P*

Smith, W. J. (1990). *Birds and beasts* (J. Hnizdovsky, Illus.). Boston: Godine. K–2;3–4. P

Humorous verses.

Soto, G. (2006). *A fire in my hands.* New York: Harcourt. 3–4;5–6. P

The fire is an orange.

Swann, B. (1998a). *The house with no door: African riddle-poems* (A. Bryan, Illus.). New York: Browndeer Press/Harcourt Brace. 1–4. P*

    A collection of African poetry.

Swann, B. (1998b). *Touching the distance: Native American riddle-poems*. New York: Browndeer Press/Harcourt Brace. K–2;3–4. P*

    Riddle poems.

Withers, C. (Comp.). (1988). *A rocket in my pocket: The rhymes and chants of young Americans* (S. Suba, Illus.). New York: Henry Holt. K–2;3–4. P

    A collection of rhymes and chants.

Worth, V. (2007). *Animal poems*. New York: Farrar. K–2. P

    Unique ways to talk about animals.

Yolen, J. (1990). *Dinosaur dances* (B. Degen, Illus.). New York: Putnam. K–2;3–4. P

    Dinosaurs dance ballet in a chorus line.

Professional References

Bagert, B. (1992). *Act it out: Making poetry alive.* In B. Cullinan (Ed.), *Invitation to read: More children's literature in the reading program.* Newark, DE: International Reading Association.

Behr, C. C. (1995). Jack Prelutsky. In A. Silvey (Ed.), *Children's books and their creators.* Boston: Houghton Mifflin.

Bridge, E. (1966). *Using children's choices and reactions to poetry as determinants in enriching literary experience in the middle grades.* University microfilm no. (67–6246) Philadelphia Temple University.

Cullinan, B., Scala, M., & Schroder, V. (1995). *Three voices: An invitation to poetry across the curriculum.* York, ME: Stenhouse Publishers.

Fisher, C., & Natarella, M. (1982). Young children's preferences in poetry: A national survey of first, second, and third graders. *Research in the Teaching of English, 16,* 339–354.

Fleischman, P. (1986). Sound and sense. *The Horn Book, 62,* 551–555.

Frye, N. (1964). *The educated imaginations.* Bloomington: Indiana University Press.

Hearne, B. (1991). *Choosing books for children: A commonsense approach.* New York: Delacorte.

Hopkins, L. B. (1998). *Pass the poetry, please!* New York: Harper.

Larrick, N. (1991). *Let's do a poem!* New York: Delacorte.

Ingham, R. (1980). The poetry preferences of fourth- and fifth grade students in a suburban setting 1980. Unpublished doctoral dissertation, University of Houston, Texas.

Lenz, L. (1992). Crossroads of literacy and orality: Reading poetry aloud. *Language Arts, 69,* 597–603.

Livingston, M. C. (Ed.). (1968). Editor's note. In *A tune beyond us.* New York: Harcourt.

Livingston, M. C. (1981). Nonsense verse: The complete escape. In B. Hearne & M. Kaye (Eds.), *Celebrating children's books* (pp. 122–142). New York: Lothrop, Lee, & Shepard.

Livingston, M. C. (1991). *Poem-making: Ways to begin writing poetry.* New York: HarperCollins.

Livingston, M. C. (1997). *I am writing a poem about—A game of poetry.* New York: McElderry.

McClure, A. A. (2002). Poetry. In A. McClure & J. Kristo (Eds.), *Adventuring with books: A booklist for PreK–Grade 6.* Urbana, IL: National Council of Teachers of English.

Morner, K., & Rausch, R. (1991). *NTC's dictionary of literary terms.* Lincolnwood, IL: National Textbook Company.

Parsons, L. (1992). *Poetry themes and activities.* Portsmouth, NH: Heinemann.

Peck, P. (1979). Poetry: A turn-on to reading. In J. Shapiro (Ed.), *Using literature and poetry.* Newark, DE: International Reading Association.

Perrine, L. (1969). *Sound and sense*: An introduction to poetry (3rd ed.). New York: Harcourt.

Sebesta, S. (1983). Choosing poetry. In N. Roser & M. Frith (Eds.), *Children's choices: Teaching with books children like* (pp. 56–70). Newark, DE: International Reading Association.

Silvey, A. (1995). *Children's books and their creators.* Boston: Houghton Mifflin.

Simmons, M. (1980). *Intermediate-grade children's preferences in poetry.* Unpublished doctoral dissertation, University of Alabama, Birmingham.

Terry, A. (1974). *Children's poetry preferences: A national survey of upper elementary grades.* Urbana, IL: National Council of Teachers of English.

Tiedt, I. M. (2002). *Tiger lilies, toadstools, and thunderbolts: Engaging K–8 students with poetry.* Newark, DE: International Reading Association.

6

Traditional Literature: Stories Old and New

KEY TERMS

ballad   legend
fable   myth
folktale   pourquoi tales

GUIDING QUESTIONS

Did you hear stories like "Goldilocks and the Three Bears," "Tom Thumb," "Jack and the Beanstalk," or "Cinderella" when you were a child? Do you think children continue to enjoy these stories? Have you read any of the new generation of folktales, the "Fractured Fairy Tales"?

1. Why is traditional literature (such as folktales, etc.) related to culture?

2. What are the major characteristics of traditional literature?

3. How is the plot in traditional literature different from other genre of literature?

4. How are characters in traditional literature different from those in realistic fiction?

Introduction to Traditional Literature

Traditional literature grew out of the experiences, imaginations, and lives of ordinary people who made up stories, ballads, and legends to explain and understand natural phenomena, human nature, and their relation to the spiritual world. Traditional literature was oral literature because that was the only media available for sharing stories with one another. These stories entertained audiences around evening fires. Storytellers, bards, minstrels, poets, and rhymers of old were welcomed into palaces and huts alike. Good storytellers changed their stories as they entertained different audiences; frequently listeners adapted stories they heard and told them to other audiences, adding their own flourishes and thus creating variants. The Cinderella story alone has nearly 1,000 variants (Thompson, 1951).

Entertainment, sharing wisdom, and telling the news were some of the original values of traditional literature; however, the tales also mirrored the values, beliefs, and mores of the culture in which the story originated. The wisdom of mankind is in traditional stories; they teach about greed, jealousy, love, and honor, which are part of the human condition. Some of the original tales were "teaching" stories and other cautionary tales that instructed children about appropriate behavior. For example, the theme of *True Friends: A Tale from Tanzania* by John Kilaka is friendship. In this story, when a drought makes food scarce, an elephant steals a rat's grain but later apologizes to the rat, who tells him, "True friends don't think only of themselves even when times are hard."

Traditional stories were committed to print after the brothers Grimm and Charles Perrault listened to storytellers and collected the tales. Folktale collectors listened to storytellers and wrote the stories they heard. They sought to collect the stories in settings that maintained the authenticity of the tales. The Grimms collected folktales in natural settings and made notes identifying the original settings in which the stories were told. Richard Chase, who collected Appalachian folktales including the *Jack Tales*, made notes about the families who told stories and where they were when they listened to the storyteller. *James Houston's Treasury of Inuit Legends* by James Houston, who lived among the Inuit people for 14 years, brings the Inuit culture to life through his writing. The people who collect traditional stories are retellers.

Human beings have shared, celebrated, and remembered experiences through story, art, and dance throughout history; traditional literature includes all of these forms of expression. Folk literature did not end with the past. Grandparents tell stories about life in their youth—before television, computers, Ipods, the Internet, and Gameboys. We tell stories about the things that happen to us and what those experiences have taught us. Parents tell children about the cute and funny things they did in their early years. Storytelling has enjoyed a revival over recent decades with storytelling festivals popping up all over the globe (Jaffe, 1999). There is even a center for the "Preservation and Perpetuation of Storytelling" in Jonesboro, Tennessee.

Folktales

Folktales are stories of the "folk," who tell about their lives and dreams. Folktales often feature impressive feats, such as escaping from powerful enemies, outwitting wicked people, earning a living, securing food, and protecting the weak. For example, the "Jack and the Beanstalk" story is a hero tale about a young boy who overcomes a larger, stronger character to prove himself. In Evelyn Nesbit's modern version of *Jack and the Beanstalk,* Jack gets advice from a fairy; otherwise, his version is like its predecessors. Jane Yolen has created two interesting folktale collections. In *Mightier than the Sword*, she demonstrates the triumph of brains over brawn. These stories are about brothers, sons, kings, trolls, men, and boys united by strength of character, wisdom, and compassion. The second collection is *Not One Damsel in Distress*, which includes world folktales for strong girls. In these stories, even though the characters' feats are imaginary, we enjoy believing they could happen. Traditional stories entertain as well as disseminate cultural beliefs to future generations.

Stories are a universal tradition, as all societies have literature in their culture. There is an African proverb that says, "When an old person dies, it is like an entire library has gone up in flames" (Steiner, 2001). These ageless stories include folktales, traditional literature, and folklore.

In times gone by, storytellers told stories to people gathered around campfires and to people who were working on everyday tasks. My grandmother told us stories while we shelled peas; this is how I learned about my Pennsylvania Dutch heritage. These tales reflect a people's concept of themselves—"their beliefs, hopes and fears, courage and humor, sense of delight in the odd, and fascination with the supernatural" (Miller, 1995, p. 22). The Classroom Snapshot on p. 95 illustrates the value of these time-honored tales in classrooms today.

The tales we enjoy today have been polished and edited as storytellers have shared stories from their own cultures using their own idioms, perspectives, and values. Although the names of the people who first told these tales may be lost in the mist of time, the folktales themselves outlive their creators.

Retellers and illustrators continue to create many appealing books in this genre. Some of these are picturebook versions of single tales, while others are collections of folktales. For example, *Ouch!,* Natalie Babbitt's retelling of a Grimm tale, is a single tale. In this story, Marco becomes king by using his wits. Jeanne Steig's *A Handful of Beans: Six Fairy Tales* is a collection of fairytale retellings. Michael Hague's *Kate Culhane: A Ghost Story* satisfies the appetite of intermediate-grade students for ghost stories. Primary-grade children will enjoy hearing the stories in Judy Sierra's *Can You Guess My Name? Traditional Tales Around the World*. This book includes three different versions of well-known tales.

Coleen Salley is a storyteller who lives in the French Quarter of New Orleans. She heard and now retells stories of the old Southern tale "Epaminondas." In her *Epossumondas*, she writes about a lovable possum who wears diapers and appears to be a baby. In the sequel *Epossumondas Saves the Day,* the little possum is celebrating a birthday. Mama needs "sody, sallyraytus" to make the birthday cake. She asks Baby Gator to go to the store for the sody. However, he is eaten by a Great Huge, Ugly Louisana Snapping Turtle, and so Epossumondas has to get the sody and avoid becoming lunch for the turtle.

Controversy in Folktales

Folktales have been sources of controversy throughout history. They were controversial early in the nineteenth century because they did not provide direct, specific moral instruction (Saxby & Winch, 1987). More recently, parents and teachers have expressed concerns about the violence in folktales; some versions of

UTILIZING FOLKTALES

Jim Summers took advantage of his fourth graders' physical education class to check out the *Children's Literature Web Guide.* He found 7 pages of material related to Cinderella stories, including different versions of the story, references, other Internet resources, and teaching ideas. This made his planning much easier. After the students returned, he directed them to their reading workshop groups, which the children eagerly joined. Mr. Summers said, "Last week, you read *Stone Soup* and *Nail Soup,* and quite a few of you asked to read more folktales like these. I couldn't locate additional versions of *Stone Soup,* so I collected 'Cinderella' stories, since there are over 1,000 versions of that tale. One of these is a Grimm fairy tale retold by Aaron Shepard, which is an unusual version of Cinderella. In this story, One Eye and Three Eye find their sister, Two Eyes, embarrassingly different. The theme of this Cinderella story is individual differences. You will find that the characters differ and sometimes the theme. You'll find several of these stories at each workstation. Scan the books and decide on one for your group to read and study." The workshop groups chose from the following books:

The Girl Who Wanted to Hunt by Emery Bernhard and Durga Bernhard

The Korean Cinderella by Shirley Climo

Fair, Brown & Trembling: An Irish Cinderella Story by J. Daly

The Turkey Girl: A Zuni Cinderella Story by Penny Pollock

Cendrillon: A Caribbean Cinderella by Robert San Souci

Smoky Mountain Rose: An Appalachian Cinderella by Alice Schroder

If the Shoe Fits by Laura Whipple

After reading and discussion, each group settled on a book to read.

"Why are these books called 'Cinderella' books?" Matt queried.

One of the students responded, "They don't even have 'Cinderella' in the title. This one is called *The Rough-Face Girl.*"

Mr. Summers said, "That is a Native-American Cinderella. Each of these books is from a different country or culture."

"Oh! This one is from Siberia. Where is Siberia?" Shannon asked.

"And this one is from China," Melissa said.

"How do you think we should study these Cinderella stories?" Mr. Summers asked.

Cory suggested, "We need to figure out what countries our stories are from."

"Good idea," Mr. Summers replied. "What other questions should we ask?"

Each group discussed the questions they should ask and compiled this list:

What country or culture did this story come from?

What is the name of the main character (if not "Cinderella")?

What kind of magic occurs?

Does every story have a prince?

How are the stories different?

How are the stories alike?

Can you think of any modern day Cinderellas?

How does the country of orgin make this Cinderella different?

How does each story begin and end?

---

traditional stories have been rewritten to "launder" or "sanitize" them (Rothman, 1990). In some instances, the vocabulary of traditional tales is changed; in others, the plot is altered. For example, in a puppet show of "Little Red Riding Hood," the wolf is sent to the zoo.

Trickster tales are popular in many cultures, although they are objectionable to some adults. The sly trickster characters who use questionable tactics create examples that some adults would prefer to avoid. The "Brer Rabbit" stories and the Native American tales featuring the wily coyote character are examples of trickster tales. Brer Rabbit represents the spirit of disorder in life (Hearne, 1999). Recent trickster tales have female tricksters. San Souci's *Sister Trickster's*

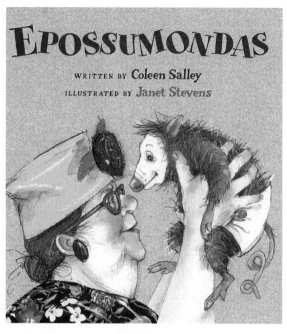

EPOSSUMONDAS

WRITTEN BY **Coleen Salley**

ILLUSTRATED BY **Janet Stevens**

Epossumondas tries to please his Mamma and Aunty.

Rollicking Tales of Clever Females has animal characters. *Clever Katarina: A Tale in Six Parts* by Ken Setterington is a book in the German and Swiss papercutting tradition. In this story, Katarina saves her father from prison and wins the King's hand in marriage by solving an apparently impossible riddle. Fortunately, strong traditional tales seem to be resilient and indestructible; they have withstood all assaults. Their popularity is ensured by their simplicity, directness, and fun.

The Contemporary Values of Traditional Literature

Traditional stories entertain modern children just as they once delighted children and adults around the campfires of long ago. Children of all ages enjoy folktales as read-alones or read-alouds, and they love storytellers. The direct simplicity of these stories appeals to children. Over the years, many of the Caldecott Medal books have belonged to this genre, including Marcia Brown's *Cinderella* and Paul Zelinsky's *Rapunzel*.

Readers learn about themselves through traditional stories, because characters can do things not permitted in real life (Dundes, 1965). Storytellers can comfort children or frighten them, depending upon the teller's purpose. They can express anger and frustration without fear of reprisal. When folktale heroes celebrate overcoming monsters, giants, dragons, and other disreputable forces, they give us heroes, wise men, wizards, and magicians. Nothing in the entire range of children's literature—with rare exceptions—can be as enriching and satisfying to children and adults alike as the folk fairytale. A child can learn more about people's inner problems and about solutions to his or her own (and our) predicaments in society than can be found in any other type of story within a child's comprehension (Bettelheim, 1975, p. 76).

The language of traditional literature is an important part of children's literary heritage. Musical elements, rhythmic language, melodic refrains, and the characters' direct dialogue punctuated with quick action excite readers' and listeners' interest. Through listening to and reading these tales, children acquire language. Moreover, traditional stories provide children with writing models.

The form and content of folktales, although grounded in vastly different cultures, are often remarkably similar, because all people share common human concerns. The details and modifications that appear in folktale variations reflect the society or culture that

Characteristics of Traditional Literature

Simple direct language

Set in the past

Stories begin with Once Upon a Time

Plots are simple

Conflicts involve good versus evil

Characters are either good or bad

Success leads to a reward

Magic and the supernatural are involved

Three is a repeated magic number,
Three wishes, three brothers

Endings: They Lived Happily Ever After

produced them. For this reason, traditional stories give anthropologists a window into other cultures. Traditional literature is a rich source of content for multicultural studies, global education, and art. For example, Leigh Casler's Native American tale, *The Boy Who Dreamed of an Acorn,* tells us that children are searching for their place in the world and that all children have dreams.

Elements of Traditional Literature

Traditional stories have the elements of character, plot, setting, theme, and style; however, they develop in different ways than other genre of fiction.

Character

Only a few characters are needed to tell folktales. The good characters are totally good, and the bad ones are altogether bad. These flat, stereotyped characters are undeveloped, so they are clearly recognizable as symbols of good or evil, kindness or meanness. Each character is a stereotype representing a part of humanity, such as courage, trickery, evil, or foolishness. The characters are introduced briefly, like Chanticleer in Helen Ward's *The Rooster and the Fox,* who is called "herald of the morning, pride of the farmyard" (p. 1). Good characters are rewarded and bad characters are punished, such as when the wolf villain in "Red Riding Hood" is killed in order to rescue the grandma he has eaten. These moralistic stories appeal to most of us, who tend to see people as completely good or completely bad. We all love to cheer when the "bad guys" get what they deserve and when dreams come true for good characters. Listeners expect good characters to reign supreme and bad characters to go down in infamy, so the good ones can live happily ever after.

The *Marvelous Mouse Man* by Mary Ann Hoberman is a retelling of the "Pied Piper of Hamelin." In this version, the Marvelous Mouse Man is portrayed as a wise older character, in contrast to many other versions that portray the Pied Piper as a young man playing an instrument.

Weak and Strong Characters

Traditional literature teaches lessons such as the importance of the inner qualities of love and kindness.

This story is a retelling of the Pied Piper of Hamelin.

Seemingly weak characters have virtues that enable them to achieve success in the face of violence and cruelty. Small, weak, hard-working characters are honored with riches, magical powers, palaces, and delicious banquets. *The Adventures of Deer Mouse: Tales of Indonesia and Malaysia* by Aaron Shepard demonstrates this theme. In this story, Deer Mouse is a small creature who knows that the big animals want to eat him, but he walks through the forest looking for tasty fruits and roots, all the while singing, "I'm quick and smart as I can be. Try and try, but you can't catch me!" Deer Mouse escapes from the most dangerous animals in the forest.

Conflict

Folktale characters experience conflicts, as do characters in other genre. Conflicts give stories suspense, because the characters have to solve a problem to end the conflict. Folktale characters have to solve problems whether they are peasants, kings, princes, woodcutters, or fools; they dramatize a part of life, such as seeking a fortune, finding a lost sibling or parent, or escaping danger. Magic often appears in folktales, but it must be logical within the story framework.

Plot and Setting in Folktales

The minimal development and description in folktale plots and settings lack subtle nuances. Plot and setting are sketched quickly, and the stereotyped characters are dropped into place. Time is developed with stock phrases such as "once upon a time" and "long ago and far away." This brevity sets a stage that is often symbolic; for example, a forest can be a symbol of confusion and losing one's way. The most important aspect of place in traditional literature is creating a backdrop for characters' actions.

Problems or conflicts put the characters into action. They have problems to solve, such as climbing a glass mountain, seeking their fortune, winning the hand of a beautiful princess, or marrying a king. Stories become boring when too many attempts are made to solve problems or conflicts; therefore, storytellers quickly introduce the conflict. Typically, there are three attempts to climb the glass mountain, three riddles to answer, three brothers who seek their fortune, or a beautiful maiden who has three wishes. Three is the magic number in the European tradition of storytelling. Zora Hurston's *Three Witches* illustrates the "magic three," as two children manage to eliminate the three witches. Asian folk tales often have a magic number of four. Three or four attempts or incidents seem to be just the right number to make most stories interesting without dragging them out too long. Figure 6.1 illustrates the components of traditional

tales and models a comparison of these tales that you may use in the classroom.

Story Structure

The typical story structures for traditional tales are as follows: sequential (beginning, middle, end), circular (ends up about where it began), and cumulative (additions and repetitions build the story). Figure 6.2, *Goldilocks and the Three Bears,* illustrates the sequential building of events to a quick resolution; Figure 6.3 shows the circular structure of *The Little Red Hen.*

Theme

Traditional stories have significant themes illustrating cultural values and mores. Characters exhibit traits of humility, courage, honesty, and patience, and demonstrate that dreams come true for good characters. *Goha the Wise Fool*, by Denys Johnson-Davies, who lives in Cairo, is a group of stories about Goha, a Middle Eastern trickster fool character. These tales illustrate the wise principles that underlie Goha's hapless ways. Tales like this facilitate cross-cultural understanding. In *Famous Korean Folktales 2, Animals*, by Ken Methold and others, readers are introduced to Korean culture. This bilingual collection will delight Korean and American children.

Style

One of the hallmarks of folktale styles is the formulaic beginnings used to establish setting and characters, as well as to invite listeners: "long ago and far away" and "once there was and was not." Folktales also have

---

FIGURE 6.1 Chart comparing *Molly Whuppie* to other traditional tales.

Title	Characters	Setting	Villain	Hero/Heroine	Conclusion
Molly Whuppie	Three girls	Woods/giant's castle/king's castle	Giant	Molly	Molly saves herself and her sisters
Jack and the Beanstalk	Jack, his mother, the giant's wife, the giant	Giant's house	Giant	Jack	Jack saves himself and gets the means to support his mother
Hansel and Gretel	Hansel and Gretel, stepmother, father, and witch	Woods, witch's hut	Wicked stepmother and witch	Hansel and Gretel	Hansel and Gretel escape and get to eat all the food they want

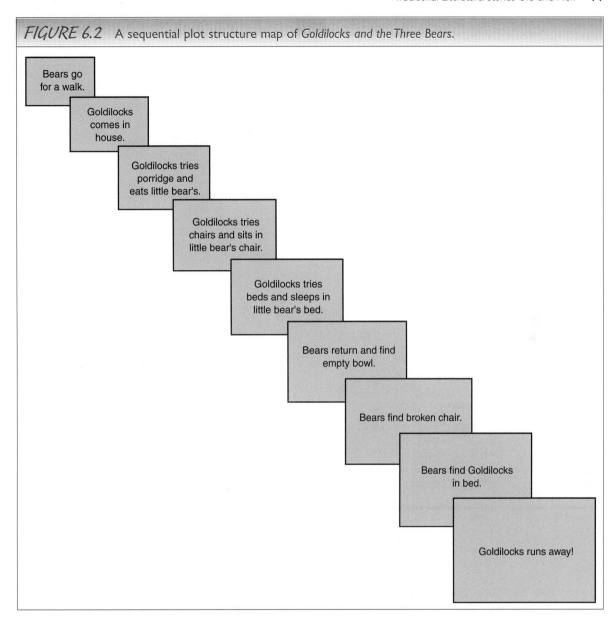

FIGURE 6.2 A sequential plot structure map of *Goldilocks and the Three Bears.*

Bears go for a walk.

Goldilocks comes in house.

Goldilocks tries porridge and eats little bear's.

Goldilocks tries chairs and sits in little bear's chair.

Goldilocks tries beds and sleeps in little bear's bed.

Bears return and find empty bowl.

Bears find broken chair.

Bears find Goldilocks in bed.

Goldilocks runs away!

formulaic endings such as "they lived happily ever after" or direct, clear endings, such as in the *Three Billy Goats Gruff*: "snip, snap, snout; this tale's told out." The language style is succinct and direct. These stories are compact; although they may be read, they retain a sense of their oral language beginnings. Some folktales include stylistic devices such as rhymes, verses, or repetition. *The Marvelous Mouse Man* by Mary Ann Hoberman, for example, is a retelling of the Hamelin story told in rhyming text.

Types of Traditional Literature

According to Dundes (1965), folklore includes many forms, such as myths, legends, folktales, jokes, proverbs, riddles, chants, charms, blessings, curses, oaths, insults, retorts, taunts, teases, toasts, tongue-twisters, greetings, and leave-taking formulas. Many of these types of folklore are found in Gerald Milnes's

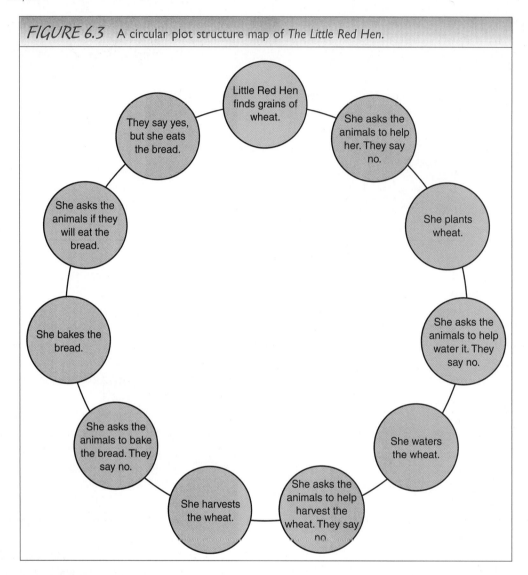

FIGURE 6.3 A circular plot structure map of *The Little Red Hen*.

Granny, Will Your Dog Bite, and Other Mountain Rhymes. To experience the folklore in this volume, Milnes, the reteller, collected the rhymes, songs, and riddles from a man in West Virginia who greeted him with, "Just throw your hat on the bed, spit on the fire, sit down on your fist, lean back against your thumb, and make yourself at home."

Folk poetry ranges from oral epics to autograph-book verse, epitaphs, latrinalia (i.e., writings on the walls of public bathrooms), limericks, ball-bouncing rhymes, jump-rope jingles, finger and toe rhymes, dandling rhymes (used to bounce children on the knee), counting-out rhymes (to determine who will be "it" in games), and nursery rhymes.

Traditional literature is classified in various ways, and authorities differ in the terminology they use. However, folktales (also called "wonder tales" and "household tales") consist of all kinds of narrative originating in the oral tradition (Thompson, 1951). In this sense, the category of folktales encompasses all traditional literature. Fairy tales, animal tales, myths, legends, tall tales, and ballads are all folk tales. The forms of folk tales, discussed in this section and summarized in Table 6.1, represent the majority of traditional literature in print for children today.

Authors who create alternate versions of classic folktales are creating "new folk tales"; in fact, some people call them "fractured fairy tales." These stories

	TABLE 6.1	
	Common types of traditional literature.	
Type	Characteristics	Example
Folktales	giants, witches, magic, tasks, ogres	*Jack and the Beanstalk* *Goldilocks and the Three Bears*
Cumulative folktales	repeat actions, refrains in sequence	*Henny Penny*
Fairy tales	magic and wonder	*Cinderella, Beauty and the Beast*
Animal tales	animals who outwit enemies	*Three Billy Goats Gruff*
Fables	animal stories that teach a lesson	*The Little Red Hen*
Trickster tales	tales in which characters (especially rabbits and coyotes) are able to dupe other characters	*Brer Rabbit*
Noodlehead tales (humorous folktales)	silly humans, stupid characters	*Simple Simon*
Myths	explain the origin of the world and natural phenomena	Greek myths
Pourquoi tales	explain why certain things are the way they are	*How the Snake Got Its Rattles*
Legends	often based on historical figures with embellished deeds	*Robin Hood, King Arthur*
Tall tales	larger-than-life characters	*Daniel Boone, Paul Bunyan*
Ballads	rhyme and rhythm set to music	*Granny, Will Your Dog Bite, and Other Mountain Rhymes*

are not true folktales, but they are fun. Both children and adults find these stories stimulating, and the stories are particularly good for stimulating writing experiences. The stories in *Fairytale News* by Colin and Jacqui Hawkins are an example of fractured fairy tales. In this book, the authors retell classic fairy tales like "Goldilocks," the "Three Little Pigs," and "Red Riding Hood." A newspaper that reports current news about fairy-tale characters is also included in the book.

The following books are also excellent examples of fractured fairy tales:

Jim and the Beanstalk by Raymond Briggs

Prince Cinders by Babette Cole

With Love, Little Red Hen by Alma Alda

The Frog Prince, Continued by Jon Scieszka, illustrated by Steve Johnson

The True Story of the 3 Little Pigs by Jon Scieszka, illustrated by Lane Smith

The Stinky Cheese Man and Other Fairly Stupid Tales by Jon Scieszka, illustrated by Lane Smith

Hammer Soup by Ingrid and Dieter Schubert

Squids Will Be Squids by Jon Scieszka and Lane Smith

The Three Pigs by David Wiesner

Fairy Tales

Fairy tales are unbelievable stories featuring magic and the supernatural. Fairies, giants, witches, dwarfs, good people, and bad people in fairy tales live in supernatural worlds with enchanted toadstools and crystal lakes. Heroes and heroines in these stories have supernatural assistance in solving problems. "Snow White and the Seven Dwarfs" is a typical fairy tale.

Animal Tales

Folk tales often feature animals with human characteristics as the main characters. "The Little Red Hen" falls into this category of folktale. *Fables* are ancient animal tales in which the animals symbolize humans, often to make a specific point or teach a moral lesson, which is explicitly stated at the end of the fable. *Aesop's Fables* are among the best-known fables in the Western culture, while the *Jataka Tales* are well-known in the Eastern culture.

Trickster tales are also animal tales. The principal character in these stories is amoral, neither good nor bad. Tricksters laugh when they should not and are always "up to" something, but tricksters are charming, likable, and tend to escape punishment. The trickster's function in folk literature is to keep us from taking ourselves too seriously (Lester, 1988). Trickster tales appear in every culture, although the trickster animal varies among cultures. Brer Rabbit is a well-known trickster character for children in the United States. Native Americans identify the coyote as a trickster, and tales from the African tradition have a spider as trickster. The trickster in Amy MacDonald's *Please Malese! A Trickster Tale from Haiti* is a devious man who is trying to get brand new shoes. This book introduces students to the culture of Haiti.

Noodlehead Tales, Drolls, and Simpleton Tales

The principal character in these types of stories is an engaging fool. Fools are popular because they represent the underdog who wins, or the good-hearted person who triumphs. A common theme in noodlehead stories is the simpleton or fool who trades something of value for a worthless object. "Lazy Jack," one of the most famous of these characters, trades a cow for some "worthless" beans in "Jack and the Beanstalk." Of course, in the end the worthless objects turn out to be valuable—they grow into a giant beanstalk. The character of Jack catches the imagination of so many people that this story continues to live in retellings, such as Shelley Fowles's *The Bachelor and the Bean.*

Myths

Myths are stories about gods and supernatural beings; myths explain human origins and natural events and tie together relationships between humans and the supernatural. Myths occur in all cultures. Perhaps the best-known myths are *pourquoi tales*, also called "why" stories. These myths explain scientific things, like why the rabbit has a short tail, why the elephant has a long trunk, and so forth.

Legends

Legends are closely related to myths, but the main characters are frequently based on actual historical figures, such as religious saints, rather than supernatural beings. Although usually based in truth about a person, place, or event, legends tend to embellish and embroider the truth in order to showcase a particular virtue so that the character's wonderful feats grow more amazing with each telling. For instance, King Arthur and his Knights of the Round Table exemplify chivalrous behavior, while Joan of Arc exemplifies courage and conviction. One of the oldest stories in the world is a Sumarian epic recorded about 4,500 years ago on a clay tablet. The tale of *Lugabanda: The Boy Who Got Caught Up In a War*, by Kathy Henderson, is the story of the King of Uruk, who sends his 8 sons to conquer the walled city of Aratta. Unfortunately, Lugabanda, the youngest, falls ill and his brothers leave him well-provisioned in a mountain cave. While he recovers, he makes friends with the fearsome Anza bird, who grants him physical strength. Then Lugabanda seeks help from the goddess Inana, who tells him to restore the city. When he returns from the campaign, the goddess breaks his shield to end war.

Published and unpublished legends exist throughout the United States; local and regional legends are especially interesting to students. *The Legend of Sleeping Bear,* by Kathy-Jo Wargin, will be familiar to people living in Michigan, as well as to those who have visited the Sleeping Bear Dunes. *Johnny Appleseed* is a legend in Ohio, and his story is well known by many. His legendary deed was his run from Mansfield, Ohio, to Mount Vernon, Ohio, to get help when Indians attacked Mansfield.

Tall Tales

Tall tales are based on lies and exaggerations about larger-than-life characters, such as Paul Bunyan, Fin M'Coul, John Henry, Mike Fink, Davy Crockett, Johnny Appleseed, and Daniel Boone. As with legends, some of the characters in tall tales actually lived, whereas others may be a composite of several people; many are entirely fictitious. These stories are probably the precursors of modern larger-than-life characters (Saxby & Winch, 1987), such as Crocodile Dundee of movie fame and the characters in Susan Isaacs's picture book, *Swamp Angel*. Tall-tale characters continue to capture our imaginations. The Internet site http://www.americanfolklore.net has a wide range of traditional stories, including tall tales, ghost stories, and stories from every state.

Paul Bunyan, a popular tall-tale character, was probably created by the American lumbering industry. The University of Minnesota has a Paul Bunyan Collection of books, newspaper clippings, photos, phonograph recordings, and memorabilia. Steven Kellogg added to the Paul Bunyan tall tales with his picture book titled *Paul Bunyan*. Paul Bunyan stories are found in the Minnesota state section of www.American Folklore.net.

Ballads

Ballads are essentially dramatic poems that tell stories handed down from one generation to the next through song. These narrative poems have marked rhythm and rhyme. They may include passages of dialogue, a repeated chorus or refrain, and formalized phrases that recur from verse to verse. Ballads usually tell stories about heroes, murders, love, tragedies, and feuds. "The Streets of Laredo" is a ballad that tells of a cowboy's exploits (Sutherland & Livingston, 1984). "Stagolee" is an African American hero who is the subject of both ballads and folktales (Lester, 1969). The popular Australian ballad "Waltzing Matilda" tells about life in the Australian bush. Traditional ballads can introduce literature and poetry.

Jokes, Riddles, and Puzzles

More Stories to Solve by George Shannon is a collection of riddles, such as these: "How did a single firefly win a fight against one hundred apes? How did the priest catch a thief with a rooster? How did a student outwit the king?" These delightful folktales will make children of all ages think.

Selecting and Evaluating Traditional Literature

The factors to consider when selecting and evaluating traditional literature are basically the same as for all literature. Some specific guidelines to keep in mind as you add to your collection are:

1. Does the book tell a good story?
2. Does the dust jacket or the foreword identify the book as traditional literature and tell the original cultural source of the selection? Does the reteller identify the source of the tale?
3. What characteristics of traditional literature does a particular book have (e.g., formulaic beginning or ending, universal setting stated briefly, little or no description, etc.)?
4. Does the story have rapid plot development?
5. Is the style simple and direct?
6. Does the story express universal values?

A Biographical Profile: John Bierhorst

John Bierhorst is an American folklorist and adapter of Native American literature for children. Many of his books have been recognized as Notable Books by the American Library Association.

As a child, Bierhorst never encountered Native American culture in any of the books he read. He discovered his interest in writing while attending college, where his interest in anthropology contributed to his desire to study native cultures. These interests led him to create an anthology of songs, prayers, orations, and languages in *The Hungry Woman: Myths and Legends of the Aztecs*. He concentrates on the Iroquois in *The Woman Who Fell from the Sky: The Iroquois Story of Creation*. He has translated eight Charles Perrault tales, which provides a sense of his diverse skills. The books identified in this profile are merely a few examples of his work.

Summary

Traditional literature is rooted in the oral tradition. The stories, ballads, and tales in this genre are descendents of the original oral stories that have traveled all over the world from storyteller to storyteller, teaching listeners about life and about people. The favorite stories of the past continue to be popular today.

The characters, settings, and events in folktales are symbolic, and they differ from other forms of fiction in that they teach more direct lessons. Other forms of literature develop themes more subtly, but folktales have very obvious themes most of the time.

Tall tales and fractured fairy tales are included in this chapter because they are closely related to traditional literature. Tall tales are about superheroes of former times, and their sources are unclear. Fractured fairy tales were created by authors as different versions of existing tales. Authors of traditional stories are considered retellers. They often collect stories in actual storytelling situations.

Research and Application Experiences

1. Develop a booktalk for introducing a folktale to a group of children, and then read the tale to the children.

2. Analyze folktales from different cultures, such as "Jack Tales," "Little Red Riding Hood," and "Sleeping Beauty," and identify how the tale changes from one culture to another.

3. Identify a folktale that you especially enjoy and prepare to tell it to a group of children.

4. Read or tell a folktale to a group of children, and then have them dramatize the tale.

5. Read two versions of a folktale to children and ask them to identify their favorite version and to explain the reasons for choosing that tale.

Classroom Activities

ACTIVITY 6.1   MAPPING

IRA/NCTE Standards: 3,4,6. Comprehension, vocabulary, knowledge of story structure.

Mapping out a story line is a good activity for developing understanding in children. This activity helps students to summarize and organize their understanding of various stories. You may have the students use their own maps using the model shown in the following figure.

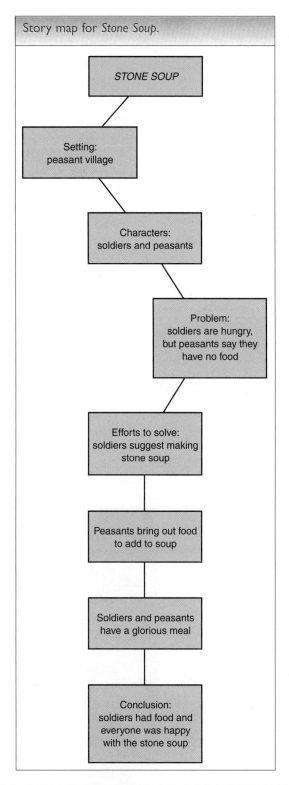

Story map for *Stone Soup*.

STONE SOUP

Setting:
peasant village

Characters:
soldiers and peasants

Problem:
soldiers are hungry,
but peasants say they
have no food

Efforts to solve:
soldiers suggest making
stone soup

Peasants bring out food
to add to soup

Soldiers and peasants
have a glorious meal

Conclusion:
soldiers had food and
everyone was happy
with the stone soup

ACTIVITY 6.2 STORYTELLING

IRA/NCTE Standards: 2,4,9. Oral language/communication.

Storytelling is a natural activity to use with traditional literature. The following guidelines help storytellers.

1. Let the children choose stories that they especially enjoy.

2. Have them learn their stories but not memorize them. Focus initially on the outline of the story. After identifying the basic plot, students can list, map, or outline these elements with drawings. A story map is a graphic display showing the organization of events and ideas in the story (see figure in Activity 6.1).

3. After the students have a map or plan for their stories, group the children in pairs and have the two paired students tell their stories to each other from the map or plan.

4. Once they can remember their story outlines, ask them to elaborate on their storytelling using these techniques:

   A. Visualize the setting, the people, and the action. Think about what you would see, hear, and feel if you were there. Choose words that will make the story more vivid so that your listeners can visualize it as you do. Retell the story with the more vivid language.

   B. Think of ways that you can make the story more exciting for the audience and get them more involved.

ACTIVITY 6.3 DRAMATIZING FOLKTALES

IRA/NCTE Standards: 5, 12. Writing to communicate and to accomplish students' purposes.

Students can compose their own folktales; for example, they can create new versions of tales such as *The dish ran away with the spoon* and so forth. This activity is a variation of one suggested by Livo and Rietz (1986). Write setting, character, and problem or conflict ideas on slips of paper and put each in a separate pile (all of the settings together, all the characters together, etc.). Organize students into groups of two or three and let each group draw one idea from each pile of slips. Then ask them to develop a spontaneous story using the setting, characters, and problem or conflict they selected. Once they are used to working this way, the activity can be varied by giving the students one slip of paper only, so they have a part of the story and must build the rest of it.

On the slips of paper you might write ideas such as:

1. Characters: mean witch, spider, trickster rabbit, good fairy.

2. Setting: enchanted forest, a peasant hut, a giant toadstool, a castle.

3. Problem: cannot break evil witch's spell, lost in a forest, cannot find family, hungry.

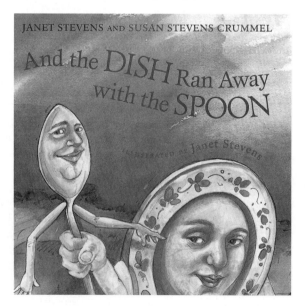

ACTIVITY 6.4   PREDICTION

IRA/NCTE Standards: 3. Comprehension and vocabulary.

Folktales are quite predictable, so anticipation and prediction are good ways to involve children with the stories. Select a story such as *Henny Penny* or *The Three Billy Goats Gruff* by Paul Galdone or *Fin M'Coul: The Giant of Knockmany Hill* by Tomie dePaola. Introduce the story to the children, and ask them to predict what the story will be about from the title and the book cover. Then read the story aloud, stopping at various points in the story to ask them to predict what will happen next. After they predict, tell them to listen to determine whether their predictions were correct. When teaching *The Little Red Hen,* you might stop for predictions after each of these points in the story:

1. The hen asks for help planting the wheat.

2. The hen asks for help watering the wheat and pulling the weeds.

3. The hen asks for help cutting the ripe wheat.

4. The hen asks someone to take the wheat to be ground into flour.

5. The hen asks for help making the wheat into bread.

6. The hen asks for help eating the bread.

A variation of this activity is to have the children write their predictions and then discuss them after the story is completed.

ACTIVITY 6.5   ILLUSTRATING FOLKTALES

IRA/NCTE Standards: 12. Interpreting written language.

Many children enjoy creating their own illustrations for their favorite folktales, many of which have variants that have been interpreted in various ways. Prepare them for this activity by presenting several picture-book versions of the same folktale (see accompanying figure for a sample list). After the students examine the tales, ask them to identify the medium, style, colors, and lines used to illustrate the tale and why they chose these specific media, colors, and so forth. They may like to add the text to their illustrations and bind the stories to make their own books.

Illustrated folktales to compare.	
Brer Rabbit	*The Tales of Uncle Remus: The Adventures of Brer Rabbit* by Julius Lester, illustrated by Jerry Pinkney
	The People Could Fly: American Black Folktales by Virginia Hamilton, illustrated by Leo and Diane Dillon
The Three Billy Goats Gruff	*The Three Billy Goats Gruff* by Peter Asbjornsen, illustrated by Marcia Brown
	The Three Billy Goats Gruff by Paul Galdone
Jack and the Beanstalk	*Jim and the Beanstalk* by Raymond Briggs
	Jack and the Beanstalk by Tony Ross
	Jack and the Bean Tree by Gail E. Haley
Cinderella	*Yeh-Shen* by Ai-Ling Louie
	Cinderella by Charles Perrault, illustrated by Errol Le Cain
	Cinderella by Charles Perrault, illustrated by Marcia Brown
	Cinderella by the Brothers Grimm, illustrated by Nonny Hogrogian
	Cinderella by Paul Galdone

ACTIVITY 6.6   WRITING FOLKTALES

IRA/NCTE Standards: 5, 6. Organizing and structuring writing, applying language conventions.

Folktales are exceptional models for writing. Folktale studies can teach story parts (beginning, middle, end), story form, and story structure, as well as the elements of story grammar (i.e., setting, problem, actions, and resolution). Folktales also provide models of story content. Through studying legends, myths, animal tales, fairy tales, and other folktales, students can learn to understand and write them.

Introduce each type of folktale to the students (i.e., fables, pourquoi tales, trickster tales, legends, myths, etc.) and give examples of each; then have the students identify additional examples of each type, specifying the characteristics that helped them identify the various types of folktales. Ways of applying this activity to specific types of folktales are listed below.

Have the students identify cumulative stories structured around repetition: *Bringing the Rain to Kapiti Plain* by Verna Aardema, *Henny Penny* by Paul Galdone, and *The House That Jack Built* by Janet

Stevens are examples. Read or have the students read the tales aloud; then discuss the cumulative aspects of the stories. Write the repeated portions on the chalkboard or charts. They may want to act out the repeated lines. Have them identify these elements of cumulative stories:

> The stories are short.
>
> The stories have a strong rhythmic pattern.
>
> The story events are in a logical order and related to the preceding events.
>
> All of the story events are in a logical order and build upon the preceding events.
>
> All of the story events are repeated and accumulated until a surprise ending is reached.

Book clusters provide a beginning point for activities and discussion, as well as materials for a variety of activities.

ACTIVITY 6.7   COMPARE FOLKTALE VARIANTS

IRA/NCTE Standards: 7, 8, 9. Research, evaluate, and synthesize data, and use a variety of information resources, critical thinking, and diversity in language and culture.

Variants exist for most popular tales. Compare variants by noting the similarities and differences in the various aspects of the story structure (e.g., setting, character, problem, resolution, and conclusion) and the way the stories are written or illustrated.

Read variants of a folktale aloud for younger students. Older students can prepare their own charts to compare variants, such as the one shown in the accompanying table.

Comparison chart for folktale variants.						
Author/ illustrator	Main character	Setting	Other characters	Beginning	Problem	Ending
Jakob and Wilhelm Grimm Nonny Hogrogian Greenwillow, 1981	Cinderella	Germany	Stepmother Doves Hazel tree	Invitation to ball	Cinderella mistreated	Marries prince
Charles Perrault Marcia Brown Scribner's 1954	Cinderella	France	Stepmother Stepsisters	Invitation to ball	Cinderella mistreated	Marries prince

ACTIVITY 6.8 AUTHOR PROFILES

IRA/NCTE Standards: 4, 6, 8. Students adjust language, apply language knowledge, and create, critique, and discuss print and nonprint texts.

Students will use a variety of technological and informational resources to access author information.

Choosing an author or reteller of traditional literature to profile is difficult because there are many excellent candidates from which to choose. Gale Haley is recognized for her interpretations of folktales, and Ed Young has often retold Asian folktales. Harold Courlander has collected tales from Native Americans, Haitians, and Africans, so his name is significant in traditional literature. Julius Lester has retold the Uncle Remus tales, while Peter and Iona Opie have retold and interpreted classic fairy tales. Steven Kellogg is a masterful writer of tall tales, and Jon Scieszka fractures fairy tales with a sure hand. John Bierhorst has written exceptional Native American folktales; a biographical profile of this author may be found on p. 103.

Children's Literature References

Note: Books designated with an asterisk (*) are recommended for reluctant readers.

Aardema, V. (1981). *Bringing the rain to Kapiti Plain*. New York: Dial. 3–4;5–6. TF

A traditional African tale.

Babbitt, N. (1998). *Ouch! A tale from Grimm* (F. Marcellino, Illus.). New York: HarperCollins. K–2;3–4. TF

A new version of a Grimm tale.

Bierhorst, J. (2002). *Is my friend at home? Pueblo fireside tales* (W. Watson, Illus.). New York: Farrar. K–2;3–4. TF

A collection of Pueblo tales.

Bini, R. (2000). *World treasury of myths, legends, and folktales: Stories from six countries* (M. Frodorow, Illus.). Milan, Italy: Abrams. K–2;3–4;5–6. TF

Briggs, R. (1970). *Jim and the beanstalk*. New York: Coward-McCann. K–2;3–4;5–6. TF

A new version of "Jack and the Beanstalk."

Brown, M. (1954). *Cinderella*. New York: Scribners. K–2. TF

A version of this well-known tale.

Casler, L. (1994). *The boy who dreamed of an acorn* (S. Begay, Illus.). New York: Philomel. 3–4. TF

A Native American tale.

Chase, R. (1943). *Jack tales*. Boston: Houghton Mifflin. K–2;3–4. TF

The author collected these tales in the mountains of North Carolina.

Coburn, J. (1996). *Jouanah: A Hmong Cinderella* (A. O'Brien, Illus.). Fremont, CA: Shen's Books. 3–4;5–6;7+. TF

This is a Cinderella tale from Southeastern Asia.

Daly, J. (2000). *Fair, brown & trembling: An Irish Cinderella story*. New York: Farrar. K–2. MF

A version of Cinderella.

Dearden, C. (2003). *Little book of Latin American folktales*. Joronto, CA: Groundwood. 3–4;5–6. TF

A collection of Latin American folktales.

DePaola, T. (1981). *Fin M'Coul: The giant of Knockmany Hill*. New York: Holiday House. K–2. TF

An Irish folk tale.

Fowles, S. (2003). *The bachelor and the bean*. New York: Farrar. K–2;3–4. TF

The central character is a grumpy old bachelor who drops his last bean in a well.

Galdone, P. (1979). *The three billy goats gruff*. New York: Clarion. K–2. TF

A well-illustrated telling of this tale.

Galdone, P. (1984). *Henny penny*. New York: Clarion. K–2. TF

A retelling of the popular tale.

Hague, M. (2001). *Kate Culhane: A ghost story*. New York: SeaStar. 3–4;5–6. TF

In this popular tale for storytellers, Kate Culhane needs help to escape.

Hamilton, V. (1985). *The people could fly: American Black folktales* (L. & D. Dillon, Illus.). New York: Knopf. 3–4;5–6;7+. TF

A superb collection of folktales.

Hawkins, C., & J. (2004). *Fairytale news*. Cambridge, MA: Candlewick. K–2;3–4;5–6. TF

A modernized newspaper version of popular fairy tales.

Henderson, K. (2006). *Lugabanda: The boy who got caught up in a war*. Cambridge, MA: Candlewick. 3–4;5–6. TF

A folktale about war.

Hoberman, M. (2002). *The marvelous mouse man* (L. Forman, Illus.). New York: Harcourt. 3–4;5–6. TF

Houston, J. (2006). *James Houston's treasury of Inuit legends*. Mt. Vernon, NH: Odyssey. 3–4; 5–6. TF

Stories about the Inuit people from a man who lived with them.

Hurston, Z. (2006). *The three witches*. New York: Harper. K–2. TF

Hurston tells the story of witches and witching.

Isaacs, A. (1995). *Swamp angel* (P. Zelinsky, Illus.). New York: Dutton. K–2;3–4;5–6. TF

The Swamp Angel is the larger-than-life heroine of this tall tale.

Johnson-Davies, D. (2005). *Goha the wise fool*. New York: Philomel. K–2;3–4. TF

The story of a Middle Eastern trickster.

Johnson, P. B. (2001). *Fearless Jack*. New York: McElderry. 3–4;5–6. TF

This story is a version of the Appalachian tale "Jack the Giant Killer."

Kellogg, S. (1984). *Paul Bunyan*. Harper: New York: K–2;3–4. TF

A woodcutting giant and his blue ox.

Kilaka, J. (2006). *True friends: A tale from Tanzania*. Berkley, CA: Groundwood. K–2. TF

After starving due to drought, the hero discovers the meaning of true friendship.

Kimmel, E. (2006). *The Frog princess: A Tinglit legend from Alaska*. New York: Holiday House. K–2;3–4. TF

This is an Alaskan version of the Frog Prince.

Lester, J. (1969). *Black folktales* (T. Feelings, Illus.). New York: Barron. 3–4;5–6;7+. TL

A collection of Black folktales including Stagolee.

MacDonald, A. (2002). *Please, Malese!: A trickster tale from Haiti* (E. Lisker, Illus.). New York: Farrar. 3–4;5–6. TF

Malese plots to avoid work and get new shoes.

Martin, R. (1992). *The rough-face girl* (D. Shannon, Illus.). New York: Putnam. K–2;3–4. TF

Methold, K., Eund-cheon Hah, Malarcher, C., and Ho-Hyun Han. (2007). *Famous Korean folktales 2, animals*. New York: Compass Publishing. K–2;3–4. TF

Korean folktales about animals.

Milligan, B. (2003). *The prince of Ireland and the three magic stallions*. New York: Holiday House. K–2;3–4. TF

The stepmother of the prince of Ireland seeks to eliminate her stepson from the throne.

Milnes, G. (1990). *Granny will your dog bite, and other mountain rhymes*. New York: Knopf. 3–4;5–6. TF

A collection of interesting mountain tales.

Nesbit, E. (2006). *Jack and the beanstalk*. Cambridge, MA: Candlewick. K–2;3–4. TF

A new version of "Jack and the Beanstalk."

Pollock, P. (1996). *The turkey girl: A Zuni Cinderella story* (D. Young, Illus.). Boston: Little Brown. K–2;3–4. TF

A Cinderella story.

Salley, C. (2006). *Epossumondas saves the day* (J. Stevens, Illus.). New York: Harcourt. K–2. TF

Epossumondas tangles with a mean old snapping turtle.

Salley, C. (2002). *Epossumondas* (J. Stevens, Illus.). New York: Harcourt. K–2. TF

A story about a baby possum who is his mamma's "Sweet Little Pootie."

San Souci, R. (2006). *Sister Trickster's rollicking tales of clever females*. Atlanta, GA: August House. 3–4;5–6;7+. TF

Women are the heroes of these tales.

Scieszka, J. (1989). *The true story of the 3 little pigs* (L. Smith, Illus.). New York: Viking. K–2;3–4;5–6;7+. MF

The wolf tells his version of this story.

Scieszka, J. (1991). *The frog prince, continued* (S. Johnson, Illus.). New York: Viking. K–2;3–4; 5–6. MF

A new version of the traditional tale.

Scieszka, J. (1992). *The stinky cheese man and other fairly stupid tales* (L. Smith, Illus.). New York: Viking. K–2;3–4;5–6;7+. MF

New versions of well-known traditional tales.

Scieszka, J., & Smith L. (1998). *Squids will be squids*. New York: Viking. K–2;3–4;5–6. MF

Fractured fairy tale.

Setterington, K. (2006). *Clever Katarina: A tale in six parts*. New York: Tundra. 3–4;5–6;7+. TF

Women heroes.

Shannon, J. (2001). *More stories to solve*. New York: Clarion. K–2;3–4. TF

Riddle stories.

Shepard, A. (2006). *One-eye!two-eyes!three-eyes: A very Grimm fairy tale*. New York: Atheneum. K–2. TF

A different version of Cinderella.

Shepard A., & Gamble, K. (2005). *The adventures of Mousedeer: Tales of Indonesia and Malaysia*. New York: Skyhook Press/Harper. K–2;3–4. TF

Trickster tales from Southeast Asia.

Sierra, J. (2002). *Can you guess my name?: Traditional tales around the world*. New York: Clarion. 3–4;5–6;7+. TF

Riddle stories.

Stevens, J. (1985). *The house that Jack built*. New York: Harcourt. K–2. TF

This is a cumulative story about building a house.

Steig, J. (1998). *A handful of beans: Six fairy tales* (W. Steig, Illus.). New York: Harper. K–2;3–4. TF

Six classic tales retold in modern language.

Sunami, K. (2002). *How the fisherman tricked the genie: A tale within a tale within a tale*. New York: Atheneum. K–3. TF

A fisherman releases a genie from a bottle, but the genie refuses to grant wishes.

Ward, H. (2002). *The rooster and the fox*. New York: Millbrook. K–2. TF.

A traditional tale.

Wargin, K. (1998). *The legend of sleeping bear* (F. Van Frankenhuyzen, Illus.). Chelsea, MI: Sleeping Bear Press. K–2;3–4. TF

The story of the formation of the Sleeping Bear Dunes.

Whipple, L. (2002). *If the shoe fits: Voices from Cinderella*. New York: McElderry. K–2;3–4. TF

The voices of Cinderella characters in poetry.

Yolen, J. (2003). *Mightier than the sword*. New York: Harcourt. 3–4;5–6. TF

A new version of a folktale.

Yolen, J. (2003). *Not one damsel in distress*. New York: Harcourt. 3–4;5–6. TF

A new version of a folktale.

Zelinsky, P. (1998). *Rapunzel*. New York: Dutton. K–2;3–4. TF

Zelinsky interprets this Grimm tale with exquisite new illustrations.

Zeman, L. (2003). *Sinbad's secret*. Toronto, CA: Tundra. 3–4;5–6. TF

A retelling of the thousand and one nights from Sinbad's point of view.

Professional References

Bettelheim, B. (1975, December 8). The uses of enchantment. *New Yorker,* pg 76.

Dundes, A. (1965). *The study of folklore*. Upper Saddle River, NJ: Prentice Hall.

Hearne, B. (1999). *Choosing books for children*. (3rd ed.). New York: Delacorte.

Hunter, M. (1975). *Talent is not enough*. New York: Harper.

Jaffe, N. (1999). Global storytelling. *Book Links, 8,* 53.

Lester, J. (1988, Summer). The storyteller's voice: Reflections on the rewriting of Uncle Remus. *New Advocate, 1,* 143–159.

Livo, N. J. & Rietz, S. A. (1986). *Storytelling process and practice*. Littleton, CO: Libraries Unlimited.

Miller, S. (1995). American folklore. In A. Silvey (Ed.), *Children's books and their creators* (pp. 22–24). Boston: Houghton Mifflin.

Rothman, R. (1990, February 21). Experts warn of attempts to censor classic texts. *Education Week,* 5.

Saxby, M. T., & Winch, G. (1987). *Give them wings: The experience of children's literature.* South Melbourne, Australia: Macmillian.

Steiner, H. (2001). Storytelling around the world. *Book Links, 10* (5), 40–48.

Sutherland, Z., & Livingston, M. C. (1984). *The Scott Foresman anthology of children's literature.* (8th ed.) Chicago: Scott Foresman.

Thompson, S. (1951). *The Folktale.* New York: Holt Rinehart Winston.

7 Modern Fantasy: Today's Magic

KEY TERMS

fantastic elements   modern fantasy

enchanted realism   science fiction

high fantasy

GUIDING QUESTIONS

1. What was your favorite fantasy when you were a child? As you read, think about a current fantasy book that is similar to your favorite story.

2. Why is fantasy such an important genre of literature for children?

3. Why is fantasy so popular today?

4. What are the elements of fantasy?

Introduction to Modern Fantasy

"Fantasy is the ultimate literature of the imagination" (Greenlaw, 2001, p. 148). According to Albert Einstein, the power to imagine is more important than simple knowledge (Shlain, 1990). In fantasy, authors create extraordinary worlds and characters who challenge and expand our sense of the norm. Imagined worlds permit readers to explore the basic truths of our own world. In this way, good fantasy helps readers understand reality. Fantasy exercises the imagination.

Fantasy helps children dream and imagine (Eisner, 1992). Fantasy stimulates students to look at life and its problems in new ways. In addition, of all the genres of children's literature, fantasy offers the greatest challenge and the greatest rewards to both readers and writers. This is why many have welcomed the blossoming interest in fantasy since the arrival of Harry Potter.

"Until quite recently fantasy writers were an outcast bunch whose work was rarely prized or rewarded" (Marcus, 2006). In the past, fantasy writers had to defend themselves to doubters who could not understand why adults spent time composing dragons and witches. When Leonard Marcus interviewed 13 well known authors of fantasy, he discovered these authors had deeply disturbing memories of World War II. Many of them said they had "intense, life-altering memories of that war" (Marcus, 2006, p. 3). They apparently found that reading and writing fantasy were ways to deal with wartime horrors that were inexpressible. They created alternative realities. Fantasy fulfills the human need to imagine alternate realities and to explore the unexplainable and the impossible (Woolsey, 2002). We live in an intense time, with the aftermath of the attacks of 9/11, terrorists, wars, the worldwide AIDS epidemic, and children around the world living in poverty. Perhaps the power of the *Harry Potter* stories is their facility to help readers imagine alternate realities where children have control.

When asked why he wrote fantasy, Lloyd Alexander responded, "Because paradoxically, fantasy is a good way to show the world as it is. Fantasy can show us the truth about human relationships and moral dilemmas because it works on our emotions on a deeper, symbolic level than realistic fiction" (Marcus, 2006, p. 13). Nancy Farmer says "The world . . . is composed of great sorrow and great joy. It has a grandeur beyond anything I can describe, but this I can say: to know what you are and where you belong is the true meaning of Magic" (Marcus, 2006, p. 49). She put the preceding words into the mouth of Rodentus, a roguish, well-traveled rat in her novel *The Warm Place*.

The Challenges of Writing Fantasy

Writers of fantasy have special challenges because "the more fantastic a piece of fiction is, the harder the writer must work to make it believable" (Hearne, 1999, p. 86). The writer's job is to make fantasy real. Writers must effortlessly use imaginary elements to create a seamless story, so real that the reader cannot avoid accepting its *fantastic elements*. Authors must adhere to strict rules; they cannot wave a wand to solve all of the dilemmas confronting the protagonist. Readers have to willingly suspend disbelief to join in the magic and believe the story could actually happen. Once they do that, they accept the magic that enables pigs to fly, animals to talk, entire villages to appear and disappear, and clocks to strike 13. The story cannot "clank," jarring the reader back to reality (Greenlaw, 1995).

Modern fantasy is the first cousin of traditional literature, which shares many characteristics with fantasy. *Modern fantasy* inherits the common themes of traditional literature: the struggle between good and evil, basic human values, and perseverance in the face of adversity. Many of the characters of traditional literature are symbols of good, beauty, and wisdom, and of bad, ugliness, and evil. The same is true of the characters in fantasy, although in fantasy, the characters' personalities are more developed.

The Nature of Fantasy

Excellent fantasy is set apart from other genres. First, the author must have a strongly realized personal vision, a perspective or belief about the meaning, significance, symbolism, and allegory. The best stories are like extended lyrical images of unchanging human predicaments: In them, life and death, as we currently understand them, exist in the physical universe (Alexander, 1991). Second, the author's personal vision leads to the moral, message, or theme in the fantasy (Langton, 1977). In fantasy, love and hate, good and evil, courage and despair are dramatized (Cook, 1969, p. 2).

Once the framework of the fantasy is created, each story must have its own self-contained logic, and that logic must be consistent throughout the story. Authors draw boundary lines outside which the fantasy may not wander. Although fantasy concerns things that cannot really happen, as well as people or creatures that do not really exist, readers have to believe that the magic and the impossible happenings are plausible. Fantasy always includes at least one element of the impossible, one element that goes against the laws of the physical universe as we currently understand them (Alexander, 1991). Katherine Paterson creates an alternate universe in her novel, *Bridge to Terabithia*[**]; although, the central characters are able to move from one universe to the other, they cannot change the laws of either universe. C. S. Lewis created another universe in *The Chronicles of Narnia*[**]. Bruce Coville created the Land of the Unicorn for the story *Into the Land of the Unicorns*[**].

In E. B. White's *Charlotte's Web*[**], the animals talk among themselves but not to the human beings. White created this logic at the outset of the story, and it is never violated. Although authors are free to create any specific boundaries or logic, writers of fantasy must be hardheaded realists. "What appears gossamer is, underneath, solid as prestressed concrete. Once committed to his imaginary kingdom, the writer is not a monarch but a subject" (Alexander, 1991, p. 143).

Alexander Key creates a character from another universe, one who drops in to visit a family, in *The Forgotten Door*[**]. When faced with this character from another universe, the people in Key's novel encounter issues that reveal the book's theme: that individuals who are different frighten some people. Alien visitors can cause us to see ourselves in new ways and to discover the importance of kindness. A truth clothed in the fantastic is often easier to understand and accept than a baldly stated fact. Fantasy gives readers the emotional distance to consider important ideas objectively (Kurkjian et al., 2006).

Readers and Fantasy

Fantasy gives children a means of verifying their understanding of the external world they share with others (their immediate world). It also gives children a means of examining their inner world and comparing

---

CLASSROOM SNAPSHOT

FANTASY BEYOND HARRY POTTER

The only sounds in Will Livingston's fifth-grade classroom were those of turning pages. Reading workshop had that effect on his students: They really enjoyed reading. When he told them it was time to stop, Josh groaned, "Our group just finished *Harry Potter and the Order of the Phoenix,* and we have read all of the other Harry Potter books. There just isn't anything as good as Harry Potter. We don't want to read anything else."

"What do you like about the Harry Potter books?" Will asked.

"The story is so interesting that I don't want to stop reading. Harry is like a real kid. He is very brave. I like the characters and the magic. They have adventures and learn how to use magic, but they can't cast spells in the world of Muggles. Quinton and James agree with me that they only want to read Harry Potter."

Will responded, "What genre is Harry Potter?"

"That's easy! It is definitely fantasy."

"Let me see if I can find some books that have some of the same qualities as Harry Potter. Then you can survey them and select another one to read," Will suggested.

Will checked several reviews and selected these titles.

The Amulet of Komondor by Adam Osterweil

Wanna Buy an Alien? by Eve Bunting

Space Race by Sylvia Waugh

Skelling by David Almond

Island of the Aunts by Eva Ibbotson

After surveying the books, the boys selected *The Amulet of Komondor.* Josh said, "We are going to read *The Amulet of Komondor,* but we don't think it will be as good as Harry Potter."

"Perhaps you could compare *The Amulet of Komondor* with Harry Potter," Will suggested. "You might also enjoy studying the authors of both books."

---

it with others' inner worlds (Britton, 1977). A theme of L'Engle's fantasy *A Wrinkle in Time*[**] is good versus evil. Despite this basic moral or lesson, the author must avoid moral pronouncements; children do not tolerate them any better than do adults. Instead, these truths must emerge naturally from the story, providing insights about the human condition without preaching (Smith, 1988).

 Types of Fantasy

Modern fantasy is perhaps the most richly varied of all genres, ranging from simple stories of magic to profoundly complex stories like those told in the *Star Wars* movies. These films are elaborate stories of good versus evil. The diversity of fantasy appeals to a broad range of readers with varying reading abilities and interests. "When children are deeply engaged with fantasy literature, we see 'live circuits' of response that reveal more about the books children read, their ways of reading and composing, and their own child worlds" (Mikkelsen, 2005, p. 22).

Classic Fantasy

Classic fantasy includes some of the most popular fantasies of all times: *Winnie-the-Pooh*[**] by A. A. Milne, *A Bear Called Paddington*[**] by Michael Bond, *Charlie and the Chocolate Factory*[**] by Roald Dahl, and *The Wonderful Wizard of Oz*[**] by Frank Baum. Each of these characters was, and is, the favorite of many children and adults.

To organize our discussion of fantasy, we will categorize stories as animal fantasies, literary fairy tales, and enchanted realism. More complex fantasy, often called *high fantasy,* is grouped into heroic fantasy, time magic, and science fiction (Woolsey, 2002). These categories are arbitrary because many stories could belong to multiple categories. For example, *Charlotte's Web*[**] is an animal fantasy, beginning in the real world but then introducing the alternative world of the animal. Moreover, the theme of friendship, as well as the comments on society, can give different perspectives on this fantasy.

Animal Fantasies

Animal fantasies are often the first stories that children encounter. In these stories, animals act and interact like human beings. When a clueless zookeeper puts the hippo sign in front of the rhino's enclosure in *Hippo! No Rhino!* by Jeff Newman, the temperamental rhino is plunged into a bad mood because he cannot stand to be mistaken for a hippo. A lonely, literate rat is the protagonist in Wersba's *Walter the Story of a Rat.* Walter lives in the home of Miss Pomeroy, an elderly author of children's books. Their friendship develps when they exchange notes.

Janell Cannon's *Stellaluna*** is a superb animal fantasy. Stellaluna is a little fruit bat who becomes separated from her mother, but Stellaluna adjusts to living with birds. Then she and her mother find one another and all is well. This fantasy is carefully structured, so that the birds and bats communicate, but they do not talk with human beings.

Literary Fairy Tales

Fantasy and traditional literature share the quality of make-believe, as well as many stylistic features, leading

Stellaluna has both real and make-believe elements.

authors of fantasy to make extensive use of the folktale style. Hans Christian Andersen, a shy man, used this style to tell stories about his own experiences. In *The Tinderbox*, Stephen Mitchell retells Andersen's classic story, following Andersen's plot telling about a soldier who tricks a witch out of her tinderbox. The soldier then uses her magic to save his life. The illustrations have the feeling of ninteenth-century engravings. Children will enjoy discussing the story, which raises the issue of justice.

Amy Lowry Poole retells Hans Christian Andersen's *The Pea Blossom.* Her retelling takes place in Beijing, and she includes Chinese mythology. The plot follows the journey of each of five sweet peas in a pod. Four of the peas are ambitious, but one plans to go wherever it is meant to. This version of Andersen's story is an excellent read-aloud.

Alice the Fairy was created by David Shannon. Alice is a temporary fairy who has to pass tests to become a permanent fairy. She changes frogs into princes and oatmeal into cake, and performs the usual fairy magic tasks with very real results that startle her parents but entertain primary-grade students.

High Fantasy

High fantasy is a complex, philosophical form of literature that focuses on themes such as the conflict between good and evil. The complexity and abstractness of high fantasy includes detailed alternate or parallel worlds that authors create through dramatic plots, fully developed characters, geographies, languages, mythologies, histories, and traditions (Greenlaw, 2001).

Creators of fantasy write of myth and legend, of science and technology, and of human life—as it is lived, as it might be lived, and as it ought to be lived (Le Guin, 1979). The characters in high fantasy are often symbolic of good people who are entangled in an endless battle between good and evil, such as what occurs in each book of the popular *Harry Potter* series.

Avi's book, *The Book Without Words: A Fable of Medieval Magic,* has the characteristics of high fantasy. In the story, the "book without words" can only be read by ones with green eyes. Thorston, the central character, is determined to avoid dying, so he sacrifices his talking raven, Odo, and his servant girl, Sybil, to use evil magic from the book to renew his life. Odo and Sybil meet characters who are so consumed with greed and desire and others who have lived such terrible lives that it seems they have not experienced life. Although humor seems remote in my description of the plot, the seriousness of the story is broken up by humor that makes readers laugh. The theme of this book is that death is a natural part of life. This book is a masterpiece that can be compared with *Tuck Everlasting*, which is the story of a family that drinks from water that makes them immortal.

Enchanted Realism

Enchanted realism has elements of both fantasy and high fantasy. These stories include magical objects, characters, and events that appear in a realistic world, creating suspense and intrigue in the story (Woolsey, 2002).

Fantasy and high fantasy are present in *Lulu's Hat* by Susan Meddaugh. Lulu, the protagonist, is adopted into a family of magicians, but they believe she has no "real magic." However, Lulu discovers an old top hat that gives her magic powers and drops her into the world of magic. She acquires a dog named Hereboy and learns the secret of her past. She thereby achieves her goal of becoming a true magician.

Ella the Elegant Elephant, by Carmela and Steve D'Amico, is another book that delights young children. Ella elephant wears her Grandma's good-luck hat, a floppy bright orange hat with flowers on it, on her first day in a new school. The uniformed students ridicule Ella. But when Ella tries to rescue her friend, Belinda, they both fall into Grandma's magic hat, which becomes a parachute and floats them to the ground.

Heroic Fantasy

Hayley, the shy heroine of *The Game* by Diana Jones, is forbidden to engage in magic. When magic finds her anyway, her grandparents kick her out of the house. Through magic, she discovers two secrets. The first secret is the world of mythosphere, a mystical layer of stories, myths, and legends that converge into a sort of path on which one can travel. She also learns that her parents are alive and trapped in the mythosphere. She is destined to overpower her Uncle Jolyon to save her parents. In this coming-of-age story, Haley explores an unknown magical world and learns about her own magical powers. Diana Jones uses wonderful

connections to Greek and Roman myths and to Irish and other magical settings to create this taut fantasy.

Dragon's Blood by Jane Yolen is also an engrossing fantasy. Jakkin, a 15-year-old bond servant, tends the beautiful dragons who are trained to fight, but he wants to earn his freedom. *Dragon's Blood* is the first book in the Pit Dragon series, which is very popular with intermediate- and middle-school students.

Science Fiction

What will life be like in 2050? How will we travel? Will there be colonies of earth people on Mars or some newly discovered planet? These are the kinds of themes explored in *science fiction*. This imaginative literature depicts plausible events that are logical extrapolations from known facts. The story builds around events and problems that would not have happened at all without the scientific content (Gunn, 1975).

Kate Thompson's *Only Human* is the sequel to *Fourth World* in the Missing Link Trilogy series. In this novel, Bernard sets out for the Himalayas to find the Yeti. His frog-human daughter stows away to help him in his odyssey. This novel, like many of the popular science fiction and fantasy books, is part of a series.

Sharp North by Patrick Cave is the story of Mira, who witnesses a murder and feels that she is somehow involved. She does not understand exactly how she is involved and sets out to learn who or what she really is. There are many cliffhangers and unexpected turns in this science fiction epic, which includes clones.

Vivien Alcock's *The Monster Garden*** is splendid science fiction for children in third through fifth grade. In the story, matter produced in the lab of a young girl's father grows into a kind-hearted and wise monster. However, Monny the monster suffers rejections when people in the community find her unacceptable because she is different. Her rescuer sadly releases Monny to find a better and kinder place.

Time Magic

In time magic stories, children read about magic that moves the story to the past or the future. Usually, a magic object launches time travel. One of my favorite time-based stories is Philippa Pearce's *Tom's Midnight Garden***. The action begins when Tom hears the grandfather clock strike 13, after which he plays with a girl who lived in the house long ago. She becomes a friend to Tom. The girl talks to Tom about the words "Time No Longer," which appear on the face of the grandfather clock. She convinces him to suspend disbelief until the mystery unfolds. She is actually the child who grew into the old woman who lives upstairs. These strange events defy the laws of time.

The heroine of Alma Alexander's novel, *The Gift of the Unma*, is Thea, the seventh child of a seventh daughter and a seventh son. Her parents are disappointed in her failure to develop extraordinary magical skills, so they decide to send her into the past to seek help from Cheveyo, an Anasazi warrior. Thea discovers that she has repressed her powers intuitively to hide them from the ruthless alien race, the Alphiri. After her return to her own life and time, she battles the Alphiri. Thea is an engaging character who is both inscrutable and haunted.

Elements of Fantasy

Authors of fantasy skillfully craft language that will cause readers to suspend their disbelief and accept an invitation to enter new and fanciful worlds. Authors must make their plots credible and consistent, and the stories must retain their inner logic, if readers are to believe in the fantasy.

Characters

Well-rounded, believable characters are essential in fantasy. To be believable, characters must be multidimensional. Neddie Wentworthstein, the protagonist in Daniel Pinkwater's *The Neddiad*, is such a character. Neddie has a sacred, stone turtle; with the assistance of a shaman and a ghost, Neddie sets out to protect the sacred turtle from Sholmos Bunyip. Neddie and his companions use a little maneuver known as the French substitution to save the world from chaos and civilization. The modern settings in this story contrast with the usual fantastic settings in books of this genre.

The principal character in a fantasy establishes the logic of the fantasy and helps readers enter into the make-believe realm by expressing a confidence and belief in the unbelievable events. In *The Neddiad*, Neddie is such a character because he believes that he must protect his sacred turtle in order to save the world from destruction.

This book has everything: humor, mystery, and turtles.

Setting

Detailed settings make readers believe in fantasy. Neil Gaiman uses graphic details in describing the characters and setting in *Coraline*. As the story unfolds, Coraline discovers a passageway to a home identical to her own, complete with two people who call themselves her "other parents." These characters look just like her parents except for the fact that their eyes are black buttons.

Plot

Characters and setting come together in an original plot to create excellent fantasy. One of the most common strategies that authors use for making a fantastic plot believable is beginning the story in reality and gradually moving into fantasy. Readers may not even realize the book is fantasy until later. Gaiman uses this technique in *Coraline*. The mood is sunny and inviting as Coraline blithely explores her new neighborhood. That setting is a dramatic contrast to the horror of her later environment.

Authors sometimes convince us to believe in their fantasy by having characters move back and forth between their real environment and the make-believe environment. This technique appears in Nicky Singer's *Feather Boy*. Robert Nobel, the central character, moves from a normal school situation to a nursing home for a class project, but then he is seized and ordered to walk to Chance House, an abandoned building that is haunted. Robert seems somehow connected to the Chance House boy. The story moves back and forth between regular life and the mystic building.

So This is How It Ends by Tui Sutherland is a futuristic fantasy. Five teenagers reach the end of their worlds and are knocked unconscious for 75 years. When they awaken, they each hear a siren calling them to New York. As they travel the long distance to reach New York, each one gains insight into this new world, in which humans cannot reproduce. They learn robots have violently rebelled, and the remaining humans are trying to find ways to extend their lives. Upon their arrival in New York, the teens discover they are to be avatars for gods and goddesses who are at war to determine who will rule the earth.

Theme

Theme is a significant aspect of fantasy. Universal themes such as wishes and dreams, the struggle between good and evil, and the importance of love are common in modern fantasy. Symbolism is often used to help further the theme of a fantasy. For example, the theme of *So This is How it Ends* is good battling evil, while the theme of *The Game* is Hayley's coming-of-age struggle (both books were discussed earlier). Many of the events in *The Game* show how Hayley has to escape her strict grandparents in order to grow into an independent, strong person who is in control of her magical powers.

Style

The language authors use is one of the major components of style. Style is especially important in fantasy because authors must find a way to tell about places,

things, and people that do not exist in such a way that readers will see them in their imaginations. Vivid descriptions of the setting, albeit imaginary, are essential. Readers must be convinced that the place exists.

Characters must also be carefully developed. They may be like Ned in *The Neddiad*, who is very much like other boys but has fantastic experiences. They may look average, even when they have unusual traits, such as the character of Dr. Who, who is 900 years old and has to save the world. Naming characters is another important part of writing. Fanny Billingsley describes searching books of baby names for a name that fit her character (Marcus, 2006). Fantasy writers often use their personal interests and passions as the subjects of their stories. Jane Yolen, for example, writes about dragons because she loves and rides horses, and she thinks of a dragon as a "large and amazing horse" (Marcus, 2006). *The Wand in the Word*, compiled by Leonard Marcus, includes interesting conversations with many writers of fantasy.

Selecting Fantasy

When selecting fantasy for your classroom, consider the following factors in addition to the guidelines for all literature.

1. Does it tell a good story?
2. What are the elements of fantasy in this story (e.g., setting, magic powers, time, etc.)?
3. How is this story different from the real world?
4. How has the author made the story believable?
5. What is the theme of this fantasy?

Fantasy in Classrooms

A great read-aloud is Deborah and James Howe's *Bunnicula*.** Harold, a dog who observes the story, is the narrator in this hilarious book. After a rabbit arrives in the home, vegetables begin to appear that have been drained of their juices. The plot thickens when Chester the cat concludes that the rabbit, Bunnicula, is a vampire rabbit, and Chester sets out to protect the family from a vampire attack. Natalie Babbitt's *The Search for Delicious* is another book guaranteed to please.

Readers in the fifth and sixth grades will enjoy the originality of plot and character in William J. Brooke's short stories featured in *Untold Tales*. One of the stories is a clever play, "A Prince in the Throat."

Kenneth Grahame's *The Reluctant Dragon*[**], a version of *St. George and the Dragon*, is one of my favorite read-alouds. A shepherd boy and a cultured, poetry writing dragon are the characters in this story. San Souci and Segal have created a new version of the story that my students enjoyed.

Summary

Modern fantasy is the literature of imagination. Fantasy has magic that develops through events, objects, characters, time, and places. Fantasy is categorized into animal fantasy, literary fairy tales, enchanted realism, science fiction, and time magic.

The themes of fantasy are often concerned with the age-old battle between good and evil. Fantasy touches our deepest feelings, and in so doing, it speaks to the best and most hopeful parts of ourselves. It can help us learn the most fundamental skill of all—how to be human (Alexander, 1991, p. 43). The abstract, imaginative nature of fantasy expands children's imagination, but children are more likely to appreciate fantasy when teachers introduce the stories and read them aloud.

Thought Questions and Applications

1. What are the major characteristics of high fantasy?
2. Why is fantasy so important today?
3. What are the major characteristics of fantasy?
4. Compare fantasy with fiction.
5. What are fantasy's values for children?

Research and Application Experiences

1. Read a fantasy book to a group of children or a class and then discuss the story. Tape the discussion so you can analyze its strengths and weaknesses.
2. Create a bibliography of fantasies for a selected grade level.

Classroom Activities

More than any other genre, fantasy needs to be introduced and read aloud. Introductions explain the context of the story and encourage listeners to predict story events.

ACTIVITY 7.1   FIND THE MAGIC

IRA/NCTE Standards: 1,2,3. Comprehension, read a wide range of print and genre.

The purpose of this activity is to identify the magic in a fantasy book. This activity can be conducted with individuals or groups. Younger students may work with one fantasy, while intermediate-grade students may compare various books.

Book: *The Amulet of Komondor* by A. Osterweil, Front Street, 2003.

Character/s	Setting	Magic	Plot	Theme
Joe and Katie	Strange mall store	DragonSteel game that transports them to Komondor via a CD	After buying a game, children have a hilarious trip to Komondor where they have to locate the five pieces needed for the game, so they can win and quit playing	Good vs. evil; family and friendship

*This story begins with a strange store
and a game of DragonSteel.*

ACTIVITY 7.2 STORY INTERPRETATION

IRA/NCTE Standard: 3. Comprehension.

A discussion that includes questions like the following will help children comprehend fantasy.

Book Title _____

1. Who are the characters?
2. Describe the protagonist.
3. Where does the story take place?
4. When does the story take place?
5. What is the magic in this story?
6. What is the story's theme?

ACTIVITY 7.3 INQUIRIES

IRA/NCTE Standards: 3, 4, 5, 7. Research, apply range of strategies, communication, and writing process.

Exploring a topic or theme develops the children's response to fantasy. An inquiry may explore the fantastic elements such as time travel, miniature worlds, futuristic settings, and other strange happenings. Through comparing the plot, theme, characterization, setting, and style, students achieve a greater understanding and appreciation for fantasy. Other units may be developed around books with themes of peace, good versus evil, or other common fantasy ideas. Group or class charts can compare thematic development in different works.

An example of a topical study about dragons follows. We selected the topic of dragons because it can be developed with children of different ages. Additionally, most dragon books are in the fantasy genre, which is our focus. The objective of this study is to identify the element or elements of the impossible that the author created. You can extend this activity for intermediate-grade students by asking them to examine the strategy that authors use to make readers believe the impossible.

Lesson

Preview the read-alouds by asking what the children know about dragons. Show the students pictures of dragons, which you can locate in art books and from various museums' web sites. The CD-ROM *The Dragon in Chinese Art* (CDR Software ed., 1998; C/W95/ww) is also very useful.

Ask primary-grade children if they have ever discovered anything exciting on a walk or while they were playing. Ask intermediate-grade students if they have ever seen a dragon dance or a dragon in art. After discussion, read aloud *Raising Dragons* for primary-grade students and *Behold . . . the Dragons!* to intermediate-grade students.

Discussion Questions: Primary Grades

1. What is the best part of this story? Why do you think that?
2. Which character is your favorite? Why?
3. Do you think you could find a dragon egg?
4. Would you like to have a dragon of your own? Why or why not?
5. How do you know this story is make-believe (fantasy)?
6. What did you learn from this story?
7. How did the author make you like the story?
8. Art and writing:
   A. The children could draw pictures of their own dragons and dragon eggs.
   B. They could write about the things they would do with a dragon as a friend.
   C. They could draw pictures of ways that dragons could help them.
9. Music and dance: Look up "Chinese dragon dancing" on the Internet.

Books for Further Study: Primary Grades

- *Dragon School* by Cara J. Cooperman
- *Aja's Dragon* by Diane Fisher
- *Dragon Poems* by John Foster
- *Custard the Dragon and the Wicked Knight* by Ogden Nash
- *Dragon's Fat Cat: Dragon's Fourth Tale* by Dav Pilkey
- *Elvira* by Margaret Shannon
- *Chin Chiang and the Dragon's Dance* by Ian Wallace

Discussion Questions: Intermediate Grades

1. Do you believe in dragons? Why or why not?
2. Where do dragons come from?
3. What new facts did you learn from *Behold . . . the Dragons!*?
4. Why are dragons so popular?
5. Why do you think dragons are important in so many cultures?
6. What mechanical things can be compared to dragons?
7. Do you think dragons are real? Why or why not?
8. Art and music: After studying dragon dancing, have the children do a dragon dance.
9. Social studies: Discuss the types of dragons found in the art, dance, and music of different cultures. How do they differ? How are they similar? Have the children create their own artistic expressions of dragons.
10. Inquiry: Ask the students to brainstorm and come up with questions they would like to study about dragons.
11. Literature: Have the students read at least one additional book about dragons, then discuss the fantasy in the book and the writer's strategies for creating fantasy.

Books for Further Study: Intermediate Grades

- *The Dragonslayers* by Bruce Coville
- *Dragon's Milk* by Susan Fletcher
- *The Reluctant Dragon* by Kenneth Grahame
- *The Book of Dragons* by Michael Hague
- *The Dragon of Lonely Island* by Rebecca Rupp
- *The Care and Feeding of Dragons* by Brenda Seabrooke
- *Backyard Dragon* by Betsy and Samuel Sterman
- *American Dragons: Twenty-Five Asian American Voices* by Laurence Yep

---

ACTIVITY 7.4   DISCUSSION

IRA/NCTE Standards: 1, 2, 3, 5. Comprehension and oral language.

Class discussion of fantasy is important to building children's understanding and response. Through discussion, students achieve a greater understanding and appreciation for fantasy.

Instead of leading the discussion, you may prefer to participate as a group member and let the students take turns starting the discussion, using significant questions such as, "What do you think?" and "Why do you think this?" The students may have enough questions in their journals to stimulate the discussion. However, they may need help in coming up with good open-ended discussion questions such as:

- What do you predict will happen next in the story?
- What did you learn about the characters, setting, and other parts of the story in today's reading?
- What experiences of your own did you remember in relation to today's reading?
- What other books could you compare this one to?

Another approach is for students to individually complete "discussion webs" such as the one shown in the accompanying figure.

Example of a discussion web.

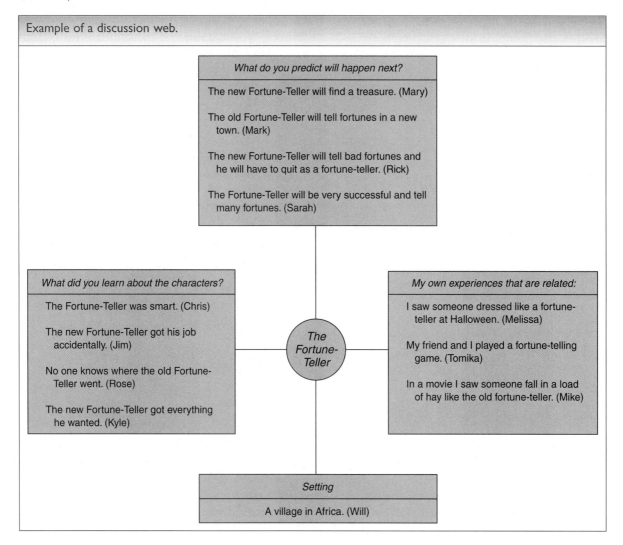

What do you predict will happen next?

The new Fortune-Teller will find a treasure. (Mary)

The old Fortune-Teller will tell fortunes in a new town. (Mark)

The new Fortune-Teller will tell bad fortunes and he will have to quit as a fortune-teller. (Rick)

The Fortune-Teller will be very successful and tell many fortunes. (Sarah)

What did you learn about the characters?

The Fortune-Teller was smart. (Chris)

The new Fortune-Teller got his job accidentally. (Jim)

No one knows where the old Fortune-Teller went. (Rose)

The new Fortune-Teller got everything he wanted. (Kyle)

The Fortune-Teller

My own experiences that are related:

I saw someone dressed like a fortune-teller at Halloween. (Melissa)

My friend and I played a fortune-telling game. (Tomika)

In a movie I saw someone fall in a load of hay like the old fortune-teller. (Mike)

Setting

A village in Africa. (Will)

Children's Literature References

Note: Books designated with an asterisk (*) are recommended for reluctant readers.

Alcock, V. (1988). *The monster garden.* New York: Delacorte. 3–4;5–6. MF

Frankie discovers an experimental matter sample that she grows into a baby monster.

Alexander, A. (2007). *The gift of the unma.* New York: Eos. 5–6;7+. MF

Thea is supposed to be magic, but she needs help to find her magic.

Avi. (2005). *The book without words: A fable of medieval magic.* New York: Hyperion. 5–6;7+. MF

An excellent example of high fantasy.

Babbitt, N. (1975). *Tuck everlasting.* New York: Farrar, Straus & Giroux. 5–6;7+. MF

Winnie Foster meets the Tucks, all of whom have drunk from the spring of everlasting life.

Babbitt, N. (2007). *The search for delicious.* New York: Farrar. 3–4;5–6. MF

The King sends people out to find a definition for "delicious."

Brooke, W. (1993). *Untold tales*. New York: Trophy. 5–6;7+. MF

Inventive retelling of familiar fairy tales.

Baum, L. F. (1987). *The wonderful wizard of Oz*. New York: Morrow. 3–4;5–6;7+. MF

The well-known story.

Berkeley, J. (2006). *The palace of laughter: The wednesday tales No.1*. 5–6;7+. MF

A humorous set of tales.

Bond, M. (1960). *A bear called Paddington*. Boston: Houghton Mifflin. K–2. MF

A bear from darkest Peru visits London.

Bunting, E. (2000). *Wanna buy an alien?* New York: Clarion. 3–4;5–6. MF

An alien is for sale in this one.

Cave, P. (2006). *Sharp north*. New York: Atheneum. 5–6;7+. MF

This story is set in the Great Britian of the future.

Coville, B. (1999). *The land of the unicorns*. New York: Scholastic. 3–4;5–6. MF

Cara has a magic amulet to protect her when she delivers a message to the queen.

Coville, B. (1995). *The dragonslayers*. New York: Pocket. 3–4;5–6. MF

Dragonslayers need training.

Dahl, R. (1964). *Charlie and the chocolate factory*. New York: Knopf. 3–4;5–6. MF

These unusual characters have vices that lead to their downfall.

D'Amico, C. & S. (2004). *Ella the elegant elephant*. New York: Levine. K–2. MF

Ella's anxious about beginning school so her grandmother gives her a magic hat.

Engdahl, S. L. (1973). *Beyond the tomorrow mountains* (R. Cuffari, Illus.). New York: Atheneum. 5–6;7+. MF

A young man is born after the Earth is to be destroyed.

Fisher, D. (1999). *Aja's dragon* (M. Levy, Illus.). New York: Mercury. K–2. MF

A bubble-blowing dragon hatches from the egg in Aja's classroom.

Fletcher, S. (1996). *Dragon's milk*. New York: Aladdin Paperbacks. 3–4;5–6. MF

These are good and loving dragons.

Foster, J. (Ed.). (1997). *Dragon poems*. New York: Oxford University Press. K–2;3–4. P

A collection of poems about dragons.

Gaiman, N. (2002). *Coraline*. New York: Harper Collins. 3–4;5–6. MF

When Coraline's family moves to another apartment, she discovers an identical family.

Grahame, K. (2004 Reissue). *The reluctant dragon*. Cambridge, MA: Candlewick. 3–4;5–6. MF

A dragon wants to be friends rather than an enemy.

Haddix, M. (1997). *Running out of time*. New York: Aladdin. 5–6;7+. MF

A young girl saves her family from a dreaded disease.

Haddix, M. P. (1998). *Among the hidden*. New York: Simon & Schuster. 3–4;5–6. MF

Families are only allowed to have two children, so they hide the third.

Howe, J. (1979). *Bunnicula* (A. Daniel, Illus.). New York: Atheneum. 3–4. MF

This book was written by a dog.

Jacques, B. (1998). *Redwall*. London, England: Ace Books. 3–4;5–6. MF

A group of mice defend Redwall from Cluny the rat.

Jones, D. (2007). *The game*. New York: Penguin. 5–6;7+. MF

Hayley is forced out of her grandparents' home. Through magic she discovers two secrets.

Key, A. (1965). *The forgotten door*. Philadelphia: Westminster. 3–4;5–6. MF

A farm family encounters a stranger who can read minds.

L'Engle, M. (1962). *A wrinkle in time*. New York: Farrar. 5–6;7+. MF

Children search for their father in an alternate universe.

Levine, G. (2006). *Fairest*. New York: Harper. 5–6; 7+. MF

The main character is not the fairest (in fact just the opposite), but she sings beautifully.

Lewis, C. S. (1956). *The chronicles of Narnia*. New York: Harper. 5–6;7+. MF

These stories have rich character and timeless themes.

Meddaugh, S. (2002). *Lulu's hat.* New York: Houghton Mifflin. 3–5. MF

Lulu is adopted by a family of magicians.

Milne, A. A. (1926). *Winnie-the-pooh* (E. H. Shepard, Illus.). New York: Dutton. K–2;3–4. MF

Classic stories of a bear who gets into great difficulties.

Mitchell, S. & Anderson, H. C. (2007). *The tinderbox.* Candlewick. K–2;3–4. MF

Mitchell tells Anderson's original story.

Newman, J. (2006). *Hippo! no, rhino.* New York: Little Brown. K–2. MF

The rhino objects to being labeled a hippo.

Paterson, K. (1977). *Bridge to Terabithia.* New York: Harper. 5–6;7+. MF

Jess and Leslie create an imaginary kingdom.

Pearce, P. (1958). *Tom's midnight garden.* Philadelphia: Lippincott. 5–6;7+. MF

Tom discovers a ghost in the garden.

Pinkwater, D. (2007). *The Neddiad.* New York: Houghton. 5–6;7+. MF

Neddie appears to be average, but he has some fantastic traveling companions.

Poole, A. (2005). *The pea blossom.* New York: Holiday House. K–2;3–4. MF

The author adapts a Hans Christian Andersen story, and the setting is China.

Roberts, G. (2005). *Dr. Who: Only human.* London: BBC Books. 5–6;7+. MF

Dr. Who looks average, but he is 900 years old and must save humanity.

Rowling, J. K. (1999). *Harry Potter and the prisoner of Azkaban.* New York: Levine. 3–4;5–6;7+. MF

Harry Potter attends the Hogwarts School.

San Souci, R. (2004). *The reluctant dragon* (J. Segal, Illus.). New York: Orchard. 3–4;5–6. MF

A dragon who doesn't want to be a dragon.

Sciezka, J. (2001). *Baloney (Henry P.).* New York: Viking. K–2. MF

Henry P. is an alien who is tardy for class.

Shannon, D. (2004). *Alice the fairy.* K–2. MF

Alice is a fairy in training.

Singer, N. (2002). *Feather boy.* New York: Delacorte. 5–6;7+. MF

Robert is kidnapped and forced into a haunted building.

Sutherland, T. (2006). Avatars book one: *So this is how it ends.* New York: Eos. 4–6;7+. MF

The beginning book of a fantasy series.

Thompson, K. (2006). *Only human.* New York: Bloomsbury USA. 5–6; 7+. MF

Christie and his stepbrother search for the missing link.

Wersba, W. (2006). *Walter the story of a rat.* Asheville, NC: Front Street. 3–4;5–6. MF

The story is told from the point of view of a rat named Sir Walter Scott.

White, E. B. (1952). *Charlotte's web.* New York: Harper.

Wilbur, the pig, and Charlotte, a spider, are friends.

Winthrop, E. (1993). *The battle for the castle.* New York: Holiday House. 3–4;5–6. MF

A sequel to *The Castle in the Attic.*

Yolen, J. (2004). *The dragon's blood: The pit dragon chronicles.* New York: Magic Carpet Books. 5–6;7+. MF

The story is set in the future. Jakkin is a bonder who must escape for freedom.

Professional References

Alexander, L. (1991). The grammar of story. In B. Hearne & M. Kaye (Eds.), *Celebrating children's books* (pp. 3–13). New York: Lothrop, Lee & Shepard.

Britton, J. (1977). The role of fantasy. In M. Meek, A. Warlow & G. Barton (Eds.), *The cool web: The pattern of children's reading.* London: Bodley Head.

Cook, E. (1969). *The ordinary and the fabulous.* Cambridge, England: Cambridge University Press.

Eisner, E. (1992). The misunderstood role of the arts in human development. *Phi Delta Kappan, 8,* 591–595.

Greenlaw, M. J. (1995). Fantasy. In A. Silvey (Ed.), *Children's books and their creators* (pp. 234–236). Boston: Houghton Mifflin.

Hearne, B. (1999). *Choosing books for children: A commonsense approach.* New York: Delacorte.

Kurkjian, C. & Livingston, N. (February, 2007). Story characters, problems, and settings. *The Reading Teacher*, *60* (pp. 494–500).

Kurkjian, C., Livingston, N., Young, T., & Avi. (February, 2006). Children's books worlds of fantasy. *The Reading Teacher*, 59 (pp. 492–503).

Langton, J. (1977). "The weak place in the cloth: A study of fantasy for children." I. P. Heins (Ed.), *Cross Currents of Criticism: Horn Book essays 1968–1977* (pp. 143–159). Boston: Horn Book.

Le Guin, U. K. (1979). National book award acceptance speech. In S. Wood (Ed.), *The language of the night: Essays of fantasy and science fiction* (pp. 60–61). New York: Putnam.

Marcus, L. (2006). *The wand in the word: Conversations with writers of fantasy.* Cambridge, MA: Candlewick.

Shlain, L. (1990). *Art and physics: Parallel visions in space, time and light.* New York: Morrow.

Whited, L. (2002). *The ivory tower and Harry Potter: Perspectives on a literary phenomenon.* University of Missouri Press.

Woolsey, D. (2002). Fantasy literature. In A. McClare and J. V. Kristo (Eds.), *Adventuring with books.* (pp. 278–297). Urbana, IL: National Council of Teachers of English.

8 People Now: Contemporary Realistic Fiction

Introduction to Contemporary Realistic Fiction

Contemporary realistic fiction and *historical fiction* (Chapter 9) both describe events, people, and relationships as they might actually happen. In these books, problems are solved through hard work, persistence, and determined efforts rather than magic, as in books of fantasy. No fantastic elements, no magical spells, and no supernatural powers appear in these types of fiction. However, we do find occasional serendipities—because truth is often unpredictable and unexpected events do impact us all. As in life, characters succeed or fail as a result of their own strengths and/or weaknesses.

Contemporary realistic fiction addresses problems and situations that could happen in today's real world. Readers can safely experience problems and tragedies—as well as the comedies—of growing up and living in the early twenty-first century. As they look at these experiences through the lens of the characters in the book, readers may be able to identify with the characters and learn from them.

Readers in middle school exhibit greater diversity than in lower grades. For instance, in teaching sixth grade, I had some girls who continued to play with Barbie dolls and others who were into make-up and boys. Therefore, their literature should reflect this diversity. As children and young adolescents read contemporary realistic fiction they have opportunities to:

- gain insights about people and events that occur in the current time;
- learn how current events may influence children and young adults;
- become aware of the similarities of the human spirit in a variety of contexts; and
- experience the ways that people have survived and learned from their challenges.

Contemporary Realistic Fiction

The challenge for writers of realistic fiction is to combine characters, contemporary events, and actions in such a way as to create a memorable story with a theme that appeals to readers. The best-written books allow readers to identify with the characters' feelings; this is done so that readers care about the characters. As authors create characters we care about, who are experiencing believable events in realistic settings, readers are drawn into seeking resolution to the problems presented. The themes that are created in this process allow readers to make connections with their lives, or the lives of others, as they read about the fictional situations.

Because readers make these connections, authors of contemporary realistic fiction must be committed to telling the truth. Fine literature portrays honest interpretations of events, characters, and conflicts. However, truth is not always obviously apparent. As Neal Shusterman (2006) says, "Truth is like the moon: even when it's full, you're really only seeing one side. You can never see all sides of the truth at once, and perhaps it's best that truth is revealed slowly, bit by bit" (p. 27). By reading books in this genre, readers have the opportunity to look at truth from a variety of vantage points.

Bushman and McNerny (2004) point out that truth or moral choices are not always easy to identify. "Trueman's teenage characters are committing armed robbery, which society correctly deems immoral. However, they are motivated to do so by a higher moral call, the desire to save their dying mother. In this case Trueman forces his readers to consider the role society plays when it denies medical care to

the poor, leading the boys to a desperate decision to commit a crime" (p. 1).

Books of contemporary realistic fiction, whether they be for primary-aged children or young adults, deal with situations that often have more than one way to resolve a problem. How characters in these books deal with difficult issues can give readers insight for recognizing and dealing with conflicts that they may face in their own lives or in the lives of someone that they know. These books can give them a vision of a better world as well as a vision of how they can be a part of changing their own world. One of the distinguishing characteristics of the best contemporary realistic fiction for children and young adolescents is the message of hope and the prospect of resolution that is presented. Life often does not turn out as we might expect but sometimes the alternatives are better than anticipated. People, especially young people, need to be able to sustain the will to live, and contemporary realistic fiction encourages positive expectations of fulfillment. "Writings for young people are about maturing in the real world. The important thing is that things do change: whatever is can be made better" (Hamilton, 1992, p. 678).

Realistic fiction does not only deal with "heavy" issues, but also includes many books with ordinary situations seen as problems by the protagonists. Authors deal with these situations sensitively and with compassion—often with a touch of humor and light-heartedness. For example, in *Agnes Parker, Happy Camper* by Kathleen O'Dell, the protagonist, Agnes, goes off to summer camp expecting to be bunk buddies with her best friend, Prejean. Instead she is paired with a girl who is *not* a happy camper. Kathleen O'Dell describes the humorous events as well as the process of changing attitudes and priorities that are a part of learning to live with a variety of people.

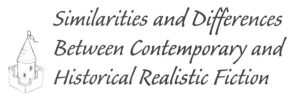

Similarities and Differences Between Contemporary and Historical Realistic Fiction

Although historical fiction and contemporary realistic fiction are different genres, they have many common features. Understanding these shared features is important if one wants to classify books into one genre or the other. Their *shared* characteristics include:

1. The plot contains events and incidents that could actually occur in the particular setting of the book. These events and incidents are possible but need not be probable (Russell, 2004).

2. The characters demonstrate both strengths and weaknesses in their actions. They are not perfect.

3. The language used is typical of the language used in the setting, either in the past or the present.

4. The theme is one that readers can relate to. They can make connections between the ideas in the book and their own lives.

Since the above characteristics hold true in well-written historical fiction and in contemporary realistic fiction, classification into one genre or the other may be difficult and depends on the reader's view. The primary *difference* between historical and contemporary realistic fiction is the setting. Historical fiction is set in a time other than the present. (See the section "When Does the Present Become the Past?" in Chapter 9.)

Values Expressed in Realistic Fiction

The values portrayed in many realistic fiction books are a concern to many parents, teachers, and librarians. Authors, of course, express values every time they write. An open marketplace of ideas encourages children to think critically and, thus, to develop their own values. The problem comes when these developing values are not ones shared by the adults around the readers. Because a few adults do not want children to read about these conflicting values, some books in this genre are challenged or even banned from being in libraries. (Challenged/banned books are discussed in Chapter 3.)

Recommended Contemporary Realistic Fiction

The categories of realistic fiction in this section have evolved from the literature itself in answer to these questions: What are the causes of the characters'

problems? What is the setting in which they are experiencing their struggles? The two primary categories that have emerged are "challenges within families" and "challenges from outside families." Within these two categories, there are, of course, several subcategories. One prevalent subcategory includes books that are labeled *series books*, many of which meet special interests held by readers of specific ages. Some of these books will be discussed later in this chapter. Another major subcategory includes books that describe children with personal challenges, such as learning problems, emotional disabilities, physical handicaps, and so forth. These books will be discussed in Chapter 12, "Literature About Children with Real-Life Challenges."

Challenges within Families

Stories grow out of authors' experiences and are greatly influenced by the times and values of the society in which they write. Taxel (1994) states, "Like other cultural artifacts, children's literature is a product of convention that is rooted in, if not determined by, the dominant belief systems and ideologies of the times in which they are created" (p. 99). Family structure in books, both past and present, gives evidence of the changing belief systems and values.

Nuclear Families

Although many families no longer consist of two parents and their children, this is still society's norm. Not surprisingly, then, we see this structure mirrored in numerous books. For many children and adults, these books confirm the belief that two-parent families are needed to provide the support necessary for growing up. Books in which the family is the focus of the story have many variations, however. They range from "happily ever after" books to those with less optimistic endings. Some of these family problems are described in the following books.

In *William's Doll*** by Charlotte Zolotow, William's family members do not understand why he wants a doll. The neighbors tease him, and he continues to get "boy" toys—but nothing dissuades him from his request. Finally someone understands—his grandmother!! She knows that he wants to practice being a dad. This classic book is as appealing now as when it was first published in 1972.

Sibling rivalry, which is common among children and especially noticeable when there is a new sibling, is the subject of Eve Bunting's *Baby Can*. When James is born and Brendan sees how his family reacts to the baby's accomplishments, Brendan demonstrates that he too is able to do everything the baby can—including burp! The author paints a realistic, humorous model of how one learns to be a big brother

Often children in large families think of themselves as disadvantaged in some way, whether they are oldest, youngest, or in the middle. Two books address the issue of being a middle child. The first is the story of an African American family in which the family members all "speak" for middle child Daisy. They let other people know what she likes and where she wants to go, rarely letting her speak for herself. When Daisy and her friend Rosa plan a sleepover, her family members must finally listen to her. This book—*Squashed in the Middle* by Elizabeth Winthrop—will be appreciated by young children who are frustrated by being a middle child.

In *Replay* by Sharon Creech, Leo is sure that being in the middle of a typical Italian family is not necessarily the best place to be. As all children do, he wants his family to be proud of him, and he fantasizes that getting a part in a school play will solve his problems. Of course his problems are not solved, but in the process, Leo discovers that there are a lot of things about his family members that he doesn't know. This is a story of a boy who tries to transform his life by using his imagination, and as he does so, he learns that there is more to life than what appears on the surface.

Having a family member in jail is a frightening situation. This is the topic addressed in *Do Not Pass Go* by Kirkpatrick Hill. Deet's father has been using drugs so that he can stay awake to work two jobs. He is then jailed for drug possession. It is a difficult situation, especially since Deet is a very judgmental person. After his mother gets a job, it is Deet who must go to the jail to visit his dad. In the process, he comes to know some of the prisoners and gains insight not only about them but about himself. He finds out that often illiteracy is a problem for many of the prisoners; in addition, Deet realizes that he is not as different as he thought he was from those for whom he previously had no respect. This book provides insight about prisons and criminals for readers.

When one thinks of bullying, it usually isn't in the context of one's family. However, for Will, a musically gifted teen in *Vandal* by Michael Simmons, his older brother is the abuser. Even after Jason returns home from serving time in a juvenile facility, he continues his destructive path. Will tries to help Jason by getting him a job in the band but even that doesn't help. Jason's behavior is devastating to the entire family and the consequences of this bullying are permanent.

Alternative Family Structures

Rather than the nuclear family structure, many children are living in families in which there are not two parents. In the past, this alternative structure was often caused by the death of a parent; this is not necessarily true today. Divorce, desertion, sexual preference, or mothers who choose to have children without being married have become more common. Homelessness, single-parent families, children raised by other family members, children whose parents are gay or lesbian, foster families, and families with stepparents are all portrayed with increasing frequency in books. The children and young people in these family structures struggle as they grow up, just as the children in two-parent families do. However, often these children may have extra responsibilities, different expectations, and circumstances over which they have no control. The ways they cope with these life conditions can give readers insights about their own lives.

Most of the characters in books that describe alternative lifestyles have some sort of adult support. Through their experiences, they develop an understanding of themselves and those with whom they interact. They realize that it may not be their family structure that causes them problems but that, instead, problems are part of daily living. Most of them learn to feel connections with both the adults and others in their environment; finding the connections is a major theme in many of these books.

Divorce

Divorce is especially hard for children to understand. After Dani's older brother dies, in *Halfway to the Sky* by Kimberly Brubaker Bradley, her parents divorce and her dad remarries. To try to forget her unhappiness, 12-year-old Dani decides to run away—to hike the entire length of the Appalachian Trail, 2,167 miles, by herself. However she barely begins when her mom finds her. Dani persuades her mom to walk part of the way, and they continue hiking for 695 miles. During this time, they come to a better understanding about themselves and their relationship with each other—and with Dani's dad and his new family. *Halfway to the Sky* is a realistic story of how attitudes and expectations can become positive, how opportunities for communication exist even when the family structure changes.

In Beverly Cleary's *Dear Mr. Henshaw*****, Leigh and his mom move to a new area after his parents divorce. It's hard for Leigh in school, at home, and with friends. In second grade, he is given the assignment to write to an author. He does so but then continues to write to Mr. Henshaw as one might write in a diary because he finds that doing so helps him come to terms with the issues in his life. *Dear Mr. Henshaw* allows readers to experience the feelings of abandonment and then acceptance of a new family situation.

Olivia Birdsall, in *Notes on a Near-Life Experience,* presents divorce as an unfortunate situation but one that, with help, can be tolerated. It comes as a shock when 15-year-old Mia's father moves out of their upper-middle-class home and moves in with another woman. Mia's mom works more, her older brother starts drinking more, and her younger sister needs more attention. Mia is challenged by the responsibility she must assume. Good things happen, however, even in this stressful situation. Mia gets a new boyfriend, and she and her dad have father-daughter "dates" as she learns to drive.

Single Parents

Single-parent families may be headed by a mother, a father, or a grandparent. Single-parent families often struggle because money and time may be in short supply. Family members may often go without things they want or need. This is the situation in *Heck Superhero* by Martine Leavitt. In this book, Heck assumes a great deal of responsibility for his mother, who has periods of extreme depression and disorientation. During one of these unstable periods, Heck's mother is unable to work, to care for him or herself, and they are evicted from their apartment. Heck is regarded by his art teacher as the best student he has ever taught—but Heck is not able to tell him about his problems for fear that someone may try to separate him and his mother. This is an engrossing novel about how a boy is able to use his inner resources to help himself and his mom. Heck believes that he is, and indeed he becomes, *Heck Superhero*.

There are now 21 "Alice" books by Phyllis Reynolds Naylor, which tell the story of Alice, whose family consists of her older brother and her single father. The books follow Alice from third grade

(*Starting with Alice)* to the summer before her junior year in high school (*Alice in the Know).* Although much of the focus of the books is on her interactions with her peers, her father and brother play significant roles in her life. For example, in *Alice on Her Way,* her father signs her up for a sexuality class at church—which actually turns out to be a good thing even though she resists going to it. Issues such as promiscuity and abuse, as well as lighter issues, give readers a glimpse that a family headed by a father does indeed "work." Her father and brother help ground her and thus she is able to achieve feelings of self-respect and self-worth. These books might be of more interest to girls than boys; other books may be more suitable for boys.

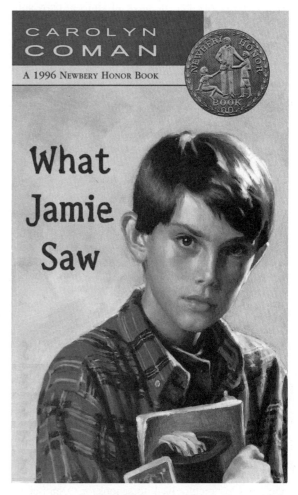

Jamie confronted violence in this suspenseful story.

Mothers sometimes need to leave abusive husbands, a subject addressed in Carolyn Coman's *What Jamie Saw.*** When Jamie wakes up in the night and sees his stepdad throw his baby sister across the room, it is time for his mother to take her two children to safety. They move to a trailer where they are constantly on the lookout for the abuser. However, with support from a battered woman's group and others, they are able to begin to get their lives together again. This sensitive book provides a picture of a family situation not often written about for younger readers.

Adoption

Eliza Thomas tells the story of adopting her daughter, PanPan, in *The Red Blanket*. The mom is so excited when she hears she has been qualified to adopt a baby girl that she buys all kinds of baby supplies, including a red blanket. When the mom goes to China to get the baby, the baby cries and cries but finally is comforted by the blanket. The blanket becomes tattered and worn but has become an integral part of their lives.

Many adoptive parents and their children are of different races. Regardless of race, what holds them together is love. *You're Not My Real Mother!* by Molly Friedrich gives lots of examples of this love in the everyday events of their lives.

In *In My Heart* by Molly Bang, a mom tells her child that throughout every day, he is always in her heart. No matter what the mom is doing, she "sees" his activities taking place. This is another story of love in a family in which the parents are blond and blue-eyed and the boy has brown skin. Author Molly Bang has created a vibrant, colorful book that children and adults will enjoy.

Children with Lesbian or Gay Parents

There is a growing number of families in which there are two parents of the same gender. Several good books have recently been published about these types of families. A typical task for a kindergarten child is to draw a picture of your family. However, when Molly does so, in Nancy Garden's *Molly's Family*, she is told by the other children that she can't have both a mommy and a mama, so she takes her picture home. When she talks about this with Mama Lu, Molly finally realizes that in her class there many kinds of families. The next day she takes her picture back to school for Open School Night. *Molly's Family* describes a situation that could happen in any alternative family structure.

Another typical task in school is to make a card for Mother's Day. When Antonio does so, in *Antonio's Card/La Tarjeta de Antonio* by Rigoberto Gonzales, he is teased because his mother's partner is a woman. He and Mami talk, and Antonio realizes that there are differences in people and in families. His family is just one variation of many. This book is one in which the text is in Spanish and English. The focus is multicultural and bilingual, rather than just a story of having two mothers.

Ken Setterington has also presented a story in which two moms are a typical family in *Mom and Mum are Getting Married*. Rosie is excited to learn that her two moms are getting married. Instead of being the flower girl, she and her brother are to carry the rings. When the rings get lost, Rosie comes up with a plan so they won't get lost again.

Blended Families

Adjustments of many kinds need to be made when families are blended. Betty Hicks, in *Out of Order*, demonstrates this in a humorous yet thoughtful way. When the mother of Lily and Parker marries the father of V and Eric, completely new family interactions are required. Lily is used to being the older daughter; now she's in the middle. V was used to taking many household responsibilities, which have now been taken over by her stepmother. Eric really misses his older brother who died, but now he has a much younger brother. Parker often makes bad decisions. Each of the chapters is told from the perspective of one of the four children as they learn to live with—and like—their new siblings.

Living with Foster Parents or Family Members Other Than a Parent

Lucky lives with her guardian, who is her father's ex-wife, after her mom dies. They live in near-poverty in the California desert. Lucky begins to worry that Brigitte is getting tired of being her guardian and decides to run away. Instead, Brigitte is trying to adopt Lucky so they will not have to be separated. This book—*The Higher Power of Lucky* by Susan Patron—is a good example of how the perceptions of adults and children are different—even if they both want the same goal.

In Glen Huser's story, *Skinnybones and the Wrinkle Queen*, foster child, Tamara, who has many problems of her own, has a required school project in which she is paired with 89-year-old rest-home resident Jean Barclay, who also has significant problems. The two of them decide that they can help each other reach their goals—a trip to Seattle for Ms. Barclay and enrolling in a modeling school in Vancouver for Tamara. They make the road trip together but each learns that their goals have not been achieved in the way that they had hoped. This story demonstrates that life does not always bring what is expected.

A very different kind of foster-care story is told in *Taking Care of Moses* by Barbara O' Connor. A baby, named Moses, is left in a box on the steps of the Baptist Church. Two potential foster mothers want him—the minister's wife and a licensed foster mother. Because the baby is black and the minister's wife is not, racial and religious issues are also part of the dilemma. The bigger problem is that 11-year-old Randall knows who left the baby, and he also knows he needs to keep the identity secret to protect his friend. Randall has a significant decision to make as he must decide what to do.

The protagonist lives with her eccentric grandmother in Mexico.

Generations of Families

In *Truth and Salsa* by Linda Lowery, 12-year-old Haley is sent to Mexico to live with her grandmother for several months after her parents' separation. While there, Haley learns a great deal about the Mexican culture and has a variety of positive experiences with her grandmother. Her grandmother is willing to take Haley on many adventures and encourages Haley to become involved with the people living in her community. Haley does so and gains a close friend as well as a great appreciation for her grandmother.

Javaka Steptoe's *The Jones Family Express* describes a closely knit family. Steven's Aunt Carolyn travels around the world and always sends him postcards from all the places she visits. Now she is coming back for the annual block party, and Steven wants to give her the perfect gift. It is difficult to find something that is perfect so he goes to his Uncle Charles's house, which is "pretty junky." Here he is able to find what he needs to create the gift. The illustrations in cut paper and a mixed-media collage create a warm, readable book.

A Tough Nut to Crack by Tom Birdseye gives readers a glimpse of three generations of a family's interactions—as well as interactions with friends and new situations. After Cassie's grandfather is in an accident, she and her widower dad go to Kentucky to help on the family farm. Her dad and her grandfather have had a feud for years: Cassie is determined to find out why and to get these two important men in her life reconciled. She finds out that the fight started because of an accusation of cheating at the game Monopoly—but that doesn't make the feud any less serious.

Samantha has to stay with her grandparents for a month while her parents are away in *Bravo Zulu, Samantha!* by Kathleen Benner Duble. Samantha's grandfather is difficult to get along with—even more so lately. Since her grandmother works, Samantha is stuck with a difficult old man every day. However, her grandfather is involved with something mysterious, and Samantha and her friend discover that he is building an airplane for a contest. Samantha becomes an accomplice, and she and her grandfather work together. This is a story of how generations of a family learn to share a common goal.

Disease of a Family Member

Alzheimer's is a disease that impacts more and more of the population as people live longer. It is hard for both children and adults to understand what is happening

Samantha is determined to discover her grandfather's secret.

the cancer, and Ida B. matures more quickly than she anticipated. In this book, Katherine Hannigan introduces readers to a young girl that many readers could be friends with. *Ida B...and Her Plans to Maximize Fun, Avoid Disaster, and (Possibly) Save the World* should become a favorite with girls.

In *The Opposite of Music*, Janet Ruth Young presents a graphic description of mental illness but also includes humorous incidents and a glimmer of hope for the future. Billy's father, an artist, is seriously depressed. He gets medical help, but that makes the situation worse, not better. The family then researches, and implements, a variety of treatments to deal with the seriousness of the father's escalating illness. The responsibilities of all family members change; for example, they need to "babysit" their father since it isn't safe to leave him alone. Billy no longer has time for his music or his friends.

Children living in a family with an alcoholic relative live with daily uncertainty. In *Spelldown* by Karen Luddy, Karlene decides that if she wins the spelling bee, she will be able to have some control over her life. When the new Latin teacher offers to coach her and makes Karlene almost a part of her family, Karlene wins not only the local spelling bees but the national one as well. Finally her father goes into rehab, and Karlene, for the first time, understands that he is proud of her, even though he has been ill. *Spelldown* shows how a young person can succeed with the help and support of others, even when there is alcoholism in his or her home.

Another excellent book for children on the subject of alcoholism is Joan Bauer's book, *Best Foot Forward*. Jenna works for Mrs. Gladstone in a shoestore that is facing a corporate takeover. Mrs. Gladstone relies on Jenna a great deal because Jenna is self-confident and competent; however she is dealing with an alcoholic father and a grandmother with Alzheimer's. Jenna attends Al-Anon to get insight into some of these issues, but she still has to deal with Mrs. Gladstone's son, who does not have the same values as his mother. Throughout the book, Jenna demonstrates maturity, insight and emotional growth.

The subject of AIDS is the focus of *Home Now* by Lesley Beake. In Africa, Sieta's parents have died from AIDS. She goes to live with Aunty but has a difficult time making the adjustment from her rural home to the village. On a field trip to the zoo, she is able to pet an orphaned baby elephant. She forms a

to loved ones who suffer from this illness. *Always My Grandpa: A Story for Children about Alzheimer's Disease* by Linda Scacco provides a good introduction to Alzheimer's and can be used as the basis for discussions about the progression of this disease. In this book, Daniel and his mom spend every summer visiting his fisherman-storytelling Grandpa. This year, however, things are different. Grandpa forgets a lot of things, and Daniel's mom says that Grandpa has Alzheimer's disease. Daniel is concerned that Grandpa may even forget who Daniel is.

In Katherine Hannigan's *Ida B...and Her Plans to Maximize Fun, Avoid Disaster, and (Possibly) Save the World*, Ida B. thinks her life is almost perfect. Her parents own an apple orchard and work in it, which leaves Ida B. with plenty of time to do all of the activities on her agenda. Then Ida B.'s mom gets cancer and their lives change dramatically. Part of the orchard must be sold to pay the medical expenses, and Ida B. acts in a mean way to the family who buys it. Mama survives special bond with the elephant after spending more time with it, and she imagines how it would be if the elephant were free. Through her interactions with the elephant, Sieta is able to see the positive aspects of living with Aunty in the village she now calls home. Lesley Beake presents Sieta in such a way that readers are able to identify with her as she observes her parents getting sicker and finally dying.

Death

In *Shelter*, Beth Cooley shows how one family emerges from a very difficult situation and is able to regain dignity. Lucy is used to attending private schools, going on expensive family vacations, and living in a big house in the suburbs. When her father dies, the family discovers that he has left many debts. They move, first to an apartment, and then to a homeless shelter. The people in the shelter are supportive, and Lucy encourages her mother to go to school so that the family can reestablish themselves.

Remembering Mrs. Rossi by Amy Hest is another good book designed to help younger readers see how one family copes with a very difficult situation. When Annie's mom, a sixth-grade teacher dies, her students create a memory book about her. Both Annie and her dad struggle as they try to adjust to life without their mom/wife. They have a difficult time understanding and accepting their loss because all of their daily routines have changed. However, they use the memory book to help remember some of the good things about her, realizing that they need to remember her but also let her go.

Nikki Grimes allows readers to experience the death of a sibling in her book, *What is Goodbye?* In a series of narrative poems, alternatively told by the two siblings left, the loss, the questions about why, and the search for understanding are shared. As the siblings also remember the good times they had together, Jerilyn and Jessie are able to come to the beginning of acceptance.

Challenges Outside the Family

As children grow up, the family—whether nuclear or alternative—may come to assume less importance while peers and other groups become more important. This change represents the children's growing need for independence. For young children, the focus of their interactions has usually been their parents, siblings, and extended family members. As they grow up, their peers, other adults, and situations outside the family are necessarily related to the issues they experience.

Many of the stories that address this changing need for independence are termed *coming-of-age* books. Coming-of-age books may be described as stories in which the characters are in the process of moving from childhood to becoming adults. They are assuming new roles, rights, and responsibilities. "All of the protagonists in these books struggle toward maturity by assuming more responsibility for themselves and their families. Coming of age also implies a search for self-definition and an exploration of several critical questions: "Who am I? Where am I going? What is my place in this world?" (Woolsey, 2001, p. 113).

Peers

In the 2006 Newbery Award winner, *Criss Cross*, Lynne Rae Perkins lets readers experience summer from the perspective of neighborhood friends who are in the process of growing up. Along with typical activities like a block party, the perpetual adolescent questions are explored: Who am I? What will be next? Is this all there is? This gentle book explores adolescence and relationships.

In *Please Write in this Book*, Mary Amato describes a strategy that makes school (and writing) fun. Ms. Wurtz starts the school year by leaving a blank journal in the writing corner; the rules for using it are to "have fun" and "sign your name." Of course, when elementary students have the opportunity to write about their peers, all sorts of things happen—feelings get hurt and unkind comments are made. At last, when the children take responsibility for their writing and choose to write a collective story, the class dynamics greatly improve. The book looks like a journal, with different kinds of handwriting and drawings.

Kirsten Smith, in *The Geography of Girlhood*, uses poetry as her writing style in this realistic account of a 14-year-old girl living with her father, sister, stepmother, and stepbrother. As Penny tries to make sense of the process of growing up, she records the events and her feelings about them. Her first kiss, her new stepmother and brother, her friendships, as well as running away with her sister's ex-boyfriend and her return—all are part of her journey through adolescence. Readers can identify with many of Penny's actions but her insights about the events make this an especially appealing book.

Bullying is never a pleasant topic but, unfortunately, it is something that happens regularly in many schools. Three books address this issue, each with a different focus. For Dexter, the protagonist in *Dexter the Tough* by Margaret Peterson Haddix, bullying happens because he is the new kid at school and he has been made fun of by some of the other students. In frustration, he punches Robin while in the bathroom. When he writes in a composition that he beat up another student, his teacher prods and pushes him to write more. When all the details come out, we learn that Dexter has recently moved to live with his grandmother in Kentucky because his dad has cancer. Margaret Peterson Haddix writes with sensitivity about the reasons for the bullying and then provides a hopeful resolution for the situation.

A very different kind of bullying takes place in *Stitches* by Glen Huser. Travis has been bullied since early elementary school because he is interested in what some of his peers consider to be girlish activities. When they are in middle school, events escalate, and Travis is almost killed. The fact that Travis is different from his peers causes him to be a scapegoat, but his differences also are his strength.

Bullying among girls is also common, especially by those girls who most popular. In *Poison Ivy* by Amy Goldman Koss, Ivy has been bullied for years. The American government teacher decides to use these incidents as a means to have the students learn about the judicial system. Through the viewpoints of several of the characters, readers see the trial unfolding in ways that the teacher did not anticipate. The book is an account of how a good-intentioned strategy may not have the desired results.

Survival

Hatchet** by Gary Paulsen is a survival book that both boys and girls will read with enthusiasm. Brian is in a small plane going to visit his father. The pilot dies and the place crashes in the Canadian wilderness. One of the last things Brian's mom gives him before the trip is a hatchet—and it is the hatchet that allows him to survive. With the hatchet, he is able to create a shelter and get food to eat.

Some people like independence and adventure. Sam Gribley, the protagonist in Jean Craighead George's *My Side of the Mountain,*** certainly demonstrates

Reading and discussing the same book increases appreciation.

those characteristics. He chooses to live by himself in a hollowed-out tree with his pet falcon and a weasel. He experiences many dangers and challenges but he is determined to make it on his own. *My Side of the Mountain* has been a favorite with readers for many, many years.

Another type of survival is described by Will Hobbs in *Crossing the Wire*. After his father dies, 15-year-old Mexican Victor Flores must work to support his family. He grows corn to sell but he learns that he will not be able to sell it for a profit because corn grown in the United States is sold more cheaply than Mexican-grown corn. When his best friend, Rico, gets money to pay the "coyotes" to help him cross the border to the United States, Victor decides he must go, too, even though he will be "crossing the wire" on his own. Victor faces death several times, but with help from people he meets and his own wits, he is finally able to get to Washington State to harvest asparagus. This is an exciting book about the perils of illegal immigration and the motivation for taking such a dangerous path.

Another book about leaving Mexico for the United States is *La Linea* by Ann Jaramillo. Miguel's father had moved north when Miguel was only 8-years-old; now on his 15th birthday, his father sends a note and instructions about how to make the journey across the border from Mexico into the United States. After a party held by his relatives, Miguel begins the dangerous journey to join his father. Death and betrayal are his constant companions on this dangerous journey.

Special Interest and Series Books

Many children develop interests during the elementary years that they retain throughout their lives; others explore a different interest each month. Whichever is true of the children you are working with, literature is a means of exploring and expanding their interests. Some of the special interests books are also series books; these books are especially popular with readers.

Sports

Many young readers are in the same kind of situation as Ty Cutter: He loves baseball, his family members are all baseball fanatics, and his dad is the coach of Ty's team. The problem is that Ty is a very poor player. In *Out Standing in My Field*, author Patrick Jennings explores Ty's feelings and Ty's interactions with his family. As the story unfolds, the team (and the readers) allow Ty to come to terms with who he really is—not who he would like to be. This insightful book examines the game of baseball from the perspective of a middle-school student who is not able to meet the expectations of his family or himself as a player.

Although the story in *Getting to First Base with Danalda Chase* by Matt Beam is set in the context of baseball (each chapter defines a baseball term), the issues raised are significant for many reasons. Darcy's friends are doing unpredictable things; his grandfather is moved to a care facility because of early Alzheimer's; and Darcy wants to date Danalda, the most popular girl in seventh grade. To do so, he gets advice from a new girl, Kamna, who will teach him about girls if he will teach her about baseball. Of course, he finds that Danalda is superficial and that he much prefers Kamna's company.

Dairy Queen by Catherine Gilbert Murdock is not only a football story but one that provides readers with respect for a person who is willing to take chances. Ever since her father was injured and her brothers went to school on football scholarships, 15-year-old D.J. Scwenk has been responsible for running the family dairy farm. During the summer, she coaches Brian, the quarterback for the neighboring high-school football team. Based on this experience, she tries out and wins a place on her high-school football team. Told in first-person narrative, D.J. is presented as a likeable, humorous teen who is able to gain insights about her family, a friend who "comes out," and her relationship with Brian.

Mysteries

David Adler has written two mysteries series for young readers. The books in the Cam Jansen series are primarily written for girls in grades 2–4 and have been very popular. The character of Cam (short for Camera because of her photographic memory) is always alert for unusual events. For example in *Cam Jansen and the Valentine Baby Mystery*, Cam recovers a stolen purse and keeps a car from being stolen. *Summer Camp Mysteries* contain three complete stories in a single book; these, too, are sure to satisfy Cam Jansen fans. The second series is more appealing to boys, the Jeffrey Bones Mysteries series. In *Bones and the Dinosaur Mystery*, Jeffrey searches for a plastic dinosaur from the museum.

Carl Hiaason has written two eco-mysteries for middle schoolers. In the first book, *Hoot*, the protagonists are trying to save a species of owls. In the second book, *Flush*, they are fighting people who are dumping sewage into Florida's waterways. Both of these well-written books provide the readers with excitement but also provide interesting factual information.

A mystery series for older students is the Bianca Balducci Mystery series by Libby Sternberg. In *Finding the Forger*, Bianca again helps her older sister solve a mystery in which there is a forgery at the museum. However, mystery is not the single focus of the book. There is also drama, romance, and teenaged relationships.

Animals

Many children are afraid of dogs. However, Daniel, in *Not Afraid of Dogs*, by Susanna Pitzer, says he just doesn't like them. When his aunt's dog, Bandit, visits, Daniel hides in his room. However, when Daniel learns that Bandit is afraid of a thunderstorm and he is not, his fear leaves and he decides that maybe he really does like dogs. Susanna Pitzer presents a realistic situation, one that younger readers can easily identify with.

Jessie Haas has written several books about horses that will appeal especially to girls in the primary grades. The most recent, *Jigsaw Pony*, is the story of twins Kiera and Fran, who care for an old pony named Jigsaw that their father brings home. The twins have to learn not only how to take care of the pony but how to get along with each other while doing so. As is true for most siblings, conflicts often arise, but they are worked out so that Jigsaw is well taken care of.

One generally doesn't think first of a crow when reading animal books. However, when author Gennady Spirin writes in *Martha* of the time his family spent with a crow with a broken wing, readers easily become involved in the story. Although advised to put the bird, Martha, to sleep, the crow is instead given a bandage, and soon she is almost a member of the family. Martha does learn how to fly again and is set free.

Summary

Contemporary realistic fiction books can be read to gain insight into one's own life or the lives of others. They can be used to convince reluctant readers that reading really is worthwhile, or they can be read just for fun. Although some of these books may include content matter that some teachers and other adults may be uncomfortable with, these books may contain the very topics some children need to read about. This is a very popular genre and one that can be utilized in all classrooms.

Thought Questions and Applications

1. Think about bibliotherapy as it was described in Chapter 3. Which of the books in this chapter might you want to read orally so that you could prepare your students for some of the tough emotional situations they may some day face?

2. How can you integrate books of contemporary realistic fiction into all of the content areas?

Research and Application Experiences

1. Choose one of the topics explored in this chapter and create a bibliography of available books. How might you use these books as you plan your reading instruction?

2. Although the books in this chapter do not include overt gender stereotyping, you decide that some of them would be more appealing to boys; others would appeal more to girls. Make a list of books (from this chapter and from other sources) that you think would be of particular interest to boys; make a similar list for girls. Now make a list of books that might be of interest to both boys and girls. Compare and contrast the books on these three lists. What are the implications for you as you choose books to use in your classroom?

3. As a primary-grade teacher, you think the David Adler books would be useful as your students are making the transition to reading chapter books. You not only want your children to read many of the different books from all of his series books, you want to study the author himself. What kinds of activities could you do for this author study? How can you integrate reading and writing in this unit of study?

Classroom Activities

ACTIVITY 8.1   CREATING BRIDGES

IRA/NCTE Standards: 1, 3, 11, 12.

In classrooms, responding to books can be part of everyday activities. Responses can be done in writing but may also involve music, art, drama, or other areas of the curriculum. Since many books of contemporary realistic fiction deal with issues that are of great importance to students, have them identify a book in which they find connections with their personal lives. Then ask them to create a bridge out of cardboard, wood, or other materials. Hanging from the bridge will be slips of paper (or halves of 3 × 5 cards). On one side of the bridge will be slips that describe events from the book; on the other side will be the personal events that are similar. At the peak of the bridge, have the students create a summary slip on which they synthesize all of the slips of paper and the connections that have been made.

ACTIVITY 8.2   READER'S THEATER

IRA/NCTE Standards: 3, 4, 9, 10, 12.

In this activity, students choose a portion of the book, such as a character's introduction, the conflict, or problem, from a book and read it dramatically. (See Chapter 14 for more description of this strategy.) In classrooms in which there are children whose first language is Spanish and English, children could read the section in either their first or second language. There are quite a few books published in which two languages are used. For example, *Antonio's Card/La Tarjeta de Antonio* by Rigoberto Gonzalez, is written in both Spanish and English. Since this is a picture book, the entire book probably would be read orally, in the Reader's Theater format. Since students in grades 5 and 6 often reject picture books, the Reader's Theater format focuses the activity.

Using Reader's Theater with older students requires a different kind of preparation. The students need to find sections of a book in which there is dialogue. Then they need to decide on the various roles individuals will take as they read. This is an opportunity for discussion and learning to work together. In *Agnes Parker, Happy Camper* by Kathleen O'Dell, there are many sections composed primarily of dialogue. Choosing the sections would allow readers to make judgments about which were the more important scenes. The discussion is also an important part of the response.

Children's Literature References

Adler, D. A. (2005). *Cam Jansen and the valentine baby mystery* (S. Natti, Illus.). New York: Viking. K–2;3–4. CRF

 Cam recovers a stolen purse and keeps a car from being stolen.

Adler, D. A. (2007). *The summer camp mysteries* (S. Natti, Illus.). New York: Viking. K–2;3–4. CRF

 Three Cam Jansen stories are in this single book.

Adler, D. A. (2005). *Bones and the dinosaur mystery* (B. Newman, Illus.). New York: Viking. K–2;3–4. CRF

 Jeffrey solves a mystery in a museum.

Adler, D. A. (2007). *Bones and the birthday mystery* (B. Newman, Illus.). New York: Viking. K–2;3–4. CRF

 Jeffrey solves another mystery.

Amato, M. (2006). *Please write in this book* (E. Brace, Illus.). New York: Holiday House. 3–4;5–6. CRF

 A teacher leaves a blank journal in the classroom for students to write in.

Bang, M. (2006). *In my heart*. New York: Little, Brown. K–2. CRF; PB

 A child is always in a mother's heart, no matter what the mom is doing.

Bauer, J. (2005). *Best foot forward*. New York: Putnam. 5–6;7+. CRF

 There are serious problems in Jenna's family and in her place of employment.

Beake, L. (2007). *Home now*. Watertown, MA: Charlesbridge. K–2;3–4. CRF; PB

 When a child's parents die from AIDS, she must live with an aunt.

Beam, M. (2007). *Getting to first base with Danalda Chase*. New York: Dutton. 5–6;7+. CRF

 Darcy's world is changing as he grows up and gets "love" advice from a friend.

Birdsall, O. (2007). *Notes on a near-life experience*. New York: Delacorte. 5–6;7+. CRF

 Children can stay close to both parents even after they are divorced.

Birdseye, T. (2006). *A tough nut to crack.* New York: Holiday House. 3–4;5–6. CRF

Cassie's dad and granddad have had a feud for years; she tries to determine why.

Bradley, K. B. (2002). *Halfway to the sky.* New York: Dell Yearling. 5–6;7+. CRF

Dani and her mom walk 695 miles of the Appalachian Trail together.

Bunting, E. (2007). *Baby can* (M. Chambliss, Illlus.). Honesdale, PA: Boyds Mills. K–2. CRF; PB

An older brother experiences jealousy when a sibling is born.

Cleary, B. (1983). *Dear Mr. Henshaw.* New York: Morrow. 3–4;5–6. CRF; New

Leigh starts writing to an author for an assignment but continues writing because it helps him come to terms with his life.

Coman, C. (1995). *What Jamie saw.* New York: Puffin. 3–4;5–6;7+. CRF; NewH

Jamie's mom moves away from an abusive husband, and the family starts over.

Cooley, B. (2006). *Shelter.* New York: Delacorte. 5–6;7+. CRF

After the death of her father, Lucy's family has serious financial problems, and they have to live in a homeless shelter.

Creech, S. (2005). *Replay.* New York: HarperCollins. 5–6,7+. CRF

Leo imagines that when he gets a part in a school play his problems will be solved. Of course they are not.

Duble, K. B. (2007). *Bravo zulu, Samantha!* Atlanta, GA: Peachtree. 5–6;7+. CRF

Samantha and her grandfather learn to work together to accomplish a major project.

Friderich, M. (2004). *You're not my real mother!* (C. Hale, Illus.). New York: Little, Brown. K–2. CRF; PB

Even when parent and child are of different races, love still abounds in their lives.

Garden, N. (2005). *Molly's family* (S. Wooding, Illus.). New York: Farrar Straus Giroux. K–2. CRF; PB

When told to draw a picture of her family, Molly draws a picture of her two mothers.

George, J. C. (1959). *My side of the mountain.* New York: Dutton. 3–4;5–6;7+. CRF; NewH

Sam Gribley lives in a hollowed-out tree with his falcon and weasel.

Gonzalez, R. (2005). *Antonio's card/La tarjeta de Antonio* (C. Alvarez, Illus.). Berkeley, CA: Children's Book Press. K–2. CRF; PB

Antonio has two mothers and is teased when he makes a Mother's Day card for them.

Grimes, N. (2004). *What is goodbye?* (R. Colon, Illus.). Los Angeles, CA: Hyperion. 5–6;7+. CRF; P

Through a series of narrative poems, two teens deal with the death of a sibling.

Haddix, M. P. (2007). *Dexter the tough.* New York: Simon & Schuster. 2–3;4–5. CRF

When the reasons for bullying are understood, remedies can be applied.

Hannigan, K. (2004). *Ida B . . . and her plans to maximize fun, avoid disaster, and (possibly) save the world.* New York: Greenwilllow. 3–4;5–6. CRF

When Ida's mom gets cancer, everything changes in Ida's very predictable life.

Haas, J. (2005). *Jigsaw pony* (Y-H Hu, Illus.). New York: Greenwillow. K–2;3–4. CRF

Twins learn to get along with each other as they take responsibility for caring for a pony.

Hest, A. (2007). *Remembering Mrs. Rossi* (H. Maione, Illus.). Cambridge, MA: Candlewick. 3–4;5–6. CRF

When Annie's mom dies, the students in her mom's sixth-grade class create a memory book that helps Annie and her dad to deal with their sorrow.

Hiaason, C. (2002). *Hoot.* New York: Knopf. 5–6; 7+. CRF

Saving a species of owls is the focus of this story.

Hiaason, C. (2005). *Flush.* New York: Knopf. 5–6; 7+. CRF

Preventing the dumping of sewage in Florida's waterways is the challenge in this book.

Hicks, B. (2005). *Out of order.* New York: Scholastic. 3–4;5–6. CRF

In a blended family, all members need to learn to make adjustments.

Hill, K. (2007). *Do not pass go.* New York: Simon & Schuster. 5–6;7+. CRF

When his father is sent to jail, Deet has a lot of growing up to do.

Hobbs, W. (2006). *Crossing the wire.* New York: HarperCollins. 7+. CRF

Victor becomes an illegal immigrant so that he can help support his family.

Hunt, I. (1976). *The lottery rose.* New York: Scribner's. 5–6;7+.

Georgie is abused by his mother and her boyfriend. He is moved to a home for boys where he will be safe.

Huser, G. (2006). *Skinnybones and the wrinkle queen.* Toronto, Ont: Groundwood. 5–6;7+. CRF

When a teenaged foster child and a rest-home resident are paired up, unexpected events occur.

Huser, G. (2003). *Stitches.* Toronto, Ont: Groundwood. 5–6;7+. CRF

Travis has been bullied since he was very young because his peers sense he is different than they are.

Jaramillo, A. (2006). *La linea.* New Milford, CT: Roaring Brook Press. 5–6;7+. CRF

Miguel's father instructs him to leave Mexico for the United States, but it is very dangerous.

Jennings, P. (2005). *Out standing in my field.* New York: Scholastic. 5–6;7+. CRF

Ty is not able to meet the expectations of his baseball-minded family.

Leavitt, M. (2004). *Heck, superhero.* Honesdale, PA: Front Street. 5–6;7+. CRF

Sometimes a child of a single parent must assume too much responsibility.

Koss, A. G. (2006). *Poison ivy.* New York: Scholastic.

A good-intentioned strategy to deal with bullying goes terribly wrong.

Lowrey, L. (2006). *Truth and salsa.* Atlanta, GA: Peachtree Publishers. 5–6;7+. CRF

Haley learns a lot when she visits her grandmother in Mexico for the summer.

Luddy, K. (2007). *Spelldown.* New York: Simon & Schuster. 5–6. CRF

Even Karlene's alcoholic father can't prevent her from winning the spelling bee.

Murdock, C. G. (2006). *Dairy queen.* New York: Houghton. 5–6; 7+. CRF

A girl earns a place on the football team.

Naylor, P. R. (2002). *Starting with Alice.* New York: Atheneum. 3–4;5–6. CRF

Alice is in third grade, living with her dad and older brother.

Naylor, P. R. (2005). *Alice on her way.* New York: Atheneum. 5–6;7+. CRF

Alice attends a sexuality class at church and discusses serious issues.

Naylor, P. R. (2006). *Alice in the know.* New York: Atheneum. 5–6;7+. CRF

This book is about Alice before her junior year in high school.

O'Connor, B. (2004). *Taking care of Moses.* New York: Foster/Farrar. 5–6. CRF

An abandoned baby causes problems for many people in the community.

O'Dell, K. (2006, Reprint). *Agnes Parker, happy camper.* New York: Puffin. 3–4;5–6. CRF

Agnes does not get the roommate of her choice at camp, which causes her distress.

Patron, S. (2006). *The higher power of lucky* (M. Phelan, Illus.). New York: Atheneum Books. 5–6;7+. CRF; New

Lucky lives with her guardian, who is her dad's ex-wife.

Paulsen, G. (1985). *Hatchet.* New York: Viking. 5–6;7+. CRF

Brian survives in the Canadian wilderness after his plane crashes.

Perkins, L. R. (2005). *Criss cross.* New York: Greenwillow Books. 3–4;5–6. CRF; New

Summer is a time for friends to get together and for growing up.

Pitzer, S. (2006). *Not afraid of dogs* (L. Day, Illus.). New York: Walker. K–2. CRF; PB

A dog that is afraid of thunder helps Daniel overcome his fear of dogs.

Scacco, L. (2005). *Always my grandpa: A story for children about Alzheimer's disease* (N. Wong, Illus.). Washington, DC: Magination Press. K–2;3–4. PB; CRF

Because Daniel's Grandpa has Alzheimer's, it changes the relationship they have always had.

Setterington, K. (2004). *Mom and Mum are getting married* (A. Priestly, Illus.). Toronto, Ont: Second Story Press. K–2. CRF; PB

> When Rosie's two moms are getting married, she finds the rings that they lost.

Simmons, M. (2006). *Vandal.* New York: Roaring Brook. 5–6;7+. CRF

> Bullying can take place in families as well as in other contexts.

Smith, K. (2006). *The geography of girlhood.* New York: Little, Brown. 7+. CRF; P

> Penny keeps a journal in verse, describing her feelings about events and actions in her life.

Spirin, G. (2005). *Martha.* New York: Philomel. K–2. CRF; PB

> Martha is a crow with a broken wing who almost becomes a member of the family.

Steptoe, J. (2003). *The Jones family express.* New York: Lee & Low Books. K–2;3–4. CRF; PB

> Steven wants to find the best possible present for his favorite aunt.

Sternberg, L. (2004). *Finding the forger.* Bancroft, IA: Bancroft. 5–6;7+. CRF

> Bianca helps her older sister solve a mystery at the museum.

Thomas, E. (2004). *The red blanket* (J. Cepeda, Illus.). New York: Scholastic. K–2. CRF; PB

> When adopting her daughter, the red blanket is what gives the child comfort.

Winthrop, E. (2005). *Squashed in the middle* (P. Cummings, Illus.). New York: Holt. K–2. CRF; PB

> Daisy learns to speak her mind when important events are coming.

Young, J. R. (2007). *The opposite of music.* New York: Atheneum. 7+. CRF

> The mental illness of Billy's father creates tension and serious problems in the family.

Zolotow, C. (1972). *William's doll.* New York: Harper & Row. K–2. CRF; PB; ALA; SLJ

> No one but his Grandmother can understand why William wants a doll.

Professional References

Brooks, G. W., Waterman, R., & Allington, R. (2003). A national survey of teachers' reports of children's favorite series books. *The Dragon Lode, 21,* 8–14.

Bushman, J. H., & McNerny, S. (2004). Moral choices: Building a bridge between YA literature and life. *The ALAN Review, 32.*

Hamilton, V. (1992). Planting seeds. *The Horn Book, 57,* 674–680.

Hosseini, K. (2003). *The kite runner.* New York: Riverhead Books.

National Center for Children Exposed to Violence: nccev.org

Parsons, L. (2005). *Bullied teacher, bullied student.* Portland, ME: Stenhouse.

Russell, D. L. (2004). *Literature for children: A short introduction.* (5th ed.). Upper Saddle, NY: Prentice Hall.

Shusterman, N. (2006). Fiction and poetry award winner. *The Horn Book, 82,* 23–27.

Swartz, L. (2006). *The novel experience: Steps for choosing and using fiction in the classroom.* Portland, ME: Stenhouse.

Taxel, J. (1994). Political correctness, cultural politics, and writing for young people. *New Advocate, 1,* 93–107.

Woolsey, D. P. (2001). Separating the men from the boys: Coming of age in recent historical fiction for children. In S. Lehr (Ed.), *Beauty, brains, and brawn: The construction of gender in children's literature.* Portsmouth, NH: Heinemann, 112–126.

9 People Then: Historical Fiction

Key Terms

fictionalized

The Great Depression

historical fiction

The Scott O'Dell Award for Historical Fiction

Guiding Questions

Historical fiction and contemporary fiction share many of the same characteristics. Regardless of the time period written about in historical fiction, young readers are able to identify with the characters because the problems faced are similar. As you read the chapter and become familiar with some of the recommended books, look for similarities between historical fiction and contemporary realistic fiction and consider how readers might be able to make connections.

1. What are some of the similarities between the problems presented in contemporary realistic fiction and those presented in historical fiction?

2. Why do you think there are so many similarities in the kinds of problems and situations presented?

3. Why might some of the books in this genre be challenged or banned?

4. What eras seem to have few books written about them? Why might this be so?

Introduction to Historical Fiction

"History is the collection of stories people tell about the past to explain the present, and the most memorable stories usually center on the actions and dreams of remarkable human beings" (Ives & Burns, 1996). *Historical fiction* is the genre in which these stories, based on historical facts, are presented. The stories, however, are *fictionalized*; in other words, they are not true but the events and actions actually could have happened. The time periods portrayed in these books were long enough ago that they cannot be considered "current." As is true for contemporary realistic fiction, no magical or make-believe elements can be used to solve problems (see Chapter 8).

The characters, although imagined, must act in a realistic manner, consistent with how individuals might have thought and acted at the time. Charlotte Huck (2001) suggests that this makes writing historical fiction particularly challenging. She uses *Caddie Woodlawn*** by Carol Ryrie Brink as an example of a story that has been criticized because Caddie doesn't act as a girl today might. Caddie is a tomboy, which was not typical for a girl living in the 1860s. As Caddie grows up, however, she gives up this type of lifestyle. Today she might continue this lifestyle but ". . . to be accepted in that society, she had to learn the ways of a lady. In writing fine historical fiction, it is essential to be true to historical facts and the mores of the culture" (p. *ix*).

The fictional characters may interact with actual historical figures, but no made-up conversations can occur with them. The setting, including the language used, must accurately represent the time period. The themes in historical fiction are similar to those in any well-written literature. They must connect with the life, dreams, and heart of the reader.

Historical Fiction

Historical fiction can help readers create bridges between their lives today and what it might have been like to live in previous time periods. As children and young adults read these books, they may be better able to understand past events and how those events have influenced life as we know it today. When reading historical fiction, it becomes obvious that many of the situations, arguments, family relationships, and outside events that occurred many years ago have basic similarities to those we are experiencing now. Siblings still argue—about the same as well as different issues; young men still go off to war—in each era a different war; and poverty, illness, and alienation still exist, and their causes may be only partially dissimilar. There is humor, joy, and happiness in both the worst and the best of conditions, whether the year is 1710, 1810, 1910, or 2010. Historical fiction, then, can be the means by which readers make connections and gain insights not only about themselves but about relationships over time.

Through these books, readers may come across ideas that are different from what they have learned from their parents or that contradict what they may have been taught in school. If readers have the opportunity to explore these ideas and discuss these contradictions, they have the chance to create new schemas and to develop new understandings of the world as it was, as it is now, and as it may be in the future. Because readers are likely to identify with the characters in historical fiction, the meaning of past events becomes more personalized and the connections between then and now are more easily made. Reading a book like *The Green Glass Sea* by Ellen Klages about the development of the atom bomb (from a child's naive perspective) during World War II allows readers to understand more clearly those times, the issues, and the impact of the bomb on lives. From

reading that book, it is not hard to make the connections with the development of current-day weapons.

If there are so many connections between historical and contemporary realistic fiction, what makes historical fiction unique? Simply stated, it is the setting and the time period. In historical fiction, the interactions among the characters must be true to the time period; the language must be the language used at the time; and the social traditions must be those that were observed in times past. To complicate it, all of factual elements must be accurate and not constructed from the mind of the author. Research is a very important part of writing historical fiction. About *Catherine, Called Birdy*, for example, author Karen Cushman says, "The people of the past are not just us in odd clothing . . . We have to look at Birdy through medieval eyes and see that she's the rebel, that she's the different one, and that she's struggling to create something that didn't really exist" (Cushman, 2001, p. 101). Presenting the characters in such a way as to have readers identify with them, being able to create the context for understanding the particular time period and setting, and developing a theme that resonates with current readers are the challenges that face writers of historical fiction.

In summary, historical fiction has additional characteristics that make it a unique genre:

1. The details describing the historical setting are portrayed so that readers can visualize the setting, characters, and events. These details must be historically accurate.

2. The actions, thoughts, conversations, and feelings accurately reflect the historical period.

3. Although actual historical events may be used, no conversations or actions of actual people can be included unless those conversations or actions can be documented.

4. There are descriptions of, or references to, historical events that are documented or events that could have occurred in the time period.

Issues in Historical Fiction

Experts do not always agree on the classification of some books in this genre. For example, should the Laura Ingalls Wilder books be considered historical fiction? Or should they be considered memoirs instead? Enciso (2000) suggests that because this series of books may actually have been co-authored by Laura and her daughter, Rose, that they should be considered memoirs. Other experts, however, may classify the Laura Ingalls Wilder books as nonfiction since many memoirs are considered nonfiction. Temple et al. (2002) classify the Wilder books as "fictionalized memoirs." "It is not surprising, then, that the line between historical fiction and nonfiction is a blurred one at best" (Enciso, p. 294).

Some of the events described in this genre are unpleasant, but they reflect real life in a particular historical era. Death and dying, cruelty and abuse, racism and sexism are integral elements of many plots. Although some adults believe that these topics are inappropriate for young readers, if those events were a part of the historical era, then to accurately portray the times they need to be included. Karen Cushman, in discussing her book, *The Ballad of Lucy Whipple*, which takes place in the 1800s, says, "Death was such a commonplace part of life at that time, especially in the wilds of this country. Women died in childbirth, miners died of pneumonia or injuries, or freezing to death. People died from eating bad food, children died frequently, doctors were far away, good medicine was not available, there were no hospitals. They could fall in the river or get hit by a falling tree. Death was really commonplace and I thought that I could not ignore it" (2001, p. 102).

On the other hand, sometimes it seems as if addressing these rather ugly issues is more acceptable in books of historical fiction than in books of other genres. Regardless of how unpleasant some events may be, however, if they were a common occurrence in the time period being written about, the issues must be included. For example, in *Yellow Star*, Jennifer Roy writes the fictionalized story of her Aunt Syvia's survival in the Lodz ghetto in Poland during the Holocaust. The book includes honest descriptions of the horrors of that place and time. Children are dragged from their parents' arms and sent to the death camps. Syvia herself experiences illness and starvation; she and her father hide in a hole in the cemetery night after night; they witness abuse and death. When the Russians liberate the ghetto, only 10 children survive this brutal time—and Syvia is one of them. She then learns of the deaths of her family members and friends. None of this is pleasant but presenting the horrors of the war is an honest and necessary depiction of these events.

Hazel Rochman (2006b) writes: "Accounts of the Holocaust must disturb. There is no happy ending. But the best books don't exploit the violence. Neither sensational nor sentimental, they tell the truth" (p. 551). The books reviewed in this chapter should do just that. The themes and events are ones that may stay with readers over time.

Not all books of historical fiction are this intense, however. In many of them, the stories describe life experiences that are associated with growing up and of relationships in families and with peers. The events are just set in a time period other than the present. In Richard Peck's *The Teacher's Funeral*, Tansy, one of the students, becomes the teacher after the regular teacher dies. This is a humorous story that provides some insights into the times (1903) and demonstrates that reading historical fiction can be fun.

When Does the Present Become the Past?

Readers of all ages are often uncertain about whether to classify some books as contemporary realistic fiction or historical fiction. Just when does the present become the past? Books that were contemporary when they were published may, over time, become historical. Children currently in the third grade think of the historical past as any time before they were born. Adults have a very different perspective about what is historical.

Many books are easy to classify as either historical fiction or contemporary realistic fiction. For example, Kathleen Benner Duble sets her book, *The Sacrifice*, in Salem in 1692 during the Salem witch trials. *F is for Freedom* by Roni Schotter takes place in 1850, before the Civil War, when many slaves were going north on the Underground Railroad. These obviously are historical fiction.

They contrast with *Beatrice Doesn't Want To*, a picture book by Laura Numeroff about a modern-day boy with a report to write and a difficult little sister who doesn't want to go to the library. Another contemporary book is *Makeovers by Marcia* by Claudia Mills, the story of an eighth-grade girl who learns that beauty isn't the most important part of one's identity. These two titles are examples of contemporary realistic fiction. Not all books are as easy to classify, however.

Various children's literature experts employ different schemes for categorizing books as historical or contemporary fiction. Some may use dates; others may use events. Temple et al. (2002) suggest that the views of the author should also be considered. Does the author think of his or her book as historical or contemporary realistic fiction? Regardless of these expert opinions, there is a relatively short period of time during which the classification is questionable. What may be the most sensible solution is to have readers decide whether a particular book is contemporary or historical. This permits them to use their experience and judgment when making the decision. As long as a reader can support a classification, it should be honored.

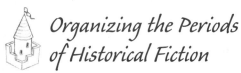

Organizing the Periods of Historical Fiction

To be most easily used, books of historical fiction need to be classified in such a way as to make them easily accessible. Readers who want to read about a particular era need to be able to quickly and efficiently find those books. However, this genre also includes many books with important themes that may not be directly related to a particular historical event; their themes are more universal in nature. For this reason, we will use a timeline as the organizational structure for the books discussed in this chapter.

During the period included in each segment of the timeline, we will include books directly related to historical events and books that focus more on universal situations. The assumption is made that readers who are looking for a specific historical event will have the knowledge, for example, that World War II occurred sometime between 1925 and 1950. Finding the historical era should not be difficult.

Historical Fiction Series Books

Recently, series of historical fiction books have been published. These works share many of the characteristics of the series books described in Chapter 2. However, there are notable differences between most of the historical series books and other series books. In many historical fiction series, the books have been written by different authors, all of whom have earned a reputation for quality writing. They are set in many different historical periods, and they do not have the same plots or the same characters. Many are written in a journal or diary format. The books are generally of great interest to students in the intermediate grades, and thus are good for reluctant readers. Series books—both those with multiple authors and those with a single author—will be reviewed here rather than in the timeline sections.

The Scraps of Time is a newer series by Patricia McKissack in which individuals in different generations of one family share their histories. In these books, African American grandchildren find artifacts in their grandmother's attic. Each artifact is the impetus for a story about a family member. The first book, *Abby Takes a Stand*, takes place in 1960 as the grandmother is involved in the Civil Rights Movement. The second, *Away West*, tells the story of the first family member who was born into freedom after the Civil War. These easy chapter books look at history from an African American perspective.

Milkweed Kids–Historical Fiction includes books from many different historical times. For example, *Hard Times for Jake Smith* by Aileen Kilgore Henderson is the story of 12-year-old MaryJake, whose parents abandon her in 1935 during the Great Depression. She makes her way to a neighboring farm and is taken in there, posing as a boy named Jake. Another book in the series, *Behind the Bedroom Wall* by Laura E. Williams, takes place during the Holocaust. *A Bride for Anna's Papa* by Isabel R. Marvin is the story of a young girl whose mother dies in 1907. She desperately wants to continue school but family responsibilities make it almost impossible. She hopes that her father will marry the school teacher. The writing style and the details provided in all of the books in this series make it easy to identify with the protagonists and to get a "feel" for the times that are presented. In addition, most of the books have won a variety of awards.

The Dear America series is written in the format of diaries of young girls who could have lived during particular times in American history. Each book in the series includes an epilogue that gives readers an idea of "what happened next"; a historical note that provides factual information about the times; and pictures of original documents, maps, and photographs. Readers can gain insight about what life might have been like for girls their own ages long ago. One of the books in this series is *Dreams in the Golden Country: The Story of Zipporah Feldman* by Kathryn Lasky. This is the story of a Jewish immigrant family from Russia, during 1903 and 1904. Another title in the series is *I Walk in Dread: The Diary of Deliverance Trembly, Witness to the Salem Witch Trials: 1691* by Lisa Rowe Fraustino, which details what it was like to see friends accused of being witches.

Another series of books, My Name Is America, has boys as the main characters. These books, like those in the Dear America series, are written in diary form, but they describe the lives of young men and boys, not girls. They also include the same kinds of notes and photographs at the end of each book. One book in this series is *The Journal of Patrick Seamus Flaherty: United States Marine Corps Khe Sanh, Vietnam 1968* by Ellen Emerson White. The book details how a young man who enlists finds out that war is awful, especially as he sees his buddies wounded or killed.

The Time Line: 1600–1750

This time period, although rich in historical events, includes relatively few recently published historical books for children and young adults. The three books that are described in this section all document the founding of Jamestown; each provides a different perspective.

In the first, *Surviving Jamestown: The Adventures of Young Sam Collier* by Gail Langer Karwoski, Sam is excited, having been chosen to be the page to Captain John Smith. Through his eyes, readers understand how unprepared the colonists are for this new life. They suffer from disease, hunger, and the harsh cold. The book includes pencil drawings of maps and illustrations of the setting. An author's note provides other facts about this endeavor.

In *Blood on the River: James Town 1607* by Elisa Carbone, Sam is a selfish boy, seeing things only from his perspective. As he learns to respect those around him, including the Natives, he begins to mature. This book presents many details about the other characters, including the scheming that takes place among them, the food, and the daily routines. Each chapter begins with a historical quotation so readers have a good sense of the places and the times.

The third book, *1609: Winter of the Dead: A Novel of the Founding of Jamestown* by Elizabeth Massie,

presents the same context but from the perspectives of two laborers who were thieves in London. They see Sam Collier as arrogant and someone who looks down on them. They experience more hardships, of course, and they see things that those in charge would obviously miss. The hardships and deprivation are especially severe for them. There are humorous incidents that make the book very readable.

The Time Line: 1750–1800

Not often do readers have the opportunity to find a book written from the Native American perspective in matters relating to various wars. However, *The Winter People* by Joseph Bruchac provides such a perspective. The story takes place during the French and Indian War, when 14-year-old Saxso tells of the raid against his Abenaki village. Saxso's mother and sisters are taken captive, and their home is destroyed. The story describes his search for the captives as well as their struggle to survive and continue their lifestyle.

There are several books and accompanying DVDs from the PBS series *Liberty's Kids*, which focuses on the American Revolution. The stories are told from the perspectives of various characters: Sarah, the daughter of a British officer; Moses, a free man of color; Henri, a boy who lives on the streets; and James, an apprentice to Ben Franklin. Two of the books, *Freedom at any Price* and *Justice for All* (by Amanda Stephens), and the accompanying DVDs (narrated by Walter Cronkite and others), present some of the most important events during 1773–1774 from the children's perspectives. Topics presented in the books include Patrick Henry's speech, the first Continental Congress, Paul Revere's ride, and many of the famous patriots, such as Samuel, John, and Abigail Adams.

During any war, each side has its own spies. In *The Scarlet Stockings Spy* by Trinka Hankes Noble, young Maddy Rose and her brother, Jonathan, have worked out a signal system so that he will know which and how many British boats are docked in the harbor; he then informs General Washington. Using red stockings and her white petticoats, Maddy Rose's information contributes to the British defeat. After Jonathan's death, she creates an American flag as a remembrance of him. This picture book can be used both with older and younger readers.

The Revolutionary War story presented in Janet Hickman's *The Valley of the Shadow*[**] provides a very different perspective of that conflict. This book is about a tribe of Native Americans who were massacred by American soldiers. This perspective is not often acknowledged or remembered.

Philadelphia was still the political and social center of the new country immediately after the conclusion of the American Revolution. During this time, sanitary conditions and medical knowledge were not well understood topics and, thus, conditions were ripe for disease. In *Fever: 1793,* Laurie Halse Anderson writes a compelling book about the yellow fever epidemic, with 16-year-old Mattie Cook telling the story. After her mother dies, Mattie and her grandfather leave the city, as do the political leaders. While they are gone, members of the African Free Society are among the only ones who give any help to those in need. *Fever: 1793* is the story of survival at a time in which survival was often questionable.

After the American Revolution, feelings were still raw from the events that took place during the war. These feelings are the focus of *Where the Great Hawk Flies* by Liza Ketchum. The family of Hiram Coombs suffers greatly from a raid by Indians, who are on the side of the British. They now have a new neighbor, Daniel Tucker, who has a Pequot Indian mother and an English immigrant father. Their cultural and language differences lead to animosity between the boys and their families. Partly because of the dignity and tolerance Daniel's healer-grandfather demonstrates, there comes resolution. The story unfolds as each boy tells of the events from his perspective. Point of view is an important aspect in the telling of the events in this book.

The Time Line: 1800–1850

The Lewis and Clark Expedition, 1803–1806, had a great impact on the expansion of this country. The youngest person who went with Lewis and Clark was a teenager named George Shannon. Kate McMullan, Shannon's distant relative, has created a fictional journal based on both family and library research. In *My Travels with Capts. Lewis and Clark by George Shannon*, the reader can see the hardships, the excitement, and the maturation of George as the group travels to the Pacific.

Marc Simmons's book, *Molly Cooper's Ride*, presents details of life at a time when every person in the community had great responsibilities. The story takes place during the War of 1812. Settlers living at

Fort Cooper on the Missouri frontier are attacked by a group of Indians, who are allied with the British. As food and supplies are depleted, the outlook is grim. A 12-year old girl rides to Fort Hempstead for help. Because of her actions, the settlers are not defeated.

A very different series of events takes place in Gloucester, Maine, in 1817, in *The Serpent Came to Gloucester* by M. T. Anderson. The story focuses on the villagers, who often see a larger-than-life creature swimming in the ocean. The sea serpent disappears when it gets cold but comes back a second year. The men in the village go to hunt it but find only a huge mackerel. The story, told in stanzas of four lines, and the illustrations give children a picture of life in a fishing village long ago.

Unscrupulous ship captains were running a brisk business of bringing Africans to this country to sell as slaves in 1818. In *Voyage of Midnight*, author Michelle Torrey depicts the brutality of slavery. Philip has been orphaned and is horrified to find that his only relative is one of these cruel, heartless ship captains. Philip has signed on as surgeon's mate on his uncle's ship and is expected to perpetuate the inhumane behavior. While on board, slaves and sailors alike get conjunctivitis; Philip recovers his sight before most of the others and is able to redirect the ship back to Africa.

Wintering Well by Lea Wait is another book set in Maine. The story, set in 1819, centers on Cassie and her farming family. When Cassie's 12-year-old brother, Will, has an accident and loses his leg, his chance for farming is gone. Cassie has the responsibility of being the caretaker for Will while he is recovering. When they move to town to live with their older sister for the summer, Will gets a wooden leg, and Cassie assists the local doctor. Both children find that they have options other than farming: Will has a talent for woodcarving, and Cassie wants to follow up with her experiences with the doctor. Details are provided about what life was like in the early part of the century.

After Josette's mother, an Ojibwe woman, dies, in Norma Summerdorf's *Red River Girl*, Josette's father is restless and moves away from the things that are most important to her. Josette had hoped to continue her education but instead she and her father join a buffalo hunt and finally move to St. Paul, where there is no school. A teacher finally comes, and Josette is able to help her with the younger children. *Red River Girl* is not only Josette's story but also gives information about the founding of St. Paul, Minnesota.

The Underground Railroad is thought to have started as early as the 1600s. We know that after the 1830s the movement of the slaves escaping to the north became more active. Before the beginning of the Civil War, there were regular "routes" that the escaping slaves followed. Three books for younger readers provide insight into these escapes. *A Good Night for Freedom* by Barbara Olenyik Morrow tells of a young white girl who accidentally sees two run-away slave girls in the cellar kitchen of Levi and Catharine Coffin. When this girl leaves the home, she meets four slave hunters who are trying to catch the slave girls, and she sends them off in another direction so the girls are not found. In *The Patchwork Quilt: A Quilt Map to Freedom,* Bettye Stroud tells the story of how Hannah and her father escape from Georgia by following secret signs sewn into quilt patterns and hiding in various places on their journey into Canada. The last of the three books, *Under the Quilt of Night* by Deborah Hopkinson, tells of the journey of a young slave girl and her family as they travel along the Underground Railroad to freedom. They, too, are in constant danger from those who are hunting them. In all three of these books, the illustrations are an integral part of the stories; they make the stories come alive for younger readers.

Harriet Tubman's name is associated with leading slaves to freedom. In *Moses: When Harriet Tubman Led Her People to Freedom,* Carole Boston Weatherford presents Tubman's source of strength and inspiration as her faith in God. The illustrations demonstrate the terror and desperation she and the other slaves experienced. The harshness of the Underground Railroad is presented honestly.

The Time Line: 1850–1900

In 1859, the largest slave auction ever was held to pay off the master's gambling debts so he wouldn't have to go to prison. Instead of writing a narrative account of this event Julius Lester, in *Day of Tears*, has created dialogue and monologues that let readers see into the minds of the characters. The story takes place over a number of years as some of the characters look back to the inhumane auction and its consequences. The characters in *Day of Tears* tell of their sadness, anger, and disbelief. This is a powerful book to read, and

because of its writing style, it would be easy to adapt to sharing in dramatic ways.

An interesting introduction to the Civil War is written by Carolyn Reeder in *Before the Creeks Ran Red*. She presents the perspectives of three 14-year-old boys, none of whom ever meet but whose actions are bridges that lead inevitably to the fighting of the Civil War. Timothy is a U. S. Army bugler at Fort Sumter at the time that South Carolina secedes from the Union; Joseph is a working-class boy who hides his family's poverty from his peers in Maryland; and Gregory's family's loyalties are divided between the north and the south. All three of them must decide what they believe and where their loyalties lie.

The Civil War, as other wars, had many boy-soldiers. In the Civil War, these young boys were often the buglers. In *The Last Brother*, Trinka Hakes Noble tells the story of Gabe, an 11-year-old who enlists so that he can look after his one remaining older brother after all of the other brothers have been killed. Gabe meets another young soldier, a Confederate, and because of this new friendship, his simplistic ideas about war change. Although *The Last Brother* is a picture book, the issues raised are ones that could be discussed by older children.

After the ending of the Civil War, former slaves often were in as much danger as they were before and during the war. *Fires of Jubilee* by Alison Hart presents what it was like to be "free" at this time. At first Abby plans to immediately leave and try to find her mother; she thinks that every other former slave should leave also. Her grandmother detains her, however, and Abby takes a much more reasoned approach to leaving as she gains insight into some of the events that preceded her mother leaving. There is still danger from patrollers as well as overt discrimination. The end of the war did not change long-held attitudes of many Americans toward former slaves.

Immigration had a great impact on the country as well as on the lives of individuals during this time period. There are many books describing the difficulties of the immigrants' trip itself as well as the hardships experienced after the immigrants arrived. Three books by Patricia Reilly Giff present the story of generations of one family. *Nory Ryan's Song* tells why Nory's family had to leave Ireland during the potato famine. Although several members of her family make the voyage to America, Nory remains in Ireland, where she becomes friends with Anna, a healer. In

MAKING HISTORICAL CONNECTIONS

The two fourth-grade classes had just returned from a field trip to the Underground Railroad Museum Center, which was one of the activities for their study of the Civil War. Before going on the trip, Miss Campbell had asked the classes to be looking for the connections between the exhibits that they saw and the books they had been reading, including Alison Hart's *Fires of Jubilee*, about the lives of several former slaves after the end of the Civil War. Now the children were talking about those connections.

Josh said, "Boy, when we read about slave hunters and patrollers, I didn't realize that it would be as scary as it was. That videoclip really made me think of what we read about in *Fires of Jubilee*. I'm glad that we don't have to worry about things like that."

Several children echoed with similar comments. Then Mr. Daly asked, "Do you think that you could create a short play about similar incidents?"

The children brainstormed for a while and agreed that they would like to create the play, using information from the books and their trip. They also wanted to share the play with the other classes at school.

The focus then changed to attention to the quilts and their role in the Underground Railroad. Martha noted that story told in *The Patchwork Quilt* supported what they saw in the Museum Center. She then suggested that since her mom quilted, perhaps she would come in and show the classes how it was done. Almost everyone wanted to learn more about quilts.

By the time the debriefing was over, the children had made many connections, they had lined up a number of follow-up projects they wanted to do, and they were eager to continue reading to find information that would support their activities. Each of the children was able to choose an activity that was of particular interest to him or her. The field trip had accomplished the objectives Miss Campbell and Mr. Daly had planned.

Maggie's Door, Nory, her little brother Patch, and her friend Sean Red Mallon make the dangerous voyage and finally arrive at her sister's home. This story, told in alternating chapters by Nory and Sean, demonstrates that simply surviving the trip on a ship took stamina and persistence. Nory and Sean's daughter is the focus of the third book, *Water Street*. Nory is a healer and midwife, and Bridgit (Bird) is her helper. Bird finds that the healing profession is one that is difficult but she, like her mother, is persistent. This book, too, is told in alternating chapters by Bird and her friend Thomas. During this time, the Brooklyn Bridge is being built, which symbolizes the hopes and dreams of the immigrants.

Another book by Patricia Reilly Giff tells the story of Dina and how much she is looking forward to moving from Germany to America to live with her uncle, whom she believes is rich. When Dina arrives, she finds that not only is her uncle not rich, but she must work harder—not only as a seamstress but also as a mother's helper—than she did in Germany. At first, Dina wants nothing more than to return to Germany but as she makes some friends, creates hats

and dresses to sell, and becomes more independent, she decides to remain in America. *A House of Tailors* gives readers insights into the illnesses, poverty, and other hardships immigrants faced.

Westward expansion was also a very great influence on people in the United States during this time period. Native Americans in all parts of the country were particularly impacted. Two books by Louise Erdrich chronicle the events of Omakayas, an Ojibwa girl living on an island in Lake Superior. In the first book, *The Birchbark House*, Omakayas is 7 years old as the white settlers are encroaching more and more on the tribal land. Nonetheless, the families try to keep their annual routines as they build a new birchbark house, and grow and harvest their gardens. One night a stranger comes to their lodge and brings smallpox— and, the lives of the tribe change dramatically. In the second book, *The Game of Silence*, Omakayas discovers that she has the gift of telling dreams. She goes off by herself and learns to accept the fate of her people, as they are forced from their homes and food supplies. This book, the winner of the 2006 Scott O'Dell Award for Historical Fiction, is provocative as readers consider the issue of expansion from the perspective of those being displaced.

In *Worth*, by A. LaFaye, 11-year old Nathaniel and his family live in Nebraska in the late 1800s, trying to make a living farming. Nate is crippled by a farm accident. When the Orphan Train comes to Nebraska, carrying children whose parents had abandoned them or had died, Nate's dad adopts one of the boys, John Worth, to do the chores Nate can no longer do. Nate is furious and makes life hard for John. However, since both boys have the goal of saving the family farm, they learn to tolerate each other and finally become friends. The power struggles between the ranchers and the farmers also help them see that they share common interests. This book was the winner of the 2005 Scott O'Dell Award for Historical Fiction.

A very different perspective on westward expansion is told in *Nothing Here but Stones* by Nancy Oswald, which tells the story of a group of Russian immigrants who settle in Cotopaxi, Colorado, in 1882. Emma, the middle child of a widower, narrates the story and tells of the great difficulties they have as they try to set up an agricultural community—crop failure, severe winters, wild animals, and isolation from their Jewish culture. Once help arrives from a Jewish group in Denver, there is a possibility of success for the families.

The Time Line: 1900–1925

The San Francisco earthquake in 1906 was a major natural disaster. Several stories have been written about the event from children's perspectives. In *Quake! Disaster in San Francisco, 1906* by Gail Langer Karwoski, Jewish immigrant Jacob Kaufman's mother has just died. He has found a stray dog but his father forbids him to keep it. As a result, Jacob is out on the street with the dog at the time the big earthquake hits. The dog saves his life and helps Jacob find others who have been buried. One of those he saves is San, a young Chinese boy. As the boys work together, Jacob begins to understand, first, how badly the Chinese immigrants are treated, and, second, how in times of great upheaval, a variety of cultural groups can learn to work together.

Laurence Yep, in *The Earth Dragon Awakes: The San Francisco Earthquake of 1906*, presents the same events but the author writes in a different format. One

Quakes occurred long ago and today.

chapter is told by 8-year-old Henry Travis; the next one by Chin, the son of the Travis's houseboy; and interspersed in the boys' first-hand accounts are informational sections about earthquakes. The friendship of the boys grows as they work together in this time of disaster.

On the opposite side of the country, young Lionel, son of Jewish immigrants, lives in New York with his family, eking out a living. Although discouraged by his parents, Lionel is constantly drawing on whatever kind of paper he can find. A teacher recognizes his talent and takes him to visit the Metropolitan Museum of Art. The visit changes his future. Sharon Reiss Baker bases this book, *A Nickel, A Trolley, A Treasure House,* on events in her family history.

The 1912 Bread and Roses strike in Lawrence, Massachusetts, is the context for Katherine Paterson's book *Bread and Roses, Too.* After Rosa's father dies, her mother and older sister have to work in the mill; to protest the unfair labor practices, they join in the strike. At school, Rosa's teacher calls the strikers uneducated and violent, which is very conflicting for Rosa. When the strike becomes more dangerous, Rosa is sent to Vermont for safety. On the way, she renews her acquaintance with a street orphan, Jake Beal, who convinces her to claim that he is her brother. She does so, and they stay together with the Gerbati family. Both learn that they must take responsibility for their actions. Readers get insight into the conditions that workers faced at that time.

A book dealing with a different social issue is *Operation Clean Sweep* by Darleen Bailey Beard. Cornelius Sanwick's father is mayor of the town when Cornelius discovers that his mother is also planning to run for mayor. In 1916, Oregon is only one of 11 states in which women can vote. Cornelius is forced to consider the issue of women's suffrage as well as his relationships with his parents. This book is based on an actual event, which makes it even more realistic to readers.

In 1918, teenagers were able to make decisions and take responsibilities that would not be possible today. One book that illustrates this is *Hattie Big Sky* by Kirby Larson. Hattie, at age 16, has lived with many different relatives since her parents died. Finally, she decides to move to the Montana homestead that she inherited from her uncle. By herself, she works hard to make the farm into a working operation, but she faces many obstacles. Hattie is lucky to have neighbors who welcome her, but because they are from Germany, others have a strong bias against them. As Hattie writes articles for the newspaper and letters to her friend Charlie who is fighting in France, readers are able to understand what it was like living on the prairie as a homesteader. *Hattie Big Sky* provides readers with details that creates a believable context for this period of time.

A book with a very different focus is *Monkey Town: The Summer of the Scopes Trial* by Ronald Kidd. In order to bring publicity to the town, Frances Robinson's father convinces John Scopes to admit that he has been teaching evolution, which is forbidden in Tennessee at the time, 1925. Frances loves her father and has a crush on John Scopes so the conflict for her is very personal. As members of the American Civil Liberties Union (ACLU), a number of famous lawyers, and many renowned journalists come in for the trial. Frances's beliefs, opinions, and feelings are seriously challenged.

The Time Line: 1925–1950

The years leading up to, and included in, *the Great Depression* were difficult for many people. In October 1929, the sharp drop in the stock market marked the beginning of sustained economic problems. Between 1929 and 1940, as many as one-third of the workforce was out of work. Not until war production started did the economy recover. This economic depression is reflected in several books for children.

An easy chapter book, *Grandma's General Store: The Ark* by Dorothy Carter, tells the story of an African American family in a segregated town in Florida. After the father loses his job and moves to Philadelphia with their mother, Pearl and Prince are left behind with their grandmother. Not only do they miss their parents terribly but there is danger from the Ku Klux Klan, the Jim Crow laws, and a hurricane. Throughout all of this, their grandmother provides the stability and safety they need as they wait to join their parents.

The Bicycle Man by David L. Dudley gives an African American perspective to this period of time. Times are hard for 12-year-old Carissa and her widowed mother. To earn a living, they do laundry for white people in their town. Because of previous experiences, Carissa's mother teaches her not to trust anyone. However, when Bailey, riding his bicycle, comes into their lives, Carissa and her mother learn to confront their past, make accommodations to it, and begin the process of moving on. The bicycle man, with secrets of his own, also faces his past and his secrets.

Another book that looks at the Great Depression from the perspective of those who are living in poverty is *The Truth About Sparrows* by Marian Hale. Sadie's father can't make a living in Dust Bowl, Missouri, so the family moves to Texas. There Sadie has many problems adjusting to others her age as well as living in a tar-paper shack. However, her parents are able to keep a positive attitude, and Sadie does have some good friends to help her through these hard times.

The segregation and the Ku Klux Klan were an integral part of the Depression. In *Mississippi Morning* by Ruth Vander Zeel, James's dad makes it perfectly clear that he does not like whites and "colored" spending time together. James, however, is friends with

LeRoy, a sharecropper's son, so when the two boys go fishing together, they go where no one will see them. When James sees his dad take off his Ku Klux Klan robes one morning, he loses respect for his dad and knows that things will never be the same between them. This powerful book story is in a picture-book format and is illustrated by Floyd Cooper. *Mississippi Morning* creates opportunities for discussion and reflection about historical events as well as family relationships.

During the Depression, President Hoover made the decision to build schools in the mountains of some of the isolated areas in the Appalachians. The impact of these schools made a great difference on the lives of people living there. One story, *Ghost Girl* by Delia Ray, tells of 12-year-old April and her eagerness to attend one of these schools. However, her mother blames April for the accidental death of her younger brother and refuses to let her attend. Only through the intervention of several people, including the teacher, is April able to attend. April also must work through her own anger and sadness as she tries to gain her mother's approval.

World War II had a lasting impact on individuals, families, politics, and most countries in the world. It is not surprising that there have been many books written for children and young adults about these events from a variety of perspectives.

One such book is Gloria Wheelan's *Summer of the War*. Summer is a special time—especially if you are going to spend the summer on an island in Lake Huron with your grandparents while your parents work in Detroit to support the war effort. Belle and her three siblings have looked forward to this—but then their sophisticated cousin comes to stay because the cousin's mother has been killed and her father is in Washington. There is tension, disappointment, and frustration because of the differences in expectations and past experiences. Author Gloria Whelan creates a picture not only of 1942 but of relationships among family members who are in crisis. *Summer of the War* presents opportunities for many connections with current events.

Elise Weston, in *Coastwatcher*, has written an interesting mystery that presents information about World War II. Because polio was a true danger in the 1940s, Hugh's parents, like many at the time, took him out of the big city, where he might encounter the disease. The entire family moves to the South Carolina shore for the summer. While there, Hugh spends much time on the beach looking for enemy submarines. Most of those around him make fun of his endeavor, even when he sees what he believes is a periscope in the ocean. Of course, Hugh is right, and he prevents a plot to destroy the Charleston Naval Base.

Being a Japanese American during World War II was a harrowing experience. Cynthia Kadohata, in *Weedflower*, describes the experiences of Sumiko and her family as they are moved from their Southern California flower farm to an internment camp in Arizona. The camp is on land taken from the Mohave reservation, so there is also conflict with the natives. As Sumiko matures in this setting, she is able to gain a sense of community as she makes friends with a Mohave boy, has a garden, and makes other new friends. Prejudice is confronted in many events in this book.

Flowers from Mariko by Rick Noguchi and Deneen Jenks is the story of a young Japanese American girl and her family who have to live in an internment camp after the bombing of Pearl Harbor. Mariko's father is a gardener and assumes he will continue this after their release, but he then finds that his truck and materials had been sold. Even though the family has to live in a dismal trailer park, Mariko plants a small flower garden, which gives them hope that things will soon be better. Indeed, they find some gardening equipment, and Mariko's father is able to start his business again.

All Japanese Americans did not have the same reactions to the atrocious treatment given to them by other Americans and by the U. S. government. Although David Patneaude's book, *Thin Wood Walls*, is told from the perspective of 11-year-old Joe Hanada, other views are given. For example, to show his patriotism, Joe's older brother enlists in the Army and fights in Europe; others in the internment camp don't want their children to speak English; still others request repatriation to Japan. Joe finds some relief from the boredom of confinement as he writes both narrative and poetry. The prejudice and hardships endured by those who were confined are well documented in this book.

The African American squadron of pilots known as the Tuskegee Airmen gained a reputation for competence and success. They boasted that they had not lost a single plane that they were escorting. Angela Johnson's book *Wind Flyer*, with illustrations by

Loren Long, lets young readers have a snapshot of how one man's desire to be a pilot is successful. The narrator tells about how his great-great-uncle, whose interest in flying begins when he is only 5 years old, becomes a *Wind Flyer*.

One of the lesser known groups of soldiers involved in the World War II were the Navajos, who were recruited by the Marine Corps. These soldiers were responsible for communications among various branches of the armed services in Japan because, using their native language, they had an unbreakable code. *Code Talker* by Joseph Bruchac is written in the format of a story being told to grandchildren, so there is ample description of the Navajos' time in school settings, of how the code talkers gained the trust and respect of those in command, and their feelings and insights about their contributions on the battlefields. Not until 1969 were the code talkers able to talk about their experiences; this information was classified until computers began to be used for communication. After that, the code talkers were given medals and were recognized by the government.

Europe was obviously disastrously impacted by World War II. Stories of resistance and the coping strategies adopted by residents of many countries provide insight about human survival. In *The Greatest Skating Race: A World War II Story from the Netherlands*, Louise Borden writes of the bravery of three children in Holland. The father of Johanna and Joop has been arrested, and the safety of the children is in question. Piet, a 10-year-old who is a skating fan, helps the children escape by skating with them on the frozen canals to Belgium where they will be safe. On their trip, they have to be aware of the German soldiers and find ways to avoid being caught. *The Greatest Skating Race* is a good introduction to this time period for younger children.

Karen Hesse has written a book of narrative poetry also set in Europe during World War II. In *The Cats of Krasinski Square*, a few Jews escape from having to live in the ghetto in Poland. They plan to sneak food into those still confined by passing food through holes in the wall. The Gestapo try to foil this humanitarian aid effort by bringing in dogs that will find the food. However, the residents gather the cats that have been abandoned, and the cats distract the dogs so that the food can be delivered. This story will appeal to all ages.

Andrea Cheng

Marika is a young girl in Budapest during the 1930s.

Another book, *Marika* by Andrea Cheng, is based on the author's mother's life growing up. Living in Budapest in the 1930s, Marika's family, although of Jewish heritage, is living as Roman Catholics. Although the family celebrates Christian holidays and goes to mass, their heritage is not forgotten. As the unrest of the war heightens, Marika experiences many instances of bigotry. When the Nazis occupy Poland, she assumes the identity of the Catholic niece of one of the family's friends.

The Time Line: 1950–1975

The time period from 1950 to 1975 includes many events that have changed the way people live and interact today. Two of the most influential events of this era are the Civil Rights Movement and the Vietnam War.

Segregation and the Civil Rights Movement

For many African Americans living in the south, opportunities for advancement were lacking. For this reason, many families packed up and moved north. In Janice Harrington's *Going North*, Jessie's family has planned their move to Lincoln, Nebraska, for some time, leaving Jessie with ambiguous feelings. She will miss her extended family but she begins to understand why the move is necessary. As the family travels north, they can stop only at gas stations and stores that serve African Americans. *Going North* is based on the author's family's experiences.

Freedom on the Menu: The Greensboro Sit-ins by Carole Boston Weatherford is a good introduction to the Civil Rights Movement. Like many mothers and daughters on a shopping trip, Connie and her mother like to go to Woolworths for a cool drink. Because of the Jim Crow laws, however, they must stand as they drink their sodas. Connie often complains that there are places she can't go and things she can't do. However, after Dr. Martin Luther King, Jr. comes and speaks in the chapel in Greensboro, her family gets very much involved in the NAACP. Connie's siblings participate in the lunch-counter sit-ins, and changes finally do come to their city.

Many of the complex issues of integration are made evident in *Yankee Girl* by Mary Ann Rodman. Alice Ann's father, an FBI agent, is sent to Jackson, Mississippi, to protect the civil rights workers and those who are trying to register to vote. When Alice Ann starts school, she must make some decisions about joining the "in" group or being kind to African American classmates and neighbors. Her father is under attack from various groups, including the Ku Klux Klan, and as the school is integrated, the situation becomes more and more difficult. Middle-school readers of this book will have much they can identify with even if the events described happened in 1964.

The Vietnam War

During the **Vietnam War**, many families, groups, and politicians did not agree about this country's involvement in Vietnam. *Summer's End* by Audrey Couloumbis presents complex emotions including anger, sadness, forgiveness, and love. Shortly after the Kent State shootings, Grace's brother, Collin, burns his draft card. The family erupts into dissension, similar to the dissension about the war typical in the country at large. Collin is thrown out of the house, and his parents fight over the issue. Grace is able to escape some of the tension by going to her grandmother's farm, where she is able to receive support. When an uncle dies, the family begins the process of coming back together, accepting the fact that families don't always agree about issues.

A very different book about Vietnam is a picture book for older readers: *Patrol: An American Soldier in Vietnam* by Walter Dean Myers. A young American soldier is in the jungles of Vietnam, looking for the enemy; what he sees is an old woman and man, the beauty of the natural environment, and a young man much like himself. Implicitly, this book raises lots of questions about war and those people who are involved both directly and indirectly. It would be a good discussion starter in classrooms.

Other Events of this Period

Although the Civil Rights Movement and the Vietnam War are the events of this era with the most books written about them that will be of interest to children and young adults, there were other issues occurring as well, such as the treatment of the mentally ill.

Ann M. Martin's book, *A Corner of the Universe* is a portrait of growing up in the 1960s, when mental illness was dealt with by sending the person to an institution. Mental illness is often as difficult to deal with in a family as physical illnesses. When Hattie's Uncle Adam comes home after living in an institution for most of his life, the dynamics of her entire family change. Because of Adam's often inappropriate behavior, Hattie's grandparents are ashamed of him. Hattie's parents are kind but they know how unpredictable he can be. Hattie seems to be one of the few people who respects him. After Adam hangs himself, Hattie divides her life into "Before Adam" and "After Adam."

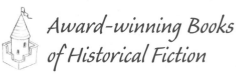

Award-winning Books of Historical Fiction

In 1982, *The Scott O'Dell Award for Historical Fiction* was established. Its purpose is to encourage writers to focus their writing on this genre. All of the books that have won this award are highly recommended. Several of them have been reviewed in this chapter. Many books of historical fiction have also won the Newbery Award. Patricia MacLachlan wrote a series of books about a family living in the prairie in the late 1800s. The first, *Sarah, Plain and Tall*[**], won both the 1987 Newbery and Scott O'Dell awards. The most recent book, *More Perfect than the Moon*, continues with the family saga. There are other books in this series, also. This series is also available in audiocassettes from Digital.

Summary

Historical fiction books are enjoyed by most people because of the connections readers can make between their lives and the lives of people who lived in other times and places. We can relate to the characters' problems, joys, and sorrows because these are the feelings of the human condition. In addition, teachers find this to be a very useful genre because there are so many connections that can be made to the curriculum.

Teachers should exercise care, however, and inform parents when choosing these books. Some of them depict events and conditions that may be considered violent, racist, or stereotyped. Parents can be involved in classroom activities, such as listening to and discussing the ideas in the books with their children.

Research and Application Experiences

1. Explore ways that social studies and historical fiction could be integrated in the curriculum.

2. What are some of the themes that occur most often in books of historical fiction? Hypothesize why this might be so.

3. Take a book of historical fiction and one from contemporary realistic fiction. Using a Venn diagram, compare and contrast the settings in each.

4. Identify your favorite books of historical fiction. Why are they your favorites?

Classroom Activities

ACTIVITY 9.1   VIETNAM WAR: COMPARE AND CONTRAST: FICTION AND INFORMATIONAL BOOKS

IRA/NCTE Standards: All standards can be accomplished because there is a wide variety of books and activities involved.

Many historical events are so complicated that it is difficult for students to see the big picture and the relationships with groups of people and other events. The Vietnam War is one of these complex events. What may help middle-school students to understand the nuances related to the war would be to read a selection of informational books and fictional accounts. As students read in these different genres, they are able to make connections that they can document in writing, performance, or other kinds of responses.

Informational Books about the Vietnam War (Rochman, 2006a).

> *African Americans in Vietnam* by Diane Canwell and Jon Sutherland
>
> *10,000 Days of Thunder* by Philip Caputo

The Vietnam War: A Primary Source History by Andrew Mason

Vietnam War Battles and Leaders by Stuart Murray

Escape from Saigon by Andrea Warren

The Valiant Women of the Vietnam War by Karen Zeinert.

Historical Fiction Books about the Vietnam War

> *Amaryllis* by Craig Crist-Evans
>
> *Song of the Buffalo Boy* by Sherri Garland
>
> *Fallen Angels* by Walter Dean Myers
>
> *LiLun, Lad of Courage* by Carolyn Treffinger

ACTIVITY 9.2   POINT OF VIEW

IRA/NCTE Standards: All standards can be accomplished because there is a wide variety of books and activities involved.

Books of historical fiction offer opportunities to view events and happenings from more than one perspective. For example, when studying the Civil War period, most people assume that all slaves would be happy to be free. Although this was probably true for many, others may have been unsure about what the future held for them. Read books like those written by Mildred D. Taylor (*The Friendship, Song of the Trees*) or Alison Hart (*Fires of Jubliee*) and try to find a variety of perspectives about what it meant to be "free." Other books in different genres, such as informational books or poetry, can also offer insights about being free at that time in history. Activities to follow the research may include debates, readers' theater, writing poetry, or dramatic presentations. A data collection chart may be used to help collect information.

Focus of study: freedom of the slaves after the Civil War.				
Book	fact/idea found	fact/idea found	fact/idea found	fact/idea found
1.				
2.				
3.				
4.				

Children's Literature References

Anderson, L. H. (2000). *Fever: 1793*. New York: Aladdin. 5–6;7+. HF

A book about yellow fever, which was rampant in Philadelphia after the Revolutionary War.

Anderson, M. T. (2005). *The serpent came to Gloucester* (B. Ibatoulline, Illus.). Cambridge, MA: Candlewick. K–2;3–4. HF; P

Maine villagers regularly see a large creature swimming offshore.

Baker, S. R. (2007). *A nickel, a trolley, a treasure house* (B. Peck, Illus.). New York: Viking. K–2;3–4. HF; PB

The life of a young immigrant boy is forever changed when his teacher takes him to the Metropolitan Museum of Art.

Beard, D. B. (2004). *Operation clean sweep*. New York: Farrar, Straus and Giroux. 3–4;5–6. HF

Both Corneilius's mother and father run for mayor of the town.

Borden, L. (2004). *The greatest skating race* (N. Daly, Illus.). New York: Margaret K. McElderry. K–2;3–4; 5–6. HF; PB

Children skate to safety in Holland to avoid capture by the Germans.

Brink, C. R. (2005, reprint). *Caddie Woodlawn*. New York: Aladdin. 3–4;5–6;7+. HF; New

Tomboy Caddie is an atypical girl in 1864, as she and her brothers have many adventures.

Bruchac, J. (2002). *The winter people*. New York: Dial. 5–6;7+. HF

During the French and Indian War, an Abenaki village is destroyed.

Bruchac, J. (2005). *Code talker*. New York: Dial. 5–6;7+. HF

Navajos are recruited to do communications during World War II.

Carbone, E. (2006). *Blood on the river: James Town 1607*. New York: Viking. 5–6;7+. HF

Sam Collier is the page to John Smith during the settling of Jamestown.

Carter, D. (2005). *Grandma's general store: The ark*. New York: Farrar, Straus and Giroux. K–2;3–4. HF

A grandmother provides safety and stability after the children's parents move north to find work.

Cheng, A. (2002). *Marika*. Asheville, NC: Front Street. 3–4;5–6;7+. HF

A family of Jewish heritage assumes the characteristics of being Catholic during World War II.

Couloumbis, A. (2005). *Summer's end*. New York: Putnam. 5–6;7+. HF

Grace's brother burns his draft card, which causes dissension in the family.

Cushman, K. (1994). *Catherine, called Birdy*. New York: Clarion. 5–6;7+. HF; NewH

The daughter of an English nobleman rebels against the regulations of the medieval times.

Cushman, K. (1996). *The ballad of Lucy Whipple*. New York: Clarion. 5–6;7+. HF

Lucy's widowed mother moves her family to take part in the Gold Rush.

Duble, K. B. (2005). *The sacrifice*. New York: Margaret K. McElderry/Simon & Schuster. 5–6;7+. HF

A story during the time of the Salem witch trials.

Dudley, D. L. (2005). *The bicycle man*. New York: Clarion. 5–6;7+. HF

Carissa and her widowed mother begin to learn to trust again after they befriend Bailey, who comes into town on his bicycle.

Erdrich, L. (2002, reprint). *The birchbark house*. New York: Hyperion. 3–4;5–6. HF

Omakayas is 7 years old as the white settlers begin to encroach on the tribal lands.

Erdrich, L. (2005). *The game of silence*. New York: HarperCollins. 3–4;5–6. HF; SO

Omakayas discovers she has special powers as her tribe is forced from their lands.

Forbes, E. (1943). *Johnny Tremain*. New York: Houghton Mifflin. 5–6;7+. HF; New

A Revolutionary War story told by one of Paul Revere's apprentices.

Fraustino, L. R. (2004). *I walk in dread*. New York: Scholastic. 3–4;5–6. HF

Friends are accused of being witches during the Salem witch trials.

Giff, P. R. (2000). *Nory Ryan's song*. New York: Delacorte. 5–6;7+. HF

Nory remains at home even though her family immigrates because of the potato famine.

Giff, P. R. (2003). *Maggie's door*. New York: Random House. 5–6;7+. HF

Nory, her brother, and her friend make the dangerous journey to the United States.

Giff, P. R. (2004). *A house of tailors*. New York: Random House. 5–6;7+. HF

Dina moves from Germany to live with her uncle. She works harder than she did before, as a seamstress.

Giff, P. R. (2006). *Water Street*. New York: Random. 5–6;7+. HF

Nory's daughter follows in her mother's footprints and becomes a healer.

Hale, M. (2004). *The truth about sparrows*. New York: Henry Holt. 5–6;7+. HF

Sadie's family moves from Missouri to Texas during the Dust Bowl.

Harrington, J. (2004). *Going north* (J. Lagarrique, Illus.). New York: Farrar, Straus, Giroux. K–2;3–4; 5–6. HF; PB; P

Jessie's family moves from the south to Nebraska because there are more job opportunities.

Hart, A. (2003). *Fires of jubilee*. New York: Aladdin. 3–4;5–6;7+. HF

After the Civil War ends, many former slaves are unsure about what to do with their lives.

Henderson, A. K. (2004). *Hard times for Jake Smith*. Minneapolis, MN: Milkweed. 3–4;5–6. HF

A 12-year-old girl is abandoned by her parents during the Depression.

Hesse, K. (2004). *The cats in Krasinski Square* (W. Watson, Illus.). New York: Scholastic. K–2;3–4; 5–6. HF; P; PB

Cats are used to distract dogs when citizens sneak food to Jews living in a ghetto.

Hickman, J. (1974). *The valley of the shadow*. New York: Atheneum. 5–6;7+. HF

A tribe of peaceful Native Americans is massacred during the Revolutionary War.

Hopkinson, D. (2005, reprint). *Under the quilt of night* (E. Ransome, Illus.). New York: Aladdin. K–2;3–4. HF; PB

A slave family travels the Underground Railroad to freedom.

Johnson, A. (2007). *Wind flyers* (L. Long, Illus.). New York: Simon & Schuster. K–2;3–4. HF; PB

A story of the Tuskegee Airmen, African American pilots in World War II.

Kadohata, C. (2006). *Weedflower*. New York: Atheneum. 5–6;7+. HF

Sumiko and her family are moved to an internment camp during World War II.

Karwoski, G. L. (2001). *Surviving Jamestown: The adventures of young Sam Collier*. Atlanta, GA: Peachtree. 5–6;7+. HF

Readers see Jamestown being settled through the eyes of Sam, page to Captain John Smith.

Karwoski, G. L. (2004). *Quake! Disaster in San Francisco, 1906* (R. Papp, Illus.). Atlanta, GA: Peachtree. 3–4;5–6. HF

Jacob finds a stray dog that saves his life and helps find others who are buried in an earthquake.

Ketchum, L. (2005). *Where the great hawk flies*. New York: Clarion. 5–6;7+. HF

At the conclusion of the Revolutionary War, former enemies have a hard time learning to live as neighbors.

Kidd, R. (2006). *Monkey town: The summer of the Scopes trial*. New York: Simon and Schuster. 5–6;7+. HF

Frances's father brings publicity to the town when he gets John Scopes to admit that he is teaching evolution.

Klages, E. (2006). *The green glass sea*. New York: Viking. 5–6;7+. HF; SO

Dewey's dad is working on a secret project, which she finds out is the atomic bomb.

Larson, K. (2006). *Hattie big sky*. New York: Delacorte. 5–6;7+. HF; NewH

Hattie is an orphan who tries to homestead her uncle's Montana property.

LaFaye, A. (2004). *Worth*. New York: Simon and Schuster. 5–6;7+. HF; SO

After Nate's farm accident, his dad gets an Orphan Train boy to help with the chores; this causes great problems.

Lasky, K. (2003). *Dreams in the golden country*. New York: Scholastic. 3–4;5–6. HF

The diary of a Jewish immigrant girl in 1903–1904.

Lester, J. (2005). *Day of tears*. New York: Jump at the Sun/Hyperion. 5–6;7+. HF

Reflections about the largest slave auction ever held.

Lowry, L. (1989). *Number the stars*. New York: Houghton Mifflin. 5–6;7+. HF; New

A Danish family is part of the Resistance efforts.

MacLachlan, P. (1986). *Sarah, plain and tall*. New York: HarperCollins. 3–4;5–6. HF; New; SO

A mail-order bride comes to live with a dad and his two children.

MacLachlan, P. (2005). *More perfect than the moon*. New York: HarperCollins. 3–4;5–6. HF

When Sarah becomes pregnant, the entire family is happy.

Martin, A. M. (2002). *A corner of the universe*. New York: Scholastic. 5–6; 7+. HF

Hattie's mentally ill uncle comes back home to live, which causes many problems.

Marvin, I. R. (2004, reprint). *A bride for Anna's papa*. Minneapolis, MN: Milkweed. 3–4;5–6. HF

Anna hopes her widower father will marry the school teacher.

Massie, E. (2007). *1609: Winter of the dead* (P. Casale, Illus.). New Milford, CT: Tor Teen. 5–6; 7+. HF

Two teenagers are taken to be laborers during the settlement of Jamestown.

McKissack, P. (2005). *Abby takes a stand* (G. James, Illus.). New York: Viking Juvenile. 3–4. HF

Abby is involved in the Civil Rights Movement.

McKissack, P. (2006). *Away west* (G. James, Illus.). New York: Puffin. 3–4. HF

The story of an African American born into freedom.

McMullan, K. (2004). *My travels with Capts. Lewis and Clark by George Shannon.* New York: Cotler/HarperCollins. 5–6;7+. HF

Teenager George Shannon is the youngest person to travel with Lewis and Clark.

Mills, C. (2005). *Makeovers by Marcia.* New York: Farrar, Straus and Giroux. 5–6;7+. CRF

An eighth grader learns that beauty isn't the only virtue that is important.

Morrow, B. O. (2003). *A good night for freedom* (L. Jenkins, Illus.). New York: Holiday House. K–2;3–4. HF; PB

When slave hunters ask for information, a young girl sends them off in the wrong direction.

Myers, W. D. (2002). *Patrol: An American soldier in Vietnam* (A. Grifalconi, Illus.). New York: Harper Collins. 5–6;7+. HF; PB

A young soldier in Vietnam raises questions about his mission.

Noble, T. H. (2004). *The scarlet stockings spy* (R. Papp, Illus.). Chelsea, MI: Sleeping Bear Press. 3–4;5–6. HF; PB

A young girl and her soldier brother work out a secret communication system during the Revolutionary War.

Noble, T. H. (2006). *The last brother* (R. Papp, Illus.). Chelsea, MI: Sleeping Bear Press. 3–4;5–6. HF; PB

The story of an 11-year-old bugler in the Civil War.

Noguchi, R., & Jenks, D. (2001). *Flowers from Mariko* (M. R. Kumata, Illus.). New York: Lee and Low. K–2;3–4. HF; PB

After the Japanese internment camp, Mariko's family had great financial difficulties.

Numeroff, L. (2004). *Beatrice doesn't want to* (L. Munsinger, Illus.). Cambridge, MA: Candlewick. K–2. PB; CRF

A little sister makes it difficult for her older brother to get his report done.

Oswald, N. (2004). *Nothing here but stones: A Jewish pioneer story.* New York: Henry Holt. 3–4;5–6. HF

A group of Russian immigrants tries to create a Jewish community in Colorado.

Paterson, K. (2006). *Bread and roses, too.* New York: Clarion. 5–6;7+. HF

Rosa's mother and sister are involved in the mill strike; Rosa is sent to Vermont for safety.

Patneaude, D. (2004). *Thin wood walls.* New York: Houghton Mifflin. 5–6;7+. HF

Eleven-year-old Joe Hanada writes of the prejudice and hardships experienced in a Japanese internment camp.

Peck, R. (2004). *The teacher's funeral: A comedy in three parts.* New York: Dial. 5–6;7+. HF

When the regular teacher dies, an older student becomes the teacher that year.

Ray, D. (2003). *Ghost girl: A Blue Ridge mountain story.* New York: Clarion. 5–6;7+. HF

During the Depression, April's mom does not want her to attend school because she blames April for the death of her brother.

Reeder, C. (2003). *Before the creeks ran red.* New York: HarperCollins. 5–6;7+. HF

Three separate stories tell of the times and events just before the Civil War begins.

Rodman, M. A. (2004). *Yankee girl.* New York: Farrar, Straus and Giroux. 3–4;5–6. HF

Alice Ann's dad is an FBI agent sent to Mississippi to protect civil rights workers.

Roy, J. (2006). *Yellow star.* Tarrytown, NY: Marshall Cavendish. 5–6;7+. HF

Syvia was one of only 10 children who survives in the Lodz ghetto during World War II.

Schotter, R. (2000). *F is for freedom.* New York: Scholastic. 3–4;5–6. HF

A story about slaves going north on the Underground Railroad.

Simmons, M. (2002). *Molly Cooper's ride* (R. Kil, Illus.). Albuquerque, NM: University of New Mexico Press. 3–4;5–6. HF

A brave young girl rides for help during the War of 1812.

Speare, E. G. (1973). *The witch of Blackbird Pond.* New York: Dell. 5–6;7+. HF; New

Being accused of doing witchcraft was dangerous in Salem.

Stephens, A. (2003). *Liberty's kids: Freedom at any price*. New York: Grosset & Dunlap. 3–4;5–6. HF

> Four young people are involved in Revolutionary War events.

Stephens, A. (2003). *Liberty's kids: Justice for all*. New York: Grosset & Dunlap. 3–4;5–6. HF

> Four young people are involved in Revolutionary War events.

Stroud, B. (2005). *The patchwork path: A quilt map to freedom* (E. S. Bennett, Illus.). Cambridge, MA: Candlewick. K–2;3–4. HF; PB

> Escaping slaves follow the directions in quilts as they make their way to Canada.

Summerdorf, N. (2006). *Red River girl*. New York: Holiday House. 5–6;7+. HF

> After Josette's mother dies, her restless father moves; finally they are part of a group of people who found St. Paul.

Taylor, M. D. (1987). *The friendship*. New York: Dial. 3–4;5–6. HF

> The long-term friendship between an elderly black man and a white store keeper ends in an unexpected way.

Taylor, M. D. (1975). *Song of the trees* (J. Pinkney, Illus.). New York: Dial. 3–4;5–6. HF

> A white man tries to force a rural black family to sell the valuable trees on their property.

Torrey, M. (2006). *Voyage of midnight*. New York: Knopf. 5–6;7+. HF

> Philip is horrified to learn that his only relative runs a slave ship in 1818.

Vander Zee, R. (2004). *Mississippi morning* (F. Cooper, Illus.). Grand Rapids, MI: Eerdmans Books. 3–4;5–6. HF; PB

> James has his world turned upside-down when he discovers his dad is a Ku Klux Klan member.

Wait, L. (2006). *Wintering well*. New York: Aladdin. 5–6;7+. HF

> A farming accident causes Cassie's brother to lose his leg; the family's lives are drastically changed because of this.

Weatherford, C. B. (2005). *Freedom on the menu: The Greensboro sit-ins* (J. Lagarrigue, Illus.). New York: Dial. K–2;3–4. HF; PB

> Connie's family becomes involved in the Civil Rights Movement.

Weatherford, C. B. (2006). *Moses: When Harriet Tubman led her people to freedom* (K. Nelson, Illus.). New York: Jump at the Sun. K–2;3–4. HF; PB; CalH; CSK

> An account of how slaves escaped with the help of Harriet Tubman.

Weston, E. (2005). *Coastwatcher*. Atlanta, GA: Peachtree. 3–4;5–6. HF

> Hugh prevents a plot to destroy a naval base during World War II.

Whelan, G. (2006). *Summer of the war*. New York: HarperCollins. 5–6;7+. HF

> Belle and her siblings stay with their grandparents while their parents work during World War II.

White, E. E. (2002). *The journal of Patrick Seamus Flaherty*. New York: Scholastic. 5–6;7+. HF

> The journal of a young soldier in Vietnam.

Williams, L. E. (2005). *Behind the bedroom wall*. Minneapolis, MN: Milkweed. 3–4;5–6. HF

> A Holocaust story.

Yep, L. (2006). *The earth dragon awakes: The San Francisco earthquake of 1906*. 3–4;5–6. HF; INF

> Two boys become friends as they work together during the aftermath of the earthquake.

Other Resources

Liberty Kids DVDs, narrated by Walter Cronkite and others. United American Video.

> *Give me liberty* (2005)
> *The first Fourth of July* (2002)
> *The Boston Tea Party*, vol.1. (2002)

Professional References

Cushman, K. (2001). Author profile, in *Beauty, brains, and brawn: The construction of gender in children's literature,* Susan Lehr, ed. Portsmouth, NH: Heinemann, 99–103.

Enciso, P. E. (2000). *Historical facts and fictions: Representing and reading diverse perspectives on the past. The New Advocate, 13,* 279–296.

Huck, C. (2001). Introduction. In *Beauty, brains, and brawn: The construction of gender in children's literature,* Susan Lehr, ed. Portsmouth, NH: Heinemann, vii–xi.

Ives, S., & Burns, K. (1966). Introduction. In D. Duncan, *People of the west* (pp. vi–viii). Boston: Little, Brown.

Rochman, H. (2006a). *The Vietnam war: Facts*. *Booklist, 102*, 16, p. 63.

Rochman, H. (2006b). *Beyond oral history*. *Hornbook, LXXXII*, p 547–551.

Temple, C. Martinez, M., Yokota, J., & Naylor, A. (2002). *Children's books in children's hands*. Boston: Allyn and Bacon.

10 Truth Is Stranger than Fiction: Nonfiction

Introduction to Nonfiction

What Is Nonfiction?

Nonfiction, informational writing, and *exposition* are synonyms for text that is written to convey information, to impart facts, and to explain. Informative text comprises most of the reading material in classrooms, the workplace, magazines, and on the Internet sites we access. Tony Stead (2002) examined the kinds of content that students commonly encounter and found that 80 percent is nonfiction. Today's children will have to read and understand massive amounts of information throughout their lives.

Information drives our society, giving nonfiction an important role in any examination of children's literature. Today's nonfiction for children is exciting and creative. It is well-written, well-researched, has attractive layouts, and addresses a wide range of subject matter. Nonfiction authors comb archives, look at documents, gather photographs, interview, research topics on the Internet, and read books in order to piece together their own work. In writing *The Great Fire*, Jim Murphy gathered information about the Chicago fire from letters, journals, published accounts, and other sources. To breathe life into this information, he wrote about the fire from the points of view of four individuals (Jensen, 2001).

Another indication that nonfiction is assuming a place of greater prominence in the world of children's literature is evidenced by the growing number of awards for nonfiction. The Horn Book Graphic Gallery competition honors outstanding nonfiction books for excellence in design. The National Council of Teachers of English bestows the Orbis Pictus Award to an outstanding children's nonfiction book each year, and the American Library Association honors nonfiction with the Sibert Medal.

Winners in the Nonfiction Genre

Nonfiction literature should be a model of quality writing that engages children's interests; after all, nonfiction is a work of art, just as poetry and fiction are works of art. Nonfiction authors create interesting, stimulating text using rich, vivid language. Writers'enthusiasm for their subjects should be apparent in their writing style and use of detail. The contrast between quality nonfiction and ordinary writing is illustrated in these passages from a textbook and a trade book:

Textbook

"So the Pilgrims decided to look for a place where they could have their own church and also live as English men and women.

After thinking about a number of places, the Pilgrims decided to go to North America. . . ."

In 1620, about a hundred people crowded onto a small ship called the Mayflower" (McAuley & Wilson, 1987, p. 69).

Trade book

"The Sparrowhawk's crew set sail from London in hopes of reaching Jamestown, Virginia. Amongst the 26 passengers, mostly Irish servants, were Masters Fells and Sibsey. I was indentured to Captain Sibsey by my unscrupulous uncle. On November 6 our ship crashed in fog on what the captain told us was a New England shore" (Bowen, *Stranded at Plimoth Plantation, 1626,* p. 1).

Values of Nonfiction

Informational books provide up-to-date facts. Students can explore timely topics such as Hurricane Katrina, which is the topic of *Hurricane Katrina Strikes the Gulf Coast* by Mora Miller. Nonfiction authors present this topic in ways that children can comprehend, increasing their awareness of issues as they impinge on the global community.

Informational books make readers aware of problems that can occur when they lack a full understanding of the possible issues. Mary Batten reveals some examples of this in *Aliens from Earth*. She identifies aliens as plant and animal species that came from outside; sometimes, these species create serious and ongoing problems in the environment. For instance, kudzu is an example of an alien plant that was deliberately introduced in the United States. Unfortunately, kudzu grew much faster in the southern United States than it did in Japan. In fact, kudzu grows a foot a day in the south where it damages forests.

Why do animals and plants invade the United States?

Expands Background Knowledge

Through wide reading on content area topics, children learn associated concepts and terms. Nonfiction books present topics in greater depth and detail than textbooks. Social studies textbooks tell facts about Hitler, but nonfiction trade books can provide readers with depth and context. For example, James Cross Giblin's compelling narrative, *The Life and Death of Hitler*, traces his rise and fall. Another perspective on Hitler is provided in *Hitler Youth: Growing Up in Hitler's Shadow* by Susan Bartoletti. *The Cat with the Yellow Star: Coming of Age in Terezin* by Susan Rubin and Ela Wiessberger provides the perspective of Jewish captives in a prison camp. *Always Remember Me: How One Family Survived World War II* by Marisabino Russo is the story of a Polish Jewish family that moves to Germany for a better life and is caught in the war. This true story tells about invasion, internment in a concentration camp, survival, death, and coming to America. Nonfiction gives children a rich context for understanding many aspects of a certain time, place, animal, person, or event, thereby enhancing their schemata. Frequently, trade books can be used to introduce topics that are in the students' textbooks.

Promotes Exploration

A good book simulates direct experience—it makes a child want to go out and experience the observation or discovery firsthand (Harvey, 1998). Many of today's nonfiction books for young readers promote firsthand discovery by explaining how to participate in particular activities through clear, easy-to-follow directions. For example, Stephen Kramer's *Hidden Worlds: Looking Through a Scientist's Microscope* provides easy directions for a variety of fascinating experiments to guide children as they examine fingerprints, dollar bills, and crystals with a magnifying glass. As students read nonfiction, they develop a basis for organizing ideas and writing in the nonfiction genre. For example, Albert Marrin's *Dr. Jenner and the Speckled Monster: The Search for the Smallpox Vaccine* traces the history of smallpox, including its weapon potential. The author includes books to read and web sites. A topical book like this will stimulate children to read and write about their interests.

Nonfiction books summarize and organize information. In *Give Me Liberty! The Story of the Declaration of Independence,* Russell Freedman chronicles the events associated with the writing and signing of this document. He includes a detailed description of the role of the militia, as well as that of ordinary citizens. Another related book is *The Signers: The 56 Stories Behind the Declaration of Independence* by Dennis Fradin. This book includes interesting materials related to the Declaration of Independence, as well as a replica of it. Christopher Manson's book, *Uncle Sam and Old Glory: Symbols of America*, explains each of these symbols in detail. The text is informative, interesting, and serves as a springboard to further reading. The Internet also provides excellent sources related to the Declaration of Independence and the Bill of Rights.

Types of Nonfiction

Informational books appear in a variety of formats: concept books, nature identification books, life-cycle books, experiment and activity books, books derived from original documents and journals, photographic essays, and reference books and periodicals. Picture books are plentiful in this genre. Nonfiction books focus on many subjects, including the arts, animals,

---

CLASSROOM SNAPSHOT

USING NONFICTION BOOKS IN THE CLASSROOM

After a workshop about nonfiction, Jan Miller, the second-grade teacher in an inner-city school, decided to delve into nonfiction with her class. The workshop leader had cited research that concluded that literacy instruction in schools concentrates on fictional texts (Venezky, 2002). Another researcher found that in the classrooms she observed only 3.6 minutes per day is devoted to informational books (Duke, 2000).

Jan collected nonfiction related to her classroom studies for reading aloud to her students. She chose *May I Pet Your Dog?: The How-to Guide for Kids Meeting Dogs (and Dogs Meeting Kids)* by Stephanie Calmenson, because the local community had concerns about dangerous dogs and dogs running loose.

She introduced the book by asking, "How many of you have a pet dog?" Rob answered, "I have two dogs."

Then Mary said, "My grandma has a little poodle."

Chris raised his hand and answered, "My dog barks a lot and likes to play with me and my sister."

Jan then asked, "Do you ever see strange dogs?"

Chris continued, "Where I live we see them all the time and my Mom said to stay away from them."

Jan replied, "That is good advice, and I chose a book for our read-aloud that tells about meeting dogs." She held up the book, so the children could see the photographs; then she read the book aloud while showing the pictures.

The children were very interested, and after she completed the book, the children dramatized the behavior *they should exhibit* when meeting dogs and how to help friends meet their dog.

On the following day, she read the book again and asked the children if they knew why dogs wag their tails and why they bark. After a lively discussion the children drew pictures of how they would act when they meet a dog. The next day, she read *Is My Dog a Wolf? How Your Pet Compares to Its Wild Cousin* by Jenni Bidner.

mathematics, manmade objects, language, sex, the life cycle, and every other topic imaginable.

Concept Books

Concept books explore both concrete and abstract ideas to develop conceptual understanding. *Seeds* by Ken Robbins, for example, is illustrated with photographs that show many different kinds of seeds and how seeds are dispersed and grow. This book is an excellent introduction to planting seeds, an activity that first-grade teachers often do as a science project with students. The children can take photographs of their seeds and create photo essays. This project gives teachers the opportunity to introduce cameras and photography. Sometimes older students will assist the teachers in projects like this.

Stars Beneath Your Bed: The Surprising Story of Dust by April Sayre and Ann Jonas is an elegant picture book that introduces the concept of dust. The author shows how it travels and how it stays with us through time. The author's poetic language presents the story of dust. She explains that the dusty film on your computer screen might have muddied a dinosaur. This book is so interesting that you won't be able to put it down. The author provides excellent documentation and the illustrator, Ann Jonas, uses watercolor to create impressionistic pictures.

Joy Cowley's *Chameleon, Chameleon* is a picture book for primary-grade children who are developing a concept of chameleons. Nic Bishop's colorful illustrations contribute to children's understanding.

Nature Identification Books

These books help students identify leaves, plants, animals, ocean life, and so forth.

The latest science information is in trade books.

Life-Cycle Books

Life-cycle books explain and illustrate the life cycles of animals, insects, and so forth. For example, *The Prairie Builders: Reconstructing America's Lost Grasslands* by Sneed Collard documents the restoration of the prairie ecosystem. The project to reconstruct grasslands found and introduced the growth of plants and reintroduced the regal fritillary butterfly to re-create America's tall grass prairies. Children will learn about the complex web of plants and animals comprising the ecosystem.

Pandas are fascinating animals that attract large audiences at zoos throughout the world. However, they are among the most endangered species in the world. John Butler illustrates the beauty and wonder of these exotic creatures with exquisite paintings in *Pi-shu the Little Panda*. Butler's text follows the growth and development of a baby panda. Pi-shu began life as a very tiny baby, just four inches long, and he grew into a large bear.

Experiment and Activity Books

Experiment and activity books, another category of nonfiction, provide children with hands-on exploration of a variety of concepts. Such books may include safety precaution statements, lists of sequential steps to follow, lists of required materials or equipment, and illustrations of the finished projects. A good example

Pi-shu's mother teaches him to eat bamboo.

of this type of book is Vicki Cobb's *You Gotta Try This! Absolutely Irresistible Science*, which includes several dozen experiments with observations and clear warnings about potential problems.

Books Derived from Original Documents and Journals

Books derived from research involving original documents and journals interest children because of their authenticity. Dennis Fradin's *The Signers: The 56 Stories Behind the Declaration of Independence* provides a reference for the Declaration of Independence based on original documents. Students will find *Ben Franklin's Almanac: Being a True Account of the Good Gentleman's Life* by Candace Fleming very interesting. The author uses a scrapbook structure to narrate Franklin's life and anecdotal boxes to highlight various events. Fleming uses Franklin's words along with period engravings and documents.

Onward: A Photobiography of African-American Polar Explorer Matthew Henson by Dolores Johnson is technically a biography, but it is also an important historical document. Henson was the first person to reach the North Pole, but he did not receive recognition until 2001. Prior to that time he was considered Peary's servant, and Peary received the recognition for reaching the North Pole first. The author uses photographs from the original exploration to illustrate the book, and Henson's face on the cover is striking.

Reference Books and Periodicals

Reference books are on disks and and online, so they are readily available to students. For example, Encarta has thousands of online encyclopedia articles, and Encyclopedia Brittanica can be downloaded from a disk.

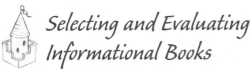

Selecting and Evaluating Informational Books

Certain qualities distinguish excellent informational books from mediocre ones. First and foremost, the best informational books make us think. Facts abound in our information-dense world, but books that make

readers think are uncommon. The qualities of excellent nonfiction include: thought-provoking text; text that raises questions; literary style; technique; and the authority of the author, as well as the accuracy, appropriateness, and attractiveness of the book.

Interesting, Thought-Provoking Text

Interest is an important factor in the quality of nonfiction. Writers select topics that are interesting to themselves and that will generate students' interest. Authors such as Bryn Barnard must be amazingly creative to think of topics like *Outbreak: Plagues That Changed History*. Everyone who reads this book will learn surprising information. For example, "In Japan, tuberculosis was thought to be lovesickness." Bryn Barnard not only researched the text, but he researched the illustrations to ensure accuracy. He identifies his sources and includes a glossary in *Outbreak*. This information should be included in all quality nonfiction.

Jim Murphy's *An American Plague: The True and Terrifying Story of the Yellow Fever Epidemic of 1793* is well documented and offers another perspective on plagues and their impact on history. Studying these books will provide students with an opportunity to compare two outstanding authors of nonfiction.

Nonfiction Raises Questions

Fine nonfiction raises questions in readers' minds, thereby leading them to make connections to other topics and experiences. Moreover, it encourages readers' curiosity and wonder (Jensen, 2001). An example of a book that raises questions in readers' minds is *Let It Begin Here! Lexington and Concord: First Battles of the American Revolution* by Dennis Fradin. In this book, the author explains that the citizens of Lexington were unprepared for the British attack, but that the overconfident British were surprised when the residents of Concord were prepared and forced the British to retreat. This is an excellent introduction to the American Revolution. This book immediately raises questions about the lack of preparation for the British and how the defeat at Lexington could have been avoided.

Style

Literary style refers to a subtle concept—the author's use of language, which is sometimes called voice.

Nonfiction prose should engage readers with a distinctive, interesting voice. Informational texts are written in narrative style, expository style, or a combination of the two. Many primary-grade nonfiction books are written in the narrative style because young children learn best from this style.

Factual accuracy and currency are very important, but rich language, appropriate terminology, and an interesting, stimulating style bring topics to life (Jensen, 2001). To achieve this, authors combine factual information with literary devices. A concise style that presents facts in simple, direct language is appropriate for most informational books. Nonfiction authors use correct terminology and do not talk down to their readers.

Nonfiction is organized with headings and subheadings, and technical vocabulary is identified. Frequently, photographs, drawings, charts, and graphs are included to make content clear to readers. Clearly organized text enables children to understand the author's presentation of information. An author may organize the text by moving from the familiar to the unfamiliar, moving from the general to the specific, or through a question-and-answer format. A common organizational pattern is presenting facts in chronological order.

Bibliographic data, which includes tables of contents, indices, glossaries, appendices, and lists of related readings, help children understand the information presented. These aids can help readers locate specific information within a book. Effective bibliographic aids provide the starting point for gathering additional information on a particular topic.

Technique

Authors often use the journalistic device of a "hook" to capture children's interest. Sally Ride and Susan Okie take readers into space in *To Space & Back*. They begin the book with "Launch morning. 6 . . . 5 . . . 4 . . . . The alarm clock counts down. 3 . . . 2 . . . 1 . . . . Ring! 3:15 A.M. Launch minus four hours" (Ride & Okie, p. 14). The countdown, juxtaposed with the alarm-clock ring, draws children's interest. It also relates the unfamiliar countdown with the familiar ring of an alarm clock.

Catherine Thimmesh uses a somewhat different approach in *Team Moon: How 400,000 People Landed Apollo 11 on the Moon*. She captures readers' interest through identifying the many individuals who were responsible for landing Apollo 11 on the moon. This detailed presentation answers questions that puzzle would-be astronauts and makes them aware of the many professionals who are involved in space exploration.

Authority

The author's qualifications for writing an informational book are usually given on the back flap of the book jacket or the book itself. Readers can also consult reviews in journals such as the *Horn Book, Language Arts, Book Links*, and the *Bulletin of the Center for Children's Books* to learn more about an author's expertise.

Accuracy

Accuracy is essential in nonfiction. Clear, correct, and up-to-date facts and concepts are the hallmarks of fine children's nonfiction, and illustrations, diagrams, charts, maps, and other material in the book should meet these requirements as well. Checking the copyright date will help determine the currency of information. Accuracy of information can be checked with a recent encyclopedia or a current textbook. I recently skimmed a book about the solar system that was incorrect due to the fact that new information became available after the book was in print. Authors must distinguish between theories and facts and make it clear that various points of view exist regarding controversial subjects.

Appropriateness

The concept of appropriateness in informational books encompasses several issues. Excellent informational books suit their audience. The literary style corresponds to the subject and the audience for which the book is intended. Information should be presented in a way that readers can relate to. Also, the information should not be disturbing to readers. In *Rescues*, author Sandra Markle has written an appropriate book for her audience. She interviewed survivors and rescuers of 11 disasters, including avalanches, coal mining accidents, capsized sailboats, stranded mountain climbers, and a tsunami. With vivid narrative and photographs the author introduces relevant information. She creates suspense while chronicling what people in various positions were doing to respond to the emergency situation.

Attractiveness

Attractiveness or appeal is important to children, who are more likely to pick up an attractive book. Television and videos have conditioned children to respond to visual images and fast-paced information with dramatic impact. Illustrations prepare readers to understand the text while photographs add a sense of direct reporting and authenticity. Nonfiction illustrations range from photographs to paintings to line drawings.

Leonard Everett Fisher (1988), who has illustrated many nonfiction books, explains his goal when illustrating books. He gives students a visual understanding of a concept, instead of merely presenting a fact. He goes on to say:

> I am trying to present a factual mood. The Tower of London, for instance, is a creepy place, and if I can establish the creepiness of the place so that the youngster gets an unsettled feeling about the tower . . . I'm trying to create the emotion of the history, the dynamics of history, together with the facts of history. I'm trying to communicate what events in history felt like. (p. 319)

Nonfiction in the Classroom

Reading nonfiction aloud establishes children's familiarity with this genre and enables them to read with confidence. Read-alouds help children learn to read and write informational materials (Duthie, 1994; Stoodt & Amspaugh, 1994). Research shows that students who lack background with nonfiction have more difficulty comprehending *exposition* (nonfiction) and are less sensitive to important information in the text. When reading nonfiction, children do not have characters to follow through the story. In general, the elements of fiction hold a story together, while nonfiction is generally explaining concepts, main ideas, and relevant details.

Exploring a theme or topic through trade books permits students to discover the connections among the types of knowledge belonging to particular domains; for example, fiction, poetry, and nonfiction convey meaning in different ways. Recognizing these differences increases fundamental understanding of science, social studies, mathematics, art, and music. Nonfiction literature has distinct benefits in developing students' learning (Shanahan, 1992).

Trade Books and Science

What makes a good science trade book? Accuracy, first and foremost, is essential (Ford, 2002). After researching for accuracy to ensure error-free text, authors use their writing skills and design talents to create a high-quality science text. *ER Vets: Life in an Animal Emergency Room* by Donna Jackson is a high-quality science book. In this book, readers learn about the kinds of emergencies that occur to animals and the various treatments.

Mosquito Bite by Alexandra Siy is a book that most of us can relate to. Mosquito bites make our skin itch, and some mosquitos carry the West Nile disease, which infects animals and people; therefore, knowing more about mosquito bites can help everyone.

Each year the *Science Teacher* publishes Outstanding Science Trade Books for Children, a list selected by a committee from the National Science Teachers Association. A number of excellent authors write science trade books: Aliki, Caroline Arnold, Jim Arnosky, Joanna Cole, Russell Freedman, Jean Craighead George, Patricia Lauber, Laurence Pringle, and Seymour Simon, to name but a few. To get a sense of what makes a science trade book outstanding, read some of the titles discussed in this chapter or select books by the authors listed above.

For a list of other high-quality titles, search the following online sources:

> Internet Science Resources: http://school.discovery.com/sciencefaircentral/
>
> Internet Public Library: http://www.ipl.org/youth/projectguide/
>
> The World Wide Web Virtual Library: http://vlib.org

Trade Books and Social Studies

Milton Meltzer (1994), a master of nonfiction, not only believes that disasters of nature (hurricanes, floods, droughts) and of human society (Vietnam, the Holocaust, poverty) are worthy of attention as causes of suffering to human victims, but that all children will encounter fundamental problems of race, class, and tyranny in their lifetimes—and so should prepare for these problems by reading about such things. An example of this challenge is presented in *Forbidden Schoolhouse: The True and Dramatic Story of Prudence*

Crandall and Her Students by Suzanne Jurmain, the story of African Americans' struggle for education.

Literature contains all the great stories of humanity and helps students develop a sense of history, a sense that the past influences the present, and a sense that various cultures each contribute in an important way to the global society. *Global literature* reflects the global community in which we all live and helps students understand the relations in their immediate environment and in the world. Nonfiction trade books create an awareness of society and culture that reaches beyond mere facts.

A diverse collection of books is listed in the "Notable Children's Trade Books in the Field of Social Studies," titles selected each year by the National Council for the Social Studies in conjunction with the Children's Book Council. This listing appears in *Social Education*. One award-winning book is *Secrets of a Civil War Submarine: Solving the Mysteries of the H.L. Hunley* by Sally M. Walker. This is a fascinating book for history buffs and will be of particular interest to those studying the Civil War.

Guidelines for selecting picture books for the social studies are shown in Figure 10.1.

Trade Books and Mathematics

Nonfiction trade books can be an important avenue for promoting talking and writing in the mathematics classroom. Literature helps readers see the relationship between mathematics and their lives (Whitin & Whitin,

2002). Math makes more sense when it is functional and purposeful, as it is in the following books:

Anderson, L., *Tea for Ten*

Brown, R., *Ten Seeds*

Hoban, T., *Let's Count*

Markle, S., *Discovering Graph Secrets: Experiments, Puzzles, and Games Exploring Graphs*

Schmandt-Besserat, D., *The History of Counting*

Schwartz, D., *Millions to Measure*

Tang, G., *The Best of Times: Math Strategies that Multiply*

Tang, G., *The Grapes of Math: Mind-Stretching Math Riddles*

Zaslavsky, C., *Number Sense and Nonsense*

Trade Books and the Language Arts

All literature enhances the language arts; however, nonfiction has specific values. Books like the following enhance the language arts:

Agee, J., *Palindromania*

Agee, J., *Who Ordered the Jumbo Shrimp? And Other Oxymorons*

Heller, R., *Behind the Mask: A Book About Prepositions*

Heller, R., *Merry-Go-Round: A Book About Nouns*

Parr, T., *The Feelings Book*

FIGURE 10.1   Picture books for social studies.

Guideline	Example
The text and illustrations should appeal to readers.	Osband, G., & Andrew, R. (1991). *Castles*. New York: Clarion.
The facts and information are accurate, authentic, and current.	Towle, W. (1993). *The Real McCoy: The life of an African-American inventor* (W. Clay, Illus.). New York: Scholastic.
The content extends the social studies topic under study.	Burleigh, R. (1991). *Flight* (M. Wimmer, Illus.). New York: Philomel.
The illustrations are accurate.	Cherry, L. (1992). *A river ran wild: An environmental history*. San Diego: Harcourt Brace Jovanovich.
The book is free of stereotypes.	Myers, W. D. (1999). *At her majesty's request: An African princess in Victorian England*. New York: Scholastic.
The language is rich and clear.	Bruchac, J., & London, J. (1992). *Thirteen moons on turtle's back* (T. Locker, Illus.). New York: Philomel.
The book motivates further reading, thinking, and studying.	Ancona, G. (1999). *Charro: The Mexican cowboy*. New York: Harcourt.

Trade Books and the Arts

A wide range of trade books is available to promote children's interest in the arts. Through the arts, children learn to create their own visions of things by carving, painting, dancing, singing, and writing (Greene, 1992). A list of suggested books follows:

> Chertok, B., Hirshfeld, G., & Rosh, M., *Learning About Ancient Civilizations Through Art*
>
> Jenkins, J., *Thinking About Colors*
>
> Prokofiev, S., *Peter and the Wolf*
>
> Ryan, P. M. *When Marian Sang: The True Recital of Marian Anderson: The Voice of a Century.*
>
> Turner, R., *Portraits of Women Artists for Children: Mary Cassatt*

Summary

Nonfiction and informational literature are synonyms. The majority of reading in school and outside of school is nonfiction. Therefore, nonfiction in the classroom is very important. Fortunately, children's nonfiction books are interesting because they answer children's natural questions about the world around them. Nonfiction trade books include a wide variety of well-written, interesting nonfiction. Informational books are accurate, up-to-date, and include references and documentation. Nonfiction builds background information for topics in textbooks that students are studying in classrooms. Children comprehend nonfiction better when they have opportunities to hear it read aloud, as well as to read it themselves.

Thought Questions and Applications

1. Why do you think nonfiction is not available in many classrooms?

2. Why is it important to read nonfiction aloud?

3. How does a nonfiction author ensure accuracy and authenticity in a work?

Research and Application Experiences

1. Compare three informational books on the same topic. What are the differences in the facts presented? What are the similarities?

2. Identify a topic you would like to know more about. Then identify the types of information you would collect about the topic. Create a data chart for the topic.

3. Read a nonfiction book and write a synopsis of it. Then evaluate it and list the standards you used. What were the book's strong points? What were its weak points?

4. Prepare a booktalk for a nonfiction book you enjoy. Give the booktalk to a group of children or to a group of classmates.

5. Find a nonfiction author on the Web and learn why he or she chooses to write nonfiction. Find out how the author chooses his or her topics. Write an author profile.

6. Select a topic that you would like to explore in a classroom and use the Internet to identify books and create a bibliography.

Classroom Activities

The following activities can be adapted to a variety of subject matter and content area classes.

ACTIVITY 10.1   DATA CHARTS

IRA/NCTE Standards: 1, 3, 5, 7, 8, 10, 11, 12. Comprehension, writing, higher-order thinking.

Data charts are excellent tools for summarizing data from multiple sources for writing. Read Tomie DePaola's *The Quicksand Book* as preparation for data organization and presentation. Data charts help students integrate collected information (Hennings, 1994; Stoodt, 1989). The steps in preparing a data chart are:

1. Identify the topic, problem, or question.

2. Brainstorm questions regarding the topic, problem, or major question, which become the labels for each column.

3. Identify the sources of information in the left-hand column.

4. Have the students complete the chart (see figure).

Data chart for summarizing information from different sources.				
Source	Questions			
	Why was Houdini famous?	What words describe his personality?	What was his best magic?	Why are people today interested in him?
Escape! The Story of the Great Houdini by Sid Fleischman Greenwillow, 2007				
Houdini the Handcuff King by Jason Lutes Hyperion, 2007				
Internet site http://www.houdinitribute.com				

ACTIVITY 10.2   BOOKTALK: BIRDS, SPIDERS, AND BUTTERFLIES (3RD GRADE UP) THE BOOK: THE AMATEUR NATURALIST BY NICK BAKER

Booktalks will spur students to read. Books like *Gotcha! Nonfiction Booktalks to Get Kids Excited About Reading* by Kathleen Baxter and Marcia Kochel and *Gotcha Again!* by the same authors are invaluable aids for teachers and librarians.

IRA/NCTE Standards: 1, 3, 4, 5, 6, 7, 8, 10, 11, 12. Higher-order thinking skills, comprehension, research in print and nonprint texts, communicate to various audiences, range of strategies, apply knowledge, use language.

Hold the book up and explain that this book is *The Amateur Naturalist.*

Ask "Do any of you know what a naturalist does?"

Answer: "Yes, they study nature including birds, insects, animals." Explain to students that Nick Baker, the author, is knowledgeable about studying nature. Nick Baker lives in England and is involved in the BBC's popular *Really Wild Show.* After students read this book, they will know how to put a spider web on a cardboard, make their own snake stick, create a pitfall trap, and more.

Book Talk: Civil Rights

(Show the students photos from *Kids at Work* by Russell Freedman and *Kids on Strike* by Susan Bartoletti. Have available *Kids with Courage: True Stories About Young People Making a Difference* by Barbara Lewis and *Lyddie* by Katharine Paterson. All of these books are photo essays except *Lyddie.* Students will find these books available in most libraries.) Explain to students:

> The kids in these books have worked in terrible conditions. They knew they lacked power, but they resisted inhumane treatment. Who do you think has the most power? The kids or the bosses? The children in *Kids at Work* were also working in terrible conditions. How do you suppose they tried to make conditions better? In *It's Our World, Too!,* there are stories of kids doing remarkable things throughout history: newspaper boys who went on strike for better pay, children who led slaves to freedom, youngsters who protested working conditions. Some of the kids in *Kids Have Courage* expressed their courage through fighting crime; others took social action, while others tried to save the environment.

ACTIVITY 10.3 PROFILING AN AUTHOR

IRA/NCTE Standards: 3, 4, 5, 6, 7, 11, 12. Comprehension, interpretation, critical thinking, use a variety of resources, and use language to achieve purposes.

Learning about authors and their interests helps readers understand how they get story ideas. After studying an author or illustrator through one of the methods described in previous activities, students can write biographical profiles. The profile of Jim Arnosky focuses on his ways of bringing the natural world to life.

A Biographical Profile: Jim Arnosky

Jim Arnosky has an uncanny connection to nature. He communicates a reverence for and a passionate love of nature using realistic illustrations and lyrical text. He thinks of himself as a naturalist; perhaps this is why his writing leads readers to explore nature and to learn from their own experiences. His best research is done through observation and journals. Visiting different places and comparing them is a part of his research. He believes that "doing" is the best part of his research.

His books have been cited for excellence by the Bank Street of Education, the John Burroughs Association, the National Council of Teachers of English, the National Science Teachers Association, and *Smithsonian Magazine.* He has a web site at: www.jimarnosky.com.

Children's Literature References

Note: Books designated with an asterisk (*) are recommended for reluctant readers.

Arnosky, J. (2002). *Field trips: Bug hunting, animal tracking, bird watching, shore walking with Jim Arnosky*. New York: HarperCollins. 3–4;5–6. INF*

   Arnosky uses interesting drawings and field notes.

Baker, N. (2006). *The amateur naturalist*. Washington, DC: National Geographic Press. K–2;3–4. INF

   This book gives children the information they need to become naturalists.

Barnard, B. (2006). *Outbreak: Plagues that changed history*. New York: Crown. 3–4;5–6;7+. INF

   This amazing book includes well-documented information with striking illustrations.

Bartoletti, S. (2006). *Hitler youth: Growing up in Hitler's shadow*. New York: Scholastic. 3–4;5–6;7+. INF

   This book is based on the perspective of a young man who grows up under Hitler's power.

Batten, M. (2003). *Aliens from earth*. Atlanta: Peachtree. 3–4. INF

   Alien plants and animals come from another place and upset the balance of an ecosystem.

Bausum, A. (2006). *Freedom walkers: John Lewis and Jim Zwerg on the front lines of the Civil Rights Movement*. Washington, DC: National Geographic Children's Books. 5–6;7+. INF

   Lewis and Zwerg are not as well-known as other leaders of the Civil Rights Movement.

Bidner, J. (2006). *Is my dog a wolf? How your pet compares to its wild cousin*. Lark Books. 3–4;5–6. INF*

   The author identifies wolf characteristics that appear in modern dogs.

Bowen, G. (1994). *Stranded at Plimoth Plantation, 1626*. New York: Harper Collins. 3–4.

   The daily life on a Plimoth Plantation is told from the point of view of an indentured servant.

Butler, J. (2001). *Pi-shu the little panda*. Atlanta: Peachtree. K–2;3–4. INF

   Illustrations and text follow the growth and development of a baby panda.

Calmenson, S. (2007). *May I pet your dog?: The how to guide for kids meeting dogs (and dogs meeting kids)* (J. Omerod, Illus.). New York: Clarion. K–2. INF*

   This book shows children how to react appropriately to dogs they are not acquainted with.

Cobb, V. (1999) *You gotta try this! Absolutely irresistible science* (T. Kelley, Illus.). New York: Morrow. 3–4;5–6. INF*

   Very interesting experiments and activities.

Collard, S. (2006). *The prairie builders: Reconstructing America's lost grasslands*. New York: Houghton. 3–4;5–6;7+. INF

   This book describes a project to bring back the prairie grasslands.

Cowley, J. (2006). *Chameleon, chameleon* (N. Bishop, Illus.). New York: Scholastic. K–2. INF*

   A beautifully illustrated picture book.

Curlee, L. (2003). *Capital*. New York: Simon & Schuster. 2–6. INF

   The author illustrates and explains the building of the capital.

Davidson, S., & Morgan, B. (2002). *Human body revealed*. New York: DK Publishing. 3–4;5–6. INF

DePaola, T. *The quicksand book*. New York: Holiday House. K–2;3–4;5–6. INF

   DePaola gives a lot of information in this book.

Dewey, J. (2002). *Paisano, the roadrunner*. Brookfield, CT: Millbrook. 3–4;5–6. INF

   Develops readers' concepts of the roadrunner.

Fleischman, J. (2002). *Phineas Gage: A gruesome but true story about brain science*. Boston: Houghton Mifflin. 3–4;5–6;7+. INF

   The story of an actual person's brain injury.

Fleming, C. (2006). *Ben Franklin's almanac: Being a true account of the good gentleman's life*. New York: Simon and Schuster. 3–4;5–6. INF

   This book is based on Franklin's almanac.

Fradin, D. (2002). *The signers: The 56 stories behind the Declaration of Independence* (M. McCurdy, Illus.). New York: Walker. 4–8. INF

Fradin, D. (2006). *Let it begin here! Lexington and Concord: First battles of the American Revolution*. New York: Walker. 3–4;5–6;7+. INF

   This book discusses the first battle of the Revolutionary War.

Frank, M. (2001). *Understanding September 11th: Answering questions about the attacks on America.* New York: Viking. 3–4;5–6;7+. INF

Provides discussion about some of the big questions arising from September 11.

Freedman, R. (2000). *Give me liberty! The story of the Declaration of Independence.* New York: Holiday House. 3–4;5–6. INF

Helps children understand the setting and politics surrounding the Declaration of Independence.

Freedman, R. (2006). *Children of the Great Depression.* New York: Clarion. 5–6;7+. INF

Excellent photos of children in the Depression era and text that helps reader understand this time period.

Giblin, J. C. (2000). *The amazing life of Benjamin Franklin* (M. Dooling, Illus.). New York: Scholastic. K–2;3–4. INF

Interesting treatment of Franklin's life.

Giblin, J. C. (2002). *The life and death of Adolf Hitler.* New York: Clarion. 5–6;7+. B

A well-researched, accurate presentation of Adolf Hitler.

Hampton, W. (2001). *Meltdown: A race against nuclear disaster at Three Mile Island: A reporter's story.* Cambridge, MA: Candlewick Press. 3–4;5–6;7+. INF

Sensitizes everyone about the power of nuclear energy.

Hatkoff, I., Hatkoff, C., & Kahumbu, P. (2006). *Owen & Mzee: The true story of a remarkable friendship.* New York: Scholastic. K–2. INF*

A true story of a friendship between a hippo and a tortoise.

Jackson, D. (2006). *ER Vets: Life in an Animal Emergency Room.* New York: Houghton Mifflin. K–2; 3–4. INF

Develops an understanding of what happens in a pet emergency room.

Johnson, D. (2006). *Onward: A photobiography of African-American polar explorer Matthew Henson.* Washington DC: National Geographic Children's Books. 3–4;5–6;7+. INF

Although he accompanied an explorer to the pole, he was not recognized until much later.

Jurmain, S. (2006). *Forbidden schoolhouse: The true and dramatic story of Prudence Crandall and her students.* New York: Houghton Mifflin. 3–4;5–6. INF

A story about Florence Crandall, who established a school for African American girls.

Kramer, S. (2006). *Hidden worlds: Looking through a scientist's microscope* (D. Kunkel, Illus.). New York: Houghton Mifflin. 1–4. INF*

The author shows students how microscopes help them see their world.

Le Rochais, M. (2001). *Desert trek: An eye-opening journey through the world's driest places.* New York: Walker. 3–4;5–6. INF

This book helps readers understand the nature of deserts.

Logan, C. (2002). *The 5,000-year-old puzzle: Solving a mystery of ancient Egypt.* New York: Farrar. 3–4;5–6. INF

Readers go on an archaeological dig.

Manson, C. (2000). *Uncle Sam and Old Glory: Symbols of America.* New York: Atheneum. 3–4;5–6. INF*

Introduces symbols of America that children may not know.

Markle, S. (2001). *Growing up wild: Wolves.* New York: Atheneum. 3–4;5–6. INF

Markle shows how wolves and wolf families live in the wild.

Markle, S. (2006). *Rescues.* Millbrook. 3–4;5–6. INF

Markle shows how birds and animals are rescued in disasters.

Marrin, A. (2002). *Dr. Jenner and the speckled monster: The search for the smallpox vaccine.* New York: Dutton. 3–4;5–6;7+. INF

Explores Jenner's search for a smallpox vaccine.

Miller, M. (2006). *Hurricane Katrina strikes the Gulf Coast.* New York: Enslow. 3–4;5–6. INF

Photos and information about Hurricane Katrina.

Montgomery, S. (2006). *Quest for the tree kangaroo: An expedition to the cloud forest of New Guinea* (N. Bishop, Illus.). K–2;3–4. INF

A very interesting animal story with superb illustrations.

Murphy, J. (2006). *An American plague: The true and terrifying story of the yellow fever epidemic of 1793.* New York: Clarion. 3–4;5–6. INF

A timely book that relates to current health concerns.

Murphy, J. (1995). *The great fire*. New York: Scholastic. 3–4;5–6. INF

The story of the Chicago fire.

Nelson, P. (2002). *Left for dead: A young man's search for the USS Indianapolis*. New York: Delacorte. 5–6;7+. INF

A young man searches for information about his father.

Posada, M. (2002). *Ladybugs: Red, fiery, and bright*. Minneapolis: Carolrhoda. K–2. INF

Excellent information and illustrations.

Ride, S. & Okie, S. (1986). *To space and back*. New York: Harper. K–2;3–4. INF

The authors take readers on a trip to space.

Robbins, K. (2006). *Seeds*. Firefly. K–2. INF

An informative book about seeds.

Russo, M. (2005). *Always remember me: How one family survived World War II*. New York: Atheneum. 3–4;5–6. INF

A true story about one family's survival of World War II.

Rubin, S. G., & Wiessberger, E. (2006). *The cat with a yellow star* (A. Jonas, Illus.). New York: Holiday House. 4–6. INF

The cat helped the family survive.

Sayre, A. (2005). *Stars beneath your bed: The surprising story of dust* (A. Jonas, Illus.). New York: Greenwillow. K–2;3–4. INF

The author states that the dust under the bed may have come from dinosaurs.

Schwartz, D. (2003). *Millions to measure* (S. Kellogg, Illus.). New York: HarperCollins. K–2;3–4. INF

A math book about the concept of "millions."

Siy, A. & Kunkel, D. (2006). *Mosquito bite*. New York: Charlesbridge. K–2;3–4. INF

Explains mosquito bites.

Tang, G. (2001). *The grapes of math: Mind-stretching math riddles*. New York: Scholastic. K–2;3–4. INF

Math games for children.

Tang, G. (2002). *The best of times: Math strategies that multiply*. New York: Scholastic. K–2;3–4. INF

Math games.

Thimmesh, C. (2007). *Team moon: How 400,000 people landed Apollo 11 on the moon*. Boston: Houghton. 3–4; 5–6. INF

A detailed portrayal of an expedition to the moon.

Vogel, C. (2000). *Nature's fury: Eyewitness reports of natural disasters*. New York: Scholastic. 4–5; 5–6. INF

The author describes disasters that were precipitated by nature.

Walker, S. (2006). *Secrets of a Civil War submarine: Solving the mysteries of the H. L. Hunley*. Minneapolis, MN: Carolrhoda Books. 3–4;5–6;7+. INF

This book explores the Civil War submarine that was raised to the surface.

Zaslavsky, C. (2001). *Number sense and nonsense*. Chicago: Chicago Press. 3–4;5–6. INF

Professional References

Ballantyne, M. M. (1993). The effects of narrative and expository discourse on the reading comprehension of middle school-aged good and poor readers (University Microfilms No. 94–06, 749). Dissertation Abstracts International 54, 4046.

Baxter, K., & Kochel, M. (1999). *Gotcha! Nonfiction booktalks to get kids excited about reading*. Englewood, CO: Libraries Unlimited.

Baxter, K., & Kochel, M. (2002). *Gotcha again! More nonfiction booktalks to get kids excited about reading*. Englewood, CO: Libraries Unlimited.

Daniels, H. (2002). *Literature circles: Voice and choice in book clubs and reading groups*. Portland, ME: Stenhouse.

Duke, N. (2000). 3.6 minutes per day: The scarcity of informational text in first grade. *Reading Research Quarterly, 35* (202–224).

Duthie, C. (1994). Nonfiction: A genre study for the primary classroom. *Language Arts*, *71*, 588–595.

Fisher, L. E. (1988). The artist at work: Creating non-fiction. *The Horn Book*, *78*, 315–323.

Ford, D. (2002, May/June). More than the facts: Reviewing science books. *The Horn Book*, *78*, 265–271.

Giblin, J. C. (1987). A publisher's perspective. *Horn Book, 63,* 104–107.

Greene, M. (1992). Texts and margins. In M. Boldberg & A. Phillips (Eds.), *Arts as education.* Cambridge, MA: Harvard Educational Review. Reprint Series No. 24, 1–18.

Harvey, S. (1998). *Nonfiction matters.* York, ME: Stenhouse.

Hennings, D. (1994). *Language arts.* Boston: Houghton Mifflin.

Jensen, J. (2001). The quality of prose in Orbis Pictus Award books. In M. Zarnowski, R. Kerper, & J. Jensen (Eds.), *The best in children's nonfiction.* Urbana, IL: National Council of Teachers of English, 2–21.

Leavitt, J., & Sohn, D. (1964). *Stop, look, and write!* New York: Bantam.

McAuley, K., & Wilson, R. H. (1987). *The United States: Past to present.* Lexington, MA: D. C. Heath.

Meltzer, M. (1994). *Nonfiction for the classroom.* New York: Teachers College Press.

Palmer, R., & Stewart, R. (2005). Models for using nonfiction in the primary grades. *The Reading Teacher, 58* (426–434).

Pappas, C. C., Kiefer, B., & Levstik, L. (1990). *An integrated language perspective in the elementary school.* White Plains, NY: Longman.

Shanahan, T. (1992). Nine good reasons for using children's literature across the curriculum. In T. Shanahan (Ed.), *Distant shores resource packages, IV* (pp. 10–22). New York: McGraw-Hill School Division.

Stead, T. (2002). *Is that a fact?* Portland, ME: Stenhouse Publishers.

Stoodt, B. (1989). *Reading instruction* (2nd ed.). New York: HarperCollins.

Stoodt, B., & Amspaugh, L. (1994, May). Children's response to nonfiction. A paper presented at the Annual Meeting of the International Reading Association, Toronto, Canada.

Venezky, R. (2002). *Scientific studies of reading.* Mahwah, NJ: Lawrence Erlbaum.

Walmsley, S. A. (1994). *Children exploring their world: Theme teaching in elementary school.* Portsmouth, NH: Heinemann.

Whitin, P., & Whitin, D. (2002). Mathematics in our world. In A. McClure, & J. Kristo (Eds.), *Adventuring with books* (13th ed.). Urbana, IL: National Council of Teachers of English.

11 Biography: Fascinating Real Life

KEY TERMS

authentic biography   biographical fiction
autobiography   fictionalized biography
biography

GUIDING QUESTIONS

1. How do biographies differ from other genres?

2. What person is most interesting to you?

3. Would you like to read a biography of that individual?

4. What values does biography have for children?

Introduction to Biography

One of the most enjoyable ways to learn about real life is to read a biography. A *biography* is the story of a life. Reading a well-written biography becomes an absorbing human encounter with a person whose achievement is out of the ordinary. That person may be famous, as in Andrea Pinkney's *Ella Fitzgerald*; infamous, as in James Cross Giblin's *The Life and Death of Hitler;* or unknown to the general public, as in Lois Lowery's *Aunt Clara Brown: Official Pioneer*. Reading a well-written biography allows students to tap into the life experiences of others as they learn about their own lives. They will discover people who overcame obstacles such as ignorance, poverty, misery, fear, and hate,

which shows us all how to overcome problems (Zarnowski, 1990). In biography, children can meet people with spirit and integrity, like Babe Ruth. Matt Christopher's *Legends in Sports: Babe Ruth* is just such a biography. Readers come to know Babe Ruth as an athlete who never lost sight of the reality that baseball was a game that he played and enjoyed.

Biography is more popular than many people realize; this is the reason why copies of *People* magazine are in waiting rooms around the country, and why the copies are usually dog-eared. Teachers can excite students' interest in biography, as illustrated by the vignette on p.182, a personal reflection showing the roots of my life-long love of biography.

Writing Biography

Accuracy and authenticity are the hallmarks of fine biography. Biographers must research their subjects carefully, then assume an attitude or theme regarding the subject, which guides them in selecting the events and details to include. The writer then shapes the biography to make the subject come alive. Biography may appear to be a simple writing task, essentially a reporting of actual people, events, and life stories. However, the writer has to decide the amount of detail to include, whether to use illustrations, which friends or enemies of the subject to write about, and many other details. Biographers use many of the same techniques as other storytellers: They "set their scenes descriptively, develop their characters completely, and give us the impression of life unfolding" (Zarnowski, 1990, p. 6). Finally, they determine which facts to include and

A Teacher Ignites a Lifelong Interest in Biography

Picture this . . . , Monday, 10 A.M., in a one-room school with six rows, one for each grade. This scene is from rural Ohio of the 1940s. A teacher-fired stove stands at the right side of the classroom, with a bucket of water and tin cups for the students and an outhouse in back of the school. It's read-aloud time! The teacher, Miss Minshall, removes a book from the corner of her desk and continues reading from the Lincoln biography started the preceding week. The story was Lincoln's courtroom defense of an accused murderer. I held my breath as she read the testimony of the first witness, "I saw him do it in the light of the full moon." However, Lincoln proved he was innocent when the *Farmers Almanac* showed there was no full moon on the night in question. Awestruck at Lincoln's brilliance, this first grader began reading biographies of Lincoln, then ventured into stories of Benjamin Franklin, another hero. Recently, she read a brand new biography of Franklin with the same relish as long ago.

Postscript: I now realize that Miss Minshall read from adult biographies and translated the text into language that young children could understand. This was an important factor because the few biographies of that era were poorly written and lacked research. When Miss Minshall read biography, she focused on myths that appealed to children, such as George Washington and the cherry tree. She also read from American history and the daily newspaper. When she read about German casualties, we cheered. She told us that was wrong because these were innocent civilians who probably did not want to fight. Perhaps she chose these subjects because this was the time of World War II, but biography and history have remained my major reading interests throughout life. I owe this to my first-grade teacher. She proved teachers can make a difference!

which to exclude. When reading Katherine Krull's *The Boy on Fairfield Street: How Ted Geisel Grew up to Become Dr. Seuss,* readers are surprised to learn that the creator of *Sam-I-Am* and *Yertle the Turtle* was taunted in World War I due to his Germanic background. Then his art teacher scolded him for breaking the rules of art. At Dartmouth, he was named "Least Likely to Succeed." These experiences and others contributed to developing him into the beloved Dr. Seuss. When reading biography, students have to realize that all of the subject's experiences contribute to the person he or she becomes.

Biography subjects do not live isolated lives. Rather, their lives are shaped through their interactions with other people and through events that form the backdrop of their story. As Milton Meltzer said, "When you write biography, you present history through the prism of a single life, a life, that is, of course, connected to other lives." (Meltzer, 1981, p. 15). In *John Lewis in the Lead: A Story of the Civil Rights Movement,* James Haskins and Kathleen Benson follow their subject through his life, beginning with his student years. During his student years, he was aspiring to become a minister and was an admirer of Martin Luther King, Jr. Then he played an important role in the Selma to Montgomery marches of 1964. The authors' style makes readers aware of John Lewis and the courage of both Lewis and his fellow nonviolent protesters.

Types of Biography

One of the most important decisions a biographer must make is the type of biography to write: complete or partial, single or collective.

Complete Biography

Complete, or cradle-to-grave, biographies address the theme of an individual's life. The theme of James Cross Giblin's *The Amazing Life of Benjamin Franklin,* for example, was Franklin's amazing accomplishments throughout his life. Barbara Kerley's *Walt Whitman: Words for America,* another complete biography, is a compelling portrait of America's well-known poet. Brian Selznick's illustrations and Kerley's text show how Whitman's life was filled with words. Whitman's experiences as a typesetter and a battlefield volunteer who nursed wounded soldiers prepared him to write the free verse that honored America's people, soldiers, and losses. Walter Dean Myers chose to write a complete biography of Muhammad Ali in *The Greatest: Muhammad Ali* because a complete biography enabled him to show all the accomplishments of this complex man. This fascinating book is difficult to put down once you start reading it because the writer chronicles Ali's early years in poverty and shows how his determination led to success. *Jane Addams: Champion of Democracy* by Dennis Fradin and Judith Fradin, the story of a gallant woman who started Hull House in Chicago, is another example of a complete biography. Hull House was a settlement house that supported immigrants and others who needed assistance. Citizenship classes guided people who hoped to become citizens. Many other classes were offered to orient people to life in the United States.

Partial Biography

When biography focuses on a portion of the subject's life, it is a partial life story. For example, James Rumfeld has written a partial biography about Sequoyah's adult life in *Sequoyah: The Man Who Gave His People Writing.* Rumfeld and the book's translator, Anna Sixkiller Huckaby, portray Sequoyah as a giant among the Cherokees. He was unable to speak or write English, but he realized that he had to create a writing system that would create a written record of his people. To achieve this goal he developed a unique symbol for each Cherokee word. His people believed the symbols were evil, so they burned his cabin. Subsequently, he developed a syllabary of 84 symbols, one symbol for each sound in the Cherokee language. This system was accepted by the Cherokee people.

In *When Marian Sang*, author Pam Munoz Ryan brings Marian Anderson, the great American singer, to life. This partial biography tells about her early life. Anderson grew up in humble circumstances and was rejected by schools of music. A related book, Deborah Hopkinson's *Sweet Land of Liberty*, is the partial biography of Oscar Chapman, who was Assistant Secretary of the Interior when Franklin Delano Roosevelt was President. This biography tells about his role in arranging Marian Anderson's concert. Oscar fought against

This biography shows how the United States grew into the sweet land of liberty.

injustice all of his life. When he learned that members of the Daughters of the American Revolution (DAR) refused to allow Marian Anderson to sing in Constitution Hall because the hall was available to "white artists only," he met with a friend and arranged for her to give a concert at the Lincoln Memorial. The author's note is very interesting. After reading this biography, you will wish you had been there in 1939 when she sang "America."

Collective Biography

Collective biography includes life stories of more than one individual. *American Heroes*, a collective biography by Mafe Delano, represents heroes from all walks of life throughout U.S. history. Delano introduces the cultural attitudes of the time to create a setting for understanding each hero. *Honky-Tonk Heroes & Hillbilly Angels: The Pioneers of Country & Western Music* by Holly George-Warren is a collection of American heroes from a different venue—country and western music. Each of the artists is presented in a basic biography, including song titles associated with the individual and little known facts, such as that Jimmie Rodgers's fans lined the railroad tracks from New York to Mississippi to pay respect to his funeral train.

Elizabeth Kimmel's collective biography is *Ladies First: 40 Daring American Women Who Were Second to*

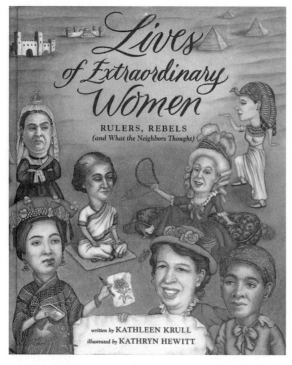

These women triumphed over adverse attitudes and conditions.

None. This group includes female scientists, writers, politicians, educators, artists, singers, explorers, and rabbis. Among these celebrated women are Georgia O'Keeffe, Jane Addams, Jane Roberts, and Brenda Berkman. Kimmel's biographies join an earlier collective biography, *Lives of Extraordinary Women*. Each profile is three pages long and celebrates the achievements of these remarkable women. *Famous Hispanic Americans* by Wendy Dunn and Janet Morey is a collective biography of contemporary Hispanic subjects. They include people who come from a wide variety of businesses and professions including athletes, fashion designers, dancers, comics, and others.

Autobiography

Autobiographies are actually written by the book's subjects. For example, in *Through My Eyes* Ruby Bridges chronicles her life as a 6-year-old, when she was one of the nation's first black children to attend school in the deep south. *Over a Thousand Hills I Walk with You* by Hanna Jansen is her story as an 8-year-old Rwandan Tutsi whose family is destroyed by genocide. She is later adopted by the Jansens; her story is

translated by Elizabeth Crawford, who maintained the childlike narrative with its emotions and personal reflections.

Authentic Biography and Fictionalized Biography

Interpreting an individual's life is a very important decision on the biographer's part. The author may adhere to the facts in an *authentic biography* or dramatize the subject's life through a *fictionalized biography*. In authentic biography, the only facts included are those verifiable through research. Any dialogue must be able to be substantiated by historical documents (David Russell, 1994). Biographer Jean Fritz (1990) explains her stance: "I would make up nothing, not even the dialogue, and I wouldn't even use dialogue unless I had a source. I would be honest. If there was a fact I wasn't sure of, or if it was unknown, I would say so" (p. 25).

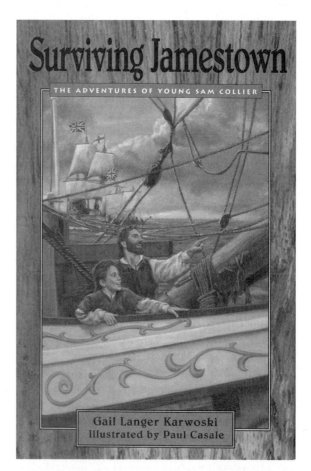

Surviving Jamestown was a challenge.

Surviving Jamestown by Gail Karwoski is a carefully researched, fictionalized biography of 12-year-old Sam Collier. The historical information is accurate, but the author has created incidents and conversations that make it a fictionalized biography. In this book, readers learn about the founders of Jamestown through the eyes of Sam Collier, who was apprenticed to John Smith.

Most children's biography is fictionalized, which represents a middle position between strict adherence to known facts and completely invented narrative. In this case, "facts are the bricks with which a biographer builds" (Coolidge, 1974, p. 141). In fictionalized biography, dialogue and events can be invented based upon historical documents (Sutherland & Arbuthnot, 1991).

Selecting and Evaluating Biography

Many current biographies are of excellent quality. When selecting biography, consider the following guidelines:

1. Does the book tell a **good story.**
2. The **subject** should be relevant to students and their interests or studies.
3. The information should be accurate. This is insured when the subject is **well-researched and documented.** Authors should include a bibliography and source notes.
4. The subject of the biography should be presented as **a three dimensional person** with strengths and flaws.
5. The book should use photographs, drawings, and paintings that support the text, orient the reader, and build interest.
6. The writing style should make the subject interesting. Using descriptions, anecdotes, and details creates interest in readers.

Biography for English Language Learners

Students who are English language learners (ELL) are affirmed when they read biography that reflects their culture (Lesesne, 2002). This is an important consideration because ELL students have not had opportunities to acquire the cultural background necessary to understand subjects in American biography. This factor also points up the need for a good collection of multicultural biography.

Subject

James Cross Giblin explains that, when choosing subjects for biography, he is drawn to complicated people, which he then has to make understandable and meaningful to young people. He adds that he is fascinated with the complexities of human nature (Harris & McCarthy, 2002). For many years, the subjects of children's biographies were historical figures. However, more and more writers are now choosing to write about a broader range of subjects (Lukens, 1995). The biography *Aunt Clara Brown: Official Pioneer*, for example, by Lois Lowery, tells the dramatic story of Clara Brown, a former slave who travels to Colorado to find a better life. Ultimately she becomes the first official Colorado pioneer who is neither white nor male.

Members of minority cultures have often been omitted from biography and history. For many years, American children learned history minus black people, women, Hispanics, and Native Americans (Hearne, 1990, p. 136). However, newer biographies include a broader range of subjects. For example, the biography *Dizzy*, by Jeanette Winter, is the biography of Dizzy Gillespie, who was fired from bands due to his lack of seriousness. But this characteristic enabled him to innovate be-bop as well as become a great jazz trumpeter. Although Harriet Tubman has been the subject of a number of biographies, Carole Weatherford's *Moses: When Harriet Tubman Led Her People to Freedom* is one of the best. The book's paintings, by Kadir Nelson, portray Tubman's role in the Underground Railroad and her life as an African American visionary. *Quiet Hero: The Ira Hayes Story*, another book by S. D. Nelson, is the story of a Native American who volunteered for the Marines and was stationed in the Pacific. He was one of the six men who raised the flag over Iwo Jima. Ira was an idealist, but the author honestly portrays his alcoholism.

Accuracy

Accuracy is the linchpin of excellent biography. The best biographers conduct exhaustive research to document their books. Biographers often choose to use the most important characteristic of a subject as a focal point and theme for the biography. Russell Freedman does this in his biographies of Abraham Lincoln[**] and Eleanor Roosevelt.[**] Dennis Fradin and Cynthia Fradin use pictures and careful documentation to tell the story of the humanitarian, Jane Addams. She was awarded the Nobel Peace Prize, but she was despised as well as admired. The authors use Addams's own writings to illustrate her concern for human life. Their careful research results in a well-developed portrayal of their subject. Another stylistic technique for helping readers "see" a subject is telling the story from a child's point of view. Allen Say, for example, compares his life and his grandfather's life in the Caldecott Award–winning book *Grandfather's Journey,* telling about his grandfather's journey to the United States and his return to Japan. His grandfather loved both countries, and when he was in one country he yearned for the other.

Theme

Biographers identify a unifying thread or theme to bind the characterization of their subject together. Identifying a theme determines which facts to include and exclude and shapes the authors' interpretation of their subjects. This theme appears in the illustrations, as well as the text. The biographer's theme often appears in the biography title. The theme of Joan Dash's *A Dangerous Engine: Benjamin Franklin, from Scientist to Diplomat* is the personal history of a public man. She explores the personal, scientific, and political dimensions of Franklin's life. W. W. Law's lifelong work for civil rights is the theme of Jim Haskins's biography, *Delivering Justice: W. W. Law and the Fight for Civil Rights.* W. W. Law was a Savannah mail carrier who registered black voters, organized boycotts, and trained protesters. The theme of *Houdini: The Handcuff King* by Jason Lutes and Nick Bertozzi is Houdini's showmanship. He was probably the most famous man in the world in his time. His showman skills, obsession, and pride were his important characteristics.

Style

Children find it easier to understand biography that reads like a story, albeit a real-life story. They generally enjoy facts woven into narrative style, but the biographer must do the research needed to create authenticity in the narrative. Research involves examining the subject's daily life, food, games, clothing, newspapers, politics, and conversation. The language created in conversation

should be appropriate to the era, and discussions must reflect the issues of the time. Some of the vocabulary used may be foreign to young readers and impede their understanding. Jean Fritz (1990) explains that she does not omit important words just because they may be strange to young readers. In addition, some authors include glossaries to help children. Some biographies are illustrated in order to help readers understand the subject of the biography. Emily McCully does this successfully in her biography of *Marvelous Mattie: How Margaret E. Knight Became an Inventor.* Margaret Knight obtained 22 patents and created 90 different inventions. In this biography, McCully writes in a narrative style, which is familiar to primary-grade children, to help them understand how inventors work.

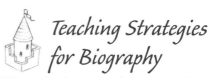

Teaching Strategies for Biography

Biography is an excellent means for enhancing language arts and social studies. Perhaps the most important contribution of teachers and librarians is providing excellent biography and reading it aloud to children at all levels.

Summary

Biography is the story of a person's life. Children learn about their own life through the lives of people who have made contributions to the world. These lives give students models of people who have overcome adverse conditions to succeed. Students also learn, from biographies of people who are not admirable, to avoid certain behaviors. Biography enriches curriculum areas because students can read about leaders in the various subject areas. These books give students the background necessary to understand the life and times of famous, infamous, and unknown people.

Thought Questions and Applications

1. Why is theme important in biography?
2. How are biography and nonfiction related?
3. How does a biographer ensure accuracy and authenticity in a work?

Research and Application Experiences

1. Create a special interest bibliography for a specific grade level based on an individual that would fit into the curriculum at the chosen grade level. These individuals might include scientists, politicians, presidents, and so forth.

2. Compare three biographies of the same person's life. What are the similarities? What are the differences?

3. Prepare a booktalk for a biography you enjoy. Present the booktalk to a group of children or to a group of classmates.

4. Find a biographer on the Web and learn why he or she chooses to write biography. Find out how the author chooses his or her subjects. Write an author profile.

Classroom Activities

ACTIVITY 11.1   DRAMA AND ROLE-PLAYING

IRA/NCTE Standards: 3, 6, 7, 8, 9, 10, 11, 12. Language arts, comprehension, vocabulary, response, knowledge, reading, and writing.

Creative drama is an excellent learning experience for students who are reading biographies. They can learn a great deal from role-playing or dramatizing biographies, as well as other books of nonfiction. Dramatizing a historical figure helps students develop a better understanding of the character. Of course, to prepare for these activities, students must research their subject using biographies and the Internet. Another drama activity involves conducting television interviews. One student prepares questions while another prepares to be the character, considering the style of dress, the issues of the day, and so forth. A camcorder or a tape recorder will add to the feeling of conducting a television interview.

Guidelines for the research, like these, will help students conduct their research.

1. Why did you choose to research this person?
2. What are the individual's outstanding characteristics?
3. What are the important facts of this individual's life?
4. What factors in this person's life led him or her to become the person he or she became?
5. What theme is appropriate for this person's life?

ACTIVITY 11.2   COMPARING BIOGRAPHIES: TIGER WOODS, BENJAMIN FRANKLIN

IRA/NCTE Standards: 1, 2, 3, 6. Read a variety of print and nonprint texts from a range of genres; use a wide range of strategies to comprehend for a variety of purposes; and apply language knowledge to critique and discuss text.

This activity may be completed with print biographies, as well as biographical material from the Internet. Students may establish their own categories for comparison or use those that follow.

1. Identify the subject for the biographical study.

2. Identify the categories of information that you expect to appear in a biography.

3. Identify the sources of information in the left-hand column, as shown in the figures on p. 188.

4. Have the students complete the chart. Older students can create their own charts on a computer.

A biographical study of Tiger Woods.						
Biography	**Childhood**	**Family**	**Personality**	**Theme**	**Honors**	**Photos**
Tiger Woods by William Durbin	precocious; played golf as toddler	close; father taught		precocious childhood		newspaper
Tiger Woods: Golf's Shining Young Star by Bill Gutman	brief discussion		emphasize	stardom	youngest golfer ever to win the Masters	color photos
Tiger Woods: Golf Superstar by David Collins	introduced as an infant who became a famous toddler	faced prejudice and bullying	emphasized positive attitude and demeanor	intelligence, athletic ability, and personality	skill	full color illustrations

A biographical study of Benjamin Franklin.						
Title & Author	**Family**	**Theme**	**Honors**	**Inventions**	**Science**	**Publisher**
B. Franklin, Printer by D. Adler, Holiday, 2001.	husband and father	our greatest American; his glory and humble pride; what he means to our country today	ambassador; helped write the Declaration of Independence			his proudest title; includes passages from his newspaper
Ben Franklin's Almanac: Being a True Account of the Good Gentleman's Life by C. Fleming, Atheneum, 2003.*		a tribute to Franklin's complexity	ambassador; author of the Declaration of Independence	includes anecdotes	includes anecdotes	includes anecdotes
Who Was Benjamin Franklin? by D. Fradin, Grossett & Dunlap, 2002.	one of 17 children	fascinating founding father; creative; inventive mind, contributed to culture, politics, and society	diplomat	national postal system, bifocals, volunteer fire department, public library	identifies contributions	

*Each of these books is an important contribution to children's literature. However, the Fleming book is exceptional in that it is done in a scrapbook style and provides unusual material related to Franklin's life.

ACTIVITY 11.3   PROFILING A BIOGRAPHER

IRA/NCTE Standards: 3, 4, 5, 6, 7, 11, 12. Comprehension, interpretation, critical thinking; use a variety of resources and use language to achieve purposes.

Learning about authors and their interests helps readers understand how writers get story ideas. After studying an author or illustrator through one of the methods described in previous activities, students can write biographical profiles.

Biographers

Russell Freedman

Jim Haskins

Elizabeth Kimmel

Kathleen Krull

Milton Meltzer

Diane Stanley

A Biographical Profile: Jean Fritz

Penguin Putnam Books calls Jean Fritz's biographies for young readers "refreshingly informal." Her widely acclaimed biographies have been described as unconventional, good-humored, witty, irrepressible, and extraordinary. Jean Fritz is an original and lively thinker who is recognized as a master of her craft. The majority of her writing is nonfiction and biography.

When asked about her choice of subjects, she suggests that she writes about the United States because she grew up in China, and she has discovered that American history is packed full of stories and people. She points out that every person has his or her own stories, and she likes to find out about them. She wants readers to realize that past times were as exciting and fun as present times.

Fritz enjoys research very much because it involves reading and traveling. She wants to find the truth and never makes up anything in her books. Research also turns up surprises, such as the fact that young Patrick Henry was remembered for wearing clean underwear. Her research has provided adventures, including her trip to London when she wrote about King George III. She has received these awards for her work: the Regina Medal by the Catholic Library Association; the Laura Ingalls Wilder Award by the American Library Association; and the Knickerbocker Award for Juvenile Literature from the New York State Library Association. A list of her books follows:

You Want Women to Vote, Lizzie Stanton?

Bully for You, Teddy Roosevelt

The Great Little Madison

Surprising Myself (autobiography)

Can't You Make Them Behave, King George?

What's the Big Idea, Ben Franklin?

Harriet Beecher Stowe and the Beecher Preachers

Traitor: The Case of Benedict Arnold

Note: The materials for this author profile were drawn from these Internet sites: Penguin Putnam Books for Young Readers; Children's Book Council; Carol Hurst's Children's Literature.

Children's Literature References

Note: Books designated with an asterisk (*) are recommended for reluctant readers.

Boomhower, R. (2006). *The soldier's friend: A life of Ernie Pyle*. Indianapolis: Indiana Historical Society Press. 5–6;7+. B

Ernie Pyle was a newspaper columnist who was close to the soldiers in WW II.

Bridges, R. (1999). *Through my eyes*. New York: Scholastic. 3–4;5–6. B

Ruby's experiences as an African American child who entered a white school.

Christopher, M. (2005). *Babe Ruth: Legends in sports*. New York: Little Brown. 3–4;5–6. B

Balanced treatment of Babe Ruth's life.

Cine-Ransome, L. (2000). *Satchel Paige* (K. Ransome, Illus.). New York: Simon & Schuster. 3–4;5–6. B

A picture-book biography of the great baseball player.

Coolidge, O. (1974). *The apprenticeship of Abraham Lincoln*. New York: Scribner's.

Dash, J. (2006). *A dangerous engine: Benjamin Franklin, from scientist to diplomat*. New York: Farrar. 3–4;5–6. B

This biography focuses on Benjamin Franklin's diverse talents.

Delano, M. (2005). *American heroes*. New York: National. K–2;3–4;5–6. B

A collective biography of American heroes.

Delano, M. (2001). *Inventing the future: A photobiography of Thomas Alva Edison*. Washington DC: National Geographic Society. 3–4;5–6;7+. B

The photos in this biography illustrate the genius of Edison's inventions.

Dunn, W., & Morely, J. (1996). *Famous Hispanic Americans*. New York: Dutton. 5–6;7+. B

A collective biography.

Fleischman, J. (2002). *Phineas Gage: A gruesome but true story about brain science*. Boston: Houghton Mifflin. 5–6;7+. B

This is the story of a man who survived after an iron bar entered his brain.

Fradin, D. (2002). *The signers: The 56 stories behind the Declaration of Independence*. New York: Walker. 3–4;5–6;7+. B*

These stories are biographies of the men who signed the Declaration of Independence.

Fradin, J., & Fradin, D. (2006). *Jane Addams: Champion of democracy*. New York: Clarion. 3–4;5–6;7+. B

Jane Addams sponsored classes for immigrants and programs to help the poor.

Freedman, R. (1987). *Lincoln: A photobiography*. Boston: Clarion. 3–4;5–6;7+. B

The author used photographs and drawings to present President Lincoln in this outstanding book.

Freedman, R. (1997). *Eleanor Roosevelt: A life of discovery*. 5–6;7+. B

This is a detailed anecdotal record of her life.

Fritz, J. (1992). *Surprising myself*. New York: Richard Owen. K–2;3–4. B

Jean Fritz, the author, writes about her own surprising life.

George-Warren, H. (2006). *Honky-tonk heroes & hillbilly angels: The pioneers of country & western music*. New York: Houghton. K–2;3–4. B

A collective biography of country and western musicians.

Giblin, J. C. (2000). *The amazing life of Benjamin Franklin* (M. Dooling, Illus.). New York: Scholastic. 3–4;5–6. B

A full-life biography of Benjamin Franklin.

Giblin, J. C. (2002). *The life and death of Hitler*. Boston: Clarion. 5–6;7+. B

The author has written an insightful historical overview.

Haskins, J. (2006). *Delivering justice: W. W. Law and the fight for civil rights*. Cambridge, MA: Candlewick. 3–4;5–6;7+. B

The story of W. W. Law's fight for civil rights.

Haskins, J., & Benson, K. (2006). *John Lewis in the lead: A story of the Civil Rights Movement*. Cambridge, MA: Candlewick. 3–4;5–6;7+. B

Biography of a leader of the Civil Rights Movement.

Hopkinson, D. (2007). *Sweet land of liberty*. Atlanta: Peachtree Publishers.

This book tells about Marian Anderson's concert.

Jansen, H. (2006). *Over a thousand hills I walk with you*. Minneapolis, MN. 5–6;7+. B

A young woman from Rwanda is adopted by an American family.

Karwoski, G., & Casale, P. (2001). *Surviving Jamestown*. Atlanta: Peachtree. 5–6;7+. B*

Sam Collier, an apprentice to Captain John Smith, tells this story.

Kerley, B. (2004). *Walt Whitman: Words for America*. New York: Scholastic. 3–4;5–6;7+. B

The great American poet.

Kimmel, E. (2006). *Ladies first: 40 daring American women who were second to none*. New York: National. 3–4;5–6;7+. B

A collective biography of adventurous American women.

Krull, K. (2000). *Lives of extraordinary women: Rulers, rebels (and what the neighbors thought)*. New York: Harcourt. 3–4;5–6. B

A collection of partial biographies about famous women.

Krull, K. (2004). *The boy on Fairfield Street: How Ted Geisel grew up to become Dr. Seuss*. New York: Viking. K–2;3–4;5–6. B

The story of Dr. Seuss's early years.

Lalicki, T. (2000). *Spellbinder: The life of Harry Houdini*. New York: Holiday House. 3–4;5–6;7+. B

Houdini the great magician.

Lowery, L. (1999). *Aunt Clara Brown: Official pioneer*. Minneapolis, MN: Carolrhoda Books. K–2;3–4. B

Aunt Clara was not famous, but she was recognized as a model pioneer.

Lutes, J. & Bertozzi, N. (2007). *Houdini: The handcuff king*. New York: Hyperion. 3–4;5–6;7+. B

An excellent biography that focuses on his showmanship.

McCully, E. (2006). *Marvelous Mattie: How Margaret E. Knight became an inventor*. New York: Farrar. K–2;3–4. B*

She was the first woman to receive a U.S. patent.

Mochizuki, K. (2006). *Be water, my friend: The early years of Bruce Lee*. New York: Lee and Low. K–2;3–4. B

Focuses on the early life of Bruce Lee.

Myers, W. D. (2001). *The greatest: Muhammad Ali*. New York: Scholastic. 3–4;5–6;7+. B

The biography of the life of Muhammad Ali, including his early life.

Nelson, S. (2006). *Quiet hero: The Ira Hayes story*. New York: Lee and Low. 3–4;5–6;7+. B

Ira Hayes was one of the soldiers who helped raise the flag in World War II.

Pinkney, A. (2002). *Ella Fitzgerald: The tale of a vocal virtuosa* (B. Pinkney, Illus.). New York: Hyperion. K–2;3–4;5–6. B

The famous musical artist.

Rumfeld, J. (2004). *Sequoyah: The man who gave his people writing* (A. Sixkiller Huckaby, Trans.). 3–4;5–6. B

Ryan, P. M. (2002). *When Marian sang* (B. Selznick, Illus.). New York: Scholastic. K–2;3–4. B

Marian Anderson's story.

Say, A. (1993). *Grandfather's journey*. Boston: Houghton Mifflin. 3–4;5–6. B

The story of Allen Say's grandfather.

Weatherford, C. (2006). *Moses: When Harriet Tubman led her people to freedom*. K–2;3–4. B

Harriet Tubman led many slaves to freedom.

Winter, J. (2006). *Dizzy*. New York: Scholastic. K–2;3–4. B

Dizzy Dean, the baseball star.

Professional References

Carr, J. (1982). What do we do about bad biographies? In *Beyond fact: Nonfiction for children and young people* (pp. 45–63). Chicago: American Library Association.

Fritz, J. (1990). The teller and the tale. In W. Zinsser (Ed.), *Worlds of childhood: The art and craft of writing for children* (pp. 21–46). Boston: Houghton Mifflin.

Harris, V., & McCarthey, S. (2002, Summer). A conversation with James Cross Giblin. *The New Advocate, 15* (3), 175–182.

Hearne, B. (1990). *Choosing books for children: A commonsense approach*. New York: Delacorte.

Hearne, B. (1999). *Choosing books for children: A commonsense approach*. (2nd ed.). New York: Delacorte.

Lesesne, T. (2002). Whose life is it, anyway? Biographies in the classroom. In *Young adult literature in the classroom. reading it, teaching it, loving it*. Newark, DE: International Reading Association.

Lukens, R. (1995). *A critical handbook of children's literature* (4th ed.). Glenview, IL: Scott Foresman.

Meltzer, M. (1981). Beyond the span of a single life. In B. Hearne and M. Kaye (Eds.), *Celebrating children's books* (pp. 87–96). New York: Lothrop, Lee, & Shepard.

Meltzer, M. (1987). The reader and the writer. In C. Bauer (Ed.), *The best of the bulletin*. Urbana, IL: National Council of Teachers of English.

Russell, D. (1994). *Literature for children*: *A short introduction.* New York: Longman.

Sullivan, E. (2002, October/November). Talking with Jim Arnosky. *Book Links.* Vol. 12. pp. 51–58.

Sutherland, Z., & Arbuthnot, M. H. (1991). *Children and books* (8th ed.). Chicago: Scott Foresman.

Zarnowski, M. (1990). *Learning about biographies*. Urbana, IL: National Council of Teachers of English.

12 Literature About Children with Real-Life Challenges

KEY TERMS

ADD/ADHD   dyscalculia
Asperger Syndrome   dyslexia
autism

GUIDING QUESTIONS

Most of us are confronted daily with challenges of one sort or another. Some of the challenges we face are merely inconveniences, but others may threaten our safety, our well-being, or how we live our lives. Many children—some of whom may be your students—live with challenges also. Think about how children learn to cope with their conditions and how you might make your classroom welcoming for them.

1. Why might it be important for all students to read about the challenges that face some children?

2. How could you use these books?

3. Would bibliotherapy be useful?

4. This chapter includes books from several genres. Why might that be so?

Introduction to Literature About Children with Real-Life Challenges

In Chapter 8, "Contemporary Realistic Fiction," we presented books in which children had to face many challenges within the family, with their peers, and in the larger world. This chapter addresses challenges that children, as individuals, may face. Physical disabilities, learning disabilities, disease, and health issues are some of the topics addressed. Children without these kinds of challenges may be afraid of children with some disabilities; they may make fun of them because they are different, or they may simply ignore them. If children are introduced to some of these challenges in books and have the opportunity to discuss the issues with their family or peers, their attitudes may change.

Additionally, it is important that the children who have the challenges see themselves in well-written literature. Sometimes children who are different, in any way, are lonely. Reading these books may help them feel less alone as they see how other children have coped with their particular challenge.

In recent years, children's books have changed a great deal in the ways they address disabilities (Saunders, 2004). In the past, books seemed to focus on the medical or rehabilitative nature of the disabilities. The focus recently, however, is on how to address equity issues for children who are in the mainstream of educational and social situations. This new focus presents opportunities for children without disabilities to make connections with children who are different from them in a number of different ways.

The Value of Literature that Addresses Real-Life Challenges

In the books in this chapter, one or more of the characters has a disability. In many cases, the disability is often just one of many characteristics—it is not always the defining one. In most of the books, the protagonists are simply trying to find a way to be like their peers and to be accepted for who they are—not pitied or made fun of because of their disability. There is an attitude of acceptance and respect in these books toward these children with challenges. A few books are informational in nature. They may help readers understand the nature of the disability so that interactions with those who have a specific characteristic can be more comfortable.

Saunders (2004) suggests that children's books can be an "agent" that is used to create, preserve, or reflect attitudes toward those with disabilities. If the protagonists are described as being "imprisoned" by their disability, readers may see them in the category of "not like us." When this happens, it is more difficult for others to make connections with them. However, if the protagonist has the problem of relating to his or her peers, and in addition has cancer, then readers are more likely to make connections with the peer issues and may gain some understanding of the cancer issue as well.

Selecting and Evaluating Literature

As is true when choosing any book to read, literary quality is the most important criteria. Unless the book tells a good story, it will not attract readers. Books that are written simply to teach or preach

rarely capture readers' interest. (See the section on didacticism in Chapter 3.)

The characters with disabilities must be portrayed as complex personalities with strengths, flaws, problems, feelings, and responses. They should not be presented as "perfect," nor should they be presented so readers feel sorry for them. Characters with challenges are capable of helping others and of having loving family relationships and friendships. They develop through their experiences, just as individuals without challenges do. Authors must avoid stereotypical behaviors in characters with disabilities or challenges and avoid superhuman portrayals, devices often used by some authors to make characters with disabilities more acceptable (Rudman, 1993). Characters with disabilities or challenges must be permitted to have ordinary flaws and to be average, non-spectacular people that readers will care about. The plot must focus on what they can do (Landrum, 1998–1999).

Landrum has developed a guide for evaluating novels written for adolescents that include challenged characters. These guidelines are also appropriate for books for younger readers as well. Using Landrum's criteria as well as our own, the following standards may be used to choose fiction books that depict challenged characters.

1. Challenged characters are strong or become stronger and more competent because of their experiences.
2. Challenged characters are portrayed through what they can do and are not confined by their disability.
3. Challenged characters are multidimensional and have emotions, strengths, and weaknesses.
4. Challenged characters are not portrayed as overly heroic or as victims.
5. Challenged characters have family and friends, just as non-challenged characters do.
6. The handicaps and challenges are accurately described.
7. The plot is realistic and avoids contrived events and miracle cures.
8. Both challenged characters and their peers have similar feelings, experiences, and conflicts.
9. All of the events are realistic and uncontrived.
10. The book should leave the challenged characters with hope.

Using These Books in the Classroom

We believe that teachers need to consider how to use the books in this chapter quite carefully. Because the characters portrayed in these books are "different" in some way, children who have not had similar or related experiences may react in inappropriate ways, just as they may react to other children in real life who may be different. Teachers need to be sensitive to both their students and the books they share so that there is both enjoyment and insight gained.

Individual Challenges

Books for children and young adults featuring characters with special challenges are categorized by the kind of challenge depicted. There are five categories of individual challenges: physical, learning, disease/health, sexuality, and emotional. In most, but not all, of the books, the main character is the person who has the challenge. Hopefully, readers will be able to connect with this person and his or her special situation. Most of the books featuring challenges are in the genres of contemporary realistic fiction or informational books.

Physical Challenges

Individuals may face a number of different physical challenges. We will discuss three in particular: challenges related to mobility, hearing, and body size.

Mobility

People with impaired mobility are sometimes identified as orthopedically disabled. They may have impaired legs, arms, or both, or may have paralyzed body parts. Mobility impairments may originate at birth, through accident, or illness. Some children are born with cerebral palsy, which can impair mobility quite seriously or very mildly. For some children, the impairment may be permanent; for others, through physical therapy or other means, the disability may be temporary.

In *Rolling Along: The Story of Taylor and His Wheelchair* by James Riggio Heelan, Taylor has cerebral palsy and uses either a walker or a wheelchair. He is a very independent boy and tries almost anything. He must have physical therapy and sometimes gets frustrated, but in general, he enjoys the same kinds of activities that other children do. This book helps younger children learn how one child copes with a physical challenge.

Stephanie Tolan in *Listen* writes about Charley, a 12-year old whose mother dies and who then badly injures her leg in a car accident. Charley has not had time to recover from her mom's death and now must also deal with her physical handicap. Her physical therapist insists that she walk, but she refuses to walk in the woods because they remind her too much of her mother. On one of her walks, she sees a stray dog, who needs help but is too afraid to make contact. Patiently, and with persistence, Charley is able to make contact with the dog she names Coyote. In doing this, she also begins her healing process and starts to work through her own grief.

In another coming-of-age story, Jean, who has cerebral palsy, goes to a summer camp for those who have this disability. At "Camp Crip," she meets others who are in wheelchairs and who have difficulty communicating. Since Jean has gone to a regular high school, she has not had the opportunity to spend time with others who are not "normal." She understands that she is a valuable person, wheelchair or not, and that she can make a difference. The book, *Accidents of Nature*, is written by Harriet McBryde Johnson, a lawyer who specializes in benefits and civil rights for people with disabilities.

In *The Winner's Walk*, Nancy Ruth Patterson has created greater understanding about how a disabled person is able to function independently with a service dog. Although Case, the protagonist in this book, does not have a disability himself, he finds an unusually talented stray golden retriever dog. For a child who never seems to do anything well enough to get positive recognition, having the dog he names Noah makes his life much more satisfying. However, Case finds out that the reason Noah can do so many things is that he is a service dog for a disabled girl. The girl has a new service dog and doesn't need Noah any longer. Now Case has a dilemma: Should he keep Noah or give him to someone who really needs him.

The Secret Garden** by Frances Hodgson Burnett was first published in 1911. It is the much loved story of Mary, an orphan, and her cousin Colin, who is in a wheelchair. Together the two find an abandoned garden, which they bring back to life. As they do so, their lives and the lives of all who live in the mansion change in very positive ways.

The classic Newbery Award–winning book *The Door in the Wall*** by Marguerite deAngeli was first published in 1949 and is still a favorite of many readers. During the plague in medieval England, Robin loses the use of his legs. He is abandoned by his servants who fear the disease. Robin is rescued by a monk and learns both acceptance and patience.

Hearing

Children with hearing impairments exhibit a full range of individual differences. Their experience, families, intelligence, and motivation are as diverse as those of other children. Their impairments may range from moderate to severe. Some live in a silent world; others may hear a few sounds. Hearing aids may help some people with hearing impairments to hear more than might be expected. However, children whose hearing is impaired usually have distorted or incomplete auditory input even with hearing aids. They may have difficulty producing and understanding speech sounds. Often deaf or hard-of-hearing children require special instruction as they learn language.

The winners of a writing competition, who are themselves deaf, contributed stories to a book sponsored by the Canadian Cultural Society of the Deaf. These stories present the frustrations and successes of children who are deaf. In one of the stories, a deaf child encounters challenges when she goes to a school where the other children can hear; in another story, the aunt of a princess will not let the princess use sign language. This book, *A Princess, a Tiger, and Other Deaf Tales*, provides insight for all readers and can be the basis for good discussions.

In *Can You Hear a Rainbow?* by James Riggio Heelan, Chris uses sign language, hearing aids, and lip reading to communicate with others. He is able to make comparisons between a friend who is deaf and one who has normal hearing. This book would be helpful to young children, especially those who have deaf friends, because Chris does not feel sorry for himself.

Body Size

Body size, whether it be height or weight, has a great impact on self-esteem and relating to peers. A topic that is not often found in literature for children and young adults is that of being a dwarf. In *The Thing About Georgie*, Lisa Graff writes about Georgie, a fourth grader and a dwarf. Georgie is lucky to be accepted as a regular person, regardless of his size. Nonetheless, he has lots of challenges—the school furniture doesn't fit, he is going to have a sibling who will probably be normal and be able to do things he cannot, and he has a fight with his best friend. When he is assigned to do a report with Jeanie the Meanie, he is very doubtful about the outcome. The outcome is surprising, and readers find that Georgie is more typical than one would first expect.

The issue of obesity is addressed in *Staying Fat for Sarah Byrnes*** by Chris Crutcher. Eric Cahloune has been a social outcast for many years because he is obese. He becomes close friends with Sarah, also an outcast because of an accident in which she was disfigured. Eric has begun competitive swimming and has slimmed down, but in so doing, his relationship with Sarah changes. This book explores more issues than weight and will appeal to young adults.

Learning Challenges

Although children and young adults may face a variety of learning disabilities, we will focus on the following: ADD/ADHD, dyslexia, autism, Asperger Syndrome, and dyscalculia.

ADD/ADHD

Attention-deficit disorder (ADD) and *attention-deficit hyperactivity disorder (ADHD)* are two learning challenges that many students have. ADD is defined as, "a developmental disorder involving one or more of the basic cognitive processes relating to orienting, focusing, maintaining attention" (Harris et al., 1995, p. 13). Attention-deficit hyperactivity disorder is ADD plus hyperactivity. Children who have ADHD are often inattentive, impulsive, and not able to follow rule-governed behavior (Harris et al., 1995). ADD/ADHD creates challenges for both the students and their teachers.

One excellent book about ADHD is *Cory Stories: A Kid's Book about Living with ADHD* by Jeanne Kraus. Cory often feels like he has jumping beans inside of him, and kids laugh at him and hurt his feelings. Cory has ADHD, and in this book he lets readers know what it is like. He tells how he takes medicine, gets help from a therapist, and gives suggestions about how he interacts with others. For younger children, this is a good introduction to ADHD.

Another book with an interesting ADD character is *Parents Wanted* by George Harrar. Andy has been turned over to the state for adoption because of a difficult family situation. Andy has lived in several foster homes and knows that in his prospective adoptive home there will be new rules. He tries to get past these rules by being dishonest—which gets him into even more trouble. Andy's process of rationalization is related to his ADD, so readers get an interesting perspective about his thinking.

Many children who have ADHD think that they are the only ones with the kinds of problems they have. *Putting on the Brakes*: *Young People's Guide to Understanding Attention Deficit Hyperactivity Disorder,* written by Patricia O. Quinn and Judith M. Stern, provides readers with suggestions that could make their lives more manageable. The suggestions are practical, and the book is very readable. The book would also be of interest to parents and teachers who may interact with children with this condition.

Dyslexia and Other Learning Difficulties

It is frustrating for a child who loves books not to be able to learn to read. In *The Alphabet War: A Story about Dyslexia* by Diane Burton Robb, not until Adam is in third grade does he learn the reason reading is so hard for him: He has *dyslexia* (a developmental reading disability). By this time, his self-confidence is low, he is acting out in a variety of ways, and he is failing. It takes a long time, but Adam does learn to read and accepts that reading will always be hard for him. This book helps to make dyslexia more understandable and perhaps can encourage those who may have this learning problem.

The esteemed author and illustrator, Patricia Polacco, was herself dyslexic. In *Thank You, Mr. Falker*, she describes how hard it was for her to learn to read and how mean the other students were as they made fun of her. When she was in fifth grade, her family moved to California. There, her teacher recognized she had a problem and with time, patience, and extra instruction, Trisha learned to read and felt the joy of being successful.

Gary L. Fisher and Rhoda Cummings do not talk about a "learning disability"; rather they focus on the fact that some students learn differently than other students. Their book, *The Survival Guide for*

Kids with LD: Learning Differences, is filled with descriptions of a variety of learning differences, how students can learn to deal with their feelings, strategies for learning how to do better in school, the rights of learning disabled students, and setting goals for the future. Parents and teachers will also learn from this book because there is a section of resources for adults who work with kids who learn differently.

Sometimes the best models for students are people who have met and overcome adversity. Jonathan Mooney and David Cole had very difficult times in school because they were learning disabled. However, both of these authors graduated from college at the top of their class. They suggest that sometimes rules must be broken and that it is possible to be a successful student regardless of the odds. The suggestions in their book, *Learning Outside the Lines*, are appropriate for students who have been given a variety of labels—including gifted students.

The following two books are helpful for parents and teachers of students who have learning difficulties. The first book is *The Secret Life of the Dyslexic Child* by Robert Frank and Kathryn E. Livingston. Frank was diagnosed as being dyslexic, and he stresses that parents are a key in helping dyslexic students be successful. The second book, *How to Reach and Teach Children and Teens with Dyslexia* by Cynthia M. Stowe, provides information about techniques to help children learn to read and be successful in school. Many resources are provided.

In *Summer of the Swans*** by Betsy Byars, Sara is a typical 14-year-old who worries about everything— her looks, her relationships, her family—especially her mentally handicapped younger brother Charlie. However, on the day that Charlie gets lost, Sara learns to separate important issues from those that are less important. This Newbery Award winner is as relevant today as it was when it was first published in 1970.

Autism

An individual who is *autistic* is one who has a developmental disorder that is characterized by language and social impairments. An autistic person is extremely self-centered and may not be able to accurately determine what is real. Some individuals with severe autism may not be able to communicate at all through language and may have little or no social interaction (Harris et al., 1995).

Two books by Marvie Ellis, a pediatric speech-language pathologist, focus on autism. In *Keisha's Doors: An Autism Story Book One*, Monica doesn't understand why her younger sister won't play with her. In *Tacos Anyone? An Autism Story Book Two*, Thomas wants to know why his younger brother Michael behaves the way he does. In both books, the younger siblings are autistic, and a therapist helps the older children learn how to interact with the younger siblings so that the family interactions are better. Both books are written in both English and Spanish. The second book won the Barbara Jordan Media Award.

The Newbery Honor book *Rules*, by Cynthia Lord, is a story of acceptance and understanding. Catherine's younger brother David is autistic. She has devised all sorts of rules for him, which she sees as her responsibility to help him and to prevent him from doing embarrassing things. The title of each chapter is a rule—which helps the reader have a sense of context for the necessity for the rule! Catherine then meets Jason, a paraplegic, who communicates by pointing at word cards. Because of her interactions with Jason, Catherine is able to look at David differently, and she begins to accept that each person is an individual, with unique strengths and weaknesses.

Asperger Syndrome

Asperger Syndrome is a neurobiological disorder and is described as an "autism spectrum disorder" (Bashe and Kirby, 2005). It includes a pattern of behaviors in which there is normal intelligence and language development but deficiencies in social and communication skills.

Thirteen-year-old Luke Jackson has Asperger Syndrome. Because Luke could find no book that addresses issues such as name calling, bullying, and problems in school, including dating, he has written a book in which he addresses some of the problems he has faced, based on interactions with his peers, family, and others. Luke hopes that his book, *Freaks, Geeks and Asperger Syndrome: A User Guide to Adolescence*, will help others learn from what he has experienced.

A second book on Asperger Syndrome, edited by Liane Holliday Willey, includes chapters by teenagers from several countries. These chapters focus on sexuality, dating, occupational therapy, and safety issues. *Asperger Syndrome in Adolescence* is an excellent follow-up to the first book because it presents a variety of perspectives from other teens.

Dyscalculia

A kind of learning problem that we do not often hear about is *dyscalculia*, the inability to do anything related to sequential processing—mathematics, spelling, or grammar. A person with this learning disability may not be able to dial a phone number, count money, or do simple adding or subtracting. In *My Thirteenth Winter: A Memoir* by Samantha Abeel, the author recounts how no matter how hard she worked on her math and spelling activities, she consistently failed at them. Because she was not diagnosed until she was a teenager, her frustration is understandable. This memoir will be helpful to students who are struggling with similar issues and to teachers who have students who may have a learning disability.

Disease and Health Challenges

Children and young adults may face a number of illnesses and diseases that affect their educational needs. We will focus on two: diabetes and cancer.

Diabetes

Many children today have diabetes. Their families, friends, and others often have lots of questions about what these children can and cannot do. Two recently published books help to answer some of these questions. *Lara Takes Charge*, written by Rocky Lang and Sally Huss, is for younger children. Lara tells readers what it is like having diabetes. She can do almost anything everyone else can do—even if she has an insulin pump and does regular blood tests. The illustrations help convey a positive message.

Another interesting book, *487 Really Cool Tips for Kids with Diabetes*, is written by brothers who were diagnosed with this disease while they were young. In response to their first book, *Getting a Grip on Diabetes*, they received lots of tips from readers about how they managed to have regular lives, even though they had significant health issues. Spike Nasmyth Loy and Bo Nasmyth Loy have compiled a book that is interesting reading for all ages.

Families of children who are diagnosed with diabetes are very much impacted by the disease. Michael Olson found this out when his younger brother, Steven, had juvenile diabetes. The family found that there were not many resources available to them. Michael decided that he needed to write a book to help

Healthful living is important for young diabetics.

his family as well as others. He did so, and the result is *How I Feel: A Book About Diabetes*, which is illustrated by his diabetic brother, Steven.

The eating patterns of children with diabetes are different from those of many others. A cookbook, *Cooking up Fun for Kids with Diabetes* by Patti Geil and Tami Ross, gives children some insights about the relationship between foods and their well-being. The recipes are ones that children, with some assistance, can make.

Cancer

In *Defiance* by Valerie Hobbs, Toby's cancer is in remission, so he and his mom have plans to spend the summer in the country. When Toby discovers a marble-like lump in his side, however, he makes the conscious decision not to tell anyone because he doesn't want to be hospitalized again. On a bicycle ride, he meets an elderly neighbor, Pearl, and forms an alliance with her. He does things for Pearl that she can't do for herself and helps her take care of her old cow, Blossom. When Blossom dies, Toby must come to terms with his disease, also. Valerie Hobbs shows readers that "defiance" can sometimes be a necessary choice in matters of life and death.

In *Runt* by V.M. Caldwell, the main character doesn't have cancer but he has been orphaned, abandoned, and abused. When Runt moves in with his older sister, he refuses to go to school and hangs around town. In the cemetery, he meets Mitch, an engaging teenager who has cancer and is in a wheelchair. Runt initially resists Mitch's attempts at friendship but then the two visit almost daily. Although Mitch is near death, he is able to share his love of life with Runt, who finally finds the strength to deal with his very real problems.

In *Side Effects,* author Amy Goldman Koss lets readers vicariously experience how a disease completely changes one's expectations about "tomorrow." Fifteen-year-old Izzy is having a normal morning fighting with her mother. As she gets ready for school, she notices that her glands are still swollen even though she had had flu some time ago. A doctor's appointment and tests reveal that she has lymphoma. Izzy deals with her cancer as best she can—hating how she feels and looks. Chemotherapy is awful as she loses her hair, her energy, and often her will to live. Of course, her interactions with her friends and family change but as they all accept the effects of the cancer, they learn to look at things with a weird sense of humor. Although the last scan that Izzy has indicates that she is cancer free, her life will always be impacted by this disease.

Sexuality

There are a number of well-written books that address issues related to sexuality. We will examine literature related to gay and lesbian issues, as well as teen pregnancy.

Gay and Lesbian Literature

In David Larochelle's *Absolutely, Positively Not*, Steven has many secrets that he hides from other people, but he finds he can't hide them from himself. For example, he really likes to square dance, and he wonders if other males think about females as often as he thinks about males. He tries to date girls but finds that that is something he just cannot do. Finally, he comes out to his best friend, Rachel. By this time, his family has made the assumption that he is gay and has accepted it. Although the book includes many incidents that are really amusing, there is also a sense of desperation as Steven tries to find someone to talk to. *Absolutely, Positively Not* is a book that might help straight students understand the dilemma a gay peer may have, and may also help the young person who is struggling with his or her sexuality.

Two books by Brent Hartinger feature Russel, a gay student in a conservative high school in which the social structure is very rigid. In the first book, *The Geography Club*, five gay students form their own group. Russel makes some questionable decisions when he is lured into a group of popular students. In the second book, *The Order of the Poison Ivy*, Russel is a camp counselor. Again he is attracted to another counselor and makes some decisions that have consequences both for himself and for the 10-year-olds that he is supervising. Regardless of Russel's problematic decisions, there is a realization of the importance of responsible behavior.

Teen Pregnancy/Parents

In *Annie's Baby: The Diary of Anonymous, a Pregnant Teenager,* edited by Beatrice Sparks, 14-year old Annie has fallen in love with 16-year old Danny, a handsome and wealthy but abusive boyfriend. She lies to her mother to be able to go out with him so they can go to parties and have sex. She writes in her diary about the relationship and how she feels when the pregnancy test comes back positive. She is lucky that her mother and teachers are supportive and that she has a good therapist. The diary format makes this book especially compelling. The book includes an appendix, which provides much relevant information.

A very different perspective on teenage pregnancy comes in two books in which the teenaged fathers take on the responsibility of raising their children. In *Hanging Onto Max* by Margaret Bechard, 17-year-old Sam keeps the baby his girlfriend, Brittany, wanted to give up for adoption. Sam is a senior at an alternative high school so he is able to continue his education while caring for Max. However, he gets little help from his widowed father, other than financial, as he struggles with his school and parenting responsibilities. Sam's senior year is certainly very different than he anticipated, but Max is an important part of Sam's life.

In *The First Part Last* by Angela Johnson, Bobby is 16 when his girlfriend, Nia, tells him that he is going to be a father. The chapters alternate between past and present, so readers don't find out until the end that Nia is in an irreversible coma, which is why the responsibility of raising his daughter falls on Bobby. We struggle with Bobby as he tries to balance all the important parts of his life—baby, school, friends. This is a very thought-provoking book for teens.

Emotional Challenges

At one time or another, most of us—children and young adults included—feel overwhelmed by our emotions. Children's literature abounds with books that can help young readers cope with their feelings. A book for younger children, *The Boy Who Didn't Want to be Sad* by Rob Goldblatt, tells how an unnamed boy decides to

STORIES ABOUT PHOBIAS

what are you afraid of?

edited by Donald R. Gallo

These short stories show readers how some people have overcome phobias.

get rid of everything that makes him sad. What he finds out, however, is that the things that make him sad are also the things that make him happy. This books lets readers look at sad/glad in a different way.

Josh's Smiley Faces: A Story about Anger by Gina Ditta-Donahue is an interesting book for younger children who may need to learn to control their feelings. Most children get angry. Josh, however, seems to get angry a lot. He throws his toys, hits, and acts out so that everyone knows when he is mad. His mom comes up with a plan: Josh will learn to use smiley faces to show his feelings. Through this strategy and with the help of his mom, Josh learns to be better able to control his anger.

In *What are You Afraid of?*, author Donald Gallo asked 11 well-known authors to write a short story about phobias. The contributors' stories deal with subjects such as the fear of gaining weight, crossing the street, and cats. The 10 stories in the book will make interesting reading for many students who may (or may not) be afraid of something relatively common. Readers can see how the characters in each story try to overcome the fear that has impacted their life.

Summary

It has been over 30 years since Public Law 94–142 was passed. This law requires that, as much as possible, children with disabilities be educated in the same classrooms as those who have not been identified as having a disability. At first, having children with a variety of challenges in classrooms was a great challenge to the teachers, as well as to all students. Over time, however, teachers and students have learned to adjust to the mainstreamed students. Perhaps this is the reason that fewer books about challenges have been published recently.

The books in this chapter are ones that address a wide variety of challenges. More of them are contemporary realistic fiction than was the case a few years ago. This might imply that rather than needing only informational books to learn about the various challenges, young people want books that have characters with whom they can identify, so that they may gain insight about their interactions with all of their peers.

CLASSROOM SNAPSHOT
ILLUSTRATING THE CHALLENGES OF CHILDREN WITH SPECIAL NEEDS

The third graders in Miss Ryan's class had just returned from a field trip to the zoo. The children, their teacher, and the parents who went with them were talking about their observations. One of their favorite exhibits was the Snake House, and they were talking excitedly about the exhibits. Then several of the children brought up the fact that there was a child in a wheelchair visiting the exhibits at the same time that they were.

"Did you notice how that boy kept pushing his way to the front of the exhibits?" asked Jamie. "I didn't think that was very nice."

"I know," said Max. "He almost ran over my foot."

Miss Ryan quickly got into the discussion. "Why do you think that he acted in such a way, trying to get to the front of the exhibit?"

Jenny suggested that maybe he couldn't see from the back and that perhaps no one was willing to move aside to let him through.

From this point, the discussion began to focus on what it might be like to have to be in a wheelchair. Everyone had an opinion!

Then one of the parents said, "I have a wheelchair at home that I had for Jenny's grandma. Would you like me to bring it to school so you could see what it might be like to be in a wheelchair?"

Miss Ryan quickly agreed that this would be an interesting activity. She also began thinking of books that she could bring to class so that the children could get more information about people with limited mobility. The trip to the zoo was the impetus for a mini-unit about a topic that was of great interest to her class—and she was going to be able to involve parents in this unit, always one of her goals!!

Thought Questions and Applications

1. Who might benefit more from reading this type of literature: challenged children or those who are not challenged?

2. Can you think of other problems and challenges that should be addressed in literature for children and young adults?

3. Why are children with challenges mainstreamed into regular classrooms?

Research and Application Experiences

1. Do an Internet search to find other books about one of the challenges that you think is particularly important for students to learn about. What kinds of hands-on experiences would you have the children do as they are reading these books?

2. Search out and find appropriate strategies to use with the children who have learning challenges. Many times, challenged children need different kinds of help than the other children in your classroom.

3. Interview the reading specialist in a school. See if he or she has suggestions for books that can be used for children with learning challenges.

4. From any collection of books, do a survey to ascertain how many of the main characters have a challenge. Are there any characters who have a challenge? What are the implications?

Classroom Activities

ACTIVITY 12.1   RESPONDING TO LITERATURE THROUGH A UNIT STUDY

IRA/NCTE Standards. Because doing a unit on the topic of challenges is conducted over a period of several weeks, it is possible to accomplish all of the standards. The standards accomplished by each of the suggested activities are in parentheses.

Planning a unit of study around the challenges of some children provides opportunities for students to identify with those who may be different. Working in pairs or small groups, the children choose a particular challenge on which to focus. Some of the choices might be hearing, vision, learning, disease, and emotional challenges. A variety of activities that might be done follow:

A. (Required) Read a variety of fiction and informational books about the topic. (#1, 2, 3)

B. Start a response journal. Write down how life would be different if you had the challenge you have been reading about. Describe all aspects of your day. (#4, 5, 6)

C. Plan a dramatic scene in which you demonstrate some of the strategies used by individuals with challenges. (#3, 4, 8, 9, 10, 12)

D. What technological devices might you create that would make the life of the challenged person easier? (#1, 7, 8, 11, 12)

E. Interview a person who has the challenge you are studying. Create the questions you want to ask before you begin the interview. Write up the responses and share them in the class. (#4, 5, 6, 7, 9)

F. Are there any songs or music about the challenge chosen? Find them and share them with the class. (#1, 3, 7, 8)

G. How might some of the games you play be modified so that a person with a challenge could play them too? (#7, 8, 12.)

As students respond to literature in a variety of ways, teachers can determine if comprehension has been gained. It is also important that positive attitudes be created about people with challenges, particularly if there has been little contact with students who are different from the students in a class.

Children's Literature References

Abeel, S. (2003). *My thirteenth winter: A memoir.* New York: Orchard Press. 7+. B

The author has dyscalculia and describes her struggles trying to learn.

Bechard, M. (2002). *Hanging onto Max.* New Milford, CT: Roaring Brook Press. 7+. CRF

A teenaged father keeps his baby while finishing high school.

Burnett, F. H. (Reprint 1998). *The secret garden.* New York: Harper Trophy. 3–4;5–6;7+. HF

Two cousins find a hidden garden and work to bring it back to life; in so doing, their lives and the lives of all who are around them are changed.

Byars, B. (1970). *The summer of the swans.* New York: Viking. 5–6;7+. CRF, New Audiocassette: Recorded Books Steady Readers (1995).

When Sara's mentally handicapped brother is lost, she learns about the things that matter most to her.

Canadian Cultural Society of the Deaf. (2006). *A princess, a tiger and other deaf tales.* Toronto, Ont: Second Story Press. K–2;3–4. CRF; MF

A collection of stories written by deaf authors about being deaf.

Caldwell, V. M. (2006). *Runt.* Minneapolis, MN: Milkweed. 5–6;7+. CRF

An abandoned boy makes friends with a boy who has cancer.

Crutcher, C. (1995). *Staying fat for Sarah Byrnes.* New York: Greenwillow. 7+. CRF

An obese teen starts swimming and begins to slim down, which impacts his friendship with a person who is disfigured.

de Angeli, M. (1949). New York: Doubleday. 5–6;7+. HF, New Audiocassette: Listening Library (1998).

Robin loses the use of his legs during the Plague but learns that he can make many contributions in his medieval society.

Ditta-Donahue, G. (2003). *Josh's smiley faces: A story about anger.* Washington, DC: Magination Press. K–2. PB; CRF

Josh and his mom work on ways to help him learn to control his anger.

Ellis, M. (2004). *Keisha's doors: An autism story book one* (J. Loehr, Illus.). Austin TX: Speech Kids Texas Press. K–2. CRF; PB

An older sister wants to know why her younger sister won't play with her. A therapist helps her and her family.

Ellis, M. (2005). *Tacos anyone? An autism story book two* (J. Loehr, Illus.). Austin, TX: Speech Kids Texas Press. K–2. CRF; PB

An older brother doesn't understand why his younger brother behaves as he does.

Fisher, G. L., & Cummings, R. (Revised and updated, 2002). *The survival guide for kids with LD: Learning differences.* Minneapolis, MN: Free Spirit Publishing. 5–6;7+. INF

A book of suggestions for students who learn differently than their peers.

Frank, R., & Livingston, K. E. (2002). *The secret life of the dyslexic child: How she thinks, how he feels, how they can succeed.* Emmaus, PA: Rodale. 5–6;7+. INF

Suggestions for being successful by a person identified as dyslexic.

Gallo, D. R., Ed. (2006). *What are you afraid of?* Cambridge, MA: Candlewick. 5–6;7+. CRF; INF

A collection of short stories about phobias people may have.

Geil, P. B., & Ross, T. A. (2003). *Cooking up fun for kids with diabetes.* Alexandria, VA: American Diabetes Association. 3–4;5–6;7+. INF

A cookbook for kids who have diabetes.

Graf, L. (2007). *The thing about Georgie.* New York: HarperCollins. 3–4;5–6. CRF

Georgie is a dwarf but he is able to interact normally with his peers.

Goldblatt, R. (2004). *The boy who didn't want to be sad.* New York: Magination Press. K–2. PB; CRF

A young boy tries to get rid of everything that makes him sad.

Harrar, G. (2001). *Parents wanted.* Minneapolis, MN: Milkweed. 5–6;7+. CRF

Andy wants to be adopted but because of his ADD, makes some bad decisions.

Hartinger, B. (2002). *Geography club.* New York: HarperTempest. 7+. CRF

Gay students form their own group in a conservative high school.

Hartinger, B. (2005). *The order of the poison oak.* New York: HarperTempest. 7+. CRF

A gay teen is a camp counselor.

Heelan, J. R. (2000). *Rolling along: The story of Taylor and his wheelchair.* Atlanta, GA: Peachtree. K–2;3–4. PB; INF

Taylor must use a walker or wheelchair. This book describes how he learns to cope with his disability.

Heelan, J. R. (2002). *Can you hear a rainbow?* Atlanta, GA: Peachtree. K–2;3–4. PB; INF

Chris uses sign language and lip reading to communicate.

Hobbs, V. (2005). *Defiance.* New York: Farrar. 5–6;7+. CRF

Toby decides not to tell that his cancer has returned while he is on vacation.

Jackson, L. (2002). *Freaks, geeks, and Asperger Syndrome: A user guide to adolescence.* Philadelphia, PA: Jessica Kingsley. 7+. INF

The author has Asperger Syndrome and wrote the book giving advice about how to live with the issues associated with it.

Johnson, A. (2003). *The first part last.* New York: Simon and Schuster. 7+. CRF

A teen-aged father takes responsibility for his child.

Johnson, H. M. (2006). *Accidents of nature.* New York: Holt. 7+. CRF

A teenager with cerebral palsy goes to a special camp with others who have this disease.

Koss, A. G. (2006). *Side effects.* New Milford, CT: Roaring Brook Press. 7+. CRF

Izzy's swollen glands are really lymphoma, which she battles vigorously.

Kraus, J. (2004). *Cory stories: A kid's book about living with ADHD* (W. Martin, Illus.). Washington, DC: Magination Press. K–2;3–4. CRF; INF

Cory tells what it feels like to have ADHD.

Lang, R., & Huss, S. (2004). *Lara takes charge.* Northridge, CA: HLPI Books. K–2. PB; INF

A girl with diabetes tells what she has to do to monitor and live with diabetes.

Larochelle, D. (2005). *Absolutely, positively not.* New York: Arthur Levine. 7+. CRF

A gay teen comes to terms with his sexuality.

Lord, C. (2006). *Rules.* New York: Scholastic. 3–4;5–6. CRF; NewH

Catherine learns to accept her brother's autism after she becomes friends with a boy who is a paraplegic.

Loy, S. N., & Loy, B. N. (2004). *487 really cool tips for kids with diabetes.* Alexandria, VA: American Diabetes Association. 3–4;5–6;7+. INF

Brothers with diabetes give tips for how they manage their lives.

Loy, S. N., & Loy, B. N. (2007). *Getting a grip on diabetes,* 2nd ed. Alexandria, VA: American Diabetes Association. 3–4;5–6;7+. INF

Brothers with diabetes tell readers about their diabetes.

Mooney, J., & Cole, D. (2000). *Learning outside the lines.* New York: Fireside. 7+. INF

Suggestions for students who have been given an educational label.

Olson, M. (2003). *How I feel: A book about diabetes* (S. Olson, Illus.). New York: Lantern Books. K–2;3–4;5–6. INF

An older brother writes about how diabetes impacts the family after his younger brother is diagnosed with it.

Patterson, N. R. (2006). *The winner's walk* (T. Yezerski, Illus.). New York: Farrar. K–2;3–4. CRF

A boy finds a service dog. Should he keep him or give him to a person who needs him?

Polacco, P. (1999). *Thank you, Mr. Falker.* New York: Scholastic. 3–4;5–6. CRF

Trisha's fifth-grade teacher discovers Trisha can't read and gives her extra help.

Quinn, P. O., & Stern, J. M. (2001). *Putting on the brakes: Young people's guide to understanding attention deficit hyperactivity disorder.* Washington, DC: Magination Press. 3–4;5–6. INF

Suggestions are given to make the lives of those with ADHD more manageable.

Robb, D. B. (2004). *The alphabet war: A story about dyslexia* (G. Piazza, Illus.). Morton Grove, IL: Albert Whitman. K–2. CRF

Adam has a hard time learning to read and finds out that he has dyslexia.

Sparks, B., Ed. (2004). *Annie's baby: The diary of anonymous, a pregnant teenager*. New York: Harper Teen. 7+. INF

The diary of a teenaged girl who gets pregnant by an abusive boyfriend.

Tolan, Stephanie. (2006). *Listen!* New York: HarperCollins. 7+. CRF

After her mother dies, a young girl is in a car accident and injures her leg. She must learn to cope with her injuries, both physical and emotional.

Willey, L. H., Ed. (2003). *Asperger Syndrome in adolescence*. New York: Jessica Kingsley. 7+. INF

Teens from around the world provide tips for living with this disease.

Professional References

Bashe, P. R., & Kirby, B. (2005). aspergersyndrome. org/oasis.

Frank, R., & Livingston, K. (2002). *The secret life of the dyslexic child: How she thinks, how he feels, how they can succeed*. Emmaus, PA: Rodale Books.

Harris, T. L., Hodges, R. E., Greene, F., & Monson, D. Eds. (1995). *The literacy dictionary: The vocabulary of reading and writing*. Newark, DE: International Reading Association.

Landrum, L. (1998–1999). Adolescent novels that feature characters with disabilities: An annotated bibliography. *Journal of Adolescent & Adult Literacy, 42*, 284–295.

Rudman, M. K. (1993). *Children's literature: Resource for the classroom*. Norwood, MA: Christopher-Gordon.

Saunders, K. (2004). What disability studies can do for children's literature. *Disability Studies Quarterly, 24.*

Stowe, Cynthia M. (2000). *How to reach and teach children and teens with dyslexia*. Hoboken, NJ: Jossey-Bass.

13 Literature About Children in Many Cultures

KEY TERMS

cultural consciousness   global literature

culture   multicultural literature

GUIDING QUESTIONS

This chapter focuses on literature that will allow children from many different cultures, families, and circumstances to find books and activities in which they may "see" themselves. It is often hard for readers to make connections with characters who share few, if any, qualities of the readers themselves. The books in this chapter were chosen to illustrate some of the many different kinds of cultures, settings, and characters that are available for children and young adults.

1. Why might some readers not make connections with some books?

2. Why might it make a difference if readers can see—or read about—characters with whom they share many common characteristics?

3. How can teachers be sure that the books they use reflect the diversity found in their classrooms, in local communities, and in this country in general?

4. Why do teachers in classrooms in which there is little cultural diversity have a responsibility

for introducing books that show a variety of cultures?

5. What will you, as a member of your culture, need to do to feel comfortable using books that are representative of other cultures?

An Introduction to Multicultural Literature

Culture is a shared way of living—acting, believing, and valuing. This shared set of ideas, behaviors, discourses, and attitudes internally and externally define a social group (Shanahan, 1994). One of the great advantages of this country is that there are many cultures, which creates richness and diversity. Sometimes, however, those in one cultural group may isolate themselves from other cultural groups. When this happens, there is little opportunity for growth or understanding. *Cultural consciousness* is awareness of and sensitivity to the diversity of other groups: It can be the beginning of gaining respect for those who are different.

Wherever we live, cultural diversity is a part of our everyday lives. Voice-mail systems offer messages in the language of our choice, while information and directions found on the Internet can be printed in several languages. Many grocery stores have "ethnic" sections where one may buy foods that are unique to

---

CLASSROOM SNAPSHOT
FOCUSING ON CULTURAL DIVERSITY

Fifth-grade teacher Libby Dranon was concerned that her team members might want to include multicultural books that present stereotypes and distortions. She had just completed a course on critical multicultural education while finishing her graduate degree and thus had developed a perspective different from that of her peers. In her classes, she learned of the "tourist approach of holidays and heroes or fun, food, and festivals" (Franquiz, 2005), which she wanted to avoid. She knew how easy it would be to just do the traditional activities, but she wanted her students to have the opportunity to have accurate information.

Libby decided to collect a group of lesson plans and activities, which she found in her graduate class as well as on the Internet. She would present these to her peers and try to convince them to create learning communities that focused on cultural diversity. She decided to use these two books: *Lies My Teacher Told Me* by James W. Loewen and *The Light in Their Eyes: Creating Multicultural Learning Communities* by Sonia Nieto. Libby knew that her teammates were always up for a challenge and, by being prepared, she hoped that they, too, would be willing to make a critical analysis of the topics they were scheduled to teach during the coming semester.

---

specific cultures, and most areas of the United States include restaurants from many different cultures; and certainly the music that we hear and the art that we see are created by individuals from a wide variety of cultures. It is impossible to remain outside of a culture, and each of us is a member of several different subcultures. The social fabric of our lives is composed of many different layers that interact within and outside of all individuals. All readers, as cultural beings, are part of this multicultural society.

In this chapter, we will talk about *multicultural literature* rather than *culturally conscious literature* because this is the term used in most professional writing. Although "multicultural" does not have the same connotation as "culturally conscious," pragmatically speaking, it is the one that is most familiar and useful to current and future teachers. Cultural consciousness often has a political connotation that may imply a different focus than we intend. Shanahan (1994) suggests that although the term *multicultural literature* may not appeal to some people, it is a useful description as long as we do not assume that multicultural refers to "other people." It is our belief that multicultural literature can demonstrate the complexity of our society and lead readers to the inescapable conclusion that we all are cultural beings.

What Is Multicultural Literature?

Grace Enriquez (2001) suggests that there are many definitions of multicultural literature. Some educators define multicultural literature to include books that depict minorities and characters from non-mainstream backgrounds, as well as books that depict women, gays, and lesbians. The members of the Cooperative Children's Book Center at the University of Wisconsin also support the notion that there is no simple definition; they "use the term to mean books by and about people of color" (p. 1). Others consider multicultural literature to be books written by and about people in groups that are outside the social or political mainstream (DeNicolo and Franquiz, 2006; Dudley-Marling, 2003; Bishop, 1992). Our definition combines many of the above aspects. We consider multicultural literature to be books in any genre that include people—both those of color and those who are not of color but who are part of a distinct cultural group, race, or religion—who, for the most part, live in the United States. For a book to be considered multicultural, it must include enough detail so that readers who may be unfamiliar with the culture will be able to create pictures in their minds of the people, setting, and events. Books that focus on cultures outside the United States are called *global literature* (Freeman & Lehman, 2001). [Only a few books with a global setting are reviewed in this chapter; they have specific ties to one of the cultural groups included later in the chapter.]

Although this chapter focuses specifically on multicultural books, books presented in all of the chapters include a variety of cultures. A point to remember is that multicultural books are found in all genres. We will begin by looking at books about the original Americans, the Native Americans. Their cultures, both past and present, are little known to many of us, although stereotypes about them abound. Our country is as diverse as it is because of the immigration of people from various countries. Many African Americans, Hispanic Americans, Asian Americans, and those from the Middle East have maintained their cultural traditions, although some of them have lived their entire lives in this country. Other cultural groups, such as members of the Jewish, Appalachian, and Amish communities, also have strong cultural traditions and have experienced prejudice because of their beliefs. We hope that reading books about these cultures will further the goal of developing cultural consciousness, respect, and appreciation of all people.

Why Use Multicultural Literature in Classrooms?

Multicultural literature is important in two very different kinds of classroom settings. The first, of course, is in elementary and middle-school classrooms. The second is in classrooms in which pre-service and in-service teachers are learning about teaching. Our hope is that if pre-service and in-service teachers become familiar with multicultural literature they will be comfortable using it in their classrooms. Teachers are the role models for children; if they read and share multicultural literature, the children will probably read it, too.

According to the United Nations' demographic data of October 1999, if the earth's population could be proportionally reduced to just 100 people, there would be 61 Asians, 12 Europeans, 14 North and South Americans, and 13 Africans. Of these 100 individuals, 70 people would be non-white and 30 would be white (Steiner, 2001). It is obvious that we live in a global world and a multicultural society; it will be to our students' advantage to feel comfortable as they interact with people who are from other cultures.

Some young people have not seen their cultural group represented in books. Goodson (2004) worked with a group of seventh graders living in a rural farming county. These students thought there was nothing unique about themselves and that nothing they could write would be of interest to other people. They viewed their culture as a liability rather than considering it positively. They saw few connections between their local culture and the values in their school culture. For these students, and others like them in very different cultures, seeing others like themselves in books may make a difference in their achievement. "Given our pressing need to produce demonstrable student improvement on standardized measures, it is more important than ever for us to better understand and account for our students' rich cultural background. Instructional interventions based purely on cognitive data can have only so much effect. To push achievement higher, we need to account for and incorporate a much more sophisticated socio-culture awareness" (n.p.).

DeNicolo and Franquiz (2006) suggest that "When students are able to see their own lives in a text, they are more likely to identify critical encounters in their reading outside the classroom" (p. 168). To have this happen, however, requires discussion and negotiating the meanings found in a text. Students and their teachers are able to support each other in developing a "critical lens—the examination of values, beliefs, and events in personal and collective lives" (p. 168).

Discussion is extremely important if teachers hope to impact attitudes and create awareness and respect about cultures other than one's own. Umber (2002) suggests that "Reading a book written for people of another culture is an interesting experience in itself" (p. 7). This is because words may be unfamiliar and the context may place the readers as "outsiders," which means that they need to infer meaning. As children and their teachers read books that are outside of their personal experiences, these inferences may be different than those anticipated by the author. The readers may not have enough prior knowledge to understand different cultures and thus they often dislike the books. For this reason, it is helpful if teachers themselves have some prior knowledge about the culture. As teachers share factual information, students may be able to construct alternative perspectives about the people and events they are reading about. Through this mediated process, students learn to look at racism, unfamiliar behaviors, and events in a more unbiased manner as they make comparisons with their own lives and develop new insights. This process can be done in a way that is enjoyable for the readers (Dressel, 2005). According to the transactional view of reading, "The author isn't boss anymore, but neither is the reader. It's what they come up with together that makes the literary experience" (Sebesta, 2001).

There are many reasons for using multicultural literature in carefully planned ways in the classrooms of children, young adults, and pre-service and in-service teachers (DeNicolo and Franquiz, 2006; Dressel, 2005; Steiner, 2001; Stoodt, 1992). Taking ideas from all of these sources, the following suggestions are made. The use of multicultural literature can:

1. create opportunities for readers to recognize that there are commonalities among all people; we share common emotions such as fear, joy, love, and so forth;

2. help readers make connections with individuals in other cultural groups so they may view themselves as members of various groups rather than identifying with just one;

3. increase readers' understanding, appreciation, and respect for different cultures and their contributions;

4. increase the development of positive self-esteem and the future goals of those outside the social and political mainstream; and,

5. facilitate positive group identity and understanding of personal heritage at the same time readers are learning to respect many different kinds of lifestyles. Developing this respect may encourage a broad range of social relationships, openness, and interest in others.

Guidelines for Choosing Multicultural Literature

As is true when choosing any book, multicultural books must be well-written. A book is not necessarily a good choice simply because it has multicultural characters or setting. The following areas need to be evaluated.

1. Is the setting accurate? Does it avoid stereotypes? For example, all African Americans do not live in urban settings. If an urban setting is necessary for the plot, then it would be appropriate; if another setting is more realistic, then it should be used.

2. Does the plot draw readers into the story? Unless readers are interested in the events, the book will not be read.

3. Are the characters presented without stereotypes? The books should reflect the lives of individuals and not general personality traits that may be associated with an entire group. Consider the roles the characters play. Are males and/or whites the only problem solvers? Are the characters three-dimensional, ones with whom the readers may identify?

4. Is the theme one that will speak to all readers? Or is it didactic, with the theme overriding the plot?

5. Is the book up-to-date and accurate? Some older books may not present the most current kinds of situations or information and may include stereotypes. However, a recent publication date does not assure readers that there are no stereotypes.

6. What language is used? If dialect is used, does it accurately portray the cultural group? Is the dialogue authentic?

7. Are the illustrations authentic? Since illustrations can have a great impact on readers, they must not be stereotypical.

8. Are the cultural values accurately portrayed? To be able to answer this question, readers must be somewhat familiar with the culture that is depicted.

Linda Pavonetti (2001) states: "Books mirror our lives. Good books speak to Africans, Asians, Europeans, Latinos, Native Americans—women and men . . . They draw readers into a person's life—flaws and feats, triumphs and tragedies. They reflect the humanity in each of us, not just the individual culture we are born into" (p. 70).

If we want books to have an impact on the lives of our students, we must choose well-written books. Readers need to be able to make connections between what they are reading and their own lives. If there is no connection, or if teachers do not create situations to help students learn to make these connections, the implicit messages that are in the books may be lost. Reading is an intensely personal process, and, because of this, well-written books can make a difference in the lives of readers.

Recommended Books

Laurence Yep (2005) is a well-known author and the winner of numerous awards for books relating to Chinese Americans. As he developed as an author, he found that it was important that he write not only historical fiction, which described the lives of Chinese

Americans, but also of their legends: "I could not understand Chinese American history without understanding the myths that shape and continue to shape a people" (p. 431). Throughout this chapter, we will review books from many genres; each genre contributes a slightly different perspective of the different groups.

Native Americans

Native Americans should not be portrayed as "generic" in culture. Although many tribes had shared values, each tribe also had its own specific culture and traditions, defined in part by the geographic location. The settings of each tribe must be accurately depicted—Native Americans living in the northwest had different homes and living styles than did those who lived on the plains. Because there are so many stereotypes about Native Americans held by individuals outside this culture, some of the best books are written by authors who have a Native American background.

The Navajo Year, Walk through Many Seasons by Nancy Bo Flood shares the activities and events that take place each month of the Navajo year. The activities are told from the perspective of a young Navajo boy, who talks about the traditions, songs, games, and events. Most children will be able to make connections with the events in their own environment, which may make the book more enjoyable.

Zinnia: How the Corn Was Saved by Patricia Hruby Powell is a traditional Navajo folktale in which a young boy, Red Bird, is sent on a journey. Because his people's crops are dying, he is to find Spider Woman to find out how to save them. On his journey, he meets all kinds of animals, but when he finds Spider Woman, she is angry because he didn't notice her at first. He makes up with her and she advises him that his people need to plant zinnias in all of their gardens. The text is written in both English and Navajo.

A young Navajo boy, Tony, has a difficult decision to make in Deborah W. Trotter's *A Summer's Trade*. Tony has worked hard and has saved almost enough money to buy a new saddle. However family problems arise; there are more bills than there is money to pay them, his uncle breaks his foot, and his grandmother becomes ill. When his grandmother pawns her precious jewelry, Tony knows that the money he has saved would be a big help to his family. The author has written a story with a universal decision that many young people must make.

Bruce Swanson writes a coming-of-age book about a young member of the Wolf Clan in *Gray Wolf's Search*. Wolf learns from the clan shaman that for him to be successful, he must find and talk to a very important person. Unsure of who this person might be, Gray Wolf goes on a journey in which he asks various animals and gets clues from each of them. At the conclusion of his journey, he comes back and shares what he has learned with the clan. *Gray Wolf's Search* takes place on the Pacific Northwest Coast and provides a view of this group of Native Americans.

An original tale based on an Iroquois folk tale, *The Sun's Daughter* by Pat Sherman tells of how the earth provides a bounty of food as Maize, Red Bean, and Pumpkin awaken each year. Maize, however, goes walking at night and finds herself held hostage by Silver (the Moon). Sun no longer provides the food until a compromise is made, and Maize is returned to Sun for half of each year. Pat Sherman has written a picture book probably better suited for slightly older children.

Sequoyah: The Cherokee Man Who Gave His People Writing, written and illustrated by James Rumford, is a beautiful picture book telling about the difficulties Sequoyah faces as he creates a written language for his people. Sequoyah creates 84 symbols, each of which stands for one of the sounds. This book, which provides the Cherokee translation of the English words, includes the complete syllabary and additional information about Sequoyah's life.

Joseph Bruchac has written two biographies about Jim Thorpe, the "Athlete of the Century" (as recognized by the U.S. Congress in 1999). The first, *Jim Thorpe's Bright Path,* is a picture book that focuses mostly on Thorpe's early years at home and then at the Carlisle Indian School. The school was not a place of support for him but through his own talent and perseverance, Jim Thorpe is able to achieve success. The second book, *Jim Thorpe, Original All-American,* a fictionalized biography, is told in the first person. Details are provided about his prowess as an athlete and about his wins in the 1912 Olympic games. Thorpe's positive qualities are demonstrated as are many of the biases and difficulties he had to face because he was a Native American. In both books, there are author's notes and other resources.

The life of other young Native Americans was not pleasant when they were forced to attend boarding schools intended to "cleanse" them of their native ways. In *Sweetgrass Basket,* Marlene Carvell tells the story of Mattie and Sarah, sisters who attend the Carlisle Indian School in Pennsylvania after their mother's death. Their story is told by the girls alternatively, as each tells about her experiences: how they are publicly shamed, wrongly accused of stealing, and beaten and abused by the adults in the school. Bullying and betrayal are the strategies used to take their culture from them. The story is based on the experiences of relatives of the author's husband.

Two other books—*Bear Dancer* by Thelma Hatch Wyss and *Sky* by Pamela Porter—are based on the actual lives of Native American women. *Bear Dancer* is the story of Elk Girl. During a raid, she is captured by a Cheyenne, then traded to the Arapaho, and finally rescued by a white soldier. This book focuses mostly on her life as she lives among the Indians rather than on her life after she marries a white man and becomes Susan Johnson. During these early years, Elk Girl learns that there are good people and those who are not so good—Indians as well as whites.

In *Sky,* a dam bursts in 1964 near a Blackfeet Reservation and floods the area. Georgia and her grandparents lose everything, and when they seek help, they are discriminated against because they are Native Americans. The whites pay nothing for food, cots, and blankets; the Indians must pay and are crowded into small classrooms. Georgia finds a colt that is rescued, and as she works to tame it, she and her grandparents begin the process of recovery. *Sky* is based on the true story of Georgia Salois and is a good book for reading aloud.

In a very different setting in *Ice Drift,* Inuit brothers Alika and Sulu are hunting seals when the ice floe on which they are working breaks off from the shore. The boys, who are 14 and 10, have to plan how they will stay alive in a setting where there is danger from the weather, the polar bears, hunger, and illness. They have only their sledge and their sled dog, Jamka. Author Theodore Taylor has written a book that will draw in readers, both boys and girls, as his protagonists struggle for survival.

African Americans

Books about the African American experience must portray the diverse settings in which real people might live or have lived. In other words, the settings need to be in all geographic areas of the United States, urban and rural communities, past and present. Like books about almost every cultural group, there is not a single African American culture—the richness created in well-written literature by individuals and their unique situations helps to avoid the stereotypes that may be found in some books.

Patricia McKissack has written an engaging book of 10 original tales that are based on stories she heard as a child. *Porch Lies: Tales of Slicksters, Tricksters, and Other Wily Characters* is amusing to read because there is always a surprise someplace in the story. The stories are all outlandish, which certainly adds to the fun of reading them, and, of course, those who are perceived as the weakest, youngest or most naive always win in the end.

*The People Could Fly: American Black Folktales*** by Virginia Hamilton is a collection of 24 stories, which celebrate the tradition of African American storytelling. These stories, illustrated by Leo and Diane Dillon, tell of slavery and freedom, of trickery and survival, and all were passed down through generations. There is also a CD, narrated by the author and by James Earl Jones; it complements the stories and makes them come alive.

A Cinderella retelling is the focus of *Mufaro's Beautiful Daughters*** by John Steptoe. This story is set in Africa and tells of one kind, helpful daughter and one who is deceitful. Of course, the good daughter wins in the end.

Circle Unbroken: The Story of a Basket and Its People by Margot Theis Raven is a tribute to what can be learned from generations past. As a grandmother teaches her granddaughter to weave a basket, so too the author weaves the history and background of slavery into this story. The child's ancestors are taken from Africa as slaves, but they bring their basket-making talent to this country. As this basket-making tradition is passed down, the new ways are solidly integrated with the old ways.

A series of three books written by Doreen Rappaport and illustrated by Shane W. Evans use first-person accounts, diaries, songs, and poetry, along with fictional vignettes, to tell the story of slavery from its early days to 1965. The first book, *No More! Stories and Songs of Slave Resistance,* tells how slaves were often successful in outwitting those who tried to control them by having secret schools, escaping on the Underground Railroad, or being spies. The second book, *Free at Last! Stories and Songs of Emancipation,* includes accounts of how former slaves and the generations that followed were able to begin to break down the color line. The 1954 Supreme Court decision made it clear that all children were entitled to a quality education. The last book in the series, *Nobody Gonna Turn Me 'Round! Stories and Songs of the Civil Rights Movement,* presents the stories of those involved in the struggle for equality from the Montgomery Bus Boycott to the Voting Rights Act of 1965. These three books are important for all students to read so that they have a picture of how powerful the desire is for equality and justice.

The *ABC's of Black History* by Craig Thompson is a compilation of portraits and lyrics describing 26 influential black Americans. This picture book gives a bit of context that tells why each person is important. It is a good beginning book for younger students.

Rosa Parks was instrumental in the Civil Rights Movement. A biography, *Rosa* by Nikki Giovanni, presents her as a well-rounded person in the context of those troubled times. Through the illustrations by Bryan Collier and the text itself, the dignity and resolve of Rosa Parks is made explicit.

Another biography, *Carver: A Life in Poems* by Marilyn Nelson, tells of the contributions of George Washington Carver, who started the agriculture department at Tuskegee Institute. The poems tell not only of his agricultural accomplishments but also his contributions as an artist, teacher, and inventor. The writing format and lyric poems make this book especially appealing.

For those who want documentation about the Underground Railroad, *Freedom Roads: Searching for the Underground Railroad* by Joyce Hansen and Gary McGowen is a good choice. This book has specific sources that pinpoint archaeological sites, describe logs from ships, and provide other written documents, such as laws that were passed during the time period. One of the projects of the Works Progress Administration (WPA) during the Depression was to record over 2,000 interviews with former slaves. These recordings support and add to information found in the documents. The format of this book is a good model to be used for Social Studies research.

Another interesting book is Pete Seeger's *The Deaf Musicians,* which is the story of Lee, a musician who loses his hearing and must give up playing the piano. Lee takes a sign language class, where he meets a saxophone player who is deaf also. The two of them together form a new band. *The Deaf Musicians* is a

The many talented Carver was a botanist, inventor, painter, musician, and teacher.

book of hope that demonstrates that even when there is a great loss something good may come from it.

The Friendly Four by Eloise Greenfield is a picture book in which four friends spend the summer together doing all kinds of activities—going to movies, having parties, and simply having fun with each other. At the end of summer, promises are made to get together the next summer, too. This book of poetry is interesting in that each child's name is designated a different color in the index and the text. A second book of poetry by Eloise Greenfield, *Honey, I Love**,* is a collection of poems about love. This American Library Association award winner is beautifully illustrated by Leo and Diane Dillon.

Walter Dean Myers's book, *Street Love,* presents a very different kind of poetry than the previous books. This narrative-verse novel, based on *Romeo and Juliet,* is set in Harlem in the present time. Damien, who has earned a scholarship to college, falls in love with Junice, a street-wise young woman who is struggling to keep her family together. The focus of the story is on their love for each other in spite of all the impediments that their situations have created. This story will appeal to older readers.

In *Brother Hood* by Janet McDonald, Nathaniel is a young African American who is caught between two cultures: that of his upper-class boarding school and his Harlem home. Where does he belong? Perhaps in both neighborhoods—or perhaps in neither. This book addresses universal questions that many young people feel as they are growing up—however, for Nathaniel, the choices may be more difficult.

The Bluford High series of books is extremely popular with young African Americans. The problems and issues presented may be similar to ones that young African Americans or their friends may be experiencing. In *Shattered (Bluford #12)* by Paul Langan, Darcy is entering her junior year of high school. Her family is having money problems so her dad takes on a second job. He has a drinking problem so there could be another serious problem. As one might expect, there are also issues outside the family with friends and school, typical of issues experienced by many readers. Because there is no graphic sex or violence and the language is appropriate, these are popular books with middle- and high-school-age students.

Books of historical fiction that depict the Africans' experiences as they were transported from their homes to slavery, as well as their status after the ships' arrivals, do not present pretty pictures. The three books reviewed here are not always easy to read, but they are very important in order to gain a balanced view of history. The first, *Freedom Ship,* by Doreen Rappaport, is based on a true incident—the black wheelman and other members of the ship's slave crew take control of the ship. In this case, the slaves are able to escape, and the ship is delivered to the Union.

Awarded the Coretta Scott King medal, *Copper Sun* by Sharon Draper is a much darker story. Fifteen-year-old Amari is captured in Africa where she is beaten and branded before being put on the slave ship. The journey is an ugly experience: She is raped, and many people die or are killed. When Amari finally reaches the Carolinas, she is sold at a slave auction to a man who gives her to his 16-year-old son, Clay. Her life is one of unrelenting work and debasement by Clay and others. Although the mistress is kind to her, freedom is always on Amari's mind, and when she makes friends with a white indentured servant girl, they work together to escape. This book presents slavery as brutal and violent but even in such horrifying situations, there may be hope for the future if one has a survivor's spirit, as Amari does.

The largest slave auction in American history was held in 1859 to pay off the gambling debts of Pierce Butler. With no regard for separating children from their parents, husbands from wives, or friends from friends, the slaves were sold to the highest bidders. *Day of Tears* by Julius Lester tells of this event. The book itself is told in the format of a play, with multiple speakers each telling his or her story. There are also reflections, written years later, by those who were involved in this event. Lists of the sale records are made by a narrator. This powerful book lends itself both to presentation and discussion.

Show Way by Jacqueline Woodson celebrates the generations of a family. When the story begins, Soonie's great-grandmother is sold as a slave; the book continues to the present, to Soonie's great-granddaughter, who is the author's daughter. Quilts are the unifying aspect of this book: They are used as the means to point north to freedom, to encourage economic stability, and to tell the stories that connect the generations. This beautiful book is a Caldecott Honor Book.

Asian/Asian Americans

Books reviewed in this section will focus on several different regions in Asia as well as books about Asian Americans. Each book presents a different perspective and culture.

A wonderful bilingual picture book, *Where Are You Going?,* has been created by Eric Carle and Kazuo Iwamura. Eric Carle wrote and illustrated the first half in English. He includes dialogue and symbols to identify the speakers—a dog, cat, rooster, goat, rabbit, and a child—each of whom invites the next animal to join the group. The second half of the book presents the same story, which is illustrated by Kakzuo Iwamura and written in Japanese, so readers can begin at either end. In the middle of the book the music and words to the song "Where Are You Going? To See My Friend" are presented.

Author Belle Yang describes what it was like to move to the United States from Taiwan in the late 1960s in *Hannah Is My Name.* She is 7 years old at the time, and one of the first things she does is to give up her Chinese name, Na-Li, to become Hannah. The family applies for green cards so they can work and stay in this country. When the cards do not come for a long time, there is great tension in the family as they fear that they will be sent back to Taiwan. Meanwhile, the family is learning to live in the very different culture of San Francisco. Hannah learns songs sung in the United States and reads typical books. There is great relief in the family when the green cards come in the mail.

In *The Name Jar* by Yangsook Choi, there is a different result when a Korean girl, who has just immigrated, considers whether to choose a new name. The girl, Unhei, is uncomfortable about her name, especially after she has been teased because it is so different. When the other children ask what her name is, she tells them that she hasn't decided yet. Her classmates try to be helpful and create a jar full of different names for her to choose from. Finally, she decides to keep her own name—especially since one of her classmates is proud of the Korean nickname he chooses for himself.

Lenore Look has created a series about a second-grader, Ruby Lu, a Chinese American girl. In both *Ruby Lu, Brave and True* and *Ruby Lu, Empress of Everything,* the main character is an energetic, inquisitive, lovable girl whose choices are not always the best but are typical of many children. She is jealous of a cousin, hates the water, and sometimes gets in trouble at school. These are good books for beginning chapter-book readers.

Another good book is *The Jade Dragon* by Carolyn Marsden and Virginia Shin-Mui Loh, which resolves the issues between the girls in the story by using humor and insight. When a new Chinese student comes into the second-grade class, Ginny, the child of Chinese parents, hopes they will become best friends. Stephanie, however, is adopted and wants nothing to do with anything Chinese. Through their interactions, which are not all positive, the girls gain respect for their native culture as well as a greater understanding of being adopted and being the child of immigrants.

Sixteen Years in Sixteen Seconds: The Sammy Lee Story by Paula Yoo tells the story of Sammy Lee, a person who demonstrated great determination and overcame many obstacles to achieve two very important goals. Sammy Lee was the first Asian American to win an Olympic gold medal as a diver. He faced great odds in his quest to swim, not only because the

Friendship is developed between two Chinese girls.

pool was not open regularly to non-whites but because his family wanted him to focus on his school work. He was able to find a coach with whom to work and was also able to earn a medical degree.

Korean Children's Favorite Stories** by Kim So-un was recently republished with new illustrations. The traditional stories have always been enjoyable, but the illustrations make the book even more attractive. The subjects are animals, which are part of the Korean culture, and the tales depict traditions in Korea. These are wonderful stories to read aloud or to read to oneself, independently.

Hispanic Americans

The Tomas Rivera Mexican American Children's Book Award is given annually "to dispel the image of a single Hispanic experience often perpetuated in literature" (Bedford and Cuellar, 2006, p. 24). The themes in these books are diverse and reflect the richness of the Latino experience. Books in all genres are recognized; each book includes text in both English and Spanish, and the illustrations are often done by Latinos from diverse Hispanic cultures. These first three books we discuss next are all winners of the Tomas Rivera Award.

In *Downtown Boy,* Juan Felipe Herrera has written a story about 10-year-old Juanito, whose parents are undocumented immigrant migrant workers. Juanito's father is not always with the family so they are often moving—with relatives and from one place to the next. When the father finally returns, his diabetes requires that his legs be amputated, which ends the traveling by the family. Juanito does have the support of a loving family as he tries to determine the course of his life. He even tries boxing, at the urging of a cousin. Juanito has problems similar to those of boys in any culture, so readers can identify with many of the issues and problems that Juanito has.

Just a Minute: A Trickster Tale and Counting Book by Yuyi Morales is the story of Grandma Beetle and how she delays a skeleton who wants her to leave with him. The 10 reasons she doesn't want to leave have to do with getting ready for her birthday party—Grandma Beetle ends up inviting the skeleton to the party—who then wants to come back for next year's birthday celebration!! The counting is done both in English and Spanish, and the illustrations are inviting.

A picture-book biography, *Jose! Born to Dance: The Story of Jose Limon* by Susanna Reich, tells of Jose's life in Mexico and his immigration to the United States. Jose faces much of the same kind of discrimination as many do who first move to the United States from Mexico, but through his determination and hard work, he succeeds. At first he wants to be a painter but then discovers his intense interest in dance. As a dancer and choreographer, he has a great impact on his field, as is explained in the notes at the end.

Another picture-book biography is *Harvesting Hope: The Story of Cesar Chavez* by Kathleen Krull. Cesar Chavez grew up in Arizona and California where he experienced discrimination by teachers and other adults. He dropped out of school after the eighth grade but had chosen several heroes by that time: Martin Luther King, Jr., Gandhi, and St. Francis of Assisi. For him, nonviolence was the only choice when he was looking for ways to gain power for his people. His 340-mile protest march to the capital of California was the impetus for changes that were made, including contracts for farm workers.

In *First Day in Grapes,* a picture book by L. King Perez, the author describes what it is like being the son of migrant workers. Chico's family is always on the move, and, once again, he must start in a new school. On his first day, he meets some bullies on the bus, and the bus driver is very grouchy. However, Chico is lucky to have a teacher who recognizes that he is gifted in math. Chico uses his mathematical intelligence to overcome the bullies and looks forward to more success in this school.

Gary Soto has written a book of stories about Mexican American teens in *Help Wanted: Stories.* Each short story has characters who have problems or issues that most teens have. The Latino culture, however, plays an important part in the setting of the stories and the reactions of the characters. Spanish words and phrases are also included, which contributes to the flavor of the stories.

Readers will get a different perspective on Latino culture as they read Tony Johnston's book of poetry, *The Ancestors are Singing.* The poems tell of ancient times, myths, and events of nature, as well as current happenings. The language used reflects the times, and the illustrations complement the language. These poems present ideas that facilitate good discussions.

Storytelling is integral to Hispanic cultures. In *Tales Our Abuelitas Told: A Hispanic Folktale Collection,* two storytellers share stories they have heard since they were children. These stories, retold by Alma Flor Ada and F. Isabel Campoy, are full of traditional themes—the younger and smaller outwit the older and bigger; animals talk and dance; love conquers all. After each retelling, there is a section that describes where the tale came from.

Another interesting book of folktales is *Horse Hooves and Chicken Feet* by Neil Philip. This collection includes 14 stories that come from Mexico or from Mexican-Americans who live in the southwest. Again, the Mexican cultures come through clearly as does the influence of the Catholic Church. The illustrations, by Jacqueline Mair, contribute greatly to the folktales in this book. There are notes about each story and a large bibliography of items for those who wish to pursue this topic.

Cinderella stories are always favorites for readers. *Domitila: A Cinderella Tale from the Mexican Tradition* by Jewell Reinhart Coburn is one that will be particularly enjoyed. As the cook for the govenor,

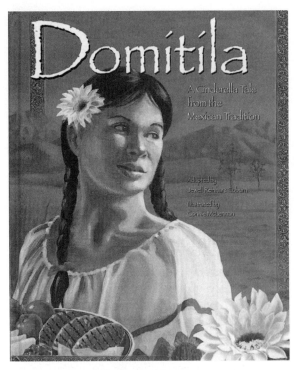

Domitila is a Mexican Cinderella.

Domitila attracts the attention of the governor's son. However, she must return home when her mother dies, and the son must search to find her—if he wants more of her good cooking!!

Jewish Literature

As is true with all multicultural literature, books set in a Jewish culture need to entertain, not preach. The plots should not be overshadowed by the theme.

Two books, each with a different perspective, describe Hanukkah. The first, *I Have a Little Dreidel* by Maxie Baum, is told in original poetry and includes the verses of the traditional song. The text and illustrations show how generations of family members celebrate the holiday together. The second book, *Papa's Latkes* by Michelle Edwards, is the story of two sisters whose mother has recently died. On the first night of Hanukkah, Papa comes home with potatoes and, together, the three try to make the latkes. Of course, they are not like those their mother made, which makes them miss her even more. However, as Papa comforts them, they feel better and try to enjoy the holiday.

The Secret Seder by Doreen Rappaport demonstrates that there is strength as people of faith gather together. During World War II, a young boy and the men in the village hold a secret Seder in an abandoned house in the forest. Because they are appearing to be Catholic, holding a secret Seder is dangerous. In spite of the danger, however, the Seder is done with traditional questions and answers and also with answers that reflect the conditions in Europe at the time.

A unique presentation of the Jewish experience in the Holocaust appears in *Memories of Survival* by Esther Nisenthal Krinitz and Bernice Steinhardt. Krinitz has demonstrated what life was like from the time she was a child in 1937 to her life in the United States by creating a series of hand-embroidered fabric collages with hand-stitched captions. This beautiful artwork illustrates the book showing some of the evils that Krinitz and her sister experienced as they escaped death in the concentration camps; it also illustrates the beauty of Poland and her family relationships. Her daughter, Bernice Steinhardt, provides notes and details about each panel, providing an additional level of understanding about the times.

In the Promised Land: Lives of Jewish Americans, by Doreen Rappaport, presents brief biographies of 13 people who have been successful in this country. The book includes individuals who are well-known (like Stephen Spielberg) and those who may not be so well-known (like Lillian Copeland, winner of an Olympic gold medal), along with illustrations of each person in a defining moment. There is additional information about each person in the reading list, on web sites, and in other resources.

The biography of Marc Chagall should be of interest to all readers—even if they do not consider themselves artists. Chagall never saw things in quite the same way as other people, and thus he was regarded as different—something many young readers can identify with. The book emphasizes Chagall's imagination and his dreams, which allowed him to create art that was different from all others. *Dreamer from the Village: The Story of Marc Chagall* also includes many Jewish terms, so the glossary is useful.

Simms Taback has collected 13 traditional stories taken from Eastern European Jewish villages. Some of the stories are humorous; others are more thought-provoking. All are beautifully illustrated and suggest lessons to be learned. The collection, *Kibitzers and Fools,* will make a good addition to other books of traditional literature.

Other Groups

Although the United States is made up of countless other cultural groups, we will end this chapter by discussing four in particular: interracial, Middle Eastern, Appalachian, and Amish communities.

Interracial/Multicultural

Books by Todd Parr always celebrate diversity—both in his illustrations, which feature faces of lots of different colors, and in the kinds of characters included. For example, in both *The Peace Book* and *The Family Book,* you can see that these books are multicultural just by looking at the covers. In the first book, examples of peace are presented that even young children can grasp—hugging a friend, keeping the street clean, and listening to different kinds of music. In the second book, the author demonstrates that there are many different kinds of families, that "family" is not a single concept—we have mixed race families, families that are big, families in which everyone eats something different, and so on. Interracial/multicultural concepts are made explicit in all of his books.

For many biracial children, finding their identity is a major challenge. Cooper's mom is Korean; his dad is white; and Cooper is called "half and half." When Cooper steals a brush from Mr. Lee's store and gets caught, Mr. Lee makes him work in the store, where Cooper learns about the difficulties Mr. Lee has had because of his language difficulties. *Cooper's Lesson* by Sun Yung shows how both Cooper and Mr. Lee learn from each other. The story is told in both Korean and English.

Another book, *Am I a Color, Too* by Heidi Cole and Nancy Vogl, tells of a young boy whose mom is white and dad is black. Tyler wonders if he, too, is a color as he explores who he is because he sees both dark and light. This book, written by his mother and grandmother, provides insight to him as well as to readers and is a good book for discussion because the value of each person is made obvious.

Children whose parents are from different races or cultural groups sometimes struggle as they try to make sense of the differences between the expectations of each of their parents. It sometimes is doubly hard if one parent is absent from the family. This is the situation in *Becoming Naomi Leon* by Pam Munoz Ryan. Naomi lives with her great-grandmother and her younger brother, Owen; her mother abandoned the children 7 years earlier. The issues Naomi has are the typical ones that many children have until the day that her mother comes to Gram's trailer and decides she wants custody of Naomi but not Owen. Gram takes the children to Mexico to find their father, and he signs the papers that make Gram their guardian. The dad had been separated from his children not by his choice, but because of the mother's choice. There is the implication that he now will be more of a part of the children's lives. This Tomas Rivera Award-winning book is the story of how Naomi loses her shyness and becomes "Naomi the Lion."

A second book in which there is an absent father takes place in a small Alaskan bush village. In Deb Vanasse's *A Distant Enemy,* a teenaged boy is close to his grandfather and assumes the values of the Eskimos, many of whom are in conflict with some of the rules of the Alaska Department of Fish and Game. The boy is angry at his Anglo father, at the restrictions placed upon the Eskimos, and at his friends and teachers. When the boy almost dies, he is finally able to work through his anger, with the help of his teacher. *A Distant Enemy* offers a balanced perspective on the clashes of the native culture and government regulations.

A book of historical fiction, *Last Child* by Michael Spooner, tells of a young girl, Last Child, whose mother is a member of the Mandan tribe and whose father is a white man who works for a fur trading company. Last Child feels torn between cultures and thinks that she belongs nowhere. When smallpox comes to her village, there is no resistance to the disease, so most of the tribe do not survive. Because of her unique background, Last Child is able to be of assistance to many, and she begins to see her heritage as an advantage.

In *Brendan Buckley's Universe and Everything in It,* author Sundee T. Frazier proposes that sometimes what a person doesn't know is better than what is known. Sundee Frazier creates likeable and humorous characters in this novel. Brendan lives with both parents; what is missing from his life is a relationship with one of his grandfathers. Secretly, Brendan makes contact with him and hopes to find a rock collector, but he stirs up problems. Brendan discovers his grandfather is white. This is why his mother has refused to discuss her father. They do resolve problems.

Another book in which the main character gets to know grandparents is Laura Resau's *What the Moon Saw*. In this story, 14-year-old Clara gets a letter from her Mexican grandparents, who invite her to visit them during the summer. There is a great contrast between Clara's suburban home and her grandparents' village, where people live in huts. However, Clara learns that her grandmother is a healer and that she, too, shares some of this skill. The story of her grandmother's coming-of-age story is interspersed with that of Clara's. There are Spanish words and phrases, which firmly grounds the story in the Oaxacan mountains.

Middle Eastern

In recent years, we have become aware of the fact that many children and adults have little knowledge about those who practice the Muslim/Islamic faith; we also know little about the countries in which they live. There are also those of other faiths living in the Middle East, about whom many readers know very little. Their stories make interesting reading. The following books should be of interest to those who want to know more about these people, their cultures, and their ways of living.

Fasting and Dates: A Ramadan and Eid-ul-Fitr Story by Jonny Zucker tells how a typical Muslim family celebrates Ramadan. The book describes the holiday, which occurs during the ninth month of the Islamic calendar, through simple text and pictures. Adults and older children fast from sun-up to sundown. Ramadan ends with a feast, Eid-ur-Fitr, which is attended by extended families; traditionally, dates and pomegranates are eaten.

Naomi Shihab Nye has collected poems from many regions of the Middle East and compiled them in two books: *19 Varieties of Gazelle: Poems of the Middle East* and *The Flag of Childhood: Poems from the Middle East.* Reading these poems makes one realize how much people are alike rather than how different they may be. Poems of family, of friends, and of interactions with the natural world give readers a more personal view of people who live in very different cultures than those who live in the United States. Connections are made with 9/11.

A series of three books for older readers by Deborah Ellis takes readers to Afghanistan. Parvana, an 11-year-old girl, and her family must stay inside their home since the Taliban has been in control. Her father is missing; in order to feed the family, Parvana disguises herself in her brother's clothes to be able to go out, find food, and earn a very modest living. *The Breadwinner* is a story of bravery and the taking on of adult responsibilities. In *Parvana's Journey,* she searches for her mother and siblings after their home is destroyed. On her search, she finds other abandoned children, and they make their way to a refugee camp. The third book, *Mud City,* features Shauzia, an Afghan refugee in Pakistan. She is unhappy there and dresses as a boy to try to find her way to France. She is returned to the refugee camp, where she comes to terms with her life in this temporary setting. Royalties from these books go to Women to Women, a relief organization that benefits women in Afghanistan.

In Suzanne Staples's book, *Under the Persimmon Tree,* Najmah's father and brother are taken by the Taliban; her mother and baby brother are killed by an American bomb. Najmah, disguised as a boy, makes her way to a refugee camp in Pakistan where she meets an American woman named Nusrat. The two women connect, each waiting for news of family members. There is no happy ending, but there is hope, as each comes to accept her loss and begins to focus on the future. *Under the Persimmon Tree* includes maps, a glossary, and notes.

Two books take place in the United States. In *Does My Head Look Big in This?* by Randa Aldel-Fattah, Amal decides that she will start wearing the hijab all the time. This does cause a few problems, but she sticks with her decision. Readers will be able to identify with the notion of being different and still getting along with peers and others. Quite a different story is *Ask Me No Questions* by Marina Budhos. This book tells of a Bangladeshi family living in the United States illegally because their visa requests have been lost in bureaucratic red tape. After 9/11, the family's problems intensify, and they try to go to Canada. The father is detained because his passport is not current so the family goes back to New York City. Fourteen-year-old Nadira takes on the responsibility of trying to work out the issues. There are unexpected challenges, and the book presents interesting perspectives on immigration.

Real Time by Pnina Moed Kass presents an Israeli perspective on the conflict with the Palestinians. Life in modern-day Israel is dangerous. Riders on a bus to Kibbutz Broshim are attacked by a young suicide bomber. As the passengers tell their stories, readers begin to connect with them. After the bomb explodes, mid-book, the focus changes to what happens in the aftermath of the explosion.

Consider how it would feel to be confined to one's house with family members and a dwindling food supply for days at a time. Tempers flare, boredom sets in, and things are thoroughly unpleasant. We experience this through the eyes of 12-year old Karim, who lives under military occupation in Ramallah. During the few times when the Israelis lift the curfew, he meets a new friend, and with another friend, the three make a soccer field. When another curfew is imposed, Karim is late leaving the soccer field and takes refuge in an abandoned car. He is wounded but survives and, after several days, makes it home safely. *A Little Piece of Ground* by Elizabeth Laird and Sonia Nimr is highly recommended.

Appalachian

The area of Appalachia is often considered to be the mountain areas from northern Georgia to southwestern Pennsylvania. The stereotype is that Appalachians are white, rural mountain people. The reality is that many Appalachians are African Americans and Native Americans. Particularly in times past, the people were quite isolated, living in "hollers" that were not often visited by outsiders. Their dialect developed from British English, which was spoken by the early settlers in these areas. Today, people with Appalachian roots are found in every segment of society, not just in the rural mountain areas of the southeast or the urban inner cities.

The Search for Belle Prater by Ruth White is the sequel to her Newbery Honor book, *Belle Prater's Boy.* Woodrow, who is living with family members after being abandoned by his mother, tries to find his mom. He receives a call one day but when he picks up the telephone and no one answers, he assumes it is from his mother. After tracing the call, he, his cousin Gypsy, and two friends take a bus and find that his mom has been traveling with the circus. The descriptions of the rural areas do create pictures in the reader's mind.

In Kerry Madden's *Gentle's Holler*, 12-year-old Livy Two takes on many family and household chores because her dad does not follow through on many of his responsibilities, and her mom, who is always pregnant, has too much to do. Livy's little sister, Gentle, is blind; her older brother runs away to earn money; the family is always hungry; and then her father has an accident and is in a coma. Nonetheless, Livy does find time to read her school books and those from the bookmobile, so she has goals and dreams. *Gentle's Holler* is a family-focused book in which there is great love even when there are many troubles.

In *Ludie's Life,* Cynthia Rylant has created a free-verse narrative that describes Ludie from the time of her birth in 1910 until her death at age 95. Her story is told in a series of vignettes that are not always in chronological order but which paint a picture of what life was like in the rural Appalachians. Poverty, hard work, family, friends, and church were all integral to Ludie's life, and readers gain an appreciation for this atypical lifestyle.

Amish

Because books about the Amish are written by those who are not themselves members of the culture, readers must remember that the "outsider" perspective, even if sensitively done, is presented.

The Amish, like other minority groups, are often the target of people who have a grudge against them. In *Simeon's Fire,* Cathryn Clinton describes the life and responsibilities of one Amish family. After a number of Amish farms have been torched by arsonists, 10-year-old Simeon finds the arsonists in his family's barn. They threaten to burn down his house if he tells on them, but Simeon figures out who the men are and shares this information.

Summary

The United States has been a multicultural society since its earliest times. Ethnic, linguistic, and racial minorities have made significant contributions to the society we have today. These contributions and the cultural groups who made them need to be respected and regarded as an integral part of American life. If first-hand experiences with different cultural groups are not available, reading about them may be an alternative means to explore and develop an appreciation for this diversity. Well-written multicultural literature can be the vehicle for creating this sensitivity about differences and similarities. This literature can be a key to allowing children and young adults from all backgrounds and cultures to see themselves and how they fit in with other cultural groups. Sensitive and knowledgeable teachers have the responsibility to create equitable educational opportunities for all of their students so that they are able to identify with characters who look like they do and to respect those who do not. Teachers will also learn that their students have much to teach—if we create the ways to make the children feel safe as they discuss issues of personal and cultural importance to them.

At this time, our society is becoming even more global in nature. Changes are occurring that will continue to impact people throughout the world. Both children and young adults may adapt to these changes more easily if they know about and respect cultures other than their own. Using multicultural literature is one practical way this process can begin.

Research and Application Experiences

1. Using the criteria listed on page 210, analyze any book that has a multicultural theme. How might you help your students use a list like this?

2. Explore web sites to look for lesson plans that will help you share accurate information about various cultural groups.

Classroom Activities

ACTIVITY 13.1   EVALUATING MULTICULTURAL LITERATURE

IRA/NCTE Standards: 1, 2, 3, 5, 9.

Middle-school students are able to evaluate the quality of books as they learn to apply all of the levels of *Bloom's Taxonomy*, which identifies learning categories. The goal of applying these categories is to help learners acquire new skills, knowledge, and attitudes. Using the criteria on page 210, teachers can begin with one or two questions chosen from this list. As the students get more comfortable evaluating literature, more items can be added.

Helpful Internet Sites for Teachers

http://officeport.com/edu/blooms.htm

http://www.teachers.ash.org.au/researchskills/dalton.htm

ACTIVITY 13.2   FAMILY HISTORY PROJECT

IRA/NCTE Standards: 1, 4, 7, 8, 9, 12.

Show Way by Jacqueline Woodson presents an approach to developing a family history that used quilts as a unifying focus. Using *Show Way* as a model, have students decide on a theme that fits their family. As the students trace the generations in their families, they need unifying threads to unite the generations. Create a collage, poster, or other form of communication to share with a larger audience.

Helpful Internet Sites for Family History

http://familyfun.go.com (This is an Internet magazine.)

http://www.familyhistoryproject.com (This address will bring up several useful sites.)

ACTIVITY 13.3 COMPARING FOLK TALES

IRA/NCTE Standards: 1,2,9,11.

Students can compare Cinderella stories from various cultures, such as *Cinderella* (European), *The Rough-Face Girl* (Native American), and *Yeh-Shen* (Chinese). The figure below illustrates a comparison chart.

Chart for comparing traditional stories.

Title and Author	Main Character	Setting	Problem	How Solved	Conclusion
Cinderella Marcia Brown	Cinderella	European house and castle	Mean stepmother and stepsisters	The prince finds her and proposes.	They marry and live happily ever after.
The Rough-Face Girl Rafe Martin	An Algonquin girl with a rough face	Native American	The tribe rejects her scarred face	She can see the Invisible Being.	She marries the Invisible Being.
Yeh-Shen: A Cinderella Story from China Al-Ling Louie	Yeh-Shen	China	Her stepmother kills the fish that is Yeh-Shen's friend and eats it	The fish's magic resides in its bones. The magic provides her with clothing for a festival.	She loses her slipper, and the King searches for her and marries her.
Cendrillon: A Caribbean Cinderella Robert D. San Souci	Cendrillon	Island of Martinique	Mean stepmother and stepsister	Godmother who is washer woman performs magic.	Cendrillon wears slipper and dances with bridegroom.
The Golden Sandal: A Middle-Eastern Cinderella Rebecca Hickox	Maha	Middle East	Mean stepmother and stepsister	Redfish is fairy godmother.	She is saved by a gold sandal: marries Tariq.
The Turkey Girl: A Zuni Cinderella Story Penny Pollock	Turkey girl	Zuni Indian, Western United States	Goes to great feast but does not return in time	Turkeys.	Turkeys are gone.

Children's Literature References

Abdel-Fattah, Randa. (2007). *Does my head look big in this?* New York: Orchard Books. 5–6;7+. CRF

Amal decides to wear the traditional hijab in the United States.

Ada, A. F., & Campoy, F. I. (2006). *Tales our abuelitas told: A Hispanic folktale collection* (F. Davalos, & S. Suevara, Illus.). New York: Atheneum. 3–4;5–6;7+. TL

Two storytellers share the stories they heard from their grandmothers.

Baum, M. (2006). *I have a little dreidel* (J. Paschkis, Illus.). New York: Cartwheel. K–2. PB; P

Original and traditional verses about Hanukkah.

Bruchac, J. (2004). *Jim Thorpe's bright path* (S. D. Nelson, Illus.). New York: Lee and Low. K–2;3–4. PB; B

A picture book biography of Jim Thorpe, Native American athlete.

Bruchac, J. (2006). *Jim Thorpe, original all-American.* New York: Dial. 5–6;7+. B

A biography of Jim Thorpe for older readers.

Budhos, M. (2006). *Ask me no questions.* New York: Ginee Seo Books. 5–6;7+. CRF

A Bangladeshi family's visas are lost, and they worry about being deported.

Carle, E., & Iwamura, K. (2003). *Where are you going? To see my friend.* New York: Orchard. K–2. F; PB

A story written in both English and Japanese with illustrations by two artists.

Carvell, M. (2005). *Sweetgrass basket.* New York: Dutton. 5–6;7+. HF

Two Native American girls live in a boarding school where they are abused and insulted.

Choi, Y. (Reprint, 2003). *The name jar.* New York: Dragonfly/Dell. K–2;3–4. CRF; PB

A Korean girl decides to keep her own name rather than taking an American name.

Clinton, C. (2007). *Simeon's fire.* Cambridge, MA: Candlewick. 3–4;5–6;7+. CRF

Simeon finds the arsonists who set fire to his family's barn; in spite of their threats, he is able to identify them.

Coburn, J. R. (2000). *Domitila: A cinderella tale from the Mexican tradition* (C. McLennan, Illus.). Walnut Creek, CA: Shen's Books. K–2;3–4. PB; TL

A Mexican Cinderella story.

Cole, H., & Vogl, N. (2005). *Am I a color, too?* (G. Purnell, Illus.). Bellevue, WA: Illumination Arts. K–2. PB

The book is about a biracial child trying to explore what color he is.

Draper, S. (2006). *Copper sun.* New York: Atheneum. 7+. HF; CSK

Amari is taken from Africa as a slave and finally escapes from her captivity.

Edwards, M. (2004). *Papa's latkes* (S. Schuett, Illus.). Cambridge, MA: Candlewick. K–2. PB; CRF

Latkes are different when made by one's father instead of one's mother.

Ellis, D. (2001). *The breadwinner.* Toronto, ON: Groundwood. 5–6;7+. CRF

Parvana dresses like a boy to get food for her family in Afghanistan.

Ellis, D. (2003). *Parvana's journey.* Toronto, ON: Groundwood. 5–6;7+. CRF

Parvana and other abandoned children look for their families in Afghanistan.

Ellis, D. (2003). *Mud city.* Toronto, ON: Groundwood. 5–6;7+. CRF

The story of a young girl, an Afghan refugee, in Pakistan.

Flood, N. B. (2006). *The Navajo year, walk through many seasons.* Flagstaff, AZ: Salina Bookshelf. K–2;3–4. PB

An account of the activities that take place within the Navajo culture during a year.

Frazier, S. T. (2007). *Brendan Buckley's universe and everything in it.* New York: Delacorte. 3–4;5–6. CRF

Brendan discovers that his grandfather is a different race than he is.

Giovanni, N. (2005). *Rosa* (B. Collier, Illus.). New York: Holt. K–2;3–4. PB; B

The story of Rosa Parks during the Civil Rights Movement.

Greenfield, E. (2006). *The friendly four* (J. S. Gilchrist, Illus.). New York: HarperCollins. K–2. PB; P; CRF

Four children are involved in a variety of activities during the summer.

Greenfield, E. (1978). *Honey, I love* (L. & D. Dillon, Illus.). New York: HarperCollins. K–2;3–4. PB; P; ALA

Love poems for the young and young at heart.

Hamilton, V. (1985). *The people could fly: American Black folktales* (L. & D. Dillon, Illus.). New York: Knopf. 3–4;5–6;7+. TL; CSK

A collection of 24 traditional folktales from the African American tradition.

Hansen, J., & McGowen, G. (2003). *Freedom roads: Searching for the Underground Railroad* (J. Ransome, Illus.). Peterborough, NH: Cricket. 3–4;5–6;7+. INF

A collection of artifacts and documents that tell how and where the Underground Railroad worked.

Herrera, J. F. (2005). *Downtown boy.* New York: Scholastic. 5–6;7+. HF; P

Juanito's family members are undocumented immigrants who worry about being found out.

Johnston, T. (2003). *The ancestors are singing* (K. Barbour, Illus.). New York: Farrar, Straus, and Giroux. 3–4;5–6;7+.

Poems about Mexican culture.

Kass, P. M. (2004). *Real time.* New York: Clarion. 5–6;7+. CRF

Riders on a bus in Israel are attacked and then tell their stories.

Krinitz, E. N., & Steinhardt, B. (2005). *Memories of survival.* New York: Hyperion. 5–6;7+. INF

The story of a Polish girl who survives the Holocaust as told in embroidered collages.

Krull, K. (2003). *Harvesting hope: The story of Cesar Chavez.* Orlando, FL: Harcourt. K–2;3–4. PB; B

A picture book biography of Cesar Chavez.

Laird, E., & Nimr, S. (2006). *A little piece of ground.* Chicago: Haymarket. 5–6;7+. CRF

A Palestinian boy and his friends make a soccer field which is destroyed by Israeli soldiers.

Langan, P. (2007). *Shattered.* West Berlin, NJ: Townsend Press. 5–6;7+. CRF

Another Bluford High School book about problems of some African American teens.

Lester, J. (2005). *Day of tears.* New York: Jump at the Sun. 5–6;7+. HF

A description of the largest slave auction ever held.

Look, L. (2004). *Ruby Lu, brave and true* (A. Wilsdorf, Illus.). New York: Atheneum. K–2;3–4. CRF

A beginning chapter book about a young Asian American girl.

Look, L. (2006). *Ruby Lu, empress of everything* (A. Wilsdorf, Illus.). New York: Atheneum. K–2;3–4. CRF

Another book in the series about the adventures of a young Asian American girl.

Madden, K. (2005). *Gentle's holler.* New York: Viking. 5–6;7+. HF

Livy's family lives in poverty in the mountains, but she still has dreams for the future.

Markel, M. (2005). *Dreamer from the village: The story of Marc Chagall* (E. Lisker, Illus.). New York: Henry Holt. K–2;3–4. PB; B

A picture-book biography of Marc Chagall.

Marsden, C., & Loh, V. S-M. (2006). *The jade dragon.* Cambridge, MA: Candlewick. K–2;3–4. CRF

Ginny tries to make friends with a new Chinese girl who joins her class.

McDonald, J. (2004). *Brother hood.* New York: Foster. 5–6;7+. CRF

An African American teen does not know if he belongs in his boarding school or in his home in Harlem.

McKissack, P. (2006). *Porch lies: Tales of slicksters, tricksters, and other wily characters* (A. Carrilho, Illus.). New York: Schwartz & Wade. K–2;3–4. TL; F

Ten original tales based on stories the author heard as a child.

Morales, Y. (2003). *Just a minute: A trickster tale and counting book.* San Francisco, CA: Chronicle. K–2. PB

Grandma Beetle tricks Death by inviting him to her birthday party.

Myers, W. D. (2006). *Street love.* New York: Amistad. 5–6;7+. CRF; P

A Romeo and Juliet love story that takes place in Harlem.

Nelson, M. (2001). *Carver: A life in poems.* Asheville, NC: Front Street. 5–6;7+. P; B; NewH; CSKH

George Washington Carver's life is described in poetry.

Nye, N. S. (2002). *The flag of childhood: Poems from the Middle East.* New York: Aladdin. 3–4; 5–6;7+. P

A book of poems collected from many regions of the Middle East.

Nye, N. S. (2002). *19 varieties of gazelle: Poems of the Middle East.* New York: HarperCollins. 3–4;5–6;7+. P

More poems about the Middle East.

Parr, T. (2003). *The family book.* New York: Little Brown. K–2. PB; INF

A collection of stories of multicultural families.

Parr, T. (2004). *The peace book.* New York: Little, Brown. K–2. PB; INF

Ways to live peacefully in multicultural settings.

Perez, L. K. (2002). *First day in grapes* (R. Casilla, Illus.). New York: Lee & Low. K–2. PB; CRF; PBH

The son of migrant workers has a challenging first day in a new school.

Philip, N. (2003). *Horse hooves and chicken feet: Mexican folktales.* New York: Clarion. 3–4;5–6;7+. TL

Fourteen folk tales from Mexico.

Porter, P. (2004). *Sky* (M. J. Gerber, Illus.). Toronto, ON: Groundwood. 3–4;5–6. HF

> After a flood, a Native American girl starts the healing process when she finds a colt.

Powell, P. H. (2004). *Zinnia: How the corn was saved* (K. Benally, Illus., P. A. Thomas, translator). K–2; 3–4;5–6. PB; TL

> An Indian youth gets advice from Spider Woman about how to save the tribe's crops.

Rappaport, D. (2005). *In the promised land: Lives of Jewish Americans* (C. Van Wright, & Y-H Hu, Illus.). New York: HarperCollins. 3–4;5–6;7+. B

> Biographies of famous and not-so-famous Jewish Americans.

Rappaport, D. (2001). *No more! Stories and songs of slave resistance* (S. W. Evans, Illus.). Cambridge, MA: Candlewick. 3–4;5–6;7+. INF; HF

> A collection of documents and fictional vignettes about slaves who escape from their masters.

Rappaport, D. (2004). *Free at last! Stories and songs of emancipation* (S. W. Evans, Illus.). Cambridge, MA: Candlewick. 3–4;5–6. INF; HF

> Accounts of how individuals work to end segregation.

Rappaport, D. (2005). *Nobody gonna turn me 'round: Stories and songs of the Civil Rights Movement.* Cambridge, MA: Candlewick. 3–4;5–6. INF; HF

> Stories of the struggle for equality during the Civil Rights Movement.

Rappaport, D. (2005). *The secret seder* (E. McCully, Illus.). New York: Hyperion. 3–4;5–6. PB; HF

> A group of men and boys secretly celebrate this holiday during the Holocaust.

Rappaport, D. (2006). *Freedom ship* (C. James, Illus.). New York: Jump at the Sun. 3–4;5–6. PB; HF

> A group of Africans takes over a ship and delivers it to the Union.

Raven, M. T. (2004). *Circle unbroken: The story of a basket and its people* (E. B. Lewis, Illus.). New York: Farrar, Straus, Giroux. K–2;3–4. PB; INF; CRF

> The basket-making tradition is passed down to a granddaughter.

Reich, S. (2005). *Jose! Born to dance: The story of Jose Limon* (R. Colon, Illus.). New York: Simon & Schuster. K–2;3–4. PB; B

> A picture-book biography of a great dancer and choreographer.

Resau, L. (2006). *What the moon saw.* New York: Delacorte. 5–6;7+. CRF

> A 14-year-old girl visits her Mexican grandparents and learns a great deal about her heritage.

Rumford, J. (2004). *Sequoyah: The Cherokee man who gave his people writing* (A. S. Huckaby, translator). New York: Houghton Mifflin. K–2;3–4. PB; B; RFSH

> Sequoyah creates a syllabary of 84 symbols to record the Cherokee language.

Ryan, P. M. (2004). *Becoming Naomi Leon.* New York: Scholastic. 3–4;5–6. CRF; NH

> A mother who abandoned her children tries to get custody of one of them.

Rylant, C. (2006). *Ludie's life.* Orlando, FL: Harcourt. 5–6;7+. INF; B

> The free-verse account of Ludie's life from her birth in 1910 to her death 95 years later.

Seeger, P. (2006). *The deaf musicians* (R. G. Christie, Illus.). New York: Putnam. K–2;3–4. PB; CRF

> After a piano player loses his hearing, he starts a band with another deaf musician.

Sherman, P. (2005). *The sun's daughter* (R. Christie, Illus.). New York: Clarion. K–2;3–4;5–6. PB; F

> The Native folktale about why summer is only six months long.

Soto, G. (2005). *Help wanted: Stories.* Orlando, FL: Harcourt. 5–6;7+. CRF

> A book of short stories about Mexican American teens.

So-un, K. (New edition, 2004). *Korean children's favorite stories* (J. Kyoung-Sim, Illus.). Boston, MA: Tuttle Publishing. K–2;3–4;5–6. TL

> A collection of traditional Korean stories.

Spooner, M. (2005). *Last child.* New York: Holt. 5–6;7+. HF

> The child of a Native American mother and white father helps many in her tribe when an outbreak of smallpox kills many people.

Staples, S. (2005). *Under the persimmon tree.* New York: Farrar, Straus and Giroux. 5–6;7+. CRF

> After her family is killed or imprisoned, Najmah goes to a refugee camp in Pakistan.

Steptoe, J. (1987). *Mufaro's beautiful daughters* (L. & D. Dillon, Illus.). New York: Amistad. K–2;3–4. PB; TL

Two sisters compete in this Cinderella variation.

Swanson, B. (2007). *Gray Wolf's search* (G. Peterson, Illus.). Toronto, ON: Second Story Press. K–2. PB; HF

A young boy goes on a journey to find out how he can be successful.

Taback, S. (2005). *Kibitzers and fools.* New York: Viking Juvenile. K–2;3–4. PB; TL

Thirteen traditional stories collected from Eastern European Jewish villages.

Taylor, T. (2005). *Ice drift.* Orlando, FL: Harcourt. 5–6;7+. HF

Two Alaskan youths are stranded on a piece of ice, which breaks off from land.

Thompson, C. (2004). *The ABC's of black history* (R. James, Illus.). Silver Spring, MD: Beckham Publications. K–2;3–4. PB; INF

A picture-book biography for younger readers.

Trotter, D. W. (2007). *A summer's trade* (Bilingual edition). Flagstaff, AZ: Salina Bookshelf. K–2;3–4. CRF

A young boy earns money for a saddle but must spend the money to help his family.

Vanasse, D. (2004). *A distant enemy.* Anchorage, AK: Alaska Print Brokers. 5–6;7+. CRF

An Alaskan biracial youth is angry at the restrictions placed upon him.

White, R. (2005). *The search for Belle Prater.* New York: Farrar, Straus & Giroux. 5–6;7+. HF

Woodrow and two others search for Woodrow's mom, who has abandoned him.

Woodson, J. (2005). *Show way* (H. Talbott, Illus.). New York: Putnam. K–2;3–4;5–6;7+. PB; B; CH

An account of generations of one African American family.

Wyss, T. H. (2005). *Bear dancer: The story of a Ute girl.* New York: Margaret K. McElderry. 3–4;5–6;7+. HF

Elk Girl is captured in a raid, traded to another tribe, and rescued by a white soldier.

Yang, B. (2004). *Hannah is my name.* Cambridge, MA: Candlewick. K–2;3–4. HF; PB

A young child from Taiwan changes her name when she comes to the United States.

Yoo, P. (2005). *Sixteen years in sixteen seconds: The Sammy Lee story* (D. Lee, Illus.). New York: Lee and Low. K–2;3–4. B; PB

A biography of the first Asian American to win a gold medal in swimming.

Yung, S. (2004). *Cooper's lesson* (K. Cogan, Illus; M. Paek, Translator). San Francisco, CA: Children's Book Press. K–2;3–4. CRF; PB

A biracial child has difficulty finding his own identity.

Zucker, J. (2004). *Fasting and dates: A Ramadan and Eid-ul-Fitr story* (J. B. Cohen, Illus.). Hauppauge, NY: Barron's. K–2;3–4. PB; INF

A description of the Muslim holiday, Ramadan.

Professional References

Bedford, A. W., & Cuellar, R. (2006). The Tomas Rivera Mexican American children's book award. *Book Links, 15,* (no. 3), 4–16.

Bishop, R. S. (1992). Multicultural literature for children: Making informed choices. In V. J. Harris (Ed.), *Teaching multicultural literature in grades K–8,* 37–53. Norwood, MA: Christopher-Gordon.

Cooperative Children's Book Center. (n.d.). http://www.education.wisc.edu/ccbc/books/multicultural.asp.

DeNicolo, C. P., & Franquiz, M. E. (2006). "Do I have to say it?": Critical encounters with multicultural children's literature. *Language Arts, 84,* 157–170.

Dressel, J. H. (2005). Personal response and social responsibility: Responses of middle-school students to multicultural literature. *The Reading Teacher, 58,* 750–764.

Dudley-Marling, C. (2003). "I'm not from Pakistan": Multicultural literature and the problem of representation. In D. L. Fox and K. G. Short (Eds.), *Stories matter: The complexity of cultural authenticity in children's literature* (304–318). Urbana, IL: NCTE.

Enriquez, G. (2001). Making meaning of cultural depictions: Using Lois Lowry's *The Giver* to reconsider what is "multicultural" about literature. *Journal of Children's Literature, 27,* 13–22.

Franquiz, M. E. (2005). Education as political work: An interview with Sonia Nieto. *Language Arts, 83,* 166–171.

Freeman, E. B., & Lehman, B. A. (2001). *Global perspectives in children's literature*. New York: Allyn & Bacon.

Goodson, F. T. (2004). A pinch of tobacco and a drop of urine: Using young adult literature to examine local culture, using local culture to enrich schools. *The Alan Review, 32.* Naperville, IL: North Central Regional Educational Laboratory.

Loewn, J. W. (1995). *Lies my teacher told me: Everything your American history textbook got wrong.* New York: Simon & Schuster.

Nieto, S. (1999). *The light in their eyes: Creating multicultural learning communities.* New York: Teachers College Press.

Pavonetti, L. M. (2001). Books about children's literature: A mirror for all our students. *Journal of Children's Literature. 27,* 70–80.

Sebesta, A. (2001). What do teachers need to know about children's literature? *The New Advocate, 14,* 241–249.

Shanahan, P. (1994). I am the canon: Finding ourselves in multiculturalism. *Journal of Children's Literature, 20,* 1–5.

Steiner, S. F. (2001). *Promoting a global community through multicultural children's literature.* Englewood, CO: Libraries Unlimited.

Stoodt, B. (1992, July). *Multicultural children's literature.* Paper presented at the World Congress on Reading. Maui, HI.

Umber, R. (2002). Reading the world and finding connections: A novel by a New Zealand author raises issues relevant to adolescent readers in America. *Signal Journal, 15,* 7–12.

Yep, Laurence. (2005). Wilder medal acceptance. *Hornbook, LXXXI,* 429–432.

14 Oral and Silent Literature

KEY TERMS

antiphonal choral reading
book-talking
choral reading
creative drama
line-a-child choral reading

reader's theater
refrain choral reading
storytelling
unison choral reading

GUIDING QUESTIONS

1. Why is reading aloud to children important in developing literary experiences?

2. How are oral and silent reading related?

3. What should you consider when selecting a book to read aloud to your class?

4. At what grade level should teachers stop reading to students?

Introduction to Oral and Silent Literature

"Does reading aloud make a difference? Yes!" (Laminack & Wadsworth, 2006.) Reading aloud to students is the most valuable component of any literature, reading, or language arts program, as well as for classes in all other types of curricula. No other activity has as many benefits. Reading aloud builds a relationship between children and adults; creates a sense of classroom community; and strengthens literature, language, grammar, vocabulary, knowledge, and writing skills. Read-alouds motivate students to read and give them opportunities to express their response to literature (Sipe, 2002). During read-alouds, students listen, question, speak, visualize, and think (Hahn, 2002).

Oral reading makes literature accessible to readers, nonreaders, and English language learners. Listening to stories frees children from thinking about word identification and word meaning, permitting them instead to think, feel, and respond to the stories, poems, or information they hear. Thinking critically about literature is easier when it is read aloud, and daily listening to stories improves children's ability to listen and to talk about and retell stories, preparing them to read and comprehend the various genres.

Discussion, another aspect of oral language, enables readers to respond to literature and to intertwine their own life "stories" with the author's story. Discussion also allows them to reflect on and revise the meaning they derived from the text by hearing and considering others' views about the story's meaning. Oral literature activities enrich children's understanding of the special conventions, devices, and effects of spoken language. In the process, they develop an ear for written language and a sense of the differences between the sound of book language and everyday speech.

Oral Reading Activities

In a warm, supportive read-aloud environment, children associate reading with pleasure; they begin to see reading as an activity to be enjoyed and valued. *Fire! Fire! Said Mrs. McGuire*** is a good read-aloud because it is a rhyme with the refrain, *Where!*,

---

FIGURE 14.1   Values of reading aloud to children.

- Makes literature available to all students
- Extends knowledge
- Builds interest in language and words
- Develops comprehension
- Creates a model of fluent reading
- Develops reading taste
- Cultivates pleasure in reading
- Builds a foundation for young children who are beginning to read
- Demonstrates the ways fiction, nonfiction, and poetry are structured

---

Where! Said Mrs. McGuire, which teacher and students can chant together. Bill Martin and Vladimir Radunsky have created a new version of this story. Another book with rhyme and refrain is *That's Good! That's Bad!* by Margery Culyer. And children will be laughing after listening to Lynne Reid Banks's

Mrs. McGuire uses rhythmic language to shout a fire warning.

book, *Harry the Poisonous Centipede Goes to Sea.* They may elect to read other books in this Harry the Centipede series.

Dick King Smith writes marvelous humorous books for reading aloud. Second-, third-, and fourth-grade students will enjoy these books. *Lady Lollipop* is a story about a pig, and *The Guard Dog* is about a very small dog that dreams of becoming a guard dog. Among his other stories are *A Mouse Called Wolf, The Invisible Dog,* and *The Water Horse.*

As children grow in their ability to read, many will choose to read a story they have heard read aloud. I observed this when reading *Little House on the Prairie*** by Laura Ingalls Wilder to fourth graders. The students checked out every copy in the library, and parents reported they had to buy copies for their children. The children read along silently as I read the story aloud. After completing this book, the students asked me to read the other books in this series. In this way, the experience of oral reading is not unlike throwing pebbles into a pond; the story creates an impetus for reading more.

Selecting Material for Reading Aloud

Read-alouds give teachers a chance to read quality literature that children might not choose for themselves or that they might be unable to read. Read-aloud materials are not confined to books; they can also include magazine articles, short stories, poems, newspaper articles, or anything of interest to both reader and listener. Read-aloud materials should be chosen carefully, in order to motivate children. The criteria for good read-aloud materials mandate that the work:

1. be of high literary quality from a variety of genres;
2. be appropriate to the age and developmental level of children;
3. be interesting enough to hold children's attention;
4. have strong plot lines and characters with whom children can identify, if fiction;
5. have accurate information, in fiction and nonfiction;
6. have a concrete subject related to children's experiences in poetry; and
7. be up to two or more reading levels above the grade level of the children, so long as the material interests them.

Books in all genres can be interesting read-alouds. Traditional literature is, of course, always a favorite because the short, direct, and lively stories lend themselves to oral presentation. Traditional literature interests a wide age range of listeners. Steven Kellogg's *I Was Born About 10,000 Years Ago* is a well-loved tall tale that appeals to many children. Jon Muth's *Stone Soup,* which is set in China, is bound to please primary-grade students. Elementary-level students will like Sherry Garland's *Children of the Dragon: Selected Tales from Vietnam.* And middle-grade students will enjoy *The Seven Voyages of Sinbad the Sailor* by John Yeoman and Quention Blake. In these stories, Sinbad explains his seven disastrous voyages; he fights storms, sea serpents, and giants but he finally finds happiness.

Many adults and children enjoy humor, such as in David Wisniewski's *The Secret Knowledge of Grown-Ups,* and in the rhyming text of Mem Fox's *Boo to a Goose.* Children in grades 2 through 4 will appreciate Lloyd Alexander's *Gypsy Rizka,* which is a perils-of-Pauline type story. In this episodic chapter book, one chapter sets up the joke and the next one resolves it. Other good read-aloud books include *Peanut's Emergency* by Cristina Salat; books by Leo Lionni, Tomie dePaola, and Arnold Lobel; and poems by Shel Silverstein and Jack Prelutsky.

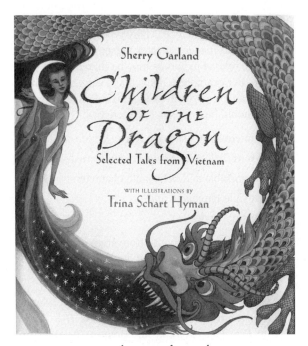

Everyone loves or fears dragons.

Successful intermediate-grade read-alouds include Wade Hudson's *Powerful Words: More than 200 Years of Extraordinary Writing by African Americans,* and *Pictures of Hollis Woods* by Patricia Giff. The Giff book, which is a real page turner, is the story of a foster child who finally finds a home where she is accepted until she suffers an accident.

The lively text of Joy Cowley's informational book *Red-Eyed Tree Frog* makes this a riveting read-aloud adventure for children in grades 1 through 3. Children will acquire information about water. Nonfiction read-alouds for primary children might also include books such as Candace Fleming's *The Hatmaker's Sign: A Story by Benjamin Franklin,* which may be considered historical fiction, although it is based on an anecdote found in Thomas Jefferson's papers and has a wonderful read-aloud quality. Many students are interested in the martial arts, so Ken Mochizuki's *Be Water, My Friend: The Early Years of Bruce Lee* is a good read-aloud for them. *The Adventures of Marco Polo* by Russell Freedman and Bagram Ibatouthice is a superb read-aloud for intermediate- and middle-school students. The authors raise two questions for readers or listeners of this story: Did Marco Polo really travel to China and beyond, as he claimed? Or was he, in fact, the man of a million lies? These questions will focus listeners.

Planning a Read-Aloud Session

Reading aloud is a sharing time. The reader selects the material, arranges the physical setting so that readers can see and hear, and looks over the materials. When reading picture books, the reader shows the illustrations at the same time he or she is reading.

A read-aloud session has three major components: First, the teacher introduces the book, identifies the author and illustrator, and helps the listeners connect with the book. Second, the teacher reads the selection, initially for understanding and appreciation; however, teachers or librarians may stop reading to encourage prediction or to connect a character, an incident, or a problem to literature students have previously read or heard. Third, depending upon the particular book in question, the teacher may conduct a follow-up discussion during which the children may raise questions or the teacher may introduce discussion points.

Activities like the following give children a chance to respond to literature, while strengthening oral and silent reading.

Reader's Theater

Reader's theater is an interpretive reading activity in which readers bring characters, story, poetry, and nonfiction text to life through their voices, actions, and words. (Black & Stave, 2007). Two or more readers characterize and narrate clearly and expressively for a reader's theater experience. Reader's theater stresses oral presentation of the text. Students learn to speak clearly and enunciate so the listeners can understand what is said. Performers read from text on the stage. Through expressive reading, posture, and limited actions, the performers suggest and enhance meaning (Black & Stave, 2007). Careful reading and discussion of the text enables readers to interpret the literature. Reader's theater gives performers the opportunity to explore meaning and interpretation in a non-threatening, controlled, and prepared situation.

The simplicity of reader's theater makes it appealing and motivating and so students enjoy practicing their oral reading. Another attraction is that reader's theater does not require rehearsal or elaborate staging; the cast may be large or small. If necessary, one individual may read several parts. During the presentation, the entire cast remains on stage, reading the various assigned portions. Movement is minimal, and actions are suggested through simple gestures and facial expressions.

Teachers or students select specific scenes from literature that convey the piece's concept or theme rather than reading the entire selection. The readers sit on stools in a circle, turning around on the stools so their backs face the audience when they are not participating in a scene. In somewhat more elaborate staging, a spotlight may be focused on the individual who is reading. Students may sit or stand side-by-side, with the narrators at one side and closer to the audience. Readers may take formal positions behind lecterns or sit on stools, often turning their backs to the audience to show that they are absent from a scene. In addition, readers may turn around or lower their heads when not participating in a scene. Readers should practice reading in a comfortable, relaxed manner at a pace that moves the scene along, but not so rapidly that the audience is lost.

The setting for reader's theater may be classrooms, libraries, nursing homes, and community centers, among others. Productions may be video- and/or audiotaped. A radio format works for productions because they are reminiscent of older radio programs.

Curriculum-Based Reader's Theater (CBRT)

In curriculum-based reader's theater (CBRT), students create narrative scripts related to their content classes, taking the script topics directly from their classroom curriculum. Flynn (2004) describes a sixth-grade production based on the U. S. Bill of Rights. She also describes a CBRT based on the American Revolution. In both of these projects, the students scored very high on the knowledge assessment after the productions. The box that follows, "A Report on a Reader's Theater Performance," describes how a fifth-grade class prepared for a reader's theater performance.

Selecting Material

Students who are becoming fluent readers need manageable texts for practice. Many types of literature are well-suited to reader's theater presentations. In some instances, related materials may be mixed in the presentation. For example, a poem and a story with related themes can be performed together. Reader's theater stories should have these characteristics:

1. an interesting, fast-paced story with a strong plot;
2. a lot of dialogue or have students create dialogue;
3. recognizable and believable characters;
4. plausible language; and
5. a distinct style.

Clearly, teachers may choose from among many appropriate pieces of literature, including the following suggestions.

- *Rolling Harvey Down the Hill* by Jack Prelutsky
- *Moses: When Harriet Tubman Led Her People to Freedom* by Carole Boston Weatherford (primary)

A Report on a Reader's Theater Performance

The students chose to read *Where the Lilies Bloom* by Vera and Bill Cleaver. Eight readers took the parts of Mary Call, the protagonist; Devola, her older sister; Roy Luther, the father; Kiser Pease, the landlord and neighbor; Mary Call's younger brother and sister; the storekeeper, who buys herbs from Mary Call; and a neighbor. The readers used stools in a circle so they could turn their backs to the audience when not participating.

They identified the following scenes as key to understanding the story.

1. Mary Call and Roy Luther discuss his impending death and burial in the grave he has prepared.
2. Mary Call and the children pretend their father is ill when a neighbor comes to call.
3. Mary Call and Devola care for Kiser Pease when he is ill.
4. Mary Call and the storekeeper interact when Mary Call sells herbs.
5. Kiser Pease brings his car to the Luthers' so that Devola can sit in it.
6. Kiser Pease asks Devola to marry him.
7. Mary Call pretends she wants to marry Kiser.
8. Devola takes charge and decides to marry Kiser.

The readers decided to serve herb tea after their performance because Mary Call earns a living for her family by gathering herbs. They also planned to read the sequel to this story, *Trial Valley*.

- *Ambergate* by Patricia Elliott (middle school)
- *Clementine* by Sara Pennypacker (primary)
- *Henny Penny* by Paul Galdone (primary)
- *The End* by Lemony Snicket (intermediate)

- *The Hare and the Tortoise and Other Fables of La Fontaine,* Translator Ranjit Bolt (primary and intermediate)

Storytelling

Storytelling is an ancient art that existed before common people had access to written language. Storytellers have preserved our past and transmitted it orally to new generations. Families pass on family lore, values and beliefs, common history, and heritage. Storytelling is a powerful, magical way of introducing and exploring literature, as storytellers make stories come to life. Oral literature includes stories, poems, and information told aloud to another person or persons. Unlike writers, who do not have a chance to interact directly with their readers, storytellers have a live, listening audience with whom to interact. Listeners hear voice effects and see their storyteller move, bend, and breathe. "As the teller looks right at the listeners, eyes meet and an interactive communication exists between them" (Livo & Rietz, 1986, p. xi). Storytelling is natural to human beings because it helps us remember and understand things that have happened; it teaches us how to behave, as well as how not to behave. It stimulates our imagination: As the storyteller spins a tale, the listeners create mental pictures of the characters, the setting, and the story events. Lawyers are storytellers, teachers are storytellers, company representatives are storytellers, visitors to historic sites listen to storytellers. Obviously, storytelling has many applications throughout one's lifetime.

Storytelling in the Classroom

Storytelling motivates children to read and write themselves. The classroom snapshot that follows shows how storytelling can be used as a model for children's own writing.

In addition to telling their own stories, children also like to join in on repeated phrases when others are telling stories. Hearing and telling different types of stories develops their awareness and comprehension of the various forms of narrative. In this way, storytelling develops thinking abilities (Roney, 1989). Teachers can tell stories to introduce literature, to help

CLASSROOM SNAPSHOT

A STORYTELLING EXPERIENCE

Jim Phillips told his first graders to make a story circle on the rug in his classroom; then he sat down on a low chair and opened the book *Brown Bear, Brown Bear* by Bill Martin. He held the book so the children could see it, told them the title and the author's name, and started reading.

"Brown Bear, Brown Bear, What do you see?" "I see a red bird looking at me."

Mr. Phillips read through the entire cumulative tale, in which each animal or bird sees another. When he finished, the children pleaded for him to read it again and he did. After the second reading, Mr. Phillips told the children they were going to make a story. They immediately asked how.

He answered, "You are going to think of new animals for the *Brown Bear, Brown Bear* story. I'll begin with 'Blue Jay, Blue Jay, What do you see?' Now, Lauren, tell us what the Blue Jay sees."

After thinking for a few moments, Lauren said, "I see a pink butterfly looking at me."

Mr. Phillips said, "Pink butterfly, pink butterfly, What do you see? Tony, tell us what the pink butterfly sees."

Tony said, "I see a striped zebra looking at me!"

Mr. Phillips and the children continued until they had completed a story, then they retold it. Afterward, Mr. Phillips said, "I am going to write your story on this chart, so you can remember it. While I am writing your story on a chart, you can draw pictures of the animals and birds that you thought of for the story, and we will paste them to the chart pages."

Later in the day, he noticed that a number of the children were writing and illustrating their own *Brown Bear* stories. When the children completed their individual stories, they read them to their classmates.

---

children learn about stories, to develop children's listening and speaking skills, and to model storytelling behavior. Teachers can also help their students learn to tell stories.

The Internet is a rich source of storytelling ideas and suggested materials. At some sites, students can actually hear storytellers sharing their favorite stories. For example, www.themoonlitroad.com is an excellent site, as is the Storytelling FAQ at www.timsheppard.co.uk/story.

Selecting Material

The first step in storytelling is selecting a story to learn. Traditional literature is a good starting point. Books such as *Teaching Through Stories: Yours, Mine, and Theirs* (Roe, Alfred, & Smith, 1998) are helpful to teachers and students. Begin with an appealing version of a traditional story that you already know, such as *Cinderella, Three Billy Goats Gruff,* or *Stone Soup.* The most important factor in choosing a story for telling is that you enjoy it.

As a beginning storyteller, a simple story will give you security as you begin. Storytellers need not feel confined to traditional stories, however. Modern tales such as Judith Viorst's *Alexander and the Terrible,*

Horrible, No Good, Very Bad Day is a delightful story that has broad appeal. You will find the following authors helpful because they retell traditional stories and write stories in a traditional literature style.

- *I, Houdini: The Autobiography of a Self-Educated Hamster* by Lynne Reid Banks, illustrated by Terry Riley
- *The Three Little Pigs* by Jean Claverie
- *Look What Happened to Frog: Storytelling in Education* by Pamela Cooper and Rives Collins
- *Hairyman* by David Holt
- *Jack and the Beanstalk* by Steven Kellogg
- *Black Folktales* by Julius Lester
- *The Tales of Uncle Remus: The Adventures of Brer Rabbit* by Julius Lester
- *The Boy Who Loved Frogs* by Jay O'Callahan

Planning Storytelling

The main ingredient in planning storytelling is learning the story. Storytelling confidence comes with story familiarity. Storytellers should know their story well. Learning the framework of a story provides a skeleton to follow in telling it. The storyteller should learn any phrases that are repeated or important to the story.

Literature becomes a living story when a storyteller talks.

Once these elements are learned, practice telling the story several times to help polish the presentation.

Learning the framework of a story is easy. As discussed in Chapter 2, stories are orderly and conform to rules recognized as story structure or story grammar (Livo & Rietz, 1986). Stories that conform to the expected structure are easier to recall and to understand (Downing & Leong, 1982).

Story patterns help readers comprehend literature; they also give form to writing. Story patterns can be mapped or diagrammed to assist storytellers in recalling and interrelating the ideas and events of a story. Story patterns and maps are especially helpful in teaching children to prepare stories for storytelling.

1. When preparing to learn a story for storytelling, a week or so in advance, read several stories. The story that comes back to you most frequently is the one to learn.

2. Divide the story into beginning, middle, and end. Learn the story in segments, such as separate scenes or units of action. Learn the story structure in order, but do not memorize it. The ways of dividing a story differ from storyteller to storyteller.

   The *Three Little Pigs* could be divided in the following way.

   ▪ *Part 1.* The three little pigs set out to find their fortune. One builds a house of straw, the next builds a house of sticks, and the third builds a house of bricks.

   ▪ *Part 2.* The wolf eats pigs one and two and goes after the third one.

   ▪ *Part 3.* The pig sends the wolf to an apple orchard and a fair and then outwits him. The wolf ends up in the kettle.

3. Do not memorize the exact words of a story, but do learn any special catch phrases and use them in telling the story. Catch phrases are phrases that may appear several times within the story or that the story hinges on, such as "I'll huff and I'll puff and I'll blow your house down" in *The Three Little Pigs*.

4. Don't worry about using the same words every time you tell the story.

5. Be expressive in storytelling, but do not be so dramatic that you overshadow the story itself (Morrow, 1988).

6. Practice telling the story several times before actually telling it to an audience to get comfortable with saying the story aloud and with the sound of your own voice.

7. Tape-record yourself. Wait a day or two to listen to the tape so you can be objective. When you evaluate the tape, think about the parts of the story and identify those that need changing or expanding. Does your voice sound pleasing? Do you speak at a speed that is appropriate to the story?

8. Look directly at your audience when you are telling the story.

9. The story should not be longer than 10 minutes. You will find helpful materials through the Internet and through storytelling associations. The National Storytelling Network (NTN) is located in Jonesborough, Tennessee. It has a web site www.storynet.org, a magazine, and many other storytelling materials, and it sponsors storytelling events such as "Tellabrations" on the Saturday before Thanksgiving. This international event takes place in elder hostels, on airplanes, in schools and colleges, in museums, and wherever people gather. Whenever you access the NTN web site, you will discover a plethora of storytelling sites from around the world. East Tennessee State University also has a storytelling program with coursework, and it publishes *Storytelling World*.

Storytelling Variations

Sitting in front of an audience and using only voice and expressions is not the only way to tell a story. Storytelling can be varied in many ways to give novelty to tried-and-true stories. Variations also can be used cooperatively with students to give them greater involvement with the story.

Flannel Board Stories

When telling stories with flannel boards, the teller sits or stands by a board covered with a flannel, indoor-outdoor carpet. Cutouts of characters backed with flannel are placed on the board as they appear in the story. Some storytellers may lay the flannel board on a table to prevent the figures from falling. Children enjoy taking turns telling stories with a flannel board.

Flannel board stories should not have large numbers of characters or complex actions. After selecting a story, the teller or tellers decide which parts to show and which to tell. For example, in preparing *Goldilocks and the Three Bears,* the teller or students could make figures for Goldilocks, the three bears, three sizes of bowls, three sizes of chairs, and three sizes of beds; some tellers may like to have a broken bowl and a broken chair to illustrate the story further. These figures can be used to present the entire story; details and actions do not have to be portrayed. The characters can be drawn or painted on cardboard, construction paper, or any other convenient material. After cutting them out, back them with flannel or sandpaper so they will stick to the flannel board. Use yarn, buttons, or fabric to decorate and develop the characters.

Prop Stories

Props such as hats, canes, stuffed animals, boxes, rocks, toys, and fruit can enhance storytelling. Beans, a small harp, and a china or plastic hen are excellent props for *Jack and the Beanstalk.* The props give the storyteller and the audience a focal point and help the storyteller remember the story.

Music Stories

Some stories are excellent when told with background music. For example, *Jack and the Beanstalk* sounds wonderful when told with the music "In the Hall of the Mountain King" (from *Legends in Music* by the Bowmar Orchestral Library) playing in the background. RCA Victor has an *Adventures in Music* record library for elementary schools that includes excellent selections for story background music. Musical storytellers may also play their own accompaniment.

Cut Stories

Cut stories are told while the storyteller cuts a piece of paper to form a character or an object in the story. The figures may be drawn ahead of time on construction paper to make the cutting easier (Morrow, 1979). Some teachers are sufficiently skilled to fold the paper and cut multiple figures while storytelling. Many picture books and folktales are good choices for cut stories because the teller can also cut objects to accompany the story. For example, a gingerbread boy cutout could accompany the story *The Gingerbread Boy,* or a pancake could accompany *The Pancake.*

Digital Storytelling

Digital stories are created on the computer. Students can create a new version of an existing story. They may choose pictures to illustrate the story or insert music into the story. Middle-school students in particular will enjoy this style, although younger children are also very knowledgeable about the digital world.

 ## Choral Reading

Choral reading is an oral literary activity in which several readers read a selection in unison with the direction of a leader. This ancient technique has been in use for centuries. For example, choral reading was an important element of Greek drama. Researchers have found evidence of choral speaking in ancient religious ceremonies and festivals, and it is still used for ritualistic purposes in church services and on patriotic occasions (McCaslin, 1990). Choral reading was used during the early history of schools because there were not enough books.

Choral reading involves listening and responding to language. Through participating in choral reading, students learn the sounds of language, predictable language patterns, and the rhythm and melody of language, which enhances their understanding (Miccinati, 1985). After choral reading experiences, children are better able to predict the words and phrases that follow one another.

The purpose of choral reading is to convey meaning through sound, stress, duration, and pitch. Choral reading also develops diction and the enunciation of speech sounds. Choral reading is a group activity that gives students opportunities for social cooperation. In a group activity such as this, students can participate without feelings of self-consciousness. Choral reading knows no age limits—kindergarten children enjoy it, as do high school students.

Selecting Material

Choral reading in the elementary classrooms can begin with short nursery rhymes in kindergarten. Rhythm and rhyme are the important factors in nursery rhymes, which help children remember them. Material for choral reading should be meaningful, have a strong rhythm, and have an easily discernible structure. The following list includes only a few of the selections that make interesting choral readings.

- "So Long as There's Weather" by Tamara Kitt
- "Godfrey, Gordon, Gustavus Gore" by William B. Rand
- "The Umbrella Brigade" by Laura Richards
- *I Know an Old Lady Who Swallowed a Fly* by Glen Rounds
- *Train Song* by Diane Siebert
- *Truck Song* by Diane Siebert
- *Laughing Time: Collected Nonsense* by William Jay Smith
- *Peanut Butter and Jelly* by Nadine Westcott

Planning a Choral Reading

When initiating a choral reading activity, prepare the students by giving them time to read the material silently, and then have them read it aloud to themselves or their peers. After reading, discuss the literature to ensure comprehension. Once the students understand the selection, they can practice reading it orally. Teachers can help young children respond to language rhythms by clapping or tapping to the rhythm. Initially, the teacher may chant most of the rhyme and have the children chime in only on the last line or a repeated refrain. Use a single selection with various choral reading methods so students learn about the various ways of expressing meaning. After students have experiences with the various choral reading types, they can choose selections and plan their own choral readings.

Four common types of choral reading exist: refrain, line-a-child, antiphonal, and unison. The easiest to learn is *refrain choral reading,* in which the teacher reads most of the lines and the students read the refrain. In *line-a-child choral reading,* individual students read specific lines while the entire group reads the beginning and ending of the selection. *Antiphonal,* or *dialogue, choral reading* is most appropriate for middle- or intermediate-level students. It enables readers to explore the pitch and duration of sound. Students vary their pitches and the sound duration for different parts of the selection.

Unison choral reading is the most difficult approach because the entire group speaks all of the lines. Without seeking perfection, the participants must practice timing so they are simultaneously producing words and sounds. Combinations of all of these types may be used for a single selection.

Tamara Kitt's poem "So Long as There's Weather" is a fine children's choice for choral reading. The spare use of words, frequent pauses, sound effects, emphasized words, and short lines ranging from one to five syllables create a feeling of changing weather and a child's joy in all kinds of weather. The appeal of this poem for children makes it an excellent choice for choral reading. Alert the students to the fact that dashes in the text represent pauses and that the emphasized words and pauses make the choral reading more interesting. A choral reading experience involving "So Long as There's Weather" for primary-grade children might proceed as indicated in the following steps.

1. The teacher begins with crashing cymbals to simulate thunder or water poured from container to container to simulate rain.

2. The teacher reads the first verse.

3. The children read the second verse in unison from a chart.

4. The teacher or a child who has practiced reads the third verse.

5. The children read the fourth verse in unison from a chart.

6. On the emphasized words in the fourth verse, designated children crash cymbals together.

As children develop their understanding of chanting in unison, they can move to longer selections. *Peanut Butter and Jelly* by Nadine Westcott is an excellent longer piece for choral reading. After children learn to chant this play-rhyme, the teacher can introduce the hand-clap and knee-slap motions that accompany it. Later, the teacher may choose to divide the poem into parts to be read by different groups.

Creative Drama

Creative drama is informal drama created by the participants (McCaslin, 1990). This kind of drama is improvisational and process-centered. It may be based on a story with a beginning, a middle, and an end. It may also, however, be an original plot that explores, develops, and expresses ideas and feelings through dramatic enactment. The players create the dialogue, whether the content is a well-known story or an original plot. "With each playing, the story becomes more detailed and better organized, but it remains extemporaneous and is at no time designed for an audience," which avoids rehearsal and memorization (McCaslin, 1990, p. 5).

Reenactments allow each member of the group an opportunity to play various parts and to be part of the audience for others. Scenery and costumes have no place in creative drama, although an occasional prop or piece of costume may be permitted to stimulate the imagination (McCaslin, 1990). Similarly, readers have no written script to follow. Creative drama emphasizes spontaneity and improvisation, although involvement in creative drama may lead students to write a script for a play later. When dialogue is written, the nature of the drama changes. Written drama can be very rewarding, as children enjoy the creative writing involved in such enterprises.

Creative drama yields fun, understanding, and learning, as well as other benefits. As children improvise in acting out a story, an episode from a story, or an experience of their own, they comprehend and express the important details of plot, character, word meanings, story sequence, and cause-and-effect relations (Miccinati, 1985). This makes story characters and story action more concrete and comprehensible. In acting out stories, they use their bodies, voices, and movements to enact literature; translating words into action encourages children to interpret and respond to literature. Dramatization increases vocabulary, syntactic flexibility, and the ability to predict aspects of the story.

Creative drama also makes strong contributions to the growth of children's communication effectiveness (Busching, 1981). It requires logical and intuitive thinking; it personalizes knowledge and yields aesthetic pleasure (Siks, 1983). Drama gives children opportunities to experiment with words, emotions, and social roles. Heathcote (1983) believes that drama expands children's understanding of life experiences and that it leads them to reflect on particular circumstances and make sense out of their world in a deeper way.

Selecting Material

A dramatized story can make a lasting impression. Both folktales and modern stories provide fine opportunities for acting. Believable characters, a well-constructed plot, and a worthwhile theme make for engrossing drama. Any story, episode, or event that children have enjoyed is a likely candidate for dramatization. Students of all ages enjoy acting out versions of the same story and comparing them. For example, they might act out three versions of *Cinderella* and compare the characterization, plot, and setting.

The following suggestions for specific stories to dramatize may stimulate you to think of others. To start, children enjoy dramatizing the traditional stories that they have heard again and again, such as Brett Johnson's *Jack Outwits the Giants* or a version of *Little Red Riding Hood* for children in kindergarten through third grade. Middle-grade students enjoy stories such as *Bunnicula* by Deborah and James Howe, *The Pushcart War* by Jean Merrill, and *The Book of Three* by Lloyd Alexander.

Planning Creative Drama

Guidelines like the following will help teachers create many opportunities for children to participate in short, unstructured drama.

1. Although props are not necessary, many teachers gather a collection of props for dramatic plays. Jewelry, fabric, hats, canes, clothing, and Halloween costumes are useful props.

2. Select a story or have the children select a favorite story. A book that includes a large number of characters gives more children opportunities to participate.

3. Discuss the main events with the students. Identify and sequence the events to be included. You may wish to outline the events using a story map.

4. Identify the characters in the story. Discuss their actions, attitudes, and feelings. Explain that the children should act the way they think the character walked, talked, and so on.

5. Discuss the action in each scene and give the children opportunities to practice it. They may need to pretend to walk in heavy boots or need to practice expressive gestures such as walking happily, sadly, or so forth. Pantomime (discussed next) is a way of preparing children to move in expressive ways.

6. Assign character roles to class members. Ask the participants to think about and visualize the characters. Children who do not want to participate can be directors or stage managers.

7. Give the audience a purpose for watching the play. For example, ask them to observe characterization, character development, or plot development.

8. Dramatize the story.

9. Discuss the dramatization.

10. Recast the characters and play the story again.

Pantomime

"Pantomime is the art of conveying ideas without words"; it sharpens children's perceptions and stimulates the imagination as the players try to remember actions and characters (McCaslin, 1990, p. 71). Children can pantomime stories as another child or the teacher reads them. They may create a character from literature or one of their own invention. Music can set the mood for people marching in a parade, horses galloping, toads hopping, cars racing on a track, or children skipping on a sunny spring day (McCaslin, 1990). Older children also enjoy pantomime, and children who have limited knowledge of English or who have speech and hearing problems can participate in it.

Puppets

Puppet shows are dramas in which the actors are puppets that come to life with the assistance of a puppeteer. Children enjoy making puppets and becoming puppeteers. Puppets are excellent for children who are shy because they can express themselves through the puppet. They also work well with children who are reluctant to participate in creative drama. A puppet show allows children to dramatize their favorite books, as well as scripts they have written. Puppetry stimulates the imagination of the children who are creating puppets and planning to dramatize a story. Children practice cooperation as they work with others to make puppets and puppet productions.

The stage can be quite simple—a youngster kneeling behind a table and moving an object along the edge of it—or as elaborate as imagination and skill can make or buy it. Similarly, you can provide commercially produced puppets, or children can make their own, possibly from nothing more than a bandanna wrapped around the first three fingers so that the thumb and little finger are the arms (McCaslin, 1990). The following list features some of the puppets students can construct (Stoodt, 1988, p. 119).

- *Stick puppets.* Draw the character on tagboard, cardboard, or construction paper and decorate it with yarn, sequins, and tissue paper. Cut out the figure and attach it to a stick, tongue depressor, or dowel for manipulation.
- *Paper-plate puppets.* Draw faces on paper plates and decorate them with yarn for hair. Glue the plates on sticks, dowels, or rulers for manipulation.
- *Sock puppets.* Add yarn hair, button eyes, and felt bits for a nose, ear, or other features to the toe

end of a sock. Put your hand inside the sock for manipulation.

- *Styrofoam-cup puppets.* Decorate a cup as a character and attach the completed puppet to a stick or dowel for manipulation.
- *Cloth puppets.* Sew fabric to fit over a child's hand. Decorate it to create a character.
- *Paper-bag puppets.* Draw the character on the bag and put the bag over your hand to manipulate it, using the folded bottom of the bag for the mouth area; or decorate the bag as the character, stuff it with newspaper or cotton, and put a stick, dowel, or ruler into the neck of the bag and tie it shut, turning it upside down and using the stick for manipulation.

Some helpful puppeteering references include *Storytelling with Puppets* by Connie Champlin and Nancy Renfro (1985); *Making Puppets Come Alive* by Larry Engler and Carol Fijan (1973); and *The Consultant's Notebook* by Puppeteers of America (1989).

Evaluating Oral Story Experiences

"Experience without reflection is hollow" (Cooper & Collins, 1992, p. 3). Guided discussion gives children an opportunity to reflect on oral experiences, respond to them, offer support to their classmates, and think about future experiences. They can also be used to elicit constructive criticism. For instance, questions such as the following, partially suggested by Cooper and Collins, could be used to evaluate a creative drama.

1. What did you like best about this play?
2. When was the imagination really at work?
3. When were the characters most believable?
4. What did you learn from the play that you did not know from the telling?
5. What did you learn about the important ideas in this story?
6. Did we leave out anything in this playing?
7. What would you like to try in our next playing of the scene?
8. What other things could our characters do or say?
9. How can we make our playing even more believable?

Silent Reading

Understanding is the goal of all reading, whether one is reading silently, reading aloud for an audience, or being read-aloud to by someone else. All reading is an interactive process. Silent reading becomes more fluent with practice. In silent reading, students can more readily perceive ideas in the text. Children who read more show large differences in their reading abilities as a result of their practice (Fractor, Woodruff, Martinez, & Teale, 1993). Silent reading, which precedes reading aloud to others, permits readers to focus on meaning without being overly involved with pronouncing words. Oral reading requires readers to think ahead of their voices and to prepare to pronounce the next word or phrase, a skill that develops over time with extensive practice in silent reading.

Literature Circles

Literature circles are small, temporary discussion groups whose members have chosen to read the same story, poem, article, or book. Each group member prepares to take specific responsibilities in the discussion, and the participants come to the group with the notes they have taken to help them with their responsibilities. The literature circles have regular meetings, with the discussion roles rotating for each meeting. After they finish a book, the circle members plan to share the highlights of their reading with others in the classroom or school. They then form different groups, select another reading, and begin a new cycle. After the readers learn to sustain their discussions, they may drop the specific roles in the discussion (Daniels, 1994).

The goal of literature circles is to create open, natural conversations about books students have read. Divergent, open-ended, interpretive questions and critical reading questions encourage reader response and discussion. When organizing literature circles, teachers give students sample questions to help them begin, but teachers point out that the best discussion questions come from their own thoughts, feelings, and concerns. Questions such as the following encourage readers to read, process, savor, and share their personal response (Daniels, 1994):

- What was going through your mind while you read this?
- What was discussed in this (a specific) part of the book?
- Can someone briefly summarize today's reading?
- Did today's reading remind you of any real-life experiences?
- What questions did you have when you finished this section?
- Did anything in the book surprise you?
- What are the one or two most important ideas in the book?
- What do you predict will be talked about next?

Children participating in literature circles may choose passages to be shared based on specific guidelines, such as when they are asked to find text that is important, surprising, funny, confusing, informative, controversial, well-written, or thought-provoking (Daniels, 1994). We recommend that you read Harvey Daniels's book because it provides excellent ideas based on teachers' experiences in developing reading circles. Another helpful book for students in middle school is *You Gotta Be the Book* by Jeffrey D. Wilhelm.

Uninterrupted Sustained Silent Reading

Uninterrupted sustained silent reading (USSR), also known as drop everything and read (DEAR) or sustained silent reading (SSR), is usually regarded as a logical counterpart to daily oral reading. USSR is predicated on the idea that teachers regularly involve children in learning the skills of reading, but they often overlook giving children time to practice reading, thereby developing reading fluency. USSR also makes children aware that reading and books are important; it allows them to experience whole books rather than fragments, and it gives them practice in sustaining attention, thinking, and reading.

Effective USSR programs require a foundation of reading materials broad enough to be appropriate to the age, development, and reading levels of all the children involved. These materials may include books, periodicals, magazines, newspapers, reference books, and any other type of reading material that might interest the children. The materials should be in the classroom library where children can readily obtain them. Select books from the school library and obtain extended loans from the local public library to stock classroom shelves.

When developing a USSR program, teachers should first explain the purpose and procedures. The students should understand that they may bring reading material to class or select from the classroom library, but they are not to move around the room, draw, talk, or do anything other than read. Everyone reads; teachers should allow no interruptions and require no reports on their reading.

At the outset, allocate 5 to 10 minutes for first and second graders, and 10 to 15 minutes for third through sixth graders. The time can gradually be increased as children grow more comfortable with the process. The time of day for USSR varies among schools and teachers. Some schools have programs that involve everyone in the school reading at the same time. In other schools, individual teachers schedule USSR when it fits best in their schedules. Some teachers have students maintain records of their reading through a log of titles, number of pages read, or through a reading journal. Some teachers give the students time to share poems or excerpts from their reading.

Fostering Silent Reading

The best way teachers can foster silent reading is to provide many opportunities for silent reading, such as USSR. Silent reading, however, is not a directly observable skill. Teaching children how to read silently through guided silent reading is important, as is providing opportunities for readers to respond to silent reading through discussion and other activities.

Guided Silent Reading

Teachers should begin by guiding children to read silently or "read with their eyes," and then encourage them to think about what they read as they read it. Demonstrate the thinking that occurs during silent reading by means of a "think-aloud," in which the teacher or fluent readers verbalize what occurs in their minds while they silently read. For example, reading "A treasure hunt—today's the day. Come on in and you can play!" (Cauley, *Treasure Hunt*) might lead a reader to think of questions such as the following:

- What kind of a treasure hunt?
- What is the treasure?
- Is it a Saturday or summer vacation, because these children should be in school?
- Who are the children inviting to the treasure hunt?

These demonstrations guide students toward understanding how to think as they read silently—which simply admonishing them to think does not do—and enhance their response to literature.

Perhaps the most important step to developing silent reading skill is helping readers develop authentic purposes for silent reading. Silent reading that is active and purposeful enhances understanding and response. Again, purpose in reading is not directly observable, so teachers must guide readers' understanding and development of purpose. Teachers can model purposeful silent reading with a group through a read-aloud activity, as shown here with *Splash!* by Ann Jonas:

1. Introduce the book to the children by reading the title, *Splash!*, and asking what they think the story will be about. Such anticipation activities will give the students something to think about as they read—a purpose.

2. Write the children's responses on the chalkboard and ask them to think, as they hear the story, whether the splash in the story is what they expected. This will develop their sense of listening purpose and help them to actively and purposefully listen as you read.

3. Ask the children which character in the story they like best. Answering this question develops purpose because readers see the story through the eyes of characters they like, which focuses their attention.

4. Ask them why they think Ann Jonas wrote this book. Thinking about why the author wrote the book will allow them to compare the author's purpose in writing with their purpose in listening and will develop their understanding of purpose.

Prereading discussions and purposeful listening activities such as these connect readers and books. Purposes based on children's own questions are the most useful and understandable. Encourage students to read the entire piece, so they can respond to the complete work.

Responding to Silent Reading

Students can respond to and organize their silent reading in many ways. Class discussion is a tried and-true method of allowing some children to respond to their reading. Prompts (discussed in Chapter 3) are useful in eliciting oral and written responses. Reflecting about a story and participating in written dialogues and discussions develop comprehension. Participating in a community of readers, dramatizing a story, or preparing for literature circles also gives opportunities for response and peer feedback. Individual response could include completing a story grammar of the book or choosing a character and explaining why this character is the favorite.

Summary

Reading aloud to students is the foundation of this chapter. Students should be read to at all grade levels. Oral and silent reading strategies give students opportunities to experience literature and to respond to it in highly motivating situations. Comprehension is the focus of both oral and silent reading. In many instances, oral and silent reading are integrated because children who are preparing for oral activities read silently in anticipation of oral reading. One of the major differences between oral and silent reading is that oral readers must think of word pronunciation and produce the appropriate sounds for a word. This makes oral reading a slower process than silent reading.

Interpreting written literature for the appreciation of listeners is the purpose of oral reading. Oral reading has a variety of other purposes; for example, in the early years of school, children have limited reading abilities that restrict their experiences with books, but oral activities like those presented in this chapter enhance their understanding and appreciation of literature. Moreover, these activities develop children's ear for the sound of written language and their understanding. In choosing literature for oral activities, teachers need to consider how it sounds.

Reader's theater, storytelling, flannel board stories, puppets, digital storytelling, and choral reading are ways of developing both oral and silent reading because they are complementary processes.

Thought Questions and Applications

1. Why are oral activities motivating for children?
2. How do oral reading activities develop literacy?
3. Which oral reading activities will you use most often? Why?
4. Why do you think some teachers neglect reading aloud?
5. Why should a teacher feel that reading aloud to children is important?

Research and Application Experiences

1. Choose a poem and plan a choral reading that involves individual and unison reading.
2. Prepare *Alexander and the Terrible, Horrible, No Good, Very Bad Day* by Judith Viorst for oral reading. Then make a tape of your reading for your own analysis.
3. Make a story map for the story. This map can serve as your guide for telling this story.
4. Invent five descriptive phrases for the characters in *Goldilocks and the Three Bears*. These phrases should add color and dramatic appeal to the story when it is told aloud.
5. Choose a story for a flannel board presentation, prepare a script, and make the flannel board and the characters. Then present it to a group of children. Write about your experiences.
6. Choose a story for a puppet dramatization. Plan the script, make the puppets, and practice the presentation. Present it to a group of children. Write about your experiences.
7. Find storytelling on the Internet and listen to a story told by a professional storyteller.

Classroom Activities

ACTIVITY 14.1   MATHEMATICAL FOLKTALES

IRA/NCTE Standards: 1, 4, 7, 9. Students read a variety of materials, conduct research, respect cultural practices.

Introduction: Students will read similar folktales from three different cultures.

Literature:

1. *One Grain of Rice: A Mathematical Folktale*, by Demi.

   Rani, a village girl, performs a good deed, and the local Raja offers her a reward. She asks for one grain of rice to be doubled each day for 30 days. At the end of the month, she has fooled the Raja and procured enough rice to feed her starving people.

2. A similar story appears in *The King's Chessboard* by David Birch. This story is set in ancient India.

3. *A Grain of Rice* by Helena Pittman is set in China.

   Divide the class into three groups. Each group studies one of the books; the groups then compare the folktales and the cultures in which they originated. Students should consider the ways that the stories are similar and different. These are excellent stories for reader's theater.

ACTIVITY 14.2 RESEARCH

Encourage students to build on Activity 14.1 by doing the following:

a. Students can research each of the cultures, including the importance of rice in their diets. What nutritional values does rice have? This activity can be structured as an individual project, incorporated into cooperative grouping, or completed with partners working together.

b. Younger students can study pictures of the characters' clothing and research their reasons for dressing as they did.

Children's Literature References

Note: Books designated with an asterisk (*) are recommended for reluctant readers.

Alexander, L. (1964). *The book of three.* New York: Holt Rinehart & Winston. 5–6. TF

The story of Taran, the assistant pig keeper.

Alexander, L. (1999). *Gypsy rizka.* New York: Dutton. 5–6. MF

A gypsy girl tricks villagers into hilarious situations.

Anderson, H. C. (1978). *The princess and the pea* (P. Galdone, Illus.). New York: Seabury. 3–4. TF

Traditional Grimm tale.

Aranda, C. (1993). *Dichos: Proverbs and sayings from the Spanish.* Santa Fe, NM: Sunstone. 3–4;5–6. TF

A collection of Spanish sayings.

Banks, L.R. (2006). *Harry the poisonous centipede goes to sea.* New York: Harper Collins. K–2;3–4. MF; HI/M

Harry, a centipede, has a busy life.

Berger, B. (2002). *All the way to Lhasa: A tale from Tibet.* New York: Philomel. K–2;3–4. TF

A traditional tale from Tibet.

Borden, L. (1997). *The little ships: The heroic rescue at Dunkirk in World War II* (M. Foreman, Illus.). New York: McElderry. 3–6. HF*

Citizens of Britain used their own boats for the D Day rescue.

Cauley, L. B. (1994). *Treasure hunt.* New York: Putnam. K–2. CRF

A clever mystery for younger children.

Claverie, J. (Reteller). (1989). *The three little pigs.* New York: North South. K–2. TF

The traditional tale.

Cleaver, V., & Cleaver, B. (1969). *Where the lilies bloom* (J. Spanfeller, Illus.). New York: Harper & Row. 5–6;7+. CRF

The story of a mountain family.

Cleaver, V. & Cleaver, B. (1991). *Trial valley.* New York: Harper Collins. 5–6. CRF

The Luther siblings raise themselves in the Great Smoky Mountains.

Cowley, J. (1999). *Red-eyed tree frog* (N. Bishop, Illus.). New York: Scholastic. K–2. INF

Information about the red-eyed tree frog.

Culyer, M. (1991). *That's good! that's bad!* (D. Catrow, Illus.). New York: Henry Holt. K–2; 3–4. PB

An old "that's good, that's bad," story.

Fleming, C. (1999). *The hatmaker's sign: A story by Benjamin Franklin.* Scholastic. K–2;3–4. HF

This story was found among Jefferson's papers.

Florian, D. (1999). *Laugh-eteria.* New York: Harcourt. 3–4. P

Funny poetry.

Fox, M. (1998). *Boo to a goose* (D. Miller, Illus.). New York: Dial. K–2. PB

The main character will say anything except "boo" to a goose.

Freedman, R., & Ibatouthice, B. (2006). *The adventures of Marco Polo.* New York: Levine. 5–6;7+. INF

The story of Marco Polo's seven voyages.

Galdone, P. (Reteller). (1984). *Henny penny.* Boston: Houghton Mifflin. K–2. TF

The traditional story.

Garland, S. (2001). *Children of the dragon: Selected tales from Vietnam* (T. Hyman, Illus.). New York: Harcourt. K–2;3–4. TF

Vietnamese traditional tales.

Giblin, J. C. (2000). *The amazing life of Benjamin Franklin* (M. Dooling, Illus.). New York: Scholastic. 3–4. B

Giblin focuses on Franklin's inventions and many different jobs.

Giff, P. (2002). *Pictures of Hollis Woods.* New York: Random House. 5–6;7+. CRF

Story of a foster child.

Greaves, M. (Reteller). (1990). *Tattercoats.* New York: Potter. K–2. TF

A Cinderella story.

Holt, D. (1994a). *Hairyman.* Fairview, NC: High Windy Audio. All ages. TF

This a traditional tale.

Holt, D. (1994b). *Tailybone.* Fairview, NC: High Windy Audio. All ages. TF

A traditional tale in rhythmic language.

Howe, D., & Howe, J. (1979). *Bunnicula* (A. Daniel, Illus.). New York: Atheneum. 3–4. F

A vampire bunny haunts a family.

Hudson, W., Edelman, M. W., & Qualls, S. (2003). *Powerful words: More than 200 years of extraordinary writing.* Natick, MA: Chrysalis. 5–6;7+. INF

Twenty-six African American leaders write about their experiences.

Jackson, D. (2002). *The bug scientists.* New York: Houghton Mifflin. K–2;3–4. INF

All kinds of bugs.

Johnson, B. (2002). *Jack outwits the giant.* New York: McElderry. K–2;3–4. TF

Another version of the Jack stories.

Kellogg, S. (Reteller). (1991). *Jack and the beanstalk.* New York: Morrow. K–2;3–4. TF

Jack climbs the beanstalk and meets the giant.

Kellogg, S. (Reteller). (1996). *I was born about 10,000 years ago.* New York: Morrow. K–2;3–4. TF

A traditional tale.

King-Smith, D. (1993). *All pigs are beautiful* (A. Jeram, Illus.). Cambridge, MA: Candlewick Press. K–2. PB

The narrator believes all pigs are beautiful.

King-Smith, D. (1995). *The invisible dog.* New York: Puffin. K–2;3–4. MF

A girl pretends that she has an invisible dog.

King-Smith, D. (1999). *A mouse called wolf.* New York: Puffin. K–2;3–4. MF

A mouse thinks he is a wolf.

King-Smith, D. (2003). *Lady lollipop.* New York: Puffin. K–2;3–4. MF

A funny pig story.

King-Smith, D. (2006). *The guard dog.* New York: Puffin. K–2;3–4. MF

A very small dog hopes to become a guard dog.

King-Smith, D., & Perkins, D. (2007). *The water horse.* New York: Harcourt. K–2;3–4. MF

Two children find an egg that hatches into a sea monster.

Kitt, T. (1988). So long as there's weather. In B. S. de Regniers, E. Moore, M. M. White, & J. Carr (Eds.), *Sing a song of popcorn.* New York: Scholastic. K–2;3–4. P

Rhythmic poetry.

Louie, A. L. (Reteller). (1982). *Yeh Shen: A Cinderella story from China* (E. Young, Illus.). New York: Philomel. K–2. TF

A Chinese version of Cinderella.

Lowry, L. (1993). *The giver.* Boston: Houghton Mifflin. 5–8. F

Award-winning high fantasy.

Martin, B. (1967). *Brown bear, brown bear, what do you see?* (E. Carle, Illus.). New York: Holt. K–2. PB

Brown Bear sees many animals.

Martin, B. (2006). *Fire! fire! said Mrs. McGuire.* New York: Harcourt. K–2. PB*

This is an old nursery rhyme.

Merrill, J. (1964). *The pushcart war* (R. Solbert, Illus.). New York: Scott. 5–6;7+. F

The story of a war between pushcarts and trucks in New York.

Milne, A. A. (1926). *Winnie-the-Pooh* (E. H. Shepard, Illus.). New York: Dutton. 1–5. F*

The adventures of Pooh and his friends.

Mochizuki, K. (2006). *Be water, my friend: The early years of Bruce Lee.* New York: Lee. K–2;3–4. INF

The author presents information about Bruce Lee.

Muth, J. (2003). *Stone soup.* New York: Scholastic. K–2. TF

The Chinese version of *Stone Soup.*

O'Callahan, J. (1994a). *Little Heroes.* Fairview, NC: High Windy Audio. K–2. TF

O'Callahan, J. (1994b). *The boy who loved frogs.* West Tilbury, MA: Vineyard Video. 1–3.

Traditional literature.

Okimoto, J., & Aoki, E. (2002). *The white swan express: A story of adoption.* New York: Clarion. K–2;3–4. CRF

A story of adoption.

O'Neill, A. (2002). *The recess queen* (L. Huliska-Beith, Illus.). New York: Scholastic. K–2. CRF

She is queen of recess until a new girl moves in.

Rounds, G. (1990). *I know an old lady who swallowed a fly.* New York: Holiday. K–2;3–4. TF

A cumulative rhyme.

Salat, C. (2002). *Peanut's emergency* (T. Lyon, Illus.). Boston, MA: Charles Bridge. K–2. CRF

"Peanut" is a dog.

Schertle, A. (1999). *I am the cat* (M. Buehner, Illus.). New York: Lothrop, Lee & Shepard. K–2;3–4. P

A collection of cat poetry.

Scieszka, J. (2001). *Baloney (Henry P.)* (L. Smith, Illus.). New York: Viking. K–2;3–4. PB

A space student is late for school.

Seuss, Dr. (1940). *Horton hatches the egg.* New York: Random House. K–2;3–4. F

A Dr. Seuss humorous fantasy.

Seuss, Dr. (1949). *Bartholomew and the oobleck.* New York: Random House. K–2;3–4. F

A Dr. Seuss fantasy.

Siebert, D. (1984). *Truck song* (B. Barton, Illus.). New York: Crowell. K–2. P

Rhythmic poetry.

Siebert, D. (1990). *Train song* (M. Wimmer, Illus.). New York: Crowell. K–2. P

Rhythmic poetry.

Smith, W. J. (1990). *Laughing time: Collected nonsense* (F. Krahn, Illus.). New York: Farrar, Straus & Giroux. K–2;3–4. P

Humorous poetry.

Viorst, J. (1972). *Alexander and the terrible, horrible, no good, very bad day* (J. Cruz, Illus.). New York: Atheneum. K–2. MRF

Describes a boy's terrible day.

Ward, H. (2003). *The dragon machine* (W. Anderson, Illus.). New York: Dutton. K–3. F

George begins to accumulate dragons and builds a dragon machine.

Westcott, N. B. (1987). *Peanut butter and jelly.* New York: Dutton. K–2. P

This book features a traditional play-rhyme.

Westcott, N. B. (1990). *I know an old lady who swallowed a fly.* New York: Dutton. 1–6. P

This book features a traditional play-rhyme.

Wilder, L. I. (1953). *Little house on the prairie* (G. Williams, Illus.). New York: Harper. 3–4. HF

This book tells the story of the Ingalls family.

Wisniewski, D. (1998). *The secret knowledge of grown-ups.* New York: Lothrop, Lee & Shepard. K–2; 3–4. MF

The author opens secret files, hidden from kids for thousands of years.

Yeoman, K., & Blake, Q. (2003). *The seven voyages of Sinbad the sailor.* Natick, MA: Chrysalis. 3–4;5–6. TF

Readers learn about Sinbad's seven shipwrecks.

Professional References

Barton, B. (1986). *Tell me another.* Portsmouth, NH: Heinemann.

Black, A., & Stave, A. (2007). An introduction to reader's theater. *A comprehensive guide to reader's theater: Enhancing fluency and comprehension in middle school and beyond.* Newark, DE: International Reading Association.

Busching, B. (1981, March). "Reader's theater": An education for language and life. *Language Arts, 58,* 330–338.

Champlin, C., & Renfro, N. (1985). *Storytelling with puppets.* Chicago: American Library Association.

Cohen, D. (1968). The effect of literature on vocabulary and reading achievement. *Elementary English, 45,* 209–213, 217.

Cooper, P., & Collins, R. (1992). *Look what happened to frog: Storytelling in education.* Scottsdale, AZ: Gorsuch Scarisbrick.

Daniels, H. (1994). *Literature circles: Voice and choice in the student-centered classroom.* York, ME: Stenhouse.

Downing, J., & Leong, C. K. (1982). *Psychology of reading.* New York: Macmillan.

Engler, L., & Fijan, C. (1973). *Making puppets come alive.* New York: Taplinger.

Flynn, R. (2004, December). Curriculum-based reader's theater: Setting the stage for reading and retention. *The Reading Teacher.*

Fractor, J. S., Woodruff, M. C., Martinez, M. G., & Teale, W. H. (1993). Let's not miss opportunities to promote voluntary reading: Classroom libraries in the elementary school. *Reading Teacher, 46,* 476–484.

Golden, J. M. (1984). Children's concept of story in reading and writing. *Reading Teacher, 37,* 578–584.

Hahn, M. L. (2002). *Reconsidering read-aloud.* Portland, ME: Stenhouse.

Heathcote, D. (1983). Learning, knowing, and languaging in drama: An interview with Dorothy Heathcote. *Language Arts, 73,* 8.

Laminack, L., & Wadsworth, R. (2006). *Learning under the influence of language and literature.* Portsmouth, NH: Heineman.

Lenz, L. (1992). Crossroads of literacy and orality: Reading poetry aloud. *Language Arts, 69,* 597–603.

Lester, J. (1988). The storyteller's voice: Reflections on the rewriting of Uncle Remus. *New Advocate, 1,* 143–147.

Livo, N. J., & Rietz, S. A. (1986). *Storytelling process and practice.* Littleton, CO: Libraries Unlimited.

Manna, A. L. (1984). Making language come alive through reading plays. *Reading Teacher, 52,* 326–334.

Martinez, M., Roser, N., & Strecker, S. (1998–1999). I never thought I could be a star: A reader's theater ticket to fluency. *Reading Teacher 52,* 326–334.

McCaslin, N. (1990). *Creative drama in the classroom* (5th ed.). New York: Longman.

Miccinati, J. (1985). Using prosodic cues to teach oral reading fluency. *Reading Teacher, 39,* 206–212.

Morrow, L. M. (1979). *Super tips for storytelling.* New York: Scholastic.

Morrow, L. M. (1988). Young children's responses to one-to-one story readings in school settings. *Reading Research, 23,* 89–107.

Naylor, A., & Borders, S. (1993). *Children talking about books.* Portsmouth, NH: Heinemann.

Perfect, K. A. (1999). Rhyme and reason: Poetry for the heart and head. *Reading Teacher, 52,* 728–737.

Puppeteers of America. (1989). *The consultant's notebook.* Chicago: Puppeteers of America.

Purcell-Gates, V. (1988). Lexical syntactic knowledge of written narrative held by well-read-to kindergartners and second graders. *Research in Teaching English, 22,* 128–160.

Rochman, H. (1989). Booktalking: Going global. *Horn Book, 58,* 30–35.

Roe, B., Alfred, S., & Smith, S. (1998). *Teaching through stories: Yours, mine, and theirs.* Norwood, MA: Christopher-Gordon.

Roney, R. C. (1989). Back to the basics with storytelling. *Reading Teacher, 42,* 520–523.

Sawyer, R. (1962). *The way of the storyteller.* New York: Harper & Row.

Siks, G. (1983). *Drama with children* (2nd ed.). New York: Harper & Row.

Sipe, L. R. (2002, February). Talking back and taking over: Young children's expressive engagement during storybook read alouds. *The Reading Teacher, 55* (5), 476–483.

Stoodt, B. D. (1988). *Teaching language arts.* New York: Harper & Row.

Teale, W. H., & Martinez, M. (1987). *Connecting writing: Fostering emergent literacy in kindergarten children.* Technical Report No. 412. San Antonio, TX: University of Texas at San Antonio.

Wilhelm, J. D. (1997). *You gotta be the book.* New York: Teachers College Press.

15 Engaging with and Responding to Children's Literature

KEY TERMS

aesthetic reading
character map
community of readers
efferent reading
engaging with literature
envisionment
inferencing
intertextuality

knowledge charts
plot
prediction charts
response
stance
story map
story pyramid

GUIDING QUESTIONS

Think about your responses to the different genres of literature you read. Do you have a favorite genre? What element of literature arouses your strongest response? As you read this chapter, think about the following questions.

1. What is engaged reading? Describe it in your own words.

2. What is the response process? Describe it in your own words.

3. How do readers' expectations influence their response to literature?

Introduction to Responding to Literature

When readers open a book, they accept an invitation to collaborate with the author or the illustrator, to explore existing meanings as well as to forge new meanings. No matter how excellent the writing may be, a book is never complete until someone reads it and brings it to life. Response to literature is many things—what readers make of a text as they read; how it comes alive and becomes personal; how readers feel and react to what they have read. Students use their knowledge of literary conventions, character, plot, setting, writing style, and theme to comprehend the story. Readers not only use what is in the text—words and their meanings—but also the meanings they bring to the text based on their life experiences and their interests (Musthafa, 1996; Thacker, 1996). Sipe (1999) described how four first- and second-graders differed considerably in the responses they offered during story time discussions. One reader, who was very logical, used textual analysis and intertextual references to support her participation in literature discussions. Another girl used text to generate creative activities. A third reader focused on the themes he perceived. A fourth reader used stories for his own performances. McGinley and Kamberelis (1996) studied readers in third and fourth grades and identified similar variations in response to literature.

This variation in response is acceptable and indicative of thoughtful reading and reflection.

Rethink and Reread

Literary experience does not stop with the book's last page (Martinez & Nash, 1991; Rosenblatt, 1978). The readers continue to respond as they rethink and reread the book or parts of the book, or even read another book that is somehow related. The reader's feelings continue to evolve after completing the book, sometimes long after the book is read (Rosenblatt, 1978; Stoodt & Amspaugh, 1994)

Intertextuality

Response includes both intertextuality and stance. Readers create intertextual connections when they relate books, magazines, movies, and television shows to events in their lives. Research reveals an incredible diversity among the links that readers make between current and previous reading. The most common intertextual links relate to genre, character, and plots (Cairney, 1990). The way in which readers apply intertextuality differs from one individual to the next, just as it does when readers create meaning. Even when reading exactly the same stories, readers identify different links. We cannot predict intertextual links with confidence, but we can encourage children to compare literary conventions—plots, characters, settings, and so forth—from story to story.

Stance

All readers have a purpose for reading, or *stance*. Stance has to do with expectations for reading, with the way in which a reader approaches a text (Galda & Liang, 2003). Whether students are reading assigned text for knowledge or reading for pleasure, adopting a stance is an active process that indicates what the reader is paying attention to while reading. Two stances have been identified: aesthetic and efferent.

Aesthetic and Efferent Stances

Aesthetic Stance

Aesthetic reading is pleasurable, interesting reading, done for its own sake. Aesthetic readers may focus on the sound and rhythm of the words and the personal feelings, ideas, and attitudes created during reading (Rosenblatt, 1982). Children create new experiences as they live through the literature: participating in the story, identifying with the characters, and sharing their conflicts and their feelings, a process Judith Langer identifies as *envisionment* (1992). Excellent fiction and nonfiction both have aesthetic values because the author's language style expresses meaning. The language in some books, such as poetry, is obviously aesthetic. For instance, *John Coltrane's Giant Steps***, remixed by Chris Raschka, creates a unique literary experience by combining John Coltrane's composition, "Giant Steps," with color and art in a picture book. Aesthetic readers may focus on the color and nature of the art.

Efferent Stance

The *efferent reading* stance focuses on the meanings and ideas in the text (Rosenblatt, 1982). Efferent readers are gathering information to use in the real world. They have a narrow focus as they seek information, directions, solutions, and conclusions. Rosenblatt points out, however, that a reading event may fall anywhere on a continuum between the aesthetic and the efferent poles. Therefore, a stance cannot be only aesthetic or only efferent, because most reading experiences have elements of both. Moreover, stance can change while reading. This happened to me when I was reading a novel; I suddenly came across a sentence that explained a reference I had been seeking for several years, and the author had very kindly included more detail in his notes.

Dimensions of Response

Readers respond to literature based on various elements. In the following section, we will explore how children respond to sound, events, and author style; when readers connect with all three of these, a "world response" occurs.

Sound

Sound is a natural response for children, who respond to a book's words and rhythms of language. They hear the text in their head as they read, listening to the dialogue as they would conversation. The dialogue in Hilary McKay's *Saffy's Angel,* for example, is like that heard in many families, so readers respond to the sounds of family talk. "Reading aloud to children of all ages is vital . . . because this is the way we learn how to turn cold print into a dramatic enactment in the theater of our imagination" (Chambers, 1996, p. 169).

Event

Readers who respond to events are sensitive to the literary forms that shape stories, poems, and nonfiction. They can anticipate events, characters, and setting when they read. They expect stories to have characters, settings, problems, and conflicts, and efforts to solve problems. Experienced readers have learned that events increase suspense in a story, and that characters usually have conflicts as they try to solve problems. Their expectations are based on genre, story elements, and story grammar.

Author Style

Author style is the quality of writing and the way the author creates plot, characters, setting, and theme. "To enter and hold the mind of a child or a young person is one of the hardest of all writers' tasks" (Zinsser, 1990). Nonfiction writers need to make information and explanations of information interesting to readers. Some readers prefer nonfiction. Authors like James Cross Giblin, who is profiled later in this chapter, is a gifted author of nonfiction. Young readers do not have the authors' breadth of experience, but they have enough experience to recognize a writer who fails to respect their experience and intelligence. They identify and reject shallow books or didactic, preachy books.

World Response

The world response occurs when readers respond to all three facets—sound, event, and author style. For instance, when reading Judith Viorst's *If I Were in Charge of the World*,** children connect the poem with their own lives and with other literature that has similar themes. The alliterative phrases in this poem create sounds that resonate with children, such as "healthy hamsters" and "basketball baskets." Anyone who has had pet hamsters can relate to the author's desire for "healthy hamsters." Children who have allergies identify with the author's desire to "cancel" allergy shots, and both children and adults identify with the poet's desire to eliminate "Monday mornings." Viorst consistently enters the children's world with her stories and poems.

Truth is a critical quality in children's books, even when the story is not literally true. E. B. White (1970) said of his own writing: "I have two or three strong beliefs about the business of writing for children. I feel I must never kid them about anything. I feel I must be on solid ground myself. I also feel that a writer has an obligation to transmit, as best as he can, his love of life, his appreciation for the world. I am not averse to departing from reality, but I am against departing from the truth" (p. 544). Fine writers express truth as they understand it, through fiction, poetry, or nonfiction. Truth in literature is also expressed in the integrity of the transaction between the writer and the reader (Zinsser, 1990). When the writer's truth resonates with the child's truth, the reader responds to the author's storytelling skill.

Truthfulness is an important part of *My Pig Amarillo* by Satomi Ichikawa. This is the story of Pablito, whose grandpa presents him with a yellow pig that he names Amarillo. Pablito is ecstatic when he receives Amarillo, but when his pet disappears he is heartbroken. Grandpa helps Pablito find an appropriate way to find comfort and say good-bye to Amarillo. Grandpa is honest and does not manipulate Pablito.

Literature as a Means of Knowing

Literary thinking develops readers' learning and knowledge (Probst, 1992). Literature plays four major roles in the curriculum: knowledge about self, knowledge about others, knowledge about books, and knowledge about contexts.

Self

Readers learn about themselves through literature when they recall experiences related to the text and then integrate them with the text, thereby developing self-understanding. For instance, after reading *Buttermilk Hill* by Ruth White, Karen realized that other girls have lost their loving family to divorce. She recognized that, like Piper Berry's parents in the story, her parents also have different dreams. Karen began to heal through her friends and her grandmother. In class discussion, Karen discovered that the experience of one of her classmates, Josh, was different from her own because his father deserted the family, making adjustment very difficult for his mother, who leaned on him for support.

Books

Literary thinking helps readers understand books and literary devices used by authors to stimulate readers' thinking. For instance, *Ruby Lu, Brave and True* by Lenore Look is the story of Ruby Lu, who loves family, friends, school, and neighborhood. Her friends are Wally, who is fluent in Cantonese; Tiger, who is faster than email; and Emma, who has a bilingual dog. Character is the important literary device in this story. Ruby's friends each have unique characteristics, and Ruby's unique character drives the story.

Contexts

Literature helps learners know about different contexts. For instance, in *Good-bye, 382 Shin Dang Dong* by Frances Park and Ginger Park, a Korean child, Jangmi, and her family move to the United States. The author helps readers understand that Jangmi is sad about leaving her grandparents, cousins, and friends to move to a strange new place. Jangmi's context leads her to view her new home as strange and different. Readers will bring different contexts and backgrounds to the book, depending on the specifics of their personal experiences. Discussion helps readers clarify and activate their contexts.

Intertextuality: Individual Connections

Literature is woven with quotations, references, and echoes of prior literary experiences—all of which give a book virtually unlimited meaning (Barthes, 1975). Meaning in each new book one reads is enriched in some measure by the shadows of previously read texts. This process, called *intertextuality,* means interpreting one text by means of another (Hartman, 1992; Lundin, 1998). Two or more texts, written or oral, are involved in the intertextuality process (Bloome & Bailey, 1992) and may include films, books, class lectures, Internet sites, conversations, and videos (Hartman, 1992).

Jazz by Walter Dean Myers gives readers intertextual connections for understanding. He and his son Christopher Myers have created what might be called a jam session that introduces great jazz musicians and the various forms and instruments of the genre. The illustrations suggest the rhythms and moods of jazz. Another book about this musical genre, *The Jazz Man* by Karen Ehrhardt, uses the traditional counting chant "This Old Man" to introduce the rhythmic feel of jazz. Teachers will find that playing a recording of "This Old Man" creates another intertextual connection. If you cannot locate a recording, introducing the song yourself will also enhance the topic. *Dizzy* by Jonah Winter marries rhythmic text with illustrations to tell the story of Dizzy Gillespie, who loved jazz because it "broke the rules." He called jazz "bebop." The illustrator uses artwork that zigs and zags in color combinations that contribute to Dizzy's story.

Stance and Response

Meaning in literature is expressed in several unique ways (Langer, 1992): through written language style; the conventions of language; genre; and literary structures such as characters, setting, plot, theme, and so forth [introduced in earlier chapters]. Meaning is expressed differently in poetry, fiction, and nonfiction. Good readers read fiction and poetry with an aesthetic stance and nonfiction with an efferent stance. (Galda & Liang, 2003). These distinct patterns of thinking enable readers to relate their prior knowledge and experiences to books in order to understand genre and the elements of literature (Langer, 1992).

Guiding Response

The literary experience is one in which teachers and children share what they read. They discover what is entertaining and engaging about books. The focus of a literary experience is discovering the reader's response, thinking about it, and discovering the reader's feelings about the experience.

Literary experiences stimulate the growing mind (Langer, 1992). The major reason for providing children with literary experiences is to help them read with more pleasure and understanding. Although we cannot directly teach literature to children, we can set the stage for them to experience literature so they actively construct their own knowledge and beliefs. There is no one correct interpretation of a literary work, but rather multiple interpretations, each of which is profoundly dependent on the reader's experience (Daniels, 2002). Literature loses its appeal when it is misused. For example, asking many pointless questions is one type of misuse; another is teaching phonics rules. As teachers we must focus on the individual reader's interpretation, the unique *response* of each reader. A child writing a letter to a friend to tell why she liked a book or an author is a response. The literary experience is not a quest for a predetermined right answer. The process of making meaning is not one of learning a correct interpretation prescribed by an authority in the field (Langer, 1995).

Reading Circles/Communities of Response

In reading circles or *communities of readers,* small groups of students who have read the same book collectively construct meaning as they respond through discussions, writing, and the arts (Hill & Noe, 2003). When readers think, rethink, reread, discuss, and write about books, they discover what a book means to them and how they feel about it. The purpose of reading circles for all of us is to read and explore books, characters, issues, and ideas and to figure out what we think (Hill, 2000). Response is individual; therefore, students must have opportunities to raise their own questions rather than answer those created by someone with different experiences and knowledge (Daniels, 2002). Teachers must encourage individuals to share their unique verbal, artistic, dramatic, and written interpretations to literature. As children share their individual understandings with one another, they learn that a story can have many interpretations. Although reading circles are predicated on students having read the same book, when students become independent readers they should have opportunities to read books they choose. Giving middle-school students choices and autonomy is especially important because they are developing individually.

Response activities sustain the reader–text interaction and nurture literary development (Martinez & Nash, 1991). Response may be written or oral, formal or informal, and may make use of a variety of media. Readers need opportunities for varied responses to literature through activities; drawing a picture to illustrate response to a book becomes boring. All students are not artistic in the same ways. In later sections, we explain strategies and activities for introducing books, experiencing books, and encouraging response.

Chambers (1996) said the need to re-create the story in our own words is so strong that "when two friends discover they have both read and enjoyed the same book their talk often consists simply of sharing retellings: 'I especially liked that part where. . . .'" Figure 15.1 summarizes the aesthetic stance for primary students.

FIGURE 15.1 A summary of the aesthetic stance for primary students.

Introduce the book	Book talk—talk about the author and the main character/s. Choose books that are in the students' range of understanding and interest.	As students become experienced, allow them to vote on which two or three books they would like to hear.
Read the book aloud	Show pictures and text together while reading. After reading, place the book where children can pick it up.	
Discuss the book	Students talk about the book. Ask students to identify words and phrases that are important.	Relate to other books or experiences. Read books with similar themes, characters, or settings, so the students can compare them.
Students raise questions	They ask about confusing points, things they liked or not.	
Students extend their response	Extend the experience through students' own stories, pictures, retelling the story. Look up the author on the Internet. Ask what happened after the story.	
Response activities	Activities include: retelling the story; making up a story and telling it; art work; dictating their own story or writing their own story; creating a collage with drawings or magazine pictures.	Refer to Chapter 2 for developing the elements of literature.

CLASSROOM SNAPSHOT

READER RESPONSE TO LITERATURE

Beth Reed selected *That's Good! That's Bad!* by Margery Culyer for storytime. She asked the children to think about a good thing that happened to them. Several of the children thought of things like birthday parties, visits to the zoo, going to the beach, visiting grandparents, and going fishing. Beth listed the students' responses on the chalkboard. She showed the book cover and the title to the children and said the story had a pattern that the children should notice. Then she read the book aloud to the children, and they chuckled as she read the book.

Response Activities

Beth asked the children why they laughed. Garth said, "Everytime something good happened, then something bad happened." Beth responded, "That was funny wasn't it."

Several of the children agreed.

Rachel volunteered that she did not like the bad things that happened, and several children agreed.

Beth asked, "Which bad things were the worst?"

Rachel said that the worst things were when the red balloon popped and the boy went in the mud and the baboons chased him.

Then Beth asked, "What were the best things that happened to the boy?"

Several children liked the red balloon and the fact that the boy could fly with the balloon.

Some of the children said they thought the book was good because the stork carried the boy back to his parents.

Discussion Follow-up

Beth suggested that the children think of their own stories using the good things they had suggested before reading. She asked them to create their own good and bad stories, telling the children who did not like that pattern that they could write about good things. She suggested that all of the children think of ways to help them remember their story. She said they could act out scenes from the book or identify key vocabulary to help them remember.

FIGURE 15.2 Reader response in middle grades.

Booktalk a group of books and ask students to select the ones they choose to read.				
Discuss aesthetic stance.	Stress the importance of individual response.			
Students read and write in journals.	Collect interesting words and phrases.	Summarize the book.	Write a book review.	Write a character study.
Discuss the book with other students who have read the same book.	Use the journal to support understanding. Quote the book to support understanding.	Discuss how the protagonist changed.	What was the tension or conflict in the book?	Write a book review.
Identify a response activity.	Author study.	How did the book make you feel?	Will the project show what the student learned?	Will the project tell about the book, so others can learn from it?

Engaging with Literature

The purpose of *engaging with literature* is to get students immersed, engrossed, absorbed, and totally involved in literature. Engagement activities focus on what the story, poem, or nonfiction work is really about so that readers can understand and respond to it. The following are some typical engagement and response activities.

Nurturing Response

All of the experiences authors have influence their writing. Paula Fox explains: "It is my view that all the moments and years of one's life are part of any story that one writes" (Elleman, 1991, p. 48). Studying authors and illustrators yields many benefits. Readers who know something about the person who wrote or illustrated a literary work have a better understanding of it. Finding connections between books and their creators challenges children to think in new ways. Because an author's experiences influence his or her writing so heavily, knowing about the author greatly enhances the response process.

Introducing Books/Booktalks

Introductions may be elaborate or very simple. They may consist of a question, discussion, or picture; a comparison to another book, film, or piece of music; a reading of the opening paragraph or paragraphs; the presentation of an object that symbolizes some aspect of the book; or a booktalk involving the teacher, librarian, or students. Introductions arouse students' interest in the text and give them background that enriches their comprehension. When introducing a book and its author, the teacher, parent, or librarian acquaints children with the genre, content, structure, and language of the text (Langer, 1995). Children usually meet the main character and identify the setting during the introduction.

Creating a relationship between a piece of literature and previous reading develops intertextuality and facilitates response. Literary experience is not based on a single book, but the ideas, experiences, and understandings that come from reading many books.

Children can learn to preview books themselves from the techniques used to introduce books to them. By the time students reach the middle grades, they are ready to independently explore a book before reading and know that the dust jacket usually provides background information.

Experiencing Books

After the introduction, the children read or listen to the book or poem. After reading the entire story, article, poem, or informational piece, children are ready to explore it in discussion or response activities. Understanding grows as readers follow the unfolding of character, the story problem and its resolution, or the full development of the theme. This is the way they learn how the story works or the way the informative pieces fit together.

Readers who immerse themselves in the literature gradually build an understanding of the text, identifying and coming to understand the main character's personality. As the story unwinds, readers recognize the escalating tension in the plot, the cause and effect, and the problem or conflict that builds suspense. Readers who ask themselves "why" and "who" can relate literature to their own experiences.

Through the comprehension of both narrative and informational text, children build a knowledge base about our world and the ways that different genre express meaning. Understanding is related to *inferencing,* or an interpretation of literature, which is concerned with meanings that are not directly stated in the text. The author suggests and hints at ideas rather than stating them directly. Authors cannot tell readers everything: The stories would be too long, and the detail would make them boring. Authors must rely on their audience to fill in the empty spaces. For example, in Louis Sachar's *Holes,* when Mr. Sir tells Stanley, "This isn't a Girl Scout Camp" (p. 14), the author is telling the reader that Camp Green Lake is a bad place. Mr. Sir also tells Stanley that he is going to be thirsty for the next 18 months. The reader can interpret these statements to mean that this is a really hard place.

Critical thinkers make judgments about the quality, value, and validity of text. They evaluate the accuracy of the material, synthesize information, make comparisons and inferences, and suspend judgment until they have all the information they need. Critical readers recognize the author's purpose, point of view, and use of language. They distinguish fact from opinion and test the author's assertions against their own observations, information, and logic. For instance, in the book *Holes,* a critical reader would probably conclude that Stanley was in a much worse place than he realized.

The activities described in this section may be conducted as individual activities, small-group activities, or whole-class activities. Pencil-and-paper activities help students organize and remember their thoughts for discussion. Activities should be varied, because even the most interesting ones become boring when overused. The major purpose in exploring literature should be simply to read.

Discussion

Discussion is an integral part of developing understanding and engagement with literature. The teacher's role is to keep the discussion going. The most useful questions are broad and open-ended because these questions help students develop a sense of the entire story, poem, or informational piece. Focusing on a few significant ideas stimulates comprehension and discussion, while focusing on trivial and obvious ideas leads to brief answers that are often as simple as "yes" and "no."

A few thoughtful questions, especially those that the students ask, will stimulate a good discussion. The inquisition approach of asking many, many questions is guaranteed to destroy children's response to literature. One teacher who commented "I feel like I have wrung the life out of this book and neither the students nor I ever want to see it again" has assuredly overanalyzed the book and ensured that her students did not enjoy it, even though the book might have been a favorite of many children who were not subjected to overteaching or overanalysis.

Discussions that focus on the characters suggest that readers wonder what kind of person the main character is. When focusing on character, develop questions to guide students' thinking, such as:

- What words describe the character?
- What character have you read about that is like the main character in this book? How are they alike?

- Do you know anyone who is like the main character? How so?
- If you met the main character, what questions would you ask?
- How do you think the main character would act in a certain situation (that the reader identifies)?

Some books are plot driven, so students read for the story events or the adventures. Many of these stories are action packed and have story events that build suspense. Guiding children's response to these stories could involve questions such as:

- What events create suspense?
- What is the main problem or conflict in this story?
- What is the climax of this story?
- How is the problem or conflict solved?

Prompts, such as the ones listed in Figure 15.3, can elicit children's oral and written responses to literature. When these prompts were used for a full year in a third-grade class, for example, the students were more actively involved in learning and more enthusiastic about literature than their peers, with an observable difference in fluency and increased reflection of emotional involvement as the students use the process (Kelly, 1990). Changing the question prompts to statements and asking students to respond, as in a study by Borders & Naylor, also leads to good class discussion. They can agree or disagree or create a better statement. Prompts are more effective the more they are used, and children as young as age 3 respond

---

FIGURE 15.3 Discussion prompts.

Kelly's (1990) prompts:

1. What did you notice about the story?
2. How did the story make you feel?
3. What does the story remind you of in your own life?

Borders & Naylor's (1993) prompts:

1. Talk about what you notice in the story, which may include any aspect of the book such as text, format, illustrations, characters, and so forth. Children will notice things that teachers never noticed.
2. Talk about how the story makes you feel. When members of a group share feelings and thoughts, they bond, and the group is a safer place to explore issues.
3. Talk about what the story reminds you of in your own life. Our own experiences help us understand a book, and the book helps us understand our experience.

to prompts. In the Borders & Naylor study, the children used the prompts on their teachers, asking what the teachers noticed in the story (Borders & Naylor, 1993).

Writing

Students who read well usually write well because they have a command of language, vocabulary, and literary knowledge. Literature gives students models for organizing writing and language to express their thoughts. The response journal is one of many appropriate writing response activities.

Literature Response Journals

Literature response journals, also called reading journals, reading logs, and dialogue journals, are a form of response activity that leads students to engage with literature. The journals consist of students' writing down their thoughts about their reading. It is a place to explore thoughts, discover reactions, and let the mind ramble. Response journals are an effective means of linking writing and thinking with the active reading process (Barone, 1990; Raphael & McMahon, 1994). Some students find it difficult to get started writing in their journal, or they may say the same things again and again, so plan ways to encourage responses when students seem to have difficulty thinking of something to write.

Janet Hancock (1991) reported an analysis of a sixth-grade girl's literature response journal. The journal revealed the student's personal meaning-making process as well as insights into her personal feelings, which the teacher had rarely seen. This student was encouraged to record all of the thoughts going on in her head as she read the book and not concern herself with correct spelling or the mechanics of writing because the objective was to capture her thoughts. Her entries were classified in these ways: (a) character interaction, (b) character empathy, (c) prediction and validation, (d) personal experiences, and (e) philosophical reflections. When writing about character interaction, the student wrote comments directly to the character she was reading about. The researcher noted that the girl's responses were of high quality and exhibited the type of reading and writing that teachers hope to inspire. After the student wrote entries, the researcher made encouraging, nonevaluative responses

that motivated the student. Then the student wrote in the same style that the researcher encouraged.

Literature response journals can have several formats. A few are suggested here, but teachers can try anything that fits the situation. Langer (1992) suggests a two-part journal with a student entry on one side and the teacher's response (or the response of another student) on the other side. Another format, which Langer suggests and which Stoodt and Amspaugh (1994) researched, shows that children's responses change over time as they relate new information, feelings, and ideas to previous knowledge. An immediate response is more detailed, whereas longer reflection permits children to relate data to a larger context. In this journal format, the students make entries under three headings: immediate reaction, later reaction, and reading and writing. Another good approach is to have students make comments in the journal and then pass the journal to another student who has read the book so he or she can respond to the comments.

Research that Raphael and McMahon (1994) conducted identified reading log entry possibilities that can be useful. These possibilities include character maps, wonderful words, pictures, special story parts, sequences of events, book/chapter critiques, relating the book to oneself, and author's writing techniques and language use. After reading nonfiction books, some students become so interested in the information that they want to learn all they can about the subject, which can lead to writing an article about it. Students may decide to develop their own original information and create a nonfiction book to share with classmates. Writing response activities are unlimited.

Oral Language

Dramatic activities are important response activities for children. These activities, explored in Chapter 14, give children opportunities to act out their interpretations of characters and events and see how the action evolved.

Maps and Charts

Literature may be mapped or charted (sometimes through *diagrams*) as a means of summarizing and organizing thoughts and responses to the text. Many kinds of maps and charts are available.

Story Maps

The sample *story map* in Figure 15.4 is based on *The White Giraffe* by Lauren St. John and represents a story grammar. Readers complete the various parts of the map based on the story structure (grammar) of the book they have read.

Character Maps

Character maps focus on the main character in a story. They assist children in developing a more thorough understanding of story characters and their actions, thereby helping readers identify character traits (Toth, 1990). They also serve to summarize the story. Students write, or cut and paste, the character's name on the map. They then write in the qualities (e.g., honesty, loyalty, bravery) that character exhibits. Finally, they identify the actions that support the qualities identified. This activity can be varied by having students draw pictures or locate magazine photographs that illustrate a character's behavior. Figure 15.5 shows a character map for *The Tale of Despereaux*.

Plot Relationships Charts

The plot relationships chart shown in Figure 15.6 is for *The Teacher's Funeral* by Richard Peck and is similar to one developed by Barbara Schmitt and Marilyn Buckley (1991). It categorizes story information under four headings: *somebody, wanted, but,* and *so.* The chart guides children as they identify the major

Martine sees a mysterious white giraffe.

elements of a selection they have heard or read and helps them understand relationships between characters, problems, and solutions.

FIGURE 15.4 A sample story map for *The White Giraffe.*

Main Characters: Martine and her Grandmother

Setting: Africa

Story Problem: Martine's parents are killed, and she has to live in Africa with a grandmother that she doesn't know.

Story Event 1: Martine's parents are killed, and she leaves for Africa.

Story Event 2: Martine meets her grandmother, who is abrupt with her.

Story Event 3: Martine discovers the white giraffe.

Story Event 4: She sees the white giraffe again and calls him Jeremy; she rides on the giraffe, who shows her his hiding place.

Problem Solution: Poachers try to capture Jeremy, but Martine is able to help him escape. Then she and her grandmother grow closer.

Theme: Loving animals and keeping them safe with any sacrifice. Understanding people and animals builds relationships.

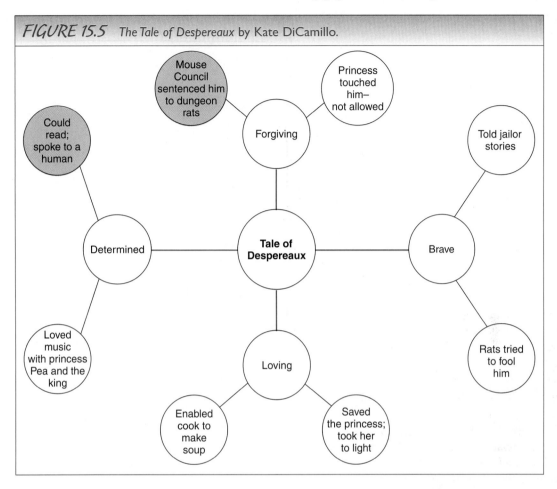

FIGURE 15.5 *The Tale of Despereaux* by Kate DiCamillo.

Story Pyramids

A *story pyramid* (Waldo, 1991) gives students a convenient way to summarize a story. Each line of the pyramid gives specific information about the story in a specific number of words: The first line has one word, the second line has two words, and so forth. Figure 15.7 shows a sample pyramid based on *Uncharted Waters* by Leslie Bulion. The lines of the pyramid force the student to encapsulate the plot and should describe the following:

1. the main character's name
2. the main character's age or grade level

FIGURE 15.6 A sample plot relationships chart for *The Teacher's Funeral*.

Somebody	Wanted	But	So
Russell Culver	To get away from school to work in North Dakota.	The school stays open with a new teacher, who is his worst nightmare . . . his sister.	The students couldn't get the school to close as they had hoped.

FIGURE 15.7 A sample story pyramid for *Uncharted Waters.*

Jonah
Eighth grade
Failed English class
Living with Uncle Nate
Does not go to school
He lied about the swim team
He worked hard on the Whaler's motor
He took the Whaler out and the engine roared

---

3. the setting

4. the problem

5. one main event

6. a second main event

7. a third main event

8. a solution to the problem

Jonah discovers his passion.

Prediction Charts

Prediction charts guide children to predict what will happen next as they move through a story. Prediction charts guide readers to activate prior knowledge and establish purposes for reading (Hammond, 1991). When using a prediction chart, the teacher introduces the book to students. Students predict orally or in writing what will happen next in the story. They also summarize what actually did happen and compare the results to their predictions. This can be an individual or group activity. Younger children who are not able to write can dictate their predictions. For longer books, predictions can be broken into smaller parts (Part I, Part II, Part III) or into the book's chapters. Figure 15.8 shows a sample prediction chart based on *Mrs. McBloom CLEAN UP Your Classroom* by Kelly DiPucchio & Guy Francis.

Knowledge Charts

Knowledge charts are quite useful with nonfiction, but they also apply to fictional materials. The purpose of knowledge charts is to engage and focus students' reading, as well as to help them access the knowledge they already have regarding the topic. If students do not have previous knowledge regarding a particular topic, then as part of this study teachers need to help them acquire background knowledge. Figure 15.9 shows a sample knowledge chart based on *Secrets of a Civil War Submarine* by Sally Walker.

Author and Illustrator Studies

Author studies can motivate students as well as stimulate their response to a favorite author's work. Author

---

FIGURE 15.8 Sample story prediction chart for *Mrs. McBloom CLEAN UP Your Classroom.*

What do you really think will happen?	What did happen?
	Mrs. McBloom is retiring; her classroom is a mess.
	The principal tells her to clean up her classroom.
	The students think of an answer.
	They have a party and ask each person to take one thing from the classroom.

---

and illustrator studies also motivate children to read and to continue reading (Jenkins, 1999).

Reading a Body of Work

The body of an author's work differs from a single work. Students can compare genre, subject, characters, plot, theme, and style in examining all of the author's books. This will help them understand the body and significance of a single author's work. For instance, James Howe's work was in the humorous fantasy genre, such as his book *Bunnicula,* until his first wife's death, when his writing took a more serious turn, as seen in Howe's *The Hospital Book.* Reading all of an author's books in the order of publication helps readers understand the ways in which the author's work has changed over time. Students may also consider whether the body of work is diverse or seems to follow a single thread. Figure 15.10 compares some of the writings of Lois Lowry.

Studying Influences on Illustrators

Artists who illustrate children's books usually have their own favorite artists. For example, Maurice Sendak (1988) identifies Randolph Caldecott, George Cruikshank, and Boutet de Monvel as favorites. Students can study an illustrator by (a) studying the illustrator's books, (b) identifying some of the major influences on the illustrator's work, and (c) comparing the various works of the illustrator. They can consider concepts such as color choice and use, style, medium, size, and shape.

Becoming an Author Expert

Reading an author's works, as well as finding articles, interviews, book reviews, and Internet sources of information about him or her, helps students become experts about their favorite authors. A student can become an expert on his or her favorite authors and illustrators by reading their works and finding articles, interviews, book reviews, and other sources of information about them. After becoming an expert on a particular author, the student may write magazine or newspaper articles about the author or write and design a new dust jacket for a favorite book. While assuming the persona of the author or illustrator, the

---

FIGURE 15.9 Sample knowledge chart based on *Secrets of a Civil War Submarine* by Sally Walker.

Know	Learned
1. Civil War sub found off the coast of South Carolina.	It was the Hunley.
2. The sub was intact. I lived in S.C., so I knew where it was found.	The Hunley was very heavy.
3. It was made of iron plates.	The Hunley weighed thousands of pounds.
4. It fired torpedoes.	The torpedo had 90 pounds of gunpowder.
5. I know it moved, but not what power it used.	The crew cranked the sub to power it.
6. The Hunley was very dangerous.	The water could pour in and drown the crew.

FIGURE 15.10   Examining an author's body of work.

Book:	*The Giver* by Lois Lowry (science fiction)		Setting:	Denmark, World War II.
Plot:	In a Utopian society where people do not want to make decisions, one person, a receiver, keeps all the memories of history. When a new receiver is being trained, he learns about war, hate, snow, trees, and color that are no longer in society.		Theme:	Courage in helping friends.
			Style:	Family conversations, especially between parents, are authentic and make the events real. The story has a vivid setting and memorable characters, especially Ann Marie.
Character:	The main character is Jonas, a young boy who is about to receive his life's assignment. However, he discovers pain as a result of learning about evil.			Both families show empathy for one another. Ann Marie demonstrates outstanding, believable courage and enterprise to help her friend.
Setting:	Utopian society.		Book:	*Rabble Starkey* by Lois Lowry (realistic fiction)
Theme:	Jonas learns that even a Utopian society with no disease, crime, and rudeness lacks something.		Plot:	Rabble (Parable Ann) and her mother (Sweet Hosanna) were deserted by her father.
Style:	Mystic style; the characters accept this world that is strange to readers, who accept it because the story characters accept it. It includes memorable characters and a vivid setting.			Rabble hopes for a more permanent and conventional family, but she learns a great deal about family through the events in the story.
			Character:	The main character is Rabble Starkey.
Book:	*Number the Stars* by Lois Lowry (historical fiction)		Setting:	A small Appalachian town.
			Theme:	Love of family, and mental illness.
Plot:	The Johansen family helps their Jewish friends, the Rosens, protect their daughter, Ellen.		Style:	Realistic fiction; the central characters are memorable, as are the many characters who inhabit the small Appalachian town. The characters' personalities and actions are very believable.
Character:	The main characters are Ann Marie Johansen and Ellen Rosen.			

---

student may participate in interviews, round-table discussions, or television talkshows staged by the class. Students can take turns conducting the interviews or directing the discussion and can film the interviews or talkshows, if possible.

Learning About Authors

Divide the class into three groups. Group 1 will read books written by the author, Group 2 will read articles or reference materials about the author, and Group 3 will read reviews of books written by the author. After the reading is completed, the students will share their information in a discussion group as a means of developing their understanding and appreciation of the author's work.

Studying Author Technique

Gaining a deeper understanding of an author's technique not only helps students understand the author, but this understanding is beneficial in developing their

own writing skills. Students can investigate an author's technique in several ways, including:

1. Use a single book to study a specific technique; for instance, explore the techniques the author used to create the character of Martine in *The White Giraffe* by Lauren St. John.

2. Compare a specific technique in several books by the same author; for instance, study setting in Kate DiCamillo's *The Tale of Despereaux* and the techniques she uses to develop it.

3. Compare how different authors achieve the same goal; for instance, study dialogue in books by two authors to see how each author develops character through conversation.

Profiling an Author

Learning about authors and their interests helps readers understand how authors get story ideas. After studying an author or illustrator through one of the methods described in the previous activities, students can write biographical

A Biographical Profile: James Cross Giblin

James Cross Giblin served as editor and publisher at Clarion Books for more than 20 years. He has also published books with several other publishers. Many of his books are nonfiction, and he points out that organizing and shaping facts into readable, interesting prose requires all the skills of a storyteller (Giblin, 1990). His books usually focus on unusual aspects of history or information, but he always blends his research with wit and drama.

In *Writing Books for Young People* (1990), he explains how he gets his writing ideas. He came up with the idea for *Chimney Sweeps* after meeting a chimney sweep on an airplane. In fact, he asked his new acquaintance to read the book manuscript for accuracy. Another book, *The Truth About Santa Claus,* resulted from seeing a picture of a contemporary Santa Claus juxtaposed next to his tall, thin ancestor, St. Nicholas. Giblin points out that an idea should not only be interesting to the writer, but it must also be an idea to which the writer is willing to devote a year or more of time. Six months of research and six months or more of writing and rewriting represent a major commitment of time and energy.

When researching a topic, Giblin looks for dramatic or amusing anecdotes that will bring the subject to life for young readers. His readers will attest to his successful use of this technique. For example, in *From Hand to Mouth* he tells how Cardinal Richelieu had his knives ground down so the points could not be used for picking teeth. When researching *The Riddle of the Rosetta Stone,* he found previously unpublished photographs to use in the book. These unusual angles on topics are a hallmark of his writing.

James Cross Giblin was awarded the Robert F. Sibert Informational Book Award in 2003 for *Adolf Hitler.* His goal in this book was to demonstrate that Hitler was a more complex person than is usually portrayed. He achieved this by posing three questions: "What sort of man could plan and carry out such horrendous schemes, win support for his deadly ventures, and why did no one stop him until it was almost too late?"

profiles to summarize their research. The profile of James Cross Giblin (see accompanying box) describes some of his strategies for selecting and developing ideas.

Summary

This chapter explores children's understanding of and response to literature. The ultimate response, of course, is pleasure in reading. Engagement, stance, and intertextuality are involved in response. Teachers and librarians can guide children's literary experiences and inspire their response to literature by selecting good literature and creating a warm, literate environment. They can introduce literature, provide activities to develop understanding, and encourage follow-up activities to enhance response, including discussion, writing, drama, and further reading. Focusing on text meaning to address students' reading purpose enhances their response to literature. Reader response is influenced by each child's stance or purpose for reading. Each reader has an individual understanding of and response to literature based upon his or her experiences and interactions with the text; however, students must also have the knowledge that enables them to share their understanding and discuss their response with a community.

Thought Questions and Applications

1. Discuss the response process that you observe in a classroom.

2. Identify the response activities that you would like to use in your own classroom.

3. What is meant by response to literature?

4. Why is response to literature important?

5. What is the teacher's role in creating literary experiences?

6. Why is discussion central to literary experience and response?

7. How are author studies related to response?

8. What is the librarian's role in creating literary experiences?

Research and Application Experiences

1. Read a book to a group of children and observe their responses to it. Note facial expressions, attentiveness, and comments. Write a paper that describes their responses. Tape-record your reading, if possible. Identify the responses that are characteristic to the grade level of the children in the experience.

2. Read a book to a small group of children. Have each child retell the story individually and tape-record the children if you can. How are their understandings alike? How are they different?

3. Create a discussion plan that fosters children's questions and comments about a book rather than a teacher-directed discussion. Conduct this discussion with a group of children and tape it for further analysis.

4. With one student or a small group of students, conduct a teacher-directed discussion. Using the same book and a different student or group, hold a student-focused discussion. Tape both discussions and compare them.

   A. Which discussion involved the most students?

   B. Which discussion revealed the greatest depth of understanding?

   C. Which students appeared to be the most interested in the book?

   D. How were the discussions similar?

   E. How were the discussions different?

5. Use one of the maps or charts presented in this chapter with a group of children as an introduction or a follow-up to a book. Bring the maps or graphics that the students developed to class and discuss them.

6. Make plans for introducing three books to a group of children, using a different technique for each. Identify the introduction needed for each book (e.g., character introduction, plot introduction, setting introduction, or story problem or conflict introduction).

7. Plan questions that could be used to guide the discussion of a book. If possible, conduct the discussion with a group of children and tape it for further analysis.

8. Select three books that are related that could be used together in the classroom.

9. Select five books that would stimulate language development,

Classroom Activities

ACTIVITY 15.1   SAMPLE BOOK INTRODUCTION FOR HISTORICAL FICTION

IRA/NCTE Standards: 2, 3, 7, 8. Students will read and comprehend a variety of literature from various periods and use various media to gather and synthesize data.

Book: *Fair Weather* by Richard Peck. Synopsis (for teachers): This historical fiction is set in 1893, the year of the World's Columbian Exposition. The central character, Rosie, is 13 years old. Rosie and her farm family are invited to Chicago to visit with Aunt Euterpe and attend the Exposition, considered the wonder of the age. The life of each family member changes forever due to their experiences. Many new and modern products were introduced at the Columbian Exposition; in addition, it generated new experiences. The focus of this literary experience is to reflect on this quotation from the book: "It was the last day of our old lives, and we didn't even know it." Another valuable focus is to analyze character growth and historical setting. The following topics will aid in the discussion and help children apply new insights gained to their own lives.

1. Identify the reasons that the characters thought this was the last day of their old lives. Students can also think of an event that affected their own lives in the way of this quotation. (Some readers have compared it to the events of 9/11.)

2. Analyze the central character and character growth (the causes and effects of character growth, as well as the relationship of setting to character development).

3. Contrast the farm family with Aunt Euterpe, the city aunt.

These steps provide organization for introducing a book:

1. Introduce Rosie and read a description of her and her feelings about going to Chicago.

   A. Ask students if they know any children who have gone to the Olympics or a World Fair.

   B. Explain the kinds of displays and shows that would occur at a World Fair.

   C. Read the quotation on page 1 and show the book cover.

   D. Show the pictures on pages 37, 71, 96, and 121.

   E. How do the views of country people differ from those of city folk?

2. If students read the story silently, discussion will prepare them to read with greater understanding.

3. Discuss the story with the students, stimulating them to think about the story. Follow-up discussion takes place after the students have read the entire story, focusing on the following:

   A. Which character changed the most? Why?

   B. Which exhibit at the Exposition interested you the most? Why?

4. Use extension activities to allow students to respond to the story. After reading the work, one class researched World Fairs and identified the kinds of exhibits and people that they would probably find in a current exposition.

5. How would a trip to a World Fair today compare to the one in this book?

> **ACTIVITY 15.2 SAMPLE BOOK INTRODUCTION FOR A NOVEL**

IRA/NCTE Standards: 2, 3, 7. Students will read and comprehend a variety of genre.

Book: *My Last Best Friend* by Julie Bowe. Synopsis (for teachers): This book relates an experience that many students encounter. After her best friend moves away, Ida May vows never to make another friend, devising a plan for avoiding best friends.

1. Introduce Ida May.
   A. Discuss how students would feel if their best friend moved away.
2. Have students listen to the book.
3. Discuss the book, focusing on the relationship between Ida and Jenna Drews.
4. Discuss the relationship between Ida and Stacey Merriweather.
   A. Ask students to identify sensory words the author uses to create the feeling of losing a friend.
   B. Ask students to identify sensory words to describe Ida's feelings about Stacey Merriweather.
   C. Ask students to think about Ida's feelings if Stacey moves.
   D. Discuss the significance of the title.
5. Use extension activities to allow students to respond to the story.

Ida May vows never to make another best friend.

Children's Literature References

Note: Books designated with an asterisk (*) are recommended for reluctant readers.

Arnold, C. (2001). *Dinosaurs with feathers: The ancestors of modern birds* (L. Caple, Illus.). New York: Clarion. 3–4;5–6. INF

   The author traces the relationship between dinosaurs and birds.

Bowe, J. (2007). *My last best friend.* New York: Harcourt. 3–4;5–6. CRF

   Ida May loses her best friend.

Bulion, L. (2006). *Uncharted waters.* Atlanta: Peachtree Publishers. 3–4;5–6. RF

   Jonah's vacation is tense because he failed English and intercepted the letter to his parents, but he discovered his passion.

Culyer, M. (1993). *That's good, that's bad.* New York: Holt. K–2. MF

A version of an old tale. The story begins with good luck, which becomes bad luck.

DiCamillo, K. (2005). *The tale of Despereaux* (T. Ering, Illus.). Cambridge, MA: Candlewick. 3–4; 5–6. MF. Newbery Award

A tiny mouse lives with a princess.

DiPucchio, K. (2005). *Mrs. McBloom CLEAN UP your classroom* (G. Francis, Illus.). New York: Hyperion. K–2;3–4. MCR

Mrs. McBloom asks her students to think of a way to clean her classroom.

Ehrhardt, K. (2006). *The jazz man* (R. Roth, Illus.). New York: Harcourt. 5–6;7+. B

The author introduces famous African American jazz musicians.

Fleming, C. (1999). *When Agnes caws* (G. Potter, Illus.). New York: Atheneum. K–3. MF

Agnes, an accomplished bird caller, travels to the Himalayan Mountains to spot the elusive pink-headed duck.

Fyleman, R. (1931). Mice. In *Fifty-one new nursery rhymes.* New York: Doubleday. K–2. P

This is a poem about mice and their activities in homes.

Giblin, J. C. (1982). *Chimney sweeps* (M. Tomes, Illus.). New York: Crowell. 3–4. INF

This book is packed with little-known information about chimney sweeps.

Giblin, J. C. (1985). *The truth about Santa Claus.* New York: Crowell. 3–4;5–6. INF

Santa Claus myths and traditions are the focus of this book.

Giblin, J. C. (1987). *From hand to mouth.* New York: Crowell. 3–4;5–6. INF

This book presents a historical study of eating implements.

Giblin, J. C. (1990). *The riddle of the Rosetta stone.* New York: Crowell. 3–4;5–6. INF

A history of the Rosetta stone, illustrated with pictures.

Giblin, J. C. (2002). *Adolf Hitler.* New York: Clarion. 5–6;7+. INF

Hitler is portrayed as a complex person in this engrossing and absorbing biography.

Grifalconi, A. (2002). *The village that vanished* (K. Nelson, Illus.). New York: Dial. 3–4;5–6. TF

An African folktale about villagers who feared the slavers, so they made their village disappear.

Hollyer, B. (Ed.) (2003). *The kingfisher book of family poems* (H. Swain, Illus.). New York: Kingfisher. K–2;3–4. P

This collection of poems includes all family members.

Hopkinson, D. (1997). *Birdie's lighthouse* (K. B. Root, Illus.). New York: Atheneum. K–2;3–4. HF

Birdie keeps the lighthouse lamps burning when her father falls ill during a storm.

Howe, D., & Howe, J. (1979). *Bunnicula: A rabbit tale of mystery* (A. Daniel, Illus.). New York: Atheneum. K–2;3–4. MF

The hilarious story of three pets: Harold, a dog; Chester, a cat; and Bunnicula, a suspicious bunny.

Howe, J., & Warshaw, M. (1994). *The hospital book.* New York: Harper. K–2;3–4. INF

This book is a guide for staying in the hospital.

Ichikawa, S. *My pig Amarillo.* New York: Philomel. K–2.

Pablito's pet pig disappeared.

Look, L. (2004). *Ruby Lu, brave and true* (L. Wilsdorf, Illus.). New York: Simon & Schuster. K–2. CRF

Ruby Lu is young girl who looks forward to school.

McKay, H. (2003). *Saffy's angel.* New York: Aladdin. 3–4;5–6. RF

Saffy lives in an eccentric British family of artists. Saffy learns she was adopted when a family member died in an auto accident.

Myers, W. D. (2006). *Jazz* (C. Myers, Illus.). New York: Holiday. 3–4;5–6. B

Myers introduces great jazz musicians, as well as the various forms and genre of jazz.

Nolen, J. (1998). *Raising dragons* (E. Primavera, Illus.). New York: Silver Whistle/Harcourt Brace. K–2. MF

A little girl finds an egg that hatches into a dragon and becomes her friend.

Park, F., & Park, J. (2002). *Good-bye, 382 Shin Dang Dong* (C. Yangsook, Illus.). Washington DC: National Geographic. K–2;3–4. CRF; PB

A Korean youngster and her family leave their home in Korea to make a new home in the United States.

Peck, R. (2006). *The teacher's funeral.* New York: Puffin. 3–4;5–6. HF*

When the teacher dies, the students make plans.

Peck, R. (2001). *Fair weather.* New York: Dial. 3–4;5–6. HF

The story of Rosie Beckett's family and their trip to the World's Columbian Exposition in 1893.

Prelutsky, J. (1984). *The new kid on the block.* New York: Greenwillow. K–2;3–4. P

This collection of poems introduces unusual things such as jellyfish stew and a bounding mouse.

Priceman, M. (1998). *My nine lives by Clio.* New York: Atheneum. K–2;3–4. MF

A cat's journal about her nine extraordinary lives in nine historical periods.

Raschka, C. (2002). *John Coltrane's giant steps.* New York: Atheneum. K–2;3–4;5–6. PB

This book presents John Coltrane's composition "Giant Steps" through language and illustrations.

Sachar, L. (1998). *Holes.* New York: Farrar, Straus & Giroux. 5–6;7+. CRF; NEW

This book tells the story of Stanley Yelnats and his bad-luck family.

Sauer, J. (1994). *The light at Tern Rock.* New York: Puffin. 3–4. HF

Ronnie and his aunt tend the Tern Rock lighthouse while the keeper takes a vacation. However, the keeper does not return.

Service, P. (1989). *Stinker from space.* New York: Scribner. 3–4;5–6. MF

When space warrior Tsynq Yr crashes his space vehicle, he must find a body to use and a power source for his return trip.

St. John, L. (2007). *The white giraffe.* New York: Dial 5–6. RF*

Martine lives with her grandmother in Africa where she sees a mysterious white giraffe.

Viorst, J. (1981). *If I were in charge of the world and other worries* (L. Cherry, Illus.). New York: Atheneum. 3–4;5–6. P

Poems about everyday children's everyday problems.

Walker, S. (2005). *Secrets of a Civil War submarine: Solving the mysteries of the H. L. Hunley.* Minneapolis, MN: Carolrhoda. 5–6;7+. INF

This book is based on the Civil War submarine that was located and brought to the surface.

White, R. (2004). *Buttermilk hill.* New York: Farrar. 5–6; 7+. CRF

Piper's life changes when her parents divorce.

Winter, J. (2006). *Dizzy* (S. Qualls, Illus.). New York: Harcourt. 3–4;5–6. B

A biography of Dizzy Dean.

Professional References

Barksdale-Ladd, M. A., & Nedeff, A. R. (1997). The worlds of a reader's mind: Students as authors. *Reading Teacher, 50,* 564–573.

Barone, D. (1990). The written responses of young children: Beyond comprehension to story understanding. *New Advocate, 3,* 49–56.

Barthes, R. (1975). *The pleasure of the text.* London: Jonathan Cape.

Barton, J. (2001). *Teaching with children's literature.* Norwood, MA: Christopher-Gordon.

Blake, R. W. (1995). *From literature-based reading to reader response in the elementary classroom.* Paper presented at the Annual Meeting of the National Council of Teachers of English, San Diego, CA.

Bloem, P. L., & Manna, A. (1999). A chorus of questions: Readers respond to Patricia Polacco. *Reading Teacher, 52,* 802–809.

Bloome, D., & Bailey, F. M. (1992). Studying language and literature through events, particularity, and intertextuality. In R. Beach (Ed.), *Multidisciplinary perspectives on literacy research* (pp. 181–210). Urbana, IL: National Conference on Research in English.

Borders, S., & Naylor, A. (1993). *Children talking about books.* Phoenix, AZ: Oryx.

Cairney, T. (1990). Intertextuality: Infectious echoes from the past. *Reading Teacher, 43,* 478–484.

Chambers, A. (1996). *The reading environment.* Portland, ME: Stenhouse.

Children's Book Council. (1994). *75 years of children's book week posters.* New York: Knopf.

Daniels, H. (2002). *Literature circles.* Portland, ME: Stenhouse.

Elleman, B. (1991). Paula Fox's *The village by the sea. Book Links, 1,* 48–50.

Enciso, P. (1998). Good/bad girls read together: Pre-adolescent girls' co-authorship of feminine subject positions during a shared event reading. *English Education, 30,* 44–62.

Galda, L. and Beach, R. (January, February, March, 2001). Response to literature as a cultural activity. *Reading Research Quarterly, 36,* 64–73.

Galda, L., & Liang, L. (April, May, June, 2003). Literature as experience or looking for facts: Stance in the classroom. *Reading Research Quarterly, 38,* 268–275.

Gambrell, L., & Almasi, J. (Eds.). (1996). *Lively discussions! Fostering engaged reading.* Newark, DE: International Reading Association.

Giblin, J. C. (1990). *Writing books for young people.* Boston: The Writer.

Hammond, D. (1991). Prediction chart. In J. Macon, D. Bewell, & M. Vogt (Eds.), *Responses to literature* (p. 3). Newark, DE: International Reading Association.

Hancock, K. J. (1991). *Teaching with picture books.* Portsmouth, NH: Heinemann.

Hansen, J. (1991, Spring). I wonder what kind of person he'll be. *The New Advocate,* 89–100.

Hartman, D. K. (1992). Eight readers reading: The intertextual links of able readers using multiple passages. *Reading Research Quarterly, 27,* 122–133.

Hill, S. (2000). *Guiding literacy learners.* Portland, ME: Stenhouse.

Holland, K., Hungerford, R., & Ernst, S. (1993). *Journeying: Children responding to literature.* Portsmouth, NH: Heinemann.

Jenkins, C. B. (1999). *The allure of authors: Author studies in the elementary classroom.* Portsmouth, NH: Heinemann.

Jewell, T., & Pratt, D. (1998–1999). Literature discussions in the primary grades: Children's thoughtful discourse about books and what teachers can do to make it happen. *Reading Teacher, 52,* 842–855.

Kelly, P. R. (1990), Guiding young students' responses to literature. *Reading Teacher 43,* 464–476.

Langer, J. (1992). Rethinking literature instruction. In J. Langer (Ed.), *Literature instruction: A focus on student response* (pp. 35–53). Urbana, IL: National Council of Teachers of English.

Langer, J. (1995). *Envisioning literature: Literary understanding and literature instruction.* New York: Teachers College Press.

Larrick, N. (1991). Give us books! . . . But also . . . Give us wings! *New Advocate, 2,* 77–84.

Lewis, C. S. (1961). *An experiment in criticism.* Cambridge, England: Cambridge University Press.

Lundin, A. (1998). Intertextuality in children's literature. *Journal of Education for Library and Information Science, 39,* 210–213.

Macon, J. M., Bewell, D., & Vogt, M. E. (1991). *Responses to literature.* Newark, DE: International Reading Association.

Many, J. (1996). Exploring the influences of literature approaches on children's stance when responding and their response complexity. *Reading Psychology, 17,* 1–41.

Martinez, M., & Nash, M. F. (1991). Bookalogues: Talking about children's books. *Language Arts, 68,* 140–147.

McClure, A. A., & Kristo, J. V. (Eds.). (1996). *Books that invite talk, wonder, and play.* Urbana, IL: National Council of Teachers of English.

McGinley, W., & Kamberelis, G. (1996). Maniac Magee and Ragtime Tumpie: Children negotiating self and world through reading and writing. *Research in the Teaching of English, 30,* 75–113.

McMahon, S., & Raphael, T. (1994). The book club program: Theoretical and research foundations. In S. McMahon, T. Raphael, V. Goatley, & L. Pardo (Eds.), *The book club connection.* New York: Teachers College Press.

Musthafa, B. (1996). *Nurturing children's response to literature in the classroom context.* ERIC NO: ED398577.

Probst, R. (1992). Five kinds of literary knowing. In J. Langer (Ed.), *Literature instruction: A focus on student response* (pp. 54–77). Urbana, IL: National Council of Teachers of English.

Raphael, T., & McMahon, S. (1994). Book club: An alternative framework for reading instruction. *Reading Teacher, 48,* 102–116.

Rosenblatt, L. M. (1978). *The reader, the text, the poem: The transactional theory of the literary work.* Edwardsville: Southern Illinois University.

Rosenblatt, L. M. (1982). The literary transaction: Evocation and response. *Theory into Practice, XXI,* 268–277.

Schmitt, B., & Buckley, M. (1991). Plot relationships chart. In J. Macon, D. Bewell, & M. Vogt (Eds.), *Responses to literature.* Newark, DE: International Reading Association.

Sebesta, S., & Iverson, W. J. (1975). *Literature for Thursday's child.* Chicago: Science Research Associates.

Sendak, M. (1988). *Caldecott and co.: Notes on books and pictures.* New York: Farrar, Straus & Giroux.

Sipe, L. (1999). Children's response to literature: Author, text, reader, context. *Theory Into Practice, 38,* 120–129.

Stoodt, B., & Amspaugh, L. (1994, May). *Children's response to nonfiction.* Paper presented at the Annual Meeting of the International Reading Association, Toronto, Canada.

Thacker, D. (1996). The child's voice in children's literature. In *Sustaining the vision: Selected papers from the annual conference of the International Association of School Librarianship,* Worcester, England, July 1995.

Toth, M. (1990). Character map. In J. Macon, D. Bewell, & M. Vogt (Eds.), *Responses to literature K–8.* Newark, DE: International Reading Association.

Waldo, B. (1991). Story pyramid. In J. Macon, D. Bewell, & M. Vogt (Eds.), *Responses to literature.* Newark, DE: International Reading Association.

White, E. B. (1970). Laura Ingalls Wilder award acceptance speech. *Horn Book, 56,* 540–547.

Wollman-Bonilla, J., & Werchadlo, B. (1999). Teacher and peer roles in scaffolding first graders' responses to literature. *Reading Teacher, 52,* 598–608.

Zinsser, W. (Ed.). (1990). Introduction. In *The art and craft of writing for children* (pp. 1–21). Boston: Houghton Mifflin.

16 Unit Studies: Learning with Literature

book clusters   theme
connections   topical units
inquiry   unit

GUIDING QUESTIONS

When you were in elementary or middle school, did you ever have a teacher who used literature in curriculum classes? If so, you were lucky. This chapter focuses on units combining nonfiction trade books, poetry trade books, and nonfiction trade books. Think about the following questions as you read this chapter.

1. What are the benefits of using literature as a resource for pleasure and for instruction?

2. What are the advantages of literature in curriculum classes?

3. How can teachers use book clusters?

Introduction to Units, Themes, and Topics

In the classroom setting, a *unit* is a collection of lessons, an organizing framework for children's inquiry and study. Units are intense learning experiences. Our goal in developing units is to help students become independent problem solvers and thinkers through direct, purposeful learning. When students are presented with a variety of ideas and a variety of ways for learning, they have more opportunities to develop individual interests. Integrating literature into all aspects of the curricula will help students make connections as they learn.

Research shows, for example, that fiction and nonfiction trade books develop students' understanding of science and the language of science (Donovan, 2001). Pappas (2006) has also found that the information book genre has an important role in integrated science literacy. Research supports the inclusion of children's literature in teaching and learning mathematics also. Ward used children's literature to develop K–8 pre-service teachers' mathematics pedagogy. She used *How Much is a Million* by David Schwartz for a demonstation lesson. She also used other trade books to enliven how students learn the place-value system and the enormity of numbers (Ward, 2005).

Fiction and nonfiction can be used together to develop concepts. Soalt (2005) has found that bringing fiction and nonfiction together on the same topic seems to motivate children to listen and think more attentively. She suggests that one genre provides a bridge to the other and that when instruction combines both types of texts students become more diverse readers who are prepared to encounter a variety of genres in school, home, and the working world (Soalt, 2005).

The purpose of this chapter is to alert current and prospective teachers to ways of connecting students with literature to enhance learning in curriculum classes. This chapter synthesizes and organizes the understandings developed in the preceding chapters. We include practical, usable guides and units in this chapter. Our text and the accompanying CD are resources for identifying books that address the themes and topics of interest to children.

Units

Well-developed curriculum units motivate students toward in-depth study of a topic, book, issue, person, idea, or theme. A unit identifies the goals (standards or objectives), experiences, activities, and materials the teacher plans to develop. Students use reading, questions, talking, listening, and thinking as tools to discover relations and to link new connections with prior understandings. The length of time involved in a unit study may be one hour, one day, one week, or longer. This text uses the term *theme* to identify the meaning, focus, or central idea of a unit of study, such as racial tension, loneliness, or survival. Topical units focus on subjects such as the solar system, the water cycle, and endangered species.

The beginning point when devising a literature unit is to determine the focus of the project. Next, locate relevant material and develop appropriate experiences. Choosing the focus may be the most difficult aspect of the process because it demands a fairly broad familiarity with the world of children's literature and an understanding of the structure of the discipline. Students who are independent readers can study textbooks, magazines, and reference books, while emergent readers can rely on stories and information read aloud.

Discussion contributes to the thinking process about a topic, as does writing. Many teachers encourage students to write in learning logs. During units, students usually participate in individual and group activities and projects related to the topic. Teachers frequently incorporate the arts, music, drama, writing, visual arts, and computerized responses into the unit. In many instances, science, math, and social studies are relevant to the unit. These connections offer opportunities for both direct and indirect teaching of the skills and strategies that we expect students to accomplish. When using fiction, nonfiction, and poetry, teachers need to make the connections clear to the students. *Science Verse* by Jon Scieszka and Lane Smith shows the connection between poetry, English, and science and is an excellent introduction to a unit.

The following classroom snapshot illustrates a unit for third grade; however, this unit would work equally

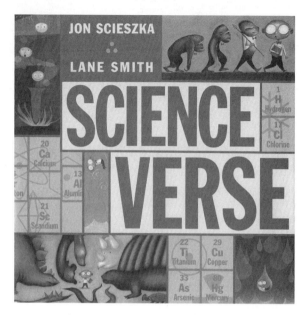

This book contains science poetry.

well with fourth-grade students. Intermediate students could study the Bill of Rights, which also has many Internet sites.

How Do Units Enhance Learning

Jean Dickinson (1995) reports that her fifth- and sixth-grade students, who used picture books, novels, and textbooks to explore World War II, developed these reading strategies:

1. to visualize while reading
2. to use prior knowledge
3. to reread interesting and exciting parts and parts with especially interesting language
4. to ask questions about what they read
5. to make predictions
6. to discuss books with friends
7. to find ideas for writing
8. to look beyond the cover
9. to relate books to other books they have read and to books by the same author
10. to put themselves in the story
11. to know when they do not understand something in the book
12. to read the rest of a paragraph to figure out word meanings

Several students in Dawn's third-grade class had fathers in the armed forces, so she decided to develop a unit entitled "What makes us Americans?" Her goal was to explore symbols, landmarks, documents, and people related to our country. The books she chose for the unit ranged from easy to difficult, so that all students could find reading material suited to their taste. She identified the following IRA/NCTE Standards to guide her study: reading a wide range of materials, understanding the United States, acquiring new information, applying a wide range of strategies, writing, spelling, punctuation, listening, speaking, generating questions, and using technology and libraries *(IRA/NCTE Standards: 1, 3, 4, 5, 6, 7, 8, 10, 11, 12)*.

To kick the unit off, she invited Noah's father, who is in the army, to talk with the students. In subsequent weeks, she invited other parents who were in the armed forces.

Dawn read selections from Caroline Kennedy's *A Patriot's Handbook* to introduce the unit's literature and its basic concepts. She also read the lyrics to "You're a Grand Old Flag" by George M. Cohan, "The Pledge of Allegiance," and the story behind the Pledge of Allegiance. She then asked, "What are some symbols of America?" After explaining the word *symbols* to some of the students, they began to identify symbols.

Chris said, "Soldiers and sailors are symbols."

"So is the flag," Delonta suggested.

"Red, white, and blue," Emily offered.

The students identified these symbols: eagle; flag; red, white, and blue; Statue of Liberty; soldiers, sailors, and marines; and the Pledge of Allegiance. Dawn gave the students a blank semantic web with the word *American* in the center to expand by adding words related to American as they read more books. She then booktalked the selected literature for the unit, which included:

> *The Pledge of Allegiance* by Francis Bellamy
>
> *America Is . . . .* by Louise Borden
>
> *We the Kids: The Preamble to the Constitution of the United States* by David Catrow
>
> *Don't Know Much About American History* by Kenneth Davis
>
> *The Declaration of Independence* by Sam Fink

> *Old Glory: An American Treasure* by Robert Lang
>
> *The Story of the Statue of Liberty* by Betsy Maestro
>
> *Uncle Sam and Old Glory: Symbols of America* by Christopher Manson
>
> *Celebrate America: In Poetry and Art* by N. Panzer
>
> *Yankee Doodle (Patriotic Songs)* by N. Owen
>
> *The Flag We Love* by Pam Munoz Ryan
>
> *A is for America* by Devin Scillian
>
> *The Impossible Patriotism Project* by Linda Skeers
>
> *The Pledge of Allegiance: The Story Behind Our Patriotic Promise (America in Words and Song)* by Liz Sonneborn
>
> *Lily and Miss Liberty* by Carla Stevens

CDs

> *God Bless America: audio CD*
>
> *United We Stand: Songs for America CD*

Related Web Sites

> National Geographic World
> [http://Nationalgeographic.com/media/world]
>
> Library of Congress (Type this term into your browser and it will pull up this site.)
>
> Smithsonian (Type this term into your browser to locate the site.)

Mathematics

The book *One Nation: America by the Numbers* by Devin Scillian is an excellent beginning point for relating math to a study of the United States. Students can create their own "America by Numbers."

Language Arts

Explore the word *symbols,* the meaning of symbols, the reasons that Americans have certain symbols, and identify common symbols of our country. Have students write in their journals after reading, and research selected topics and symbols.

Social Studies

This unit focuses on history and patriotism.

(continued)

Fine Arts

Students can view relevant art for Americans, along with related poetry, in Nora Panzer's *Celebrate America: In Poetry and Art.* Students may contact regional and local art museums to order prints and slides for classroom display; some may choose to create their own artistic treatment of American symbols and choose poetry to accompany their work.

Tapes of patriotic music will also enhance children's understanding.

Closure

At the end of each day, students will discuss their experiences and write in their learning logs. When the study is completed, they may choose to share products or performances developed during the unit.

Planning Units

When choosing the unifying theme or topic for a unit, the teacher should consider curriculum goals, standards, and objectives. For instance, first-grade teachers are usually accountable for emergent reading and writing, as well as for developing concepts of family, friends, and holidays, among others. Two periodicals that teachers can rely on when planning units are *School Library Media Activities Monthly,* which is a publication of *School Library Media Monthly*, and *Books Links*, which is a publication of the American Library Association.

Consider what the students already know and what they need to know about the selected topic or theme. In addition to prior knowledge, teachers may consider the students' interests because this motivates them and provides a sense of ownership. Other considerations include the students' learning needs, developmental levels, and previous experiences. Building background experiences for the theme or topic is necessary for students who may lack relevant experiences.

The resources available for students are another consideration. A good supply of well-written books is essential. The books must, of course, address the unit topic or theme, and they need to match the students' range of reading levels. Both print and nonprint media develop children's knowledge base and understanding. Videos, films, pictures, computer programs, and web sites are useful in units. Guest speakers or people who can demonstrate skills or materials also add interest to units.

Teachers should plan read-alouds, as well as booktalks, on the books selected for the unit. Booktalks provide students with the information they need when choosing the books they want to read.

Making Connections Through Inquiry

Knowledge does not "reside" in books. Rather, knowledge is developed when students discuss, question, and write about literature. Discussion is a social process that strengthens learning and response. It also helps readers make sense of new information (Copenhaver, 1993). Although learners can arrive at a meaning alone, they do so more often through collaboration (Barnes, 1995).

To investigate their questions, students listen, read, write, view films, listen to audiotapes, use the Internet, and watch television; they also consult with people who have special knowledge related to their questions. Students may conduct their own experiments, as a group of kindergarten students did when investigating which insects crawl fastest. All of these approaches to investigation—and more—can be used in the classroom.

The beginning or access point for *inquiry* is identifying students' knowledge about a topic. Brainstorming is an effective strategy for summarizing existing knowledge. Students can also create individual webs of knowledge. Figure 16.1 summarizes the unit activities of teachers and students, and Figure 16.2 is a planning guide. The following box shows a fantasy unit for an intermediate or middle school class.

Shared Book Experiences

Obviously, accessing literature is necessary for incorporating literature in the curriculum units. Teachers should plan to read books aloud and to identify works of literature that reflect a range of readability, so that students can independently read the books. The following guidelines will help teachers plan.

1. Select the *core literature* (literature central to the unit theme or topic) carefully. The literature should reflect a wide range of readability. Booktalk each book to help students select those they wish to read.

2. Read the books aloud, encouraging the students to discuss what is happening (Jacque, 1993).

3. Have the students use response journals, literature logs, or interactive journals. In response journals, students write about their feelings, specifically *connections* to their lives and to other literature.

FIGURE 16.1 Unit activities.

Teacher Activities

Plan:
   Identify theme or topic
   Connect to literature and/or knowledge
   Identify Standards
Select: literature, web sites, videos, audios, activities
Accept children's ideas
Engage children in meaningful activities as time allows
Initiating activities
   Closure (Culmination)
   Evaluation/Assessment

Student Activities

Ask questions
Apply background
Focus-relate
Listen, read, think, write
Discuss complete required work
Do optional activities as time allows

FIGURE 16.2 Unit planning guide.

Planning Guide

Theme or Topic: _____

Standards or Objectives: _____

Questions:

Literature and Media Selections:

Students to learn (knowledge, skills, response):

Prereading (initiating activities):

During reading (activities):

Following reading (activities): Include literature log.

Evaluation/assessment strategies:

In a literature log, students discuss their understanding of the elements of literature. In an interactive journal, the student writes and the teacher responds and/or asks questions.

4. Divide the class into four cooperative groups and have each group read a different book. Conduct a booktalk for each of the books in advance to help children choose a book that appeals to their interests.

5. Have various groups or individuals read a book and retell the high points of the parts they read.

Fantasy Unit

Fantasies permit readers to consider and speculate about experiences and themes in ways that are more palatable than in realistic fiction or nonfiction (Kurkjian et al). In fantasy we can examine profound ideas, strange characters, and imaginary worlds; however, make-believe also has the power to help us understand reality. Harry Potter has awakened the entire world to the magic of fantasy, creating a powerful interest in this genre. The following unit was created because intermediate-grade and middle-school students are interested in fantasy.

Fantasy Theme Unit

Focus: Fantasy for Intermediate and Middle School

Standards: To develop students' concepts of fantasy and the rules of well-written fantasy.
To develop students' ability to compare and contrast.
IRA/NCTE Standards: 1,2,3,7

Part I. Teacher-Planned Whole-Class Reading and Viewing

Teacher Read-Aloud: *The Neddiad* by Daniel Pinkwater. This unusual fantasy provides a good introduction to make-believe.

Books:

Atherton: The House of Power by Patrick Carman

Skin Hunger: A Resurrection of Magic, Book One by Kathleen Duey

Into the Wild by Sarah Durst

The Land of the Silver Apples by Nancy Farmer

Stonehart by Charlie Fletcher

Beowulf retold by James Rumford (graphic novel)

The Dragon's Eye by Dugald Steer

Elissa's Quest: Phoenix Rising, Book One by Erica Verrillo

H.I.V.E.: Higher Institute of Villainous Education by Mark Walden

Books to compare:

The Society of Super Secret Heroes: The Great Cape Rescue by Phyllis Shalant and *Missing Magic* by Emma Laybourn

The Wednesday Wars by Gary Schmidt and *The Neddiad* by Daniel Pinkwater

Content Activities

Writing: Journaling

Music: Students can select eerie music that they consider appropriate to books they are reading. In many instances, organ music would be apppropriate.

Art: Several of these novels are set in the time of castles, dragons, and witches.
Teachers and/or students can find posters and pictures online for the unit.

Computer/ Internet: Research the authors of the books and fantastic characters, plots, or settings.

Unit Introduction

Use the following discussion questions after reading *The Neddiad* by Daniel Pinkwater aloud. Students may generate the questions they prefer to discuss.

1. What elements of fantasy appeared in this story?

2. How did the author make you believe the fantasy?

(continued)

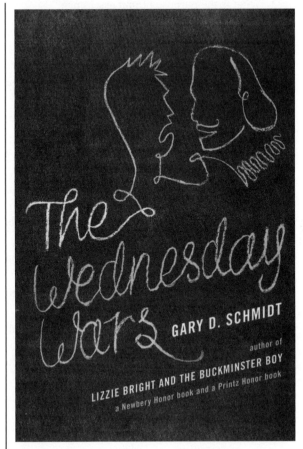

Holling bonds with his seventh grade teacher.

3. What was the theme of this fantasy?
4. What did this fantasy make you think about?

In addition to discussion, have students write their thoughts about these questions. Then have them think of questions they would like to have answered.

When the book is finished, working in small groups in pairs, have students read one of the titles listed.

Curricular Connections

Math: Have students discuss the role of math in the book they read.

Social studies: Describe the lifestyle and values of the people in the various stories. Have the students identify what kinds of things they need to consider when describing a society and its values.

Writing: Instruct students to keep journals in which they write a response to a novel they read.

Students also may use art, music, or literature to express their responses to the novels.

More and more students are interested in writing graphic novels, and most bookstores have books that will help them.

Drama: Students may do reader's theater; they may dramatize a scene from the book or act out what they believe happened after the book ends.

Assessing Unit Experiences

Assessment is an integral part of instruction. The purpose of assessment in literature is to gather information regarding students' growth in understanding and appreciating literature. Sources of information regarding student progress include work samples, journal entries, projects and displays, individual conferences, oral presentations, portfolios, and student observation forms. Portfolio assessment is a type of informal evaluation that involves student input. Portfolios may include work samples, checklists, and assignments specifically designed to collect information (Meinback, Rothlein, & Fredericks, 2000).

When using a literature checklist, the student should:

- identify the beginning, middle, and ending of stories;
- recognize the central character in a story;
- follow the sequence of events in a story;
- recognize the literary elements (plot, character, setting, theme, style);
- understand and follow plot; and
- choose to read for pleasure.

Summary

This chapter focuses on using literature in the class-room, reading aloud daily, and using an integrated curriculum, inquiry learning, units, and assessment. Units are intensive learning experiences that help students make connections as they learn. Integrated units develop language skills within a context that may involve social studies, math, science, the arts, music, and physical education. Inquiry learning focuses on students' questions as powerful stimulators of learning. Units may focus on curriculum topics, themes, authors/illustrators, current events, concepts, or student-generated ideas. A unit plan, which may be revised as it is used, serves as a road map for teachers.

Thought Questions and Applications

1. What components should teachers consider when developing units? Can you think of any additional considerations?
2. Describe a unit in your own words.

3. What is the purpose of unit assessment?
4. How are reading aloud to children and their own silent reading related to inquiry units?

Research and Application Experiences

1. Prepare a complete unit for a grade level of your choice. Teach your unit, if possible.
2. Prepare a unit that could be integrated with a specific unit in a basal reader of your choice.
3. Consult a curriculum guide or the standards for your state and list the unit topics or themes appropriate for the grade level you teach or hope to teach.
4. Read a unit ideas book and decide which units you would be interested in using and why you would use these.
5. Write a narrative plan for inquiry instruction and get children to raise important questions.
6. Determine what literature-related items you think should be included in a portfolio for your class or the class you plan to teach. Explain why you would choose these items.

Classroom Activities

There is no specific method, no process based on hard-and-fast rules, for integrating literature into curriculum units. Rather, literature experiences can be molded and adapted to fit local curricula and students. One of the most powerful ideas in teaching literature in units is to constantly seek connections. Students should think about connections in plot, characters, themes, setting, and style.

This section of the chapter is devoted to actual units that classroom teachers have developed, used, and refined. These units are organized around different formats, some narrative and others outlined. You may choose to use all or part of any unit or activity in your own teaching. Activity 16.6 illustrates a book cluster; additional book clusters are included on our Internet site.

ACTIVITY 16.1   WORDS (KINDERGARTEN, FIRST GRADE, SECOND GRADE)

IRA/NCTE Standards: 2, 3, 7, 12. Students will use a range of strategies to comprehend, evaluate and appreciate text.

This unit provides a variety of activities. When planning a thematic unit, consider the students' interests and the activities they enjoy. You should consult your specific

state standards for each grade level and identify specific curricular goals and objectives from each of the content areas that correspond to the unit.

This unit explores words. Students will learn how to explain words and their importance, both verbally and nonverbally. Many other skills can be developed during this study, such as how to use picture dictionaries and picture thesaurus. Children will make their own word collections, and they may illustrate their collections. Each of the mini-lessons in this unit can be taught separately as a stand-alone experience.

Suggested Books

Word Wizard by Cathryn Falwell

Please Bury Me in the Library by J. Patrick Lewis

Wonderful Words: Poems About Reading, Writing, Speaking, and Listening by Lee Bennett Hopkins

The Color of My Words by Lynn Joseph (Students in grades 3 to 6)

The Place My Words Are Looking For: What Poets Say About and Through Their Work by Paul B. Janeczko (Students in grades 3 to 6)

Martin's Big Words: The Life of Dr. Martin Luther King, Jr. by Doreen Rappaport

Words Are Not for Hurting by Elizabeth Verdick

Elbert's Bad Word by Audrey Wood

Skills to Develop

- alphabetic order
- using alphabetical order in organizing word collections
- using the alphabet to locate words in picture dictionary
- sequencing (story events)
- language appreciation
- letter identification
- rhyming words
- phonemic awareness
- Scrabble-type games
- fastening words to magnets to make sentences

Writing

Children dictate stories to their teacher or write their own responses to books in the following ways:

- journals
- logs
- shared writing
- dictated information, story, or poem

Science

- How is a word collection like a butterfly collection or a coin collection?

Social Studies

- Why are some words good? How do good words make people feel?

Fine Arts

- Explore different ways to print words. Alphabet books usually use different print for letters.
- Make picture puzzles that have letters hidden in them.

Physical Education

- Introduce Bill Martin's book, *Chicka, Chicka, Boom Boom*. This book has marvelous rhythm. The children can march to the rhythm and then dance to it.

Mini-Lesson One

Read *Max's Words*, by Kate Banks, aloud.

Ask students to find out why Max likes words. Students can type words on the computer using various fonts and put the words on magnets to make sentences.

Discussion Questions

- Why does Max decide to collect words?
- What happens when Max has too many words?
- How does Max use his word collection?
- Where are some good places to find words?
- Can you think of words to add to Max's collection?
- Why do you think these words belong in Max's collection?

Activities

Have children dictate a story about the ways they use words.

What words are the most important?

What words make people feel bad?

Make an "old maid" game with words on the cards and play the game.

This is the true story of a devoted librarian.

Mini-Lesson Two

Read *The Boy Who Loved Words*, by Roni Schotter, aloud. This book focuses on the power and purpose of language. Ask the students to identify examples of the power of language. Then ask them to identify the purpose of language.

Discuss the ways the boy who loved words shares his word wealth.

Make a word tree

Read *The Librarian of Basra*, by Jeanette Winter, aloud. Then discuss her devotion to books and how she showed her devotion and love of words.

ACTIVITY 16.2   EVERYBODY LOVES A GOOD MYSTERY—GRADE LEVELS 4–7

IRA/NCTE Standards: 2, 3, 4, 5, 6, 7, 11, 12.

Mysteries have wide appeal for all ages; furthermore, they give teachers opportunities to develop a sequence of story events, analysis, inferencing, critical thinking, problem solving, vocabulary, and drawing conclusions.

Objectives
1. Students will read a mystery.
2. Students will learn strategies for solving the mystery.
3. Students will identify the problem, clues, and perpetrator.
4. Students will refine their literary knowledge of plot, characterization, and motivation.

Mystery
In *The Mysterious Matter of I. M. Fine* by Diane Stanley, Franny, a fifth grader, is concerned because her classmates have psychosomatic illnesses and delusions after reading middle-grade horror novels called "Chillers." Franny and her friend, Beamer, decide to find the author of the books and stop her.

Introduction
1. Ask the students if they have ever experienced a mystery. Discuss their responses.
2. Read the first three chapters of the book aloud to the class.
3. Introduce these words: alibi, clue, deduction, delusions, evidence, perpetrator, psychosomatic illness, suspects, and witness. Apply these terms to the first three chapters of the book.
4. What is the mystery in this book? Identify the sequence of events up to this point.

5. Identify and describe the central character.

6. Explain the steps in analyzing a problem (in this instance, analyzing a mystery).

Silent Reading in Small Groups

Organize groups of four or five students and have them read the story. After the students complete it, discuss the following questions and write out the answers. Students can work out the answers as a group or assign different individuals to answer different questions.

1. Describe the main characters in the mystery, explaining how each is related to the mystery.

2. Identify the important clues to the mystery.

3. What was the most important clue to the mystery?

4. What is the solution to the mystery?

5. How did you analyze the problem? (Work backwards to the beginning; make guesses that you can support with information from the book; and draw a web of facts, events, characters, and clues.

6. How did the characters in the book solve the problem (mystery)?

Books

We recommend that students read additional mysteries, so they can use their newly developed knowledge and understanding. The asterisk (*) indicates mysteries that will appeal to challenged readers. The numbers in parentheses indicate grade levels.

> Abrahams, P. *Behind the Curtains* (4–6)
>
> Anderson, M. *The Case of the Linoleum Lederhosen* (4–6)

Avi, *Strange Happenings: Five Tales of Transformation* (4–7)

Hoobler, D., & Hoobler, T. *The Ghost in the Tokaido Inn* (4–6)

Littke, L. *Lake of Secrets* (6–9)

Manns, N. *Operating Codes* (6–9)

Moriarty, J. *The Murder of Bindy Mackenzie* (5–7)

Naylor, P. *Bernie Magruder & the Bats in the Belfry* (4–7)

Newbery, L. *Set in Stone* (5–7)

Nickerson, D. *How to Disappear Completely and Never Be Found* (6–9)

Stanley, G. *The Cobweb Confession* (All)*

Stenhouse, T. *Across the Steel River* (5–8)

Internet Sites

A number of Internet sites offer copies of mysteries that are quick reads for children, plus explanations of how each mystery was solved. Students can compare their solutions with the professionals. Students are encouraged to write mysteries and to learn from them. We recommend the following Internet sites: MysteryNet's Kids Mysteries at http://kids.mysterynet. com and Kids Love a Mystery.com at www.kidsloveamystery.com.

ACTIVITY 16.3   COUNTING (SECOND, THIRD, OR FOURTH GRADE)

IRA/NCTE Standards: 2, 3, 4, 5. Students learn to comprehend various genre, use language to accomplish purposes.

This unit, which focuses on various ways of counting and the importance of math, is presented in a unit map.

Books

> Babbitt, N. *The Search for Delicious* (4–6)
>
> Chae, I. *How Do You Count a Dozen Ducklings?* (K–3)
>
> Ekeland, I. *The Cat in Numberland* (4–6)

Fisher, V. *How High Can a Dinosaur Count?: and Other Math Mysteries* (K–3)

Frandel, J. *The Metric System* (4–6)

Goldstone, B. *Great Estimations* (4–6)

Guettier, B. *The Father Who had 10 Children* (K–2)

Merrill, J. *The Toothpaste Millionaire* (4–7)

Scieszka, J. and Smith, L. *Math Curse* (3–4; 5–6)

Questions

- What do you want or need to count?
- What is the best way to count that thing?

Math

- Why do we need to count things?
- What kinds of things need to be counted?
- What is one-to-one correspondence?

Writing

- Think of a new way to count and write it down.

Art

- Make illustrations and art to go with the project.

Social Studies

- Why is counting people important?
- What do we call it when we count people?
- What is a poll?
- Why do we conduct polls?

ACTIVITY 16.4 PIRATES (THIRD OR FOURTH GRADE)

IRA/NCTE Standards 3, 4, 7: Comprehension, use a variety of strategies, apply language to print and non-print texts.

Topic: Pirates

Objectives

- To study oceans through pirate routes.
- To study the difference between saltwater and fresh water.
- To learn about the importance of vitamin C and how sailors got vitamin C.
- To learn why pirates needed math to figure out where they were and to plot their route.
- To learn pirate songs.
- To learn pirate words and language.

Questions

1. Why did pirates live on ships? Did they always live on ships? Can you be a pirate if you do not live on a ship?
2. Why do pirates wear funny clothes?
3. How did they get their treasure?
4. Did they help other people?
5. How do you become a pirate?
6. Why do they use funny words?
7. Did all the pirates live long ago? Do pirates exist today?
8. Why did people become pirates?
9. Can girls be pirates?

Literature

The Handbook of Pirates by Terry Deary

Tough Boris by Mem Fox

Pirates: Robbers of the High Seas by Gail Gibbons

One-Eyed Jake by Pat Hutchins

Pirates by Drew Lammrate

Pirate Diary: The Journal of Jake Carpenter by Richard Platt

How I Became a Pirate by David Shannon

Do Pirates Take Baths? by Kathy Tucker

The Ballad of the Pirate Queens by Jane Yolen

ACTIVITY 16.5 INVENTORS (FOURTH OR FIFTH GRADE)

IRA/NCTE Standards: 2, 3, 4, 7. Read a variety of genre, develop comprehension, adjust use of spoken and written language.

Topic: Inventors

Questions
- What is the best invention in the world?
- What is an invention that changed the world?
- What is creativity?

Math
- Measurement
- Computers
- Probability

Thinking
- Classify inventions.

Science
- Identify important scientific inventions.

Writing
- Write to the U.S. Patent Office to get information about obtaining patents.
- Write about a needed invention that would improve your life.

Social Studies
- How did these inventions change life in the United States: automobiles, telephones, computers, computer chips?

Reading
- Review biographies of famous inventors and some who are not so famous—what made these people creative?

Literature
- *Mistakes That Worked: 40 Familiar Inventions and How They Came to Be* by Charlotte Foltz Jones
- *The Wright Brothers: How They Invented the Airplane* by Russell Freedman
- *Ice Cream Cones for Sale* by Elaine Greenstein
- *The Amazing Thinking Machine* by Dennis Haseley
- *Outward Dreams: Black Inventors and Their Inventions* by Jim Haskins
- *The Many Lives of Benjamin Franklin* by Mary Osborne
- *Pinkerton: America's First Private Eye* by Richard Wormser
- *100 Inventions That Shaped World History* by Bill Yenne

ACTIVITY 16.6 BOOK CLUSTERS

Book clusters are groups of books under a common theme or topic with a range of reading difficulty that teachers can use to develop units. The following example is a cluster of sports books.

Adler, D. (1997). *Lou Gehrig: The luckiest man*. Harcourt. 3–5. PICTURE BOOK, BIOGRAPHY.

Bunting, E. (1997). *Trouble on the t-ball team*. Clarion. K–3. FICTION.

Green, M. (2002). *A strong right arm: The story of Mamie "Peanut" Johnson*. Dial. 4–8. BIOGRAPHY.

Layden, J. (1997). *NBA game day*. Scholastic. 2–6. NONFICTION.

Telander, R. (2002). *String music*. Cricket. 4–6. FICTION.

Children's Literature References

Note: Books designated with an asterisk (*) are recommended for reluctant readers.

Ata, T. (1989). *Baby rattlesnake* (L. Moroney, Adapt.; V. Reisberg, Illus.). San Francisco: Children's Book Press. K–2. TF

A Native American teaching tale.

Babbitt, N. (1969). *The search for delicious.* New York: Farrar, Straus & Giroux. 5–6. MF

The king searches for the meaning of *delicious.*

Banks, K. (2006). *Max's words.* New York: Farrar. K–2. PB

Max collects words.

Begay, S. (1992). *Ma'ii and cousin horned toad.* New York: Scholastic. K–2. TF

A traditional Navajo story about the coyote trickster.

Begay, S. (1994). *Navajo: Visions and voices across the mesa.* New York: Scholastic. 3–4;5–6. TF

Shonto Begay combines his art with his prose and poetry in this book.

Bellamy, F. (2001). *The pledge of allegiance.* New York: Cartwheel Books. K–2;3–4. INF

Colorful photographs illustrate the pledge and our country.

Borden, L. (2002). *America is . . .* (S. Schuett, Illus.). New York: McElderry. K–2;3–4. INF

This picture book tells about our American home.

Brown, L. K., & Brown, M. (1992). *Dinosaurs to the rescue! A guide to protecting our planet.* New York: Little, Brown. K–2;3–4. INF

This informational book is a guide to conservation.

Brown, R. (2001). *Ten seeds.* New York: Knopf. K–2. PB

This seed-planting story introduces subtraction.

Bruchac, J. (2007). *Bearwalker* (S. Comport, Illus.). New York: HarperCollins. 3–4;5–6. TF

A Mohawk folktale.

Cannon, A. (2003). *On the go with Pirate Pete and Pirate Joe* (E. Smith, Illus.). New York: Viking. K–2;3–4. MF

The story of two pirates, one tall and thin and one short and round, who like to dance.

Carle, E. (1977). *The grouchy ladybug.* New York: Thomas Crowell. K–2. PB

The grouchy ladybug tries to fight with everyone she meets, but makes a friend.

Carman, P. (2007). *Atherton: The house of power.* New York: Little. 5–6;7+.

Edgar lives in the three-tiered world of Atherton and struggles with the levels.

Catrow, D. (2002). *We the kids: The Preamble to the Constitution of the United States.* New York: Dial. 3–4;5–6. NF

This is a sort of "how-to" book showing how to have happiness, safety, and comfort.

Cheney, L. (2002). *America: A patriotic primer* (R. Glasser, Illus.). New York: Simon & Schuster. 3–4;5–6. NF

This book contains alphabetical information about our country.

Cohen, C. L. (Reteller). (1988). *The mud pony: A traditional Skidi Pawnee tale* (S. Begay, Illus.). New York: Scholastic. K–2;3–4. TF

A Pawnee boy makes a pony from mud; the pony then comes to life.

Cutler, J. (1999). *'Gator aid* (T. Pearson, Illus.). New York: Farrar, Straus & Giroux. 3–4;5–6. CRF

Edward sees an alligator, but no one believes him; he solves the mystery.

Davis, K. (2003). *Don't know much about American history.* New York: Harper. 3–4;5–6. INF

A brief treatment of American history.

Duey, K. (2007). *Skin hunger: A resurrection of magic, book one.* New York: Atheneum. 5–6;7+. MF

Magic is banned in the kingdom; later it is returned, but it rests in the hands of a few.

Durst, S. *Into the wild.* New York: Anchor. 5–6; 7+. MF

A version of Rapunzel.

Erlback, A. (1997). *The kids' invention book.* Minneapolis, MN: Lerner. 2–5. INF

This book suggests science fair projects that could grow into products for manufacture.

Esbensen, B. J. (Reteller). (1994). *The great buffalo race: How the buffalo got his hump: A Seneca tale.* New York: Little, Brown. K–2. TF

This pourquoi tale explains how the buffalo got its hump.

Falwell, C. (2006). *Word wizard.* New York: Clarion. K–2. INF

Anna discovers that her cereal spells words.

Farmer, N. (2007). *The land of silver apples*. New York: Atheneum. 5–6;7+. MF

Jack causes an earthquake, and his sister is kidnapped. Then he meets a hobgoblin king.

Fink, S. (2002). *The Declaration of Independence*. New York: Scholastic. 3–4;5–6. INF

The author breaks the document into phrases and explains them.

Fletcher, C. (2007). *Stoneheart*. New York: Hyperion. 3–4;5–6. MF

George discovers the unseen half of London.

Florian, D. (1989). *Turtle day*. New York: Crowell. 1–3. INF

This book helps children learn about turtles and reptiles.

Ford, R. (1989). *Walt Disney*. New York: Walker. 3–4;5–6. B

A biography of Walt Disney.

Fox, M. (1994). *Tough Boris* (K. Brown, Illus.). New York: Harcourt Brace. K–2;3–4. PB

This book is about Boris, a pirate who is not so tough.

Freedman, R. (1991). *The Wright brothers: How they invented the airplane* (W. Wright & O. Wright, Photog.). New York: Holiday House. 3–4;5–6. B

An excellent biography of the Wright Brothers and their quest to fly.

Friedman, A. (1994). *The king's commissioners*. New York: Scholastic. 3–4;5–6. MF

Commissioners of the king find a mathematical solution to their problems.

Gibbons, G. (1993). *Pirates: Robbers of the high seas*. New York: Little, Brown. K–3;4–5. INF

Facts are presented about pirates in this descriptive book.

Goble, P. (2003). *Mystic horse*. New York: Harper Collins. K–2;3–4. TF

Pawnee story about a boy and his grandmother who rescue a sickly horse.

Goble, P. (Reteller). (1989). *Iktomi and the berries: A Plains Indian story*. New York: Orchard. K–2;3–4. TF

A trickster story from the Lakota Sioux.

Greenstein, E. (2003). *Ice cream cones for sale*. New York: Scholastic. K–2;3–4. CRF

This book tells the story of the first ice cream cones.

Guettier, B. (1999). *The father who had 10 children*. New York: Dial. K–2. CRF

The father of 10 children has to count by ones, twos, fives, and tens.

Haseley, D. (2002). *The amazing thinking machine*. New York: Dial. 3–4;5–6. CRF

The central character invents the thinking machine to support his family.

Haskins, J. (1991). *Outward dreams: Black inventors and their inventions*. New York: Walker. 5–6;7+. INF

This book details significant accomplishments of African Americans.

Hoobler, D., & Hoobler, T. (1999). *The ghost in the Tokaido inn*. New York: Philomel. 3–4;5–6. HF/M

In this complex mystery set in eighteenth-century Japan, a boy solves a crime to improve his status.

Hopkins, L.B. (2004). *Wonderful words: Poems about reading, writing, speaking, and listening*. New York: Simon. K–2;3–4. P

A collection of poems with exquisite illustrations.

Hutchins, P. (1979). *One-eyed Jake*. New York: Greenwillow. K–2. PB

This book is about one-eyed Jake, a mean-looking pirate.

Janeczko, P. (1990). *The place my words are looking for: What poets say about and through their work*. New York: Simon. 3–4;5–6;7+. P

A book of Janeczko's poetry.

Jones, C. F. (1991). *Mistakes that worked: 40 familiar inventions and how they came to be* (J. O'Brien, Illus.). New York: Doubleday. 4–6;7+. INF

This book presents the stories behind 40 things that were invented or named by accident.

Joseph, L. (2001). *The color of my words*. New York: Harper Trophy. 3–4;5–6. INF

Ana Rosa is 12 years old and dreams of becoming a writer. When she runs out of paper, she writes on paper bags.

Kennedy, C. (2003). *A patriot's handbook*. New York: Hyperion. K–2;3–4;5–6;7+. B; P; INF

The author has collected a variety of readings.

Konigsburg, E. (2000). *Silent to the bone*. New York: Atheneum. 5–6;7+. CRF

A 13-year-old boy is accused of dropping his baby sister.

Lewis, P. (2002). *ARITHME-TICKLE*. New York: Harcourt. K–2. PB

A collection of even numbers and of odd riddle rhymes.

Lewis, J. P. (2005). *Please bury me in the library*. New York: Gulliver. K–2;3–4. P

The poet writes with wordplay about words, letters, and so forth.

Littke, L. (2002). *Lake of secrets*. New York: Holt. 5–6;7+. CRF

Carlene has a lost brother, and she has peculiar experiences that she needs to solve.

Long, M. (2003). *How I became a pirate* (D. Shannon, Illus.). New York: Harcourt. K–2. MF

A young boy ventures into piracy.

Lyons, M. E. (1992). *Letters from a slave girl: The story of Harriet Jacobs*. New York: Scribner's. 5–6; 7+. HF

The experiences of a slave girl are written in the form of letters.

Maestro, B. (1989). *The story of the Statue of Liberty* (G. Maestro, Illus.). New York: Harper. K–2. INF.*

This book explains the Statue of Liberty.

Manns, N. (2001). *Operating codes*. New York: Little, Brown. 5–6;7+. CRF

After moving into a new home, Graham discovers ghosts and mysteries.

Manson, C. (2000). *Uncle Sam and Old Glory: Symbols of America*. New York: Atheneum. K–2;3–4;5–6. INF

This book identifies and explains 15 American symbols, including the Liberty Bell and Uncle Sam.

Martin, B., Archambault, J., & Ehlert, L. (2006). *Chicka, chicka, boom, boom*. New York: Simon. K–2. PB

A rhythmic alphabet race.

Martin, R. (1992). *The rough-face girl* (D. Shannon, Illus.). New York: Putnam. K–2;3–4. TF

This tale, from both the Algonquin and Comanche Indians, is the Native American version of *Cinderella*.

Martin, T. (1999). *A family trait*. New York: Holiday House. 3–4;5–6. CRF

Mae Watson solves the mystery of a neighbor's death and other family mysteries.

Merrill, J. (1972). *The toothpaste millionaire*. Boston: Houghton Mifflin. 3–4;5–6. CRF

In this book, a homemade toothpaste project becomes very profitable.

Naylor, P. (2003). *Bernie Magruder & the bats in the belfry*. New York: Atheneum. 3–4;5–7. CRF

A town is plagued by a provision in Eleanor Scuttlefoot's will, so Bernie Magruder and his companions set out to solve the mystery.

Nickerson, S. (2002). *How to disappear completely and never be found*. New York: HarperCollins. 5–6;7+. CRF

Margaret lives with a mother who doesn't talk about the past. She then discovers a mystery.

Osborne, M. P. (1990). *The many lives of Benjamin Franklin*. New York: Dial. 3–4;5–6. B

The author focuses on Franklin as a scientist, statesman, diplomat, and inventor.

Panzer, N. (Ed.). (1994). *Celebrate America: In poetry and art*. New York: Hyperion. 3–4;5–6. PB

The art is from the National Museum of American Art at the Smithsonian.

Pinkwater, D. (2007). *The Neddiad*. Boston: Houghton Mifflin. 3–4;5–6. MF

The story of Neddie and his friends—a ghost and a shaman.

Pittman, H. C. (1994). *Counting Jennie*. Minneapolis: Carolrhoda. K–2. PB

In this picture book, Jennie counts everything she sees.

Platt, R. (2001). *Pirate diary: The journal of Jake Carpenter* (G. Riddell, Illus.). New York: Candlewick Press. 3–4;5–6. MF

A pirate's journal of his experiences.

Rappaport, D. (2001). *Martin's big words: The life of Dr. Martin Luther King, Jr.* New York: Jump at the Sun. K–3;4–5. B

The author uses words of Dr. Martin Luther King, Jr.'s speeches and writing.

Rector, R. (2002). *Tria and the great star rescue*. New York: Delacorte. 3–4;5–6. MF

Tria lives in a futuristic home with a holographic friend.

Rumford, J. (Reteller). (2007). *Beowulf*. New York: Houghton Mifflin. 5–6;7+. TF

This is a graphic novel version of Beowulf.

Ryan, P. (2000). *The flag we love* (F. Masiello, Illus.). New York: Charlesbridge. K–2;3–4;5–6. INF*

This book identifies the national symbol and what it stands for.

Schwartz, D. (1985). *How much is a million?* New York: Harper. K–2;3–4. PB

Helps children understand the immensity of numbers.

Scieszka, J., & Smith, L. (1995). *Math curse*. New York: Viking. 3–4;5–6. INF

Readers learn how everything is a math problem.

Scieszka, J., & Smith, L. (2004). *Science verse*. New York: Penguin. K–2;3–4;5–6. P

Science poetry.

Scillian, D. (1995). *A is for America* (P. Carroll, Illus.). Chelsea, MI: Sleeping Bear Press. K–2;3–4. INF

An alphabet book about the United States.

Scillian, D. (2000). *One nation: America by the numbers* (P. Carroll, Illus.). Chelsea, MI: Sleeping Bear Press. 3–4;5–6;7+. INF

This counting book for all ages includes U.S. trivia related to numbers.

Stanley, D. (2001). *The mysterious matter of I.M. Fine*. New York: HarperCollins. 5–6;7+. CRF

A mystery story.

Stanley, G. (2001). *The cobweb confession* (S. Murdocca, Illus.). New York: Aladdin. K–2;3–4;5–6. CRF*

A science teacher and his students solve mysteries.

Steer, D. (2006). *The dragon's eye* (C. Darrell, Illus.). Cambridge, MA: Candlewick. 3–4;5–6;7+. MF

Daniel and his sister discover that their father is a leading dragonolist.

Stenhouse, T. (2001). *Across the steel river*. Toronto, Canada: Kids Can. 4–5;7+. CRF

This book describes a friendship between Will Samson and Siksika, a Blackfoot Indian.

Stevens, C. (1993). *Lily and Miss Liberty*. New York: Little Apple. 3–4;5–6. HF

A girl and her father discuss the Statue of Liberty and how it was given to us by the French.

Stevens, J. (2000). *The weighty word book*. New York; Rinehart. 3–4;5–6. INF

Delightful stories about words.

Verdick, E. (2004). *Words are not for hurting*. New York: Free Spirit. K–2. INF

The power of language to hurt and to help.

Verrillo, E. (2007). *Elissa's quest: Phoenix rising, book one*. New York: Random House. 5–6;7+. MF

The heroine has a secret that must be hidden. She talks with animals.

Walden, M. (2007). *H.I.V.E. Higher institute of villianous education*. New York: Simon. 5–6;7+. MF

The institute trains worldwide wickedness.

Wood, A. (1996). *Elbert's bad word*. New York: Voyager. K–2;3–4. PB

Elbert says a bad word, and mayhem ensues.

Wormser, R. (1990). *Pinkerton: America's first private eye*. New York: Walker. 5–6;7+. INF

This book begins with Pinkerton growing up in the slums of Glasgow.

Yenne, B. (1993). *100 inventions that shaped world history*. San Francisco: Bluewood Books. 3–4;5–6. INF

This book identifies and tells about 100 important inventions.

Yolen, J. (1990). *Sky dogs* (B. Moser, Illus.). New York: Harcourt. K–2;3–4. TF

The story is about how the Blackfoot Indians got horses.

Yolen, J. (1995). *The ballad of the pirate queens* (D. Shannon, Illus.). New York: Harcourt. 3–4;5–6;7+. MF

Women pirates are the subjects of this ballad.

Professional References

Altwerger, B., & Flores, B. (1994). Theme cycles: Creating communities of learners. *Primary Voices K–6, 2*, 2–6.

Barnes, D. (1995). Talking and learning in classrooms: An introduction. *Primary Voices K–6, 3*, 2–7

Copenhaver, J. (1993). Instances of inquiry. *Primary Voices K–6, 1*, 6–12.

Dickinson, J. (1995). Talk and picture books in intermediate classrooms. *Primary Voices K–6, 3*, 8–14.

Donovan, C. (2001). Genre and other factors influencing teachers' book selections for science instruction. *Reading Research Quarterly, 36*, 412–440.

Fredericks, A. (1991). *Social studies through children's literature*. Englewood, CO: Teachers' Ideas Press.

Harste, J. (1993). Inquiry-based instruction. *Primary Voices K–6, 1,* 2–5.

Hartman, D. K. (1992). Eight readers reading: The intertextual links of able readers using multiple passages. *Reading Research Quarterly, 27,* 122–123.

Hughes, S. (1993). The impact of whole language on four elementary school libraries. *Language Arts, 70,* 521–530.

Jacque, D. (1993). The judge comes to kindergarten. In *Journeying: Children responding to literature* (pp. 43–53). Portsmouth, NH: Heinemann.

Johnson, T., & Louis, D. (1990). *Bringing it all together: A program for literacy*. Portsmouth, NH: Heinemann.

Kimeldorf, M. (1994). *A teacher's guide to creating portfolios*. Minneapolis, MN: Free Spirit.

Kurkjian, C., Livingston, N., Young, T., Avi. (2006). Worlds of fantasy. *The Reading Teacher, 59,* pp. 492–495.

Laughlin, M., & Swisher, C. (1990). *Literature-based reading*. Phoenix, AZ: Oryx Press.

Meinback, A., Rothlein, L., & Fredericks, A. (2000). *The complete guide to thematic units: Creating the integrated curriculum* (2nd ed.). Norwood, MA: Christopher-Gordon.

Pappas, C. (April, May, June, 2006). The information book genre: Its role in integrated science literacy research and practice. *Reading Research Quarterly, 41,* 226–250.

Peterson, B. (1991). Selecting books for beginning readers. In D. Deford, C. A. Lyons, and G. S. Pinnell (Eds.), *Bridges to literacy: Learning from reading recovery*. Portsmouth, NH: Heinemann.

Rosenblatt, L. M. (1983). *Literature as exploration*. New York: Noble and Noble.

Soalt, J. (April, 2005). Bringing together fictional and informational texts to improve comprehension. *The Reading Teacher, 58,* 680–683.

Walmsley, S. (1994). *Children exploring their world*. Portsmouth, NH: Heinemann.

Ward, R. (October, 2005). Using children's literature to inspire K–8 preservice teachers' future mathematics pedagogy. *The Reading Teacher, 59,* 132–143.

Weaver, C., Chaston, J., & Peterson, S. (1993). *Theme exploration*. Portsmouth, NH: Heinemann.

Weston, L. (1993). The evolution of response through discussion, drama, writing, and art in a fourth grade. In K. Holland, R. Hungerford, and S. Ernst (Eds.), *Journeying: Children responding to literature* (pp. 137–150). Portsmouth, NH: Heinemann.

Appendix

BOOK AWARDS

The Caldecott Medal

This award, sponsored by the Association for Library Service to Children, a division of the American Library Association, is given to the illustrator of the most distinguished picture book for children published in the United States during the preceding year. Only U.S. residents or citizens are eligible for this award.

2007   *Flotsam* by David Wiesner. Clarion.

2006   *The Hello, Goodbye Window* by Norton Juster. Hyperion.

2005   *Kitten's First Full Moon* by Kevin Henkes. Greenwillow.

2004   *The Man Who Walked Between the Towers* by Mordicai Gerstein. Roaring Brook Press/ Millbrook.

2003   *My Friend Rabbit* by Eric Rohmann. Roaring Brook Press/Millbrook Press.

2002   *The Three Pigs* by David Wiesner. Clarion/ Houghton Mifflin.

2001   *So You Want to Be President?* by Judith St. George, illustrated by David Small. Philomel.

2000   *Joseph Had a Little Overcoat* by Simms Taback. Viking.

1999   *Snowflake Bentley* by Jacqueline Briggs Martin, illustrated by Mary Azarian. Houghton Mifflin.

1998   *Rapunzel* retold by Paul O. Zelinsky. Dutton.

1997   *Golem* by David Wisniewski. Clarion.

1996   *Officer Buckle and Gloria* by Peggy Rathmann. Putnam.

1995   *Smoky Night* by Eve Bunting, illustrated by David Diaz. Harcourt.

1994   *Grandfather's Journey* by Allen Say. Houghton Mifflin.

1993   *Mirette on the High Wire* by Emily Arnold McCully. G. P. Putnam.

1992   *Tuesday* by David Wiesner. Clarion.

1991   *Black and White* by David Macaulay. Houghton Mifflin.

1990   *Lon Po Po: A Red-Riding Hood Story from China,* translated and illustrated by Ed Young. Philomel.

1989   *Song and Dance Man* by Karen Ackerman, illustrated by Stephen Gammell. Knopf.

1988   *Owl Moon* by Jane Yolen, illustrated by John Schoenherr. Philomel.

1987   *Hey, Al* by Arthur Yorinks, illustrated by Richard Egielski. Farrar.

1986   *The Polar Express* by Chris Van Allsburg. Houghton Mifflin.

1985   *Saint George and the Dragon* retold by Margaret Hodges, illustrated by Trina Schart Hyman. Little, Brown.

1984   *The Glorious Flight: Across the Channel with Louis Blériot* by Alice and Martin Provensen. Viking.

1983   *Shadow* by Blaise Cendrars, translated and illustrated by Marcia Brown. Scribner's.

1982   *Jumanji* by Chris Van Allsburg. Houghton Mifflin.

1981   *Fables* by Arnold Lobel. Harper.

1980   *Ox-Cart Man* by Donald Hall, illustrated by Barbara Cooney. Viking.

1979   *The Girl Who Loved Wild Horses* by Paul Goble. Bradbury.

1978   *Noah's Ark* by Peter Spier. Doubleday.

1977   *Ashanti to Zulu: African Traditions* by Margaret Musgrove, illustrated by Leo and Diane Dillon. Dial.

1976   *Why Mosquitoes Buzz in People's Ears* retold by Verna Aardema, illustrated by Leo and Diane Dillon. Dial.

1975   *Arrow to the Sun* adapted and illustrated by Gerald McDermott. Viking.

The Newbery Award

This award, sponsored by the Association for Library Service to Children, a division of the American Library Association, is given to the author of the most distinguished contribution to children's literature published during the preceding year. Only U.S. citizens or residents are eligible for this award.

2007   *The Higher Power of Lucky* by Susan Patron. Simon Schuster.

2006   *Criss Cross* by Lynne Rae Perkins. HarperCollins.

2005   *Kira-Kira* by Cynthia Kadohata. Simon & Schuster.

2004   *The Tale of Despereaux* by Kate DiCamillo, illustrated by Timothy Basil Ering. Candlewick Press.

2003   *Crispin: The Cross of Lead* by Avi. Hyperion.

2002   *A Single Shard* by Linda Sue Park. Clarion/Houghton Mifflin.

2001   *A Year Down Yonder* by Richard Peck. Dial.

2000   *Bud, Not Buddy* by Christopher Paul Curtis. Delacorte.

1999   *Holes* by Louis Sachar. Farrar Straus.

1998   *Out of the Dust* by Karen Hesse. Scholastic.

1997   *The View from Saturday* by E. L. Konigsburg. Atheneum.

1996   *The Midwife's Apprentice* by Karen Cushman. Clarion.

1995   *Walk Two Moons* by Sharon Creech. HarperCollins.

1994   *The Giver* by Lois Lowry. Houghton Mifflin.

1993   *Missing May* by Cynthia Rylant. Jackson/Orchard.

1992   *Shiloh* by Phyllis Reynolds Naylor. Atheneum.

1991   *Maniac Magee* by Jerry Spinelli. Little, Brown.

1990   *Number the Stars* by Lois Lowry. Houghton Mifflin.

1989   *Joyful Noise: Poems for Two Voices* by Paul Fleischamn. Harper.

1988   *Lincoln: A Photobiography* by Russell Freedman. Clarion.

1987   *The Whipping Boy* by Sid Fleischman. Greenwillow.

1986   *Sarah, Plain and Tall* by Patricia MacLachlan. Harper.

1985   *The Hero and the Crown* by Robin McKinley. Greenwillow.

1984   *Dear Mr. Henshaw* by Beverly Cleary. Morrow.

1983   *Dicey's Song* by Cynthia Voigt. Atheneum.

1982   *A Visit to William Blake's Inn: Poems for Innocent and Experienced Travelers* by Nancy Willard, illustrated by Alice and Martin Provensen. Harcourt.

1981   *Jacob Have I Loved* by Katherine Paterson. Crowell.

1980   *A Gathering of Days: A New England Girl's Journal, 1830–1832* by Joan Blos. Scribner's.

1979   *The Westing Game* by Ellen Raskin. Dutton.

1978   *Bridge to Terabithia* by Katherine Paterson. Crowell.

1977   *Roll of Thunder, Hear My Cry* by Mildred D. Taylor. Dial.

1976   *The Grey King* by Susan Cooper. McElderry/Atheneum.

1975   *M. C. Higgins, the Great* by Virginia Hamilton. Macmillan.

Coretta Scott King Awards

These awards, founded to commemorate Dr. Martin Luther King, Jr., and his wife, Coretta Scott King, for their work in promoting peace and world brotherhood, are given to an African American author and, since 1974, an African American illustrator whose children's books, published during the preceding year, made outstanding inspirational and educational contributions to literature for children and young people. The awards are sponsored by the Social Responsibilities Round Table of the American Library Association.

2007   Author: *Copper Sun* by Sharon Draper. Simon & Schuster.
Illustrator: *Moses: When Harriet Tubman Led Her People to Freedom,* illustrated by Kadir Nelson, text by Carole Boston Weatherford. Hyperion.

2006   Author: *Day of Tears: A Novel in Dialogue* by Julius Lester. Hyperion.
Illustrator: *Rosa,* illustrated by Bryan Collier, text by Nikki Giovanni.

2005   Author: *Remember: The Journey to School Integration* by Toni Morrison. Houghton Mifflin.
Illustrator: *Ellington Was Not a Street,* illustrated by Kadir Nelson, text by Ntozake Shange. Simon & Schuster.

2004   Author: *The First Part Last* by Angela Johnson. Simon & Schuster
Illustrator: *Beautiful Blackbird* by Ashley Bryan. Atheneum.

2003   Author: *Bronx Masquerade* by Nikki Grimes. Dial.
Illustrator: *Talkin' About Bessie: The Story of Aviator Elizabeth,* illustrated by E. B. Lewis. Orchard.

2002   Author: *The Land* by Mildred Taylor. Putnam.
Illustrator: *Goin' Someplace Special,* illustrated by Jerry Pinkney. Atheneum.

2001   Author: *Miracle's Boys* by Jacqueline Woodson. Putnam.
Illustrator: *Uptown* by Bryan Collier. Henry Holt.

2000   Author: *Bud, Not Buddy* by Christopher Paul Curtis. Delacorte.
Illustrator: *In the Time of the Drums,* illustrated by Brian Pinkney, text by Kim Siegelson. Hyperion.

1999   Author: *Heaven* by Angela Johnson. Simon & Schuster.
Illustrator: *I See the Rhythm,* illustrated by Michele Wood, text by Toyomi Igus. Children's Book Press.

1998   Author: *Forged by Fire* by Sharon M. Draper. Atheneum.
Illustrator: *In Daddy's Arms I Am Tall: African Americans Celebrating Fathers,* illustrated by Javaka Steptoe. Lee & Low.

1997   Author: *Slam!* by Walter Dean Myers. Scholastic.
Illustrator: *Minty: A Story of Young Harriet Tubman,* illustrated by Jerry Pinkney, text by Alan Schroeder. Dial Books for Young Readers.

1996   Author: *Her Stories* by Virginia Hamilton, illustrated by Leo and Diane Dillon. Scholastic/Blue Sky Press.
Illustrator: *The Middle Passage: White Ships Black Cargo* by Tom Feelings, introduction by John Henrik Clarke. Dial.

1995   Author: *Christmas in the Big House, Christmas in the Quarters* by Patricia C. and Frederick L. McKissack, illustrated by John Thompson. Scholastic.
Illustrator: *The Creation,* illustrated by James E. Ransome, text by James Weldon Johnson. Delacorte.

1994   Author: *Toning the Sweep* by Angela Johnson. Orchard.
Illustrator: *Soul Looks Back in Wonder,* illustrated by Tom Feelings, text edited by Phyllis Fogelman. Dial.

1993   Author: *The Dark-Thirty: Southern Tales of the Supernatural* by Patricia McKissack, illustrated by Brian Pinkney. Knopf.
Illustrator: *The Origin of Life on Earth: An African Creation Myth,* illustrated by Kathleen Atkins Wilson, retold by David Anderson. Sights Production.

1992   Author: *Now Is Your Time! The African-American Struggle for Freedom* by Walter Dean Myers. HarperCollins.
Illustrator: *Tar Beach* by Faith Ringgold. Crown.

1991   Author: *Road to Memphis* by Mildred D. Taylor. Dial.
Illustrator: *Aïda,* illustrated by Leo and Diane Dillon, retold by Leontyne Price. Harcourt.

1990   Author: *A Long Hard Journey* by Patricia and Frederick McKissack. Walker.
Illustrator: *Nathaniel Talking,* illustrated by Jan Spivey Gilchrist, text by Eloise Greenfield. Black Butterfly Press.

1989   Author: *Fallen Angels* by Walter Dean Myers. Scholastic.
Illustrator: *Mirandy and Brother Wind,* illustrated by Jerry Pinkney, text by Patricia McKissack. Knopf.

1988   Author: *The Friendship* by Mildred D. Taylor, illustrated by Max Ginsburg. Dial.
Illustrator: *Mufaro's Beautiful Daughters: An African Tale,* retold and illustrated by John Steptoe. Lothrop.

1987   Author: *Justin and the Best Biscuits in the World* by Mildred Pitts Walter. Lothrop.
Illustrator: *Half a Moon and One Whole Star,* illustrated by Jerry Pinkney, text by Crescent Dragonwagon. Macmillan.

1986   Author: *The People Could Fly: American Black Folktales* by Virginia Hamilton, illustrated by Leo and Diane Dillon. Knopf.
Illustrator: *The Patchwork Quilt,* illustrated by Jerry Pinkney, text by Valerie Flournoy. Dial.

1985   Author: *Motown and Didi* by Walter Dean Myers. Viking.
Illustrator: No award.

1984   Author: *Everett Anderson's Goodbye* by Lucille Clifton. Holt.
Illustrator: *My Mama Needs Me,* illustrated by Pat Cummings, text by Mildred Pitts Walter. Lothrop.

1983   Author: *Sweet Whispers, Brother Rush* by Virginia Hamilton. Philomel.
Illustrator: *Black Child* by Peter Magubane. Knopf.

1982   Author: *Let the Circle be Unbroken* by Mildred Taylor. Dial.
Illustrator: *Mother Crocodile: An Uncle Amadou Tale from Senegal,* illustrated by John Steptoe, adapted by Rosa Guy. Delacorte.

1981   Author: *This Life* by Sidney Poitier. Knopf.
Illustrator: *Beat the Story-Drum, Pum-Pum* by Ashley Bryan. Atheneum.

1980   Author: *The Young Landlords* by Walter Dean Myers. Viking.
Illustrator: *Cornrows,* illustrated by Carole Byard, text by Camille Yarbrough. Coward.

1979   Author: *Escape to Freedom* by Ossie Davis. Viking.
Illustrator: *Something on My Mind,* illustrated by Tom Feelings, text by Nikki Grimes. Dial.

1978   Author: *Africa Dream* by Eloise Greenfield, illustrated by Carole Byard. Crowell.
Illustrator: *Africa Dream,* illustrated by Carole Byard, text by Eloise Greenfield. Crowell.

1977   Author: *The Story of Stevie Wonder* by James Haskins. Lothrop.
Illustrator: No award.

1976   Author: *Duey's Tale* by Pearl Bailey. Harcourt.
Illustrator: No award.

1975   Author: *The Legend of Africana* by Dorothy Robinson. Johnson Publishing.
Illustrator: No award.

Robert F. Sibert Informational Book Medal

This award was established by the Association for Library Service to Children in 2001. It is awarded annually to the author of the most distinguished informational book published during the preceding year.

2007   *Team Moon: How 400,000 People Landed Apollo 11 on the Moon* by Catherine Thimmesh. Houghton.

2006   *Secrets of a Civil War Submarine: Solving the Mysteries of the H.L. Hunley* by Sally M. Walker. Carolrhoda.

2005   *The Voice that Challenged a Nation: Marian Anderson and the Struggle for Equal Rights* by Russell Freedman. Clarion.

2004   *An American Plague: The True and Terrifying Story of the Yellow Fever Epidemic of 1793* by Jim Murphy. Clarion.

2003   *The Life and Death of Adolf Hitler* by James Cross Giblin. Clarion.

2002   *Black Potatoes: The Story of the Great Irish Famine, 1845–1850* by Susan Bartoletti. Houghton Mifflin.

2001   *Sir Walter Ralegh and the Quest for El Dorado* by Marc Aronson. Clarion.

Nonfiction Awards: Orbis Pictus Award

The Orbis Pictus Award for Outstanding Nonfiction for Children was established by the National Council of Teachers of English (NCTE) in 1990 to promote and recognize excellence in the field of nonfiction writing.

2007   *Quest for the Tree Kangaroo: A Expediion to the Cloud Forest of New Guinea* by Sy Montgomery. Houghton Mifflin.

2006   *Children of the Great Depression* by Russell Freedman. Clarion.

2005   *York's Adventures with Lewis and Clark: An African-American's Part in the Great Expedition* by Rhonda Blumberg. HarperCollins.

2004   *An American Plague: The True and Terrifying Story of the Yellow Fever Epidemic of 1793* by Jim Murphy. Clarion Books.

2003   *When Marian Sang: The True Recital of Marian Anderson: The Voice of a Century* by Pam Munoz Ryan. Scholastic.

2002   *Black Potatoes: The Story of the Great Irish Famine, 1845–1850* by Susan Bartoletti. Houghton Mifflin.

2001   *Hurry Freedom: African Americans in Gold Rush California* by Jerry Stanley. Crown.

2000   *Through My Eyes* by Ruby Bridges, edited by Margo Lundell. Scholastic.

1999   *Shipwreck at the Bottom of the World: The Extraordinary True Story of Shackleton and the Endurance* by Jennifer Armstrong. Crown.

1998   *An Extraordinary Life: The Story of a Monarch Butterfly* by Laurence Pringle, paintings by Bob Marstall. Orchard.

1997   *Leonardo da Vinci* by Diane Stanley. Morrow.

1996   *The Great Fire* by Jim Murphy. Scholastic.

1995   *Safari Beneath the Sea* by Diane Swanson. Sierra Club Books.

1994   *Across America on an Emigrant Train* by Jim Murphy. Clarion.

1993   *Children of the Dust Bowl: The True Story of the School at Weedpatch Camp* by Jerry Stanley. Crown.

1992   *Flight: The Journey of Charles Lindbergh* by Robert Burleigh. Harper.

1991   *Franklin Delano Roosevelt* by Russell Freedman. Clarion.

Other nonfiction awards not listed include the Boston Globe–Horn Book Award; the Carter B. Woodson Book Award; the Children's Book Guild Nonfiction Award; the Christopher Awards; and the Eva L. Gordon Award for Children's Science Literature.

Pura Belpré Award

The Pura Belpré Award is given every two years by the Association for Library Service to Children (ALSC) and the National Association to Promote Library Services to the Spanish Speaking (REFORMA). The award honors Latino writers and illustrators whose work best portrays, affirms, and celebrates the Latino cultural experience in a work of literature for youth. The award was named in honor of Pura Belpré, the first Latina librarian of the New York Public Library.

The first awards, given in 1996, were selected from books published between 1990 and 1995.

2006   Author: *The Tequila Worm* by Viola Canales. Random House.
Illustrator: *Dona Flor: A Tall Tale About a Giant Woman with a Great Big Heart.* Knopf.

2004   Author: *Before We Were Free* by Julia Alvarez. Knopf.
Illustrator: *Just a Minute: A Trickster Tale and Counting Book.* Chronicle.

2002   Author: *Esperanza Rising* by Pam Munoz Ryan. Scholastic.
Illustrator: *Chato and the Party Animals* by Gary Soto. Putnam.

2000   Author: *Under the Royal Palms: A Childhood in Cuba* by Alma Flor Ada. Atheneum.
Illustrator: *Magic Windows: Cut Paper Art and Stories* by Carmen Lomas Garza. Children's Book Press.

1998   Author: *Parrot in the Oven: Mi Vida* by Victor Martinez. Joanna Cotler Books/ HarperCollins.
Illustrator: *Snapshots from the Wedding,* illustrated by Stephanie Garcia, text by Gary Soto. Putnam.

1996   Author: *An Island Like You: Stories of the Barrio* by Judith Ortiz Cofer. Melanie Kroupa/Orchard.
Illustrator: *Chato's Kitchen,* illustrated by Susan Guevara, text by Gary Soto. Putnam.

Glossary

Adolescent literature   literature that addresses the interests, concerns, and problems of this age group.

Aesthetic reading   pleasurable, interesting reading done for its own sake.

Alliteration   literary device based on repetition of consonant sounds.

Animal fantasy   stories in which animals act and interact like human beings.

Antagonist   a character in a story who is in conflict with the main character or protagonist.

Antiphonal choral reading   choral reading participants vary pitch and duration of sound.

Assonance   the close repetition of middle vowel sounds between different consonant sounds.

Audio books   books that are recorded for listening.

Authentic activities   activities that have meaning for the students engaged in them.

Authentic biography   biography based entirely on the actual words and experiences of the subject. There are no imagined conversations or events.

Author   the title given to the person who writes the text in books.

Autobiography   a category of biography written by the subject of the book.

Ballads   rhymes and rhythms set to music, centering on a single character in a dramatic situation.

Benchmark   a term describing an exemplary book that is used as a standard of quality for comparing other similar books.

Bibliotherapy   literally means "helping with books"; self-examination and insights gained from reading.

Biography   the story of a particular person's life. In biography, authors conduct careful research in order to explore and record the lives and significant acts and accomplishments of a person. Three styles of biography are typical. For children (a) **authentic biography** is based on documented words, speeches, and writing of the subject; (b) the **biographical fiction style** of biography permits the author to create conversations and

portray the everyday life of the subject, but these details are based on thorough historical research into the subject's character and life as well as the time in which the person lived; and (c) when writing **fictionalized biography,** the author takes greater latitude in creating a story around the actual life of a subject.

Book cluster   groups of books based on common theme or subject.

Booktalking   the act of telling or reading highlights of a book without revealing its entire plot. The purpose of booktalking is to motivate others to read a book.

Caldecott Medal   an award presented each year by the American Library Association to the creator of an outstanding picture book.

Catharsis   books that help work out emotions.

Censorship   the act of controlling what literature is available to be read in any given setting. Censors may attempt to remove books from library shelves because they believe the works in question violate particular values, religious beliefs, or good taste.

Challenged students   individuals who face difficulties in educational situations.

Chapter books   relatively short books divided into chapters with more text than pictures. They are intended for readers who are ready to read longer books than picture books.

Character maps   a strategy for developing students' understanding of character development in a story.

Characters   the people in a story, comparable to actors in movies or on stage. Their actions, thoughts, and conversations tell the story.

Children's literature   materials written specifically with children's interests and reading abilities in mind.

Choral reading   an oral literary activity in which a selection from literature is read by several persons in unison with the direction of a leader. The most common types of choral reading are: (a) refrain, in which the teacher reads most of the lines and the children read the refrain; (b) line-a-child choral reading, in which individual students read specific lines, while the entire group reads the beginning and ending of the selection; and (c) antiphonal or dialogue choral reading, based on boys and girls (sometimes in groups) varying their voices to speak different parts of a selection.

Classroom sets   multiple copies of trade books for classroom use.

Climax   the high point of a story when conflicts are resolved.

Coming-of-age books   literature for readers who are between childhood and early adolescence, also called "tweens."

Community of readers   term that denotes shared understandings within a group of readers who discuss ideas about the same books.

Concept books   books that explore the various facets of a particular concept and in the process develop a reader's understanding of it. Geometric shapes, nature, and maps are some of the subjects of concept books.

Concrete poetry   poetry written in the shape of the topic; a poem about a boat, for example, would be written in the shape of a boat.

Conflict   the result of difficulties or opposing views between characters in a story. Conflict gives a story the tension that makes it interesting. There are a number of types of conflict, such as conflict within an individual, between individuals, or between an individual and nature.

Connections   the process of identifying ways that books are related to one another and to the experiences of the reader.

Connotative meaning   inferred meaning as opposed to literal meaning. It is meaning deduced from "reading between the lines."

Contemporary realistic fiction   events and settings that readers recognize as being in the present.

Core literature   literature that is the focus of a unit study.

Creative drama   informal drama created by the participants in the drama. It is improvisational and process-centered: The players create the dialogue, and there are no written scripts to follow.

Cultural diversity   society that includes people from many cultures and races.

Culturally conscious literature   literature that recognizes the importance of culture and shows respect for people of all cultures and races.

Culture   the context in which children develop. Culture is comprised of the values and customs that form an identifiable heritage.

Cumulative stories   stories that accumulate. Events build on events and phrases build on phrases, leading to a climax, at which point the accumulation falls apart.

Denouement   the falling action that occurs after the climax.

Developmentally appropriate   a phrase describing instruction that is compatible with the learner's stage of development.

Dialect   variations in speech patterns from what is considered the "standard."

Didacticism   obvious moral messages or values that some authors believe should be taught directly.

Diversity background   the student population of today's schools is more varied than in the past. Diversity arises from many sources, including ethnicity as well as emotional and physical development.

Dramatic plot   plot with fast-moving action that grabs readers' attention and creates enough tension to hold their interest until the climax.

Early literacy experiences   experiences with literature that occur through listening to stories and handling books and writing materials.

Efferent reading   reading that has a narrow focus and depends upon the reader's purpose; for example, efferent reading may be done to seek specific information, such as directions.

Element of literature   the structural elements of fiction that include plot, characterization, setting, style, and theme.

Emergent literacy   the beginning stages of learning to read and write.

Enchanted realism   writing that includes elements of both fantasy and high fantasy. These stories include magic objects, characters, and events that appear in a realistic world, creating suspense and intrigue in the story.

Engaging with literature   readers' response to reading in which readers' minds, interests, and feelings connect with the ideas in a text. It connotes an understanding and an emotional response to what is read.

Envisionment   the unique meaning each reader creates when reading; each reader has slight to significant differences in interpretation.

Epic   a story of a person's life and death told in poetic form.

Episodic plot   the name given to a small plot within a larger one. It usually occurs in a single chapter within a book. In some books, each chapter is an episode.

Exceptional   a descriptive word for individual differences that fall outside the average, or bell curve. Exceptional students need adjustments in their instruction in order to achieve their potential.

Experiencing literature   reading with pleasure and with understanding.

Experiment and activity books   books that give directions for experiments or activities, such as cut paper stories.

Exposition   literature that explains.

Fable   a story about an animal that teaches a lesson.

Fact frames   a strategy for organizing the facts that one acquires from reading.

Family literacy   reading and writing that occur in the home.

Fantastic element   an impossible element in a story; something that could not really happen such as a person or animal that does not really exist, or an aberration of some other aspect of the laws of the real world.

Fantasy   a genre of literature that is based on make-believe elements; it may include such factors as characters, place, events, and time.

Figurative language   language with a nonliteral meaning; it may include similes, metaphors, hyperbole, and personification.

Folktales   pieces of literature that mirror the mores and values of a culture; they are passed down from generation to generation and have no identifiable author.

Foreshadowing   a stylistic device employed to hint at future actions or events.

Free verse   poetry that does not follow a traditional form in that it does not have a regular rhythm or meter, nor does it usually rhyme.

Genre   classifications of literature that share the same basic characteristics. The genre of children's literature includes picture books, poetry, fantasy, traditional literature, historical fiction, realistic (contemporary) fiction, biography, and nonfiction.

Global literature   these books reflect the global community in which we live.

Graphic novels   novels told in comic book style but which are printed on higher quality paper. Graphic novels address many topics, but most frequently they are based on superheroes and fantastic characters.

Great books   books that have lived through several generations, usually because they express universal truths; people in different situations and circumstances can relate to the way these truths are expressed.

Haiku   a poetic form that originated in Japan and refers to nature and the seasons; it is patterned poetry of 17 syllables in which the first line contains five syllables, the second contains seven, and the third contains five.

High fantasy   complex fantasy that is grouped into heroic fantasy and science fiction.

Historical fiction   books in which the setting is in the past. Events and characters are realistic, and setting and background are true to a particular time period, but descriptions, and sometimes characters, are made up. Characters behave and react the way one would expect of people in the time period in which the story is set.

Illustrated books   books in which illustrations are used to supplement the text.

Illustrators   artists who create the illustrations for books. These artists create pictures that interpret the text; sometimes illustrations tell the whole story, as in wordless picture books.

Imagery   images that are created in the mind through the use of language; imagery appeals to the senses of sight, sound, touch, and smell.

Inclusion   a plan for teaching educationally handicapped students in the regular classroom rather than segregating them in special education classrooms.

Individual differences   variations from one individual to another.

Individualized education plan (IEP)   the plan developed by teachers, administrators, parents, and special educators to guide the education of students.

Inferencing   interpretation of literature based on meanings that are not directly stated in a text; readers must "fill in the empty spaces."

Informational books   books that explain, impart knowledge, or describe persons, places, things, or events.

Inquiry   the process of searching for information, ideas, and truth about questions the student has raised.

Inside perspective   a perspective of a culture from a member inside that culture.

Integrated units   units that address various subjects and literacy processes included in the elementary curriculum.

Interests   topics and experiences toward which individuals gravitate because they are motivated. Interests are usually developed and cultivated through experience.

Intertextuality   the process of interpreting one text by connecting the ideas in it with the ideas in all other previously read texts.

Issues in children's literature   major concerns in books written for children. Issues may include cultural diversity, authentic treatment of subjects, homosexuality and treatment of sex in the children's books, and elements of fantasy that could be construed as the occult. Other issues may concern specific groups or individuals.

KWL chart   an activity that identifies what readers know about a topic, what they want to learn, and what they eventually learn.

Legends   stories that are often based on an actual historical figure whose deeds and exploits have been embellished.

Life-cycle books   books that explain and illustrate the life cycles of animals, insects, and so forth.

Line-a-child choral reading   individual students read a line individually, and the entire group reads the beginning and end in unison.

Literary conventions   elements of form, style, or content. These fundamental patterns, conventions, or universals occur in both children's and adult literature.

Literary criticism   identifying the quality of literature. It falls into three categories: text-centered, child-centered, and issues-centered.

Literary fairy tales   stories that use the folktale style but were written by an author rather than emerging from the oral tradition.

Literary quality   well-written literature that has well-developed plots, themes, characterization, setting, and style. Nonfiction has literary quality when it is accurate, well-written, and interesting; presents main ideas and supporting details; differentiates theories from facts; and has illustrations that are appropriate to the subject.

Literate environment   a place where reading and writing are used for authentic purposes; many kinds of reading and materials are available in such a place.

Literature   a body of written works, an art form in which language is used in creative, artistic ways.

Mainstreaming   a practice that places exceptional students in the regular classroom.

Manga   Japanese comic books that are often printed and read in Japanese style, which is from back to front.

Metaphor   a figure of speech comparing two items that says one thing is the other.

Middle school   a school organization that includes grades 6, 7, and 8, although the grade levels included vary from place to place.

Modern fantasy   stories that take for granted not only the realities of the world that we see and feel, but also the supernatural aspects that lead to all sorts of possibilities; fantasies have identifiable authors.

Multicultural literature   literature that portrays the diversity of the population.

Multiculturalism   the process of developing sensitivity to the various cultures comprising a community, state, country, and world.

Myths   stories that explain the origin of the world and natural phenomena.

Narrative poetry   poems that tell a story; it includes the story elements of plot, character, setting, and theme.

Newbery   the name given to a medal that is awarded annually by the American Library Association to an outstanding children's book.

Nonfiction books   books in which all the information presented is true, such as a biography. No fictional elements are included in nonfiction.

Nonsense poetry   poems composed in lyric or narrative form. This poetry is playful and does not conform to what is expected; it pokes fun at what is usually taken seriously.

Onomatopoeia   poetry based on words that sound like their meaning, such as "bang."

Partial biographies   writing that focuses on a particular part of a person's life. For example, a partial biography may focus on either a subject's childhood or his or her adult life.

Personification   attributing human characteristics to something that does not actually have these qualities.

Physical disability   the condition of an individual who has learning challenges because of physical exceptionalities.

Picture books   books that tell stories by integrating language and pictures. Some picture books, however, are wordless.

Plot   the plan and structure of the story. Plots usually consist of introductory material, a gradual building of suspense, a climax, the falling of action, and the culmination.

Plot frames   strategies that help readers understand the plot line of a story.

Poetry   literature in its most intense, imaginative, and rhythmic form, which expresses and interprets the essence of experience through language; it is not the same as "verse."

Popular literature   in vogue at a particular time, it is usually characterized as a fad that enjoys a period of popularity and then disappears. Popular literature is produced very quickly and lacks the literary quality that would inspire readers to read and reread it.

Pourquoi   a story that explains why things are the way they are.

Prediction chart   a chart to guide readers to anticipate text, improving comprehension.

Problem resolution   the way conflicts and story problems are resolved.

Protagonist   usually the main character or hero of the book. Readers identify with this "good guy" character.

Racial and ethnic stereotyping   assuming that all members of a racial or ethnic group have the same characteristics. The characteristics assumed in stereotypes are usually negative views of people. Stereotyping interferes with the ability to see individuals as human beings.

Readability   the level at which a person can read a book (or other printed text) with comprehension.

Reader's theater   an oral presentation of literature—the oral delivery of stories, poetry, biography, or information by two or more readers who characterize and narrate clearly and expressively.

Realistic fiction   fiction that is written true to the physical and factual details of a particular time period. The problems that characters encounter are related to the realities of life during that time.

Refrain choral reading   the teacher or leader reads the lines, and students read the refrain.

Response   what readers take to a text, what happens during reading, how they feel about what they have read, how it becomes alive and personal, and the ways these feelings are displayed.

Rhyme   in poetry, rhyme occurs when the sounds of the accented syllables and all following sounds are the same.

Rhythm   the patterned flow of sound in poetry.

Schemata   expectations based on experience. Readers expect stories to have characters, setting, and so forth. These are schemata for stories.

Science fiction   stories created around events and problems that could not have happened without the scientific content.

Series books   books with the same principal character/s. These books are numbered 1, 2, 3. . . .

Setting   the time and place of the story.

Sexual stereotyping   assuming that all men or all women behave in certain ways (for example, that all women are weak and all men are strong). Sexual stereotyping functions in a negative way and interferes with the ability to appreciate individuals as human beings.

Simile   a figure of speech using the words *like* or *as* to compare one thing to another.

Social studies   one of the primary content areas studied in schools; some of the subjects within this discipline are history, geography, and anthropology.

Stance   the purpose or purposes a reader has for reading. It gives form to the literacy experience as well as the mode for expressing a response.

Stereotype   describing an entire group of people as having specific characteristics without recognizing that individuals in that group may not have those characteristics.

Story frames   strategy for developing students' understanding of story structure.

Story grammar   the structure of a story.

Story map   the map illustrating the story structure.

Storytelling   the act of telling stories. Many storytellers tell traditional stories that they have heard from other storytellers, and they often read and memorize stories and retell them.

Style   the way an author uses language and symbols to express ideas.

Survey nonfiction   a form of nonfiction that gives readers a broad overview of a topic rather than in-depth information.

Teacher-generated themes   those themes that teachers identify or suggest.

Theme   the universal meaning (big idea) that the author expresses through a literary work.

Touchstone books   books of such excellent quality that they become a standard for evaluating other books.

Trade books   books that are not textbooks.

Traditional literature   literature based on oral tradition. *Little Red Riding Hood* is an example of a traditional story.

Transaction   the interaction between a text and a reader in which both are modified and changed.

Unison choral reader   the entire group reads all of the lines in unison.

Unit   an organizing framework for children's inquiry and study.

USSR (uninterrupted sustained silent reading) sometimes called DEAR (drop everything and read), it is a specific period set aside for reading. Everyone in the class reads, including the teacher. In some schools, this is a school-wide reading time.

Values clarification   literature that encourages readers to examine their own values.

Visual art art that evokes both cognitive and aesthetic understanding and response.

Visual literacy a major avenue of communication in which understanding is gained visually by interpreting information presented on billboards, signs, television, pictures, and photographs.

Word choice a language issue that impacts literature for children and adults.

Wordless picture book a book in which the story is told entirely through the use of illustrations.

Writing style how authors put together words and sentences.

Subject Index

Poetry fairs, 89
Poetry-related Internet links, 90
Point of view, 31–32
Prediction charts, 260, 261
Prop stories, 236
Protagonists, 28
Pura Belpre Award, 9
Puzzles, 103

Reader's theater, 141, 232–233
    curriculum-based (CBRT), 232
    selecting material for, 232–233
Reading
    circles, 14–15, 253
    discussions, 14–15
    identifying children's interests in, 10–11
    interest inventory, 11
    motivation for, 10. *See also* Motivation to
        Read Profile
Reading Rainbow (television program), 12
Reading Teacher, The, 12
Realistic fiction. *See* Contemporary realistic fiction
Refrain choral reading, 237
Rethink and reread, 250
Rhyme, 73–74
Rhythm, 71, 74, 83
Riddles, 103
Riddle-poems, 86
Robert F. Sibert Informational Book Award, 8

Schemata, 24
School Library Media Activities Monthly, 13
Science fiction, 7, 117
Series books, 6–7, 139–140
Setting, 29
Setting, in fantasy, 118
Setting, Venn diagram comparing, 36
Sexuality, content, 41, 42, 44, 45–46, 199
Sibling rivalry, 132
Silent reading
    fostering, 241–242
    guided, 241–242
    literature circles, 240–241
    student response to, 242
    uninterrupted sustained silent reading
        (USSR), 241
Simpleton tales, 102
Single parents, 133–134
Sock puppets, 239–240
Sound patterns, 73
Special interest books, 139–140
Sports themes, 139

Stances, 250, 252
Static characters, 28
Stereotypes/stereotyping, 41, 46
Stick puppets, 239
Story(ies)
    grammar, 36
    introduction, 36
    mapping, 104–105, 258
    pyramids, 259–260
    structure in traditional literature, 98
Storytelling, 106, 233–236
    classroom experience with, 233–236
    flannel board stories, 236
    literary quality and, 8
    planning activities, 234–236
    selecting material for, 234
    value of, 1
    variations in, 236
Style, 30
    in biography, 186
    in fantasy, 119
    in traditional literature, 98–99
Subject Guide to Books in Print, 11
Symbolism, 31

Tall tales, 102–103
Television, 12
Themes, 29–30
    in biography, 186
    children's response to, 30
    definition, 30
    in fantasy, 119
    vs. topic, 30
    in traditional literature, 98
Third-person narrator, 31–32
Time magic, 117–118
Topic, vs. theme, 30
Trade books
    arts and, 173
    language arts and, 172–173
    mathematics and, 172
    science, 171
    social studies, 171–172
Traditional literature, 21, 23, 93–94.
        See also Folk tales
    characteristics of, 96
    contemporary values of, 96–97
    elements of, 97–99
    folk tales, 94–96
    in picture books, 55–56, 60
    themes in, 98
    types of, 99–103

Author/Title Index

Credits